*mis*Reading Plato

This book reorients the scholarship on Plato by returning readers to his most fundamental insights and reflections on the nature of the human psyche and the human condition.

By approaching the dialogue anew, as if for the first time, the book creates new intellectual pathways by opening the conversation to a clash of ideas. The contributors offer nuanced, nontraditional readings of Plato, readings that not only analyze but also build on the dialogues by bringing them into conversation with psychoanalysis, phenomenology, and contemporary continental thought more broadly. It addresses a major gap in the literature caused by reading Plato as a metaphysician or moral or political philosopher and not, primarily, as a psychologist.

Psychologists and scholars in philosophy, psychoanalysis, Platonic thought, and other humanities-related disciplines will find this new approach to Plato refreshing, accessible, and uniquely innovative.

Matthew Clemente is a husband and father of five. He lives and writes in Boston, Massachusetts, where he holds teaching appointments at Boston College and Boston University. He has published seven books, most recently *Eros Crucified: Death, Desire, and the Divine in Psychoanalysis and Philosophy of Religion*, and is the assistant editor of the *Journal for Continental Philosophy of Religion*.

Bryan J. Cocchiara is currently an adjunct professor of philosophy at Brookdale Community College. He received his MA from Boston College in 2014, where he was a research fellow at the Lonergan Institute. He received his STM from Drew University in 2021, where he specialized in philosophical and theological studies in religion. He is the co-editor of *misReading Nietzsche* (Pickwick Publications, 2018).

William J. Hendel is a teaching fellow at Boston College, who specializes in ethics, political philosophy, aesthetics, and contemporary continental philosophy.

The Psychology and the Other Book Series
Series editor: David M. Goodman
Associate editors: Brian W. Becker, Donna M. Orange and Eric R. Severson

The *Psychology and the Other* book series highlights creative work at the intersections between psychology and the vast array of disciplines relevant to the human psyche. The interdisciplinary focus of this series brings psychology into conversation with continental philosophy, psychoanalysis, religious studies, anthropology, sociology, and social/critical theory. The cross-fertilization of theory and practice, encompassing such a range of perspectives, encourages the exploration of alternative paradigms and newly articulated vocabularies that speak to human identity, freedom, and suffering. Thus, we are encouraged to reimagine our encounters with difference, our notions of the "other," and what constitutes therapeutic modalities.

The study and practices of mental health practitioners, psychoanalysts, and scholars in the humanities will be sharpened, enhanced, and illuminated by these vibrant conversations, representing pluralistic methods of inquiry, including those typically identified as psychoanalytic, humanistic, qualitative, phenomenological, or existential.

Recent titles in the series include:

Madness in Experience and History
Merleau-Ponty's Phenomenology and Foucault's Archaeology
Hannah Lyn Venable

Fanon, Phenomenology and Psychology
Edited by Leswin Laubscher, Derek Hook, and Miraj U. Desai

Self and Other in an Age of Uncertain Meaning
Communication and the Marriage of Minds
Timothy D. Stephen

For a full list of titles in the series, please visit the Routledge website at:
www.routledge.com/Psychology-and-the-Other/book-series/PSYOTH

misReading Plato

Continental and Psychoanalytic Glimpses Beyond the Mask

Edited by Matthew Clemente, Bryan J. Cocchiara and William J. Hendel

NEW YORK AND LONDON

Cover image: *Socrates reproaching Alcibiades*, Anton Petter, oil on canvas. © Alamy/The Picture Art Collection.

First published 2022
by Routledge
605 Third Avenue, New York, NY 10158

and by Routledge
4 Park Square, Milton Park, Abingdon, Oxon, OX14 4RN

Routledge is an imprint of the Taylor & Francis Group, an informa business

© 2022 selection and editorial matter, Matthew Clemente, Bryan J. Cocchiara and William J. Hendel; individual chapters, the contributors

The right of Matthew Clemente, Bryan J. Cocchiara and William J. Hendel to be identified as the authors of the editorial material, and of the authors for their individual chapters, has been asserted in accordance with sections 77 and 78 of the Copyright, Designs and Patents Act 1988.

All rights reserved. No part of this book may be reprinted or reproduced or utilised in any form or by any electronic, mechanical, or other means, now known or hereafter invented, including photocopying and recording, or in any information storage or retrieval system, without permission in writing from the publishers.

Trademark notice: Product or corporate names may be trademarks or registered trademarks, and are used only for identification and explanation without intent to infringe.

Library of Congress Cataloging-in-Publication Data
A catalog record for this title has been requested

ISBN: 9781032062693 (hbk)
ISBN: 9781032062686 (pbk)
ISBN: 9781003201472 (ebk)

DOI: 10.4324/9781003201472

Typeset in Times New Roman
by Apex CoVantage, LLC

For our siblings
Rob, Alyssa, & Victoria
In memory of Anthony Joseph and Vitoria Rae

There are indeed, as those concerned with the mysteries say, many who carry the thyrsus but the Bacchants are few.

Phaedo, 69d

Contents

List of Contributors   x
Foreword   xiv
Preface   xxiii

PART I
Aesthetics as First Philosophy   1

1 **The Multiplicity of Man: Beyond the Postmodern**   3
 MATTHEW CLEMENTE

2 **Farrago: Mythos and Logos in Plato's *Phaedrus***   33
 BRYAN J. COCCHIARA

3 **Plato at the Opera: The Sounds of Philosophia**   51
 ELISABETH LASCH-QUINN

4 **True Lies: A Defense of the Sophists**   69
 SIMON CRITCHLEY

PART II
The Ethics of Desire   85

5 **Blinded by Desire: Self-Deception and the Possibility of the True Lie in Plato's *Republic***   87
 STEPHEN MENDELSOHN

6 **Philosophical "Descent": Between the Philosopher and the Other**   101
 MELISSA FITZPATRICK

7 "Halt!": Socrates, Levinas, and the Divine Sign 115
ERIC R. SEVERSON

8 Ignorance, Flattery, and Dialectic: Philosophical Rhetoric in Plato's *Gorgias* 133
CHRISTINE ROJCEWICZ

PART III
The Desire of Ethics 149

9 Being and Seeming: On Socrates' Ontological Humiliation of the Sophists 151
WILLIAM J. HENDEL

10 The Noble Taboo: Homoerotic Desire and Philosophic Inquiry 173
ANDREW J. ZEPPA

11 Division and Proto-Racialism in the *Statesman* 188
JOHN D. PROIOS

12 Hunting in Plato: On Noticing 207
DONALD N. BOYCE

PART IV
Aesthetics as Final Philosophy 227

13 The Philosophical Poet and the Poetic Philosopher 229
M. SAVERIO CLEMENTE IN DIALOGUE WITH
RICHARD KEARNEY

14 In Search of the Natural Beginning 240
A CONVERSATION WITH STEPHEN MENDELSOHN AND
JOHN SALLIS

15 Plato's Final Dialogue DAVID ROOCHNIK	253
16 Who Is the Philosopher King? JEAN-LUC BEAUCHARD	277
Index	283

Contributors

Jean-Luc Beauchard is a Catholic priest and philosopher of religion. His first book, *The Mask of Memnon: Meaning and the Novel*, is set to be released by Cascade Books in 2022.

Donald N. Boyce is the director of the Minchin Center for Innovation and Entrepreneurship at Pacifica Christian High School, where he teaches courses in business, economics, philosophy, and theology. Donald's "day job" is to oversee partnerships for a top professional video game team, Cloud9. Donald has worked in marketing, gaming, and exports for the last eight years for top agencies and teams such as TSM, Team Liquid, and TBWA\Chiat\Day. He holds an MA in philosophy from Loyola Marymount University, where he studied Hegel and Bernard Lonergan, and an Mphil from Katholieke Universiteit Leuven, where he studied Augustine.

Matthew Clemente is a husband and father of five. He lives and writes in Boston, Massachusetts, where he holds teaching appointments at Boston College and Boston University. He has published seven books, most recently *Eros Crucified: Death, Desire, and the Divine in Psychoanalysis and Philosophy of Religion*, and is the assistant editor of the *Journal for Continental Philosophy of Religion*.

Bryan J. Cocchiara is currently an adjunct professor of philosophy at Brookdale Community College. He received his MA from Boston College in 2014, where he was a research fellow at the Lonergan Institute. He received his STM from Drew University in 2021, where he specialized in philosophical and theological studies in religion. He is the co-editor of *misReading Nietzsche* (Pickwick Publications, 2018).

Simon Critchley is the Hans Jonas Professor of Philosophy at the New School for Social Research. His work engages in many areas: continental philosophy, philosophy and literature, psychoanalysis, ethics, and political theory, among others. He has written on topics as diverse as David Bowie, religion, and suicide. As moderator of "The Stone" at *The New York Times*, Critchley asks philosophers to weigh in on contemporary issues in art, literature, politics, and popular culture. His books include *Very Little... Almost Nothing* (1997), *Infinitely Demanding* (2007), *The Book of Dead Philosophers* (2009), and *The Faith of the Faithless* (2012). Recent works include a novella, *Memory Theatre*, a book-length essay, *Notes on Suicide*, and studies of David Bowie and Football. His most recent book is *Tragedy, the Greeks and Us* (Pantheon, 2019). He is also 50% of an obscure musical combo called Critchley & Simmons. A new book, called *Bald*, is forthcoming from Yale University Press.

Melissa Fitzpatrick is an assistant professor of the Practice in Ethics for the Portico Program in Boston College's Carroll School of Management and the director of pedagogy for the Guestbook Project. Her research focuses on the intersection between contemporary virtue ethics and post-Kantian continental philosophy. She has also done integrated teaching, research, and community outreach in precollege philosophy in the Mississippi Delta and on the Mexican–American border in El Paso, Texas.

William J. Hendel is a teaching fellow and PhD candidate at Boston College who specializes in ethics, political philosophy, aesthetics, and contemporary continental philosophy. Previously, he practiced private equity mergers and acquisitions law in Boston.

Richard Kearney holds the Charles B. Seelig Chair of Philosophy at Boston College. He is the author of more than twenty books on philosophy and literature, including *Strangers, Gods, and Monsters*; *On Stories*; *The God Who May Be*; *Anatheism: Returning to God After God*; and *Touch*, as well as two novels and a volume of poetry. In addition, he has edited or coedited sixteen books, including *Carnal Hermeneutics*, *Reimagining the Sacred: Richard Kearney Debates God*, and *The Art of Anatheism*. In 2008, he launched the Guestbook Project, an ongoing artistic, academic, and multimedia experiment in hospitality.

Elisabeth Lasch-Quinn is a professor of history at Syracuse University. She is the author of a number of essays and books, including *Black Neighbors* (winner of the Berkshire Prize), *Race Experts*, and, most recently, *Ars Vitae*.

John Panteleimon Manoussakis is an associate professor of philosophy at the College of the Holy Cross (Worcester, MA), and chief coeditor of the *Journal for Continental Philosophy of Religion* (Brill). His publications focus on philosophy of religion, phenomenology (in particular post-subjective anthropology in Heidegger and Marion), Plato and the Neoplatonic tradition, Patristics (Augustine, Dionysius, Gregory of Nyssa, Maximus) and psychoanalysis (Freud, Lacan). He is the author of *God after Metaphysics: A Theological Aesthetic* (2007, translated into Russian and Romanian), *For the Unity of All* (2015, translated into Italian), and, more recently, *The Ethics of Time: Phenomenology and Hermeneutics of Change* (2017). He is the editor of six volumes, and he has published more than thirty articles in English, Greek, Italian, French, Russian, Serbian, Bulgarian, and Ukrainian.

Stephen Mendelsohn received his PhD in philosophy at Boston College in the fall of 2021. He specializes in ancient philosophy—particularly Plato—with a focus on the relationship between ethics and epistemology. He has additional research interests in late modern and contemporary continental thought. He is currently living and working in Chestnut Hill, Massachusetts.

John D. Proios is an assistant professor of philosophy at the University of Chicago. His interests include ancient Greek metaphysics, science, and epistemology, especially as they are applied to moral and political theory.

Christine Rojcewicz is a University Fellow at Boston College. Her areas of interest include philosophy of embodiment, psychoanalysis, phenomenology, Plato, and philosophy of education. She is currently working on the problem of sophistry in ancient Greek philosophy, particularly in relation to the figure of Socrates, through the lens of philosophy of education. She is coeditor of *Somatic Desire: Recovering Corporeality in Contemporary Thought* (Lexington Books, 2019).

David Roochnik is Professor Emeritus of Philosophy at Boston University. His most recent publication is *Eat, Drink, Think: What the Ancient Greeks Can Tell Us about Food & Wine* (Bloomsbury, 2020).

John Sallis is the Frederick J. Adelmann Professor of Philosophy at Boston College. He is the author of more than twenty books, including *Chorology*, *Songs of Nature*, and *Kant and the Spirit of Critique*.

Eric R. Severson is a philosopher specializing in the work of Emmanuel Levinas. He is the author of *Before Ethics* (Kendall-Hunt, 2021), *Levinas's Philosophy of Time* (Duquesne University Press, 2013), and *Scandalous Obligation* (Beacon Hill Press, 2011) and the editor of eight other books on philosophy, psychology, ethics, theology, and the philosophy of religion. He lives in Kenmore, Washington, and teaches philosophy at Seattle University.

Andrew J. Zeppa is a graduate student in philosophy at Boston College.

This work would not have been possible without the help of our diligent Associate Editor Eric David Silver to whom we are grateful.

Foreword

The Parodic Plato

"There is nothing like desire for preventing the things one says from bearing any resemblance to what one has in one's mind."[1] It is safe to assume that the desire of every man or woman who has ever put down in writing their thoughts is to be understood. There is nothing that an author would lament more, except perhaps the utter destruction of his writings, than having his work be misunderstood by his readers. And yet, there is nothing better understood, even by beginners among Plato's readers, than the curious fact that Plato writes as if his main intention was precisely to create such misunderstanding. Indeed, it is not that Plato is such a careless writer that he fails to make himself clear. On the contrary, all his art's skills—and he is perhaps one of the most skillful authors in world literature—all the literary devices made available to him whether by the fables of mythology, the epics, or lyric and tragic poetry are brought together in order to create one total artwork (*Gesamtkunstwerk*), a magnificent façade that cannot fail to impress anyone who approaches it but that also, by making such a mesmerizing impression (the philosophical θαυμάζειν), covers and hides from him what lies behind it, namely, Plato's thought.

Misinterpretation (παρερμηνεία) *is the proper interpretation* (ἑρμηνεία) *of Plato*. By saying this I don't mean that we should subject Plato to all kinds of misinterpretation. *That*, I am afraid, would happen anyway because that's what Plato intended to happen. Rather, what I mean is that, because of the very nature of Plato's writing style, the proper hermeneutics of the dialogues would be an interpretation (*hermeneia*) that has succeeded in disclosing the *para–* of the *para-hermeneia* that Plato's ingenuity has set in place, like a trap, ready to capture the reader's mind. I call *the parodic reading* of Plato, or simply, *the parodic Plato*, that reading of Plato that remains fully aware of the fact that Plato spares neither effort nor talent of his that he does not employ continuously and consistently in order to be misunderstood.[2]

The *parodic* in this case is not (not yet, not immediately in any case) the nominalization of a reference to parody. Parody in the dialogues is almost a side effect of the parodic by which I mean the operation of the *para–* through the *parables*, the *paradoxes*, and the *paradigms* of the Platonic dialogues. The meaning of the parodic then is that of the *para–*, although, as a preposition, *para–* has more of a function than a meaning, and its meaning is to be gleaned from its function in altering the meaning of the noun it governs in a sentence (which also depends on whether the noun is in the genitive, the dative, or the accusative case) or the verb to which it is prefixed. The term *parodic* was formed with reference to two Greek compound words that I thought exemplify best the function of the preposition *para–*, namely, (1) *parode* and (2) *parodia*:

1. In the structure of the classical theater, the *parode* is the passage located on either *side* of the stage. It is called πάροδος, from the preposition παρα- and ὁδός, the Greek word for the "way." As a "period" is a complete revolution around the way (*peri-hodos*), and "method" is to move on or along with the way (*met[a]-hodos*), so the parode is a way *by* or *beside* the way—in other words, *the sideway*. It would be quite accurate to say that there is no Platonic method: the parodic is Plato's method. Or, put it differently, Plato is methodic in the application of the parodic. In addition, the song that the chorus sang, in particular while making its first entrance into the theater, was also called a "parode." However, it is called a "parode" *not* from the Greek word for a song (*ode*), as one might expect since it *was* a song, but rather, it was named so after the theater's two "sideways" (*parodos*) through which the chorus entered the orchestra. In choosing the word *parode* as one of two terms to help me explain the parodic, I have not forgotten the ambiguous relationship that the Platonic corpus has with Greek tragedy to which Nietzsche first testified. But what Nietzsche forgot was that the parode of the Greek theater is also the same "stage" where comedy is also performed. That's why the parodic, as Socrates reminds his fellow symposiasts (*Symposium*, 223d), is a style capable of combining, like the symposium's drinking cups, the clear water of tragic sobriety with the wine of comic drunkenness and drunken hilarity. More on that anon.

2. *Parodia*, on the other hand, is, as the term suggests, an *ode*, a song, that imitates—in an exaggerated fashion to be sure (the element of exaggeration, as we are about to see, belongs to the parodic)—another song or the very act of songwriting. Parody is, therefore, the song *behind* the parodied song, as the palinode is the repetition and at the same time the retraction of the song repeated. In other words, parody is the "shadow" of a song or the "shadowing" of a song (the recent colloquialism "to throw shade"—which, fittingly for our discussion on Plato, originated in the drag queen subculture—might also be used to illustrate the effects of the parodic).

If the element of the parodic has been neither recognized nor analyzed so far and has remained ignored by Plato's commentators, that is because our reading of Plato is largely determined by the various layers of reception of the Platonic corpus that, superimposed over each other and taken collectively, constitute what we call the Platonic tradition or simply "Platonism." Platonism is earnest; from the outset, it has been the unsuspecting victim of Plato's desire to be misunderstood, that is, to be understood as if he wanted the reader to read the said without the saying. Platonism sees in the dialogues as a series of answers to philosophical questions or, worse, as a series of arguments on a given topic. So, the *Phaedo* becomes an essay on the immortality of the soul and the *Republic* a political theory based on the concept of justice while forgetting that the *Phaedo* is actually the narration of a broader scene in which the immortality of the soul happens to be a topic of discussion or that the *Republic* is actually a nightmare (in the sense used by Chesterton, who adds "a nightmare" as the subtitle of *The Man Who Was Thursday*). Everything else in the dialogue that is not explicitly either an answer to some question or a premise in an argument—in short, the element of the parodic—is regarded as *parasitic*. When a scholar does not know why, for example, Aristophanes has the hiccups just before his turn to speak in the *Symposium* or why the *Republic* does not end with the review of the various forms of governments—as one would expect, if this was a book on political philosophy—but rather ends with a fanciful description of the underworld, then it is assumed that the addition must be something either meaningless or a mistake. Thus, an otherwise reputed scholar of Plato concludes that "Plato failed as a literary artist," since, for no apparent reason (not apparent at least to this scholar),

Plato chooses to end the *Republic* with a "gratuitous and clumsy" book "full of oddities."³ And so, Platonism argues, if Plato writes the dialogues as a series of arguments on different topics, then it should be possible to synthesize them into one philosophical system, which is precisely what Platonism purports to be. So far, no effort to accomplish such a synthesis has been successful.

Thankfully, another Plato, other than the Plato of Platonism, has been preserved for us, kept away from philosophy's speculative eyes, hidden in the pages of those books that are placed, rather disparagingly, under the category of fiction. I refer to Plato's literary legacy of the parodic as we find it, for example, in Rabelais; in Borges; in Chesterton, whom I have already mentioned earlier; and even in Nabokov.⁴ The very first mention of any proper name in *Gargantua and Pantagruel*, the very first reference to any book, is that of Plato and his *Symposium*. In fact, the short prologue opens with a reference to the *Symposium* and ends with a reference to the *Republic*. And the question is, Why does Rabelais choose, among all the other authors and sages of antiquity, to invoke Plato's name and authority in order to introduce this grotesque and carnivalesque text—as it was aptly called by Bakhtin in his *Rabelais and His World*—to his reader? Did Rabelais think that Plato was the only analogous precedent in literature's history worth comparing to the colorful and obscene episodes that fill the biography of two gluttonous and dipsomaniac giants? That's exactly what he thinks, and I believe he is right, except that he does not compare the content of the dialogues, the material of the narrative, or the topics of the discussion but rather the *technique* of their respective narrative that operates, as Rabelais immediately recognizes, by the logic of the parodic. Here are the opening lines of the author's prologue to the First Book of *Gargantua and Pantagruel*:

> Most Noble and Illustrious Drinkers, and you thrice precious Pockified blades, (for to you, and none else do I dedicate my writings) *Alcibiades*, in that Dialogue of *Plato's*, which is entitled *The Banquet*, whil'st he was setting forth the praises of his Schoolmaster *Socrates* (without all question the Prince of Philosophers) amongst other discourses to that purpose said, that he resembled the *Silenes*. *Silenes* of old were little boxes, like those we now may see in the shops of Apothecaries . . . but within those capricious caskets were carefully

> preserved and kept many rich jewels, and fine drugs such as *Balme*, *Ambergreece*, *Amamon*, *Musk*, *Civet*, with several kindes of precious stones, and other things of great price. Just such another thing was *Socrates*, for to have eyed his outside, and esteemed of him by his exterior appearance, you would not have given the peel of an Oinion for him . . . now opening this boxe you would have found with it a heavenly and inestimable drug. . .[5]

As Alcibiades compares Socrates to a Silenus, Rabelais says, for he looked like one thing but he was another, so my text is to be compared to Socrates, for it looks like a vulgar story, but within it, "you shall finde another kinde of taste, and a doctrine of a more profound and abstruse consideration, which will disclose unto you the most glorious Sacraments, and dreadful mysteries."[6] The profound behind the base is to be retrieved by a reader who is, like Plato's dog in the second book of the *Republic*, philosophical. "Did you ever see a Dog with a marrow-bone in his mouth, (the beast of all other, saies *Plato, lib. 2, de Republica*, the most Philosophical)?" Rabelais warns his reader that he cannot hope to understand his books unless, "in imitation of this Dog," the reader "by a sedulous lecture, and frequent meditation break the bone, and suck out the marrow."[7] I think one could make a similar observation with respect to Plato's work that, like Socrates himself, shows one thing but hides another. If the Rabelaisian text hides serious matters under vulgar garb, are Plato's dialogues proper outfits for improper matters? What if the grotesque and carnivalesque aspects of the dialogues (and they are both many and frequent) disguise some sober truths, while the grandiloquent parts of the dialogues were but a façade for the ridiculous? Wouldn't this be, in fact, the best way to write comedy and tragedy at the same time?

We all have met at some point that type of person who, having developed certain mannerisms in the way they speak and move, give at times the impression, on the basis of a perceived exaggeration, that they are an actor who impersonates themselves; that, in this scene, they play themselves, and that there is something almost conscious of itself behind the (quasi-theatrical) manners, which, insofar as by *mannerism* we mean the gestures and styles one appropriates and displays unconsciously, cannot be considered as manners anymore but rather as a *poses*. In a similar fashion, there is a certain reading of Plato from which one can perceive in the dialogues an exaggeration in Plato's "Platonism" so to speak, as if Plato's style was aware of itself, aware of itself *as* Plato's style, that is, as if Plato was already copying himself and as if this self-imitation was, under pain of committing an unpardonable contradiction, his *original*.

It is only within this space that is opened up by an original that originates through the act of copying itself that Plato can write, as he does in *Letter II*, "there is no writing of Plato's, nor will there ever be" (*Letter II*, 314c).[8] All traces of Plato's writings (and that was all they were: traces) have been erased or completely covered under the dialogues, as the "endless drafts" of Pierre Menard were destroyed by their author in composing his *Don Quixote*, which, as it is well known, happens to coincide "word for word and line for line" with that other *Don Quixote* written by Cervantes. As Pierre Menard himself explains,

> The final term of a theological or metaphysical proof—the world around us, or God, or chance, or universal Forms—is no more final, no more uncommon, than my revealed novel. The sole difference is that philosophers publish pleasant volumes containing the intermediate stages of their work, while I am resolved to suppress those stages of my own.[9]

Menard is, of course, right about philosophers writing only about the "intermediate"—it is as "intermediate" after all, as the in-between, the *metaxu*, that philosophical Eros is described in the *Symposium*[10]—but he is wrong if he groups Plato among those philosophers who publish "pleasant volumes," as his earlier not-so-cryptic reference to "universal Forms" might suggest. It might be precisely on account of their intellectual affinity that Pierre Menard failed to recognize (or *recollect*, if you prefer) in Plato his family resemblance. As, perhaps, Charles Kinbote, the commentator and editor of John Shade's poem "Pale Fire" in Nabokov's novel by the same title, does not recognize Pierre Menard as *his* predecessor. One may as well imagine Plato in the evenings going for a walk on the outskirts of Athens, as Borges describes Pierre Menard doing on the outskirts of Nîmes, during which he would "often carry along a notebook [of his] and make [with it] a cheery bonfire."[11] Plato did, after all, advise others to do so with his letters: "read this letter again and again, then burn it" (*Letter II*, 314c).

"And indeed" observes Borges, "there is not a single draft to bear witness to that yearlong labor."[12] As there are none of Plato's drafts—Plato himself tells us so: "there is no writing of Plato's, nor will there ever be; those that are now called so come from an idealized and youthful Socrates" (*Letter II*, 314c). Plato's Greek is even more ambiguous than the translation: τὰ δὲ νῦν λεγόμενα Σωκράτους ἐστιν καλοῦ καὶ νέου γεγονότος. What does it mean that τὰ (and that's as much he has to say about his own works) are Socrates'? How exactly are they his? Since we are speaking of texts disowned by their author, what does it mean that "they are Socrates"? Was it Socrates who wrote them? Or is Plato calling them *his* (Socrates') because they are about him or because they are, in some sense, dedicated to him ("*ad eum autem*")? To call someone καλός meant, of course, to call him "attractive" or "good-looking." The νέος is a little more unusual in this context and a terrible pleonasm for a Greek for whom it would never cross his mind to call an old man καλός. It can mean, of course, "young" or "youthful" in which case Plato would seem to say that the dialogues are the nostalgic reminiscences of a Socrates "young and beautiful," except that, given Socrates' notorious ugliness (it is, after all, on the basis of his ugliness that one can surmise how Plato understood Socrates' trial and execution in the *Apology* and the *Phaedo*, respectively), it would be rather unconvincing, all poetic license notwithstanding, to call Socrates "beautiful" or "good-looking" during any period of his life, including his youth, assuming that at some point he was actually young (a young Socrates in the *Parmenides* thinks and speaks very much like the older Socrates). Καλός already implies νέος (since, following Diotima, who is herself expressing a commonplace of Greek mentality, physical beauty is to be found only in youth), which renders the addition of νέος superfluous and, insofar as Plato deliberately writes it, suspicious.

If, on the other hand, we take the expression καλοῦ καὶ νέου to refer not to Socrates' physical appearance but rather, as some translations have it, to Socrates' philosophy that Plato has set down in writing in these dialogues for which, as we have seen, he refuses to receive any credit, then they are not his but "the work of a Socrates embellished and modernized" (*Letter II*, 314).[13] In this case, Plato would seem to say that he could take perhaps some credit but only for the "presentation" of Socrates' ideas; he can't, however, claim authorship of the ideas themselves. In other words, the so-called Platonic dialogues present the authentic thought of Socrates, only "embellished and modernized." And so that's all that Plato is—the embellisher and modernizer of Socrates. (Lamentably, this line of interpretation is followed even today, or especially today, by many readers of Plato and—alas!—by many scholars of Plato as well.)

The phrase, however, that Plato uses as the formula of solving the mystery of the authorship of the dialogues is, significantly enough, an echo that refers the reader back to the most famous scene of recognition in Greek letters. It is the scene from Homer's *Odyssey* that describes the crucial moment when Odysseus's true identity is to be discovered, even though he is still disguised under the tatters of a wandering beggar, by his old handmaid, who recognizes his childhood wound on his thigh as she is about to wash his feet. This context makes Plato's phrase ring quite differently now, for it is as if we are to recognize the true identity of the dialogues' author, as the old handmaid recognizes Odysseus's from his wound. In the dialogues, after all, one finds often such passages that compare either Socrates specifically or, through Socrates, the philosopher in general, with Homer's stargazing, homebound navigator. It is also at this moment that Homer remembers the day Odysseus was born, the day he was named by his grandfather, Autolukos, to whom παῖδα νέον γεγαῶτα (*Odyssey*, XIX, 400). Plato's phrase καλοῦ καὶ νέου γεγονότος, insofar as it echoes the Homeric formula of announcing Odysseus's birth, could suggest that, even as Plato abdicates his authorial rights to the dialogues for the sake of Socrates, he, nevertheless, maintains for himself a different claim: that of the *paternity* of Socrates.

Therefore, that reader of Plato who, like that friend of the person with the exaggerated mannerisms, happens to catch a glimpse of that shadow that lags behind the dialogues and that gives them such a dimension of depth that makes them opaque and insincere, has to forfeit for good the earnestness of a reading that hasn't yet lost its innocence. As with all sacrifices, however, no offering is left unrewarded and so it is also with that reader of Plato for whom the ability to recognize the parodic in the dialogues is a worthy substitution for the loss of his reading's innocence.

John Panteleimon Manoussakis

Notes

1 Proust, *In Search of the Lost Time* (vol. 3), 629.
2 Is the reader, then, to approach Plato with the same caution and mistrust that Descartes has for the sensible world, which might be, after all, nothing more than a deception of an evil genius? Isn't the "awareness" of Plato's cunning already embedded in the hermeneutics of suspicion that the careful reader would anyways apply, especially when reading something presented in the

form of fiction? The parodic reading is not the skeptical reading; it doesn't decide the truth or falsehood of what Plato writes; rather, it is interested *in understanding the role of distortion and deception in the Platonic corpus and how the distorted image* (pareidolia) *contributes to the uncovering of the truth hidden therein.*

3 Annas, *An Introduction to Plato's Republic*, 335.
4 I limit myself only to those names that I happen to mention here. There are others. To support my position that in literature one finds a forgotten Plato worth discovering, I would say that the best commentary on the *Phaedrus*, for example, is Thomas Mann's *Death in Venice*, as the best reading of the *Charmides* is to be found in Oscar Wilde's eponymous poem.
5 Rabelais, *Gargantua and Pantagruel*, 19. (I retain the text's spelling and emphasis.)
6 Ibid., 21.
7 Ibid., 20–21.
8 Citations of *Letter II* come from the Morrow translation found in Cooper's *Complete Works* unless otherwise noted.
9 Borges, "Pierre Menard, Author of the *Quixote*" in *Collected Fictions*, 91.
10 See Plato, *Symposium*, 202e–203.
11 Borges, "Pierre Menard," 91 (footnote).
12 Borges, "Pierre Menard," 91.
13 This rendering comes from L. A. Post's translation in Hamilton and Cairns's *The Collected Dialogues of Plato*, 1567.

Bibliography

Annas, Julia, *An Introduction to Plato's Republic* (Oxford: Oxford University Press, 1981)

Borges, Jorge Luis, "Pierre Menard, Author of the *Quixote*" in *Collected Fictions*, trans. Andrew Hurley (New York: Penguin, 1999)

Plato, *The Collected Dialogues of Plato*, ed. Edith Hamilton and Huntington Cairns (Princeton, NJ: Princeton University Press, 1989)

Plato, *Complete Works*, ed. John M. Cooper (Indianapolis, IN: Hackett, 1997)

Proust, Marcel, *In Search of the Lost Time* (vol. 3: *The Guermantes Way*), trans. C. K. Scott Moncrieff and Terence Kilmartin (New York: Everyman's Library, 2001)

Rabelais, François, *Gargantua and Pantagruel*, trans. Thomas Urquhart (New York: Everyman's Library, 1994)

Preface

There could be no justification for adding even one page more to the 2,400-year accumulation of commentary on Plato. What aspect of the dialogues has not been remarked on by this late hour? It would be an incredible act of hubris to believe that there has been anything left unsaid. Yet, as every neglected child will tell you, what is said is not always heard. And Socrates—both his friends and accusers agree—was not one to neglect children. Can the same be said of Plato's interpreters? Or is it not that most readers today come to the dialogues devoid of childlike wonder, already anticipating the readings they will find, with ready-made answers prepared before they have even opened the books?

The canonical philosophers and philosophies are, in a sense, the most inaccessible, the most obscure. That might sound like a paradox (wide acceptance, admiration, and interminable study would, presumably, leave few mysteries) but it's easy enough to explain. Wherever you happen to be is hidden by its nearness. Think, for example, of standing in a crowd or on top of a mountain; the distant observer can see where you are better than you can yourself. It's not so different for the students of Socrates and Plato living in the West. Their ideas are so pervasive, so foundational, so integral to our governments and our religions that it would hardly be an exaggeration to say that we are living in their civilization, sitting atop their insights (or the intellectual accretions that began with their insights). To study them from on top and within is like studying a skyscraper by leaning over the side of the observation deck—there is more vertigo, distortion, and danger in that speculative craning than there is enlightenment.

Thus, in order to approach the dialogues anew, as if for the first time, we must employ a method that brings us back to our questionable beginnings, one that lets go of the comfortable abstractions that academic philosophy so often provides in order to return us to the morass of the human psyche, the enormity of our finite condition. We need to stand with a foot in the mire and not on the shoulders of hollow men, the unriddlers of the past who can answer the Sphinx but never the mirror. Only there, on the ground and on our own—without the aid or restraints of the canonical interpretations—can we appreciate Plato in his full majesty. Only when we have forgotten the principles of Platonism and recollected Plato's most forgotten principle—know thyself—can we understand the value of his philosophy, not as an intellectual exercise but as a way of life.

There is no question that the best thinkers of the past two centuries have been Platonists in the truest sense. From the existential philosophers to the psychoanalysts to the great artists and literary figures, the intellectual titans of modernity are characterized by a desire to bring human reflection back down to the level of human interaction. Dialogue, their works suggest, is the ore from which every insight is extracted. (Indeed, many—such as Freud in *The Future of an Illusion* and Nietzsche in *On the Genealogy of Morals*—were forced to invent interlocutors when no one seemed willing to take up and challenge their most audacious ideas.) The "talking cure" and the "hermeneutic wager" tell us more about human existence than any amount of armchair abstraction because they depend upon confrontation with the other, understanding born of disagreement and resistance, a kind of living truth that is refined when it is refuted.

This animating spirit, which opens new intellectual pathways by opening the conversation to the clash of ideas, is precisely what is needed if we are going to read the dialogues anew. In this volume, contributors offer nuanced, nontraditional readings of Plato, readings that not only analyze but also build on the dialogues by bringing them into conversation with psychoanalysis, phenomenology, and contemporary continental thought more broadly. It is our hope that in doing so, their work will initiate a new generation of readers whose approach to the works of Plato is markedly different from the scholars of the past, more philosophical, more psychological, and, ultimately, more human.

MSC, BJC, and WJH
Elaphebolion 17/March 31, 2021
Final Day of the City Dionysia/Spy Wednesday

Part I

Aesthetics as First Philosophy

1

The Multiplicity of Man
Beyond the Postmodern

Matthew Clemente

Preface: The American Philosopher

> "Phaedrus, my friend! Where have you been? And where are you going?"
> —*Phaedrus*, 227a

Every son pines for the death of his father. As a father of boys, I recognize the truth of this maxim more readily today than I did as a boy, living, as I was, through that exuberant carnival of feeling and drive in which experience has yet to be sublimated yet to detach itself from life like a dead autumnal leaf and flutter skyward toward the gray empyrean only to land brittle and dry on the starving sod of rational thought. Yet not just sons but peoples are thrust forth by the mania of the patricidic drive. Nations are founded on it. Temples erected in its honor. Every art, every science, every religion—in short, all that we call culture, everything civilized and refined—gives testimony to the hold it has on the human spirit.

Americans know this better than most. Or if we don't know it, we live it. The death of the father is our daily bread. We commemorate his decomposition with our national festivals, reenact his demise with our unending wars and circular political disputes, wave his severed head from the pike of our flagpoles, and march through the streets declaring our independence from his rule. What, after all, is the American freeman, as Emerson calls him, free from? The "courtly muses of Europe"? The "accepted dogmas" of bygone generations? No, such influences are felt as keenly today as they were in the time of George, even if we delude ourselves into thinking they are not. What American freedom loosens us from—the thing we have rooted out and rid ourselves of—is the awareness of our debt, the consciousness of our dependence, and the requisite gratitude that goes along with it. Having fled like rebellious children from our paternal home, we

DOI: 10.4324/9781003201472-2

feed ourselves on swine pods and insist we are better off than when we shared our father's fattened calf. In many ways, we are. The father, it must be said, is an unbearable tyrant—another maxim my life bears out daily. But a tyrant continues to tyrannize even after he's gone. Influence is harder to remove than a human head. The question we face today is not how to depose a king but what to do with the shadow he still casts over an empty throne.

This, it should be clear, is the problem facing the American philosopher. There is no need to expend precious words rehearsing the tedious argument between the so-called Anglo-American and continental schools of contemporary thought. In truth, both are thoroughly American insofar as each is predicated on the decadent denial of the past, the former refusing the import of tradition, the latter attempting to annihilate it. Do not misunderstand me. When I say that, in a sense, all the philosophy being written today is American philosophy, I am not advancing some right-wing, populist notion of American exceptionalism. Nor am I echoing the equally juvenile zeitgeist lament that America is an exceptional menace, uniquely guilty of co-opting and oppressing other lands and peoples. In truth, every society is exceptional in that society itself is the exception, the most unnatural and antinatural scourge on the face of the earth (cf. *Republic*, 369b–373e; *Genesis* 4:17; and countless other of society's great treasures that sing in unison on this point). And it is a banal truism that every city seeks to colonize every other. Even the most cursory look at human history assures us of that.

No, to say, as I do, that today's philosophy is American philosophy is only to say that it embodies the American spirit, that is founded on the American ethos, by which I mean that it takes as its starting point the violent amputation of the past. There is no Russell, no Whitehead, no Quine without William James. There is no Foucault, no Derrida, no Lyotard without Nietzsche. But neither James nor Nietzsche can be understood without Emerson, godfather to one, fatherland to the other.[1] The lineage is clear. The analytic philosopher and the continental are twin stalks growing from a single root. They are siblings, kind of like Cain and Abel, divided by temperament but heirs to the same grievous crown. What did these two inherit from their shared progenitor? What trait, what deformity, what sin? Today's philosopher may call his project a scientific investigation into what can be known or a search for meaning in the wake of the death of

God. He may claim to examine logical forms and the structures of language or to deconstruct social hegemonies and patriarchal systems. But in either case, his work is driven and defined by the oedipal impulse, the quest for autonomy, the attempt to stand security for oneself, the desire to root out influence.

Such pursuits, I will not deny, were once noble. Noble as a lie can be noble, to be sure, but worthwhile all the same. There was a time when Emersonian self-reliance was the needed potion, the witches' brew that awakened the spirit while deadening the mind to the folly of human endeavors. It had a vivacity to it, the ability to charm one back to life. The problem is that we've lived too long. Our tolerance has increased; our intoxication dwindled. We post-post-postmoderns have realized the promise of an empty promise and, like the maligned servant of the old parable, squandered our talents without producing anything of our own. What aim is there for man today? Around what values can he construct a life? It is no doubt easier to knock a statue to the ground than achieve that which merits one's erection. But do we today believe that anything might merit one's erection? Have we become so drunk on destruction that we no longer aspire to build anything at all? The past has been forgotten. The father is dead. Who will stand in his place?

This chapter, I hope, represents a first attempt at construction after destruction. There is no denying that it looks to topple certain ideals, values that have calcified and become the most monstrous of idols. But a hammer is put to ill use if used only for smashing. My chief concern is the future. Where do we go from here? What comes next? Lyotard rightly defines the postmodern as a part, perhaps even a precondition, of the modern. "All that has been received, if only yesterday . . . must be suspected."[2] True enough. But if the man who suspects everything suspects even his suspicions, if he sees something questionable in his questioning, recalls that all his ideas are only recollections received from another—what then? How will his future unfold? What will become of him? The answer, I think, is as untimely as it is obvious. We live in an age of progress that never wants to look back—and yet, here we stand at a crossroads. At this late hour, we are confronted with only two options: ruin or return. Wary of everything, wearied by everything, lacking faith and without hope, we can either continue to starve, feeding on the straw reserved for swine, or muster the humility to return to the old man's doorstep and ask for a little bit more.

The copy of *Self-Reliance* that sits open on my desk was printed by a press that calls itself "American Renaissance Books." The American Renaissance, like its European predecessor, appreciated the virtue of the past. (Even Emerson, who seems to advocate cutting ties with tradition, is steeped in it.) Its authors and artists saw that the way forward and the way backward are the same, that the one who comes after us is before us, that he who would envision his tomorrow must look to his yesterday, must examine where he has been before he can know where he is going. As I've grown older, I've appreciated more and more how indebted I am to my father, both the flesh-and-blood man and the idol of the father that stands before me in all things, looms over everything I do. The question is: Can we learn from our predecessors as men, not as boys? Can we lean forward with trust after we've cast trust aside, passed through the crucible of doubt?

The chapter that follows returns us to Plato not because it longs to go back but because it desires more than anything to forge ahead. What comes after the postmodern? What can be built when even the raw material has been destroyed? It is a question that is on the minds of us all, and yet none has an answer to it. Well, in the following pages, I venture to offer an answer to it. The picture is partial, not fully formulated or worked out, but I offer it all the same and hope that in the months and years ahead, others will take up my call to return to the wellspring of the past in order to envision anew what might be made of the future. To do so, it will be necessary to destroy, to clear the way for that which is yet to come. It is only by examining the origins of our values, the regime under which we live, that we can see our ideals for what they are—dangerous idols. And it is only when we have knocked every idol to the ground that we can erect for ourselves a new and noble ideal, sacred, wonderful, and pleasing—radiant as the sun.

Questioning the Question

> "But do you think there's some desire that's a desire not for any pleasure but for itself and the other desires?"
>
> —*Charmides*, 167e

The Platonic dialogues, Strauss tells us, are written in such a way as to say different things to different people. To those who possess "good natures"—that is, those "who are quick to learn, have a good memory and are desirous for all worthwhile subjects of learning,"[3] that is, those with philosophic natures (cf. *Republic*, 487a)—the dialogues convey startling, sometimes unsettling truths. To others, they seem merely to confirm the salutary opinions of those who use common sense as their guide. Take, for example, the passage from *Charmides* quoted above. In response to Socrates' leading question, Critias offers the all too obvious answer: "Certainly not." Desire, as everyone knows, is the desire *for* something—the desire for food, the desire for sex, the desire for wealth, and so on. And what's more, one only desires what one lacks. If I desire a good meal, that is because I am hungry. If I desire the love of a woman, that is because I am lonely. If I desire a cold glass of beer, that is because I am thirsty. Even when I desire that which I currently possess—say, good health—it is only because "I want the things I have now to be mine in the future as well" (*Symposium*, 200d). Or, said differently, I desire never to lack that which I currently possess.

Echoing his question to Critias, Socrates asks Agathon in the *Symposium*, "Is Love [Eros] the love of nothing or of something?" (199e). And Agathon, like Critias before him, answers without hesitation: "Of something, surely!" (200a). From here the argument flows on as a matter of course, and the question of erotic desire—the questionable nature of erotic desire, erotic desire as questionable, as a riddle—is left behind. To those who have not been initiated into the "Bacchic frenzy of philosophy" (*Symposium*, 218b)—those who fail to recognize that irony is the heart of philosophy—there is no reason to question any further. The obvious answer and the true answer are one. But what about us? Will we number ourselves among those who stumble upon a satisfying conclusion and question no further? Will we have our fill of argumentation and cease to search for answers? Will we become fat, glutted, complacent, ready to give up the pursuit? Or, like the erotic man who Socrates offers as an image of the true philosopher (*Republic*, 474d–475d), will we follow our insatiable appetite, give ourselves over to an endless longing, allow our lust for truth to carry us beyond all limitations (cf. *Republic*, 485b; 490a)?

The brilliance of the questions raised by Socrates is that they immediately bring us beneath the surface of the text and point beyond the surface answers provided by Socrates' interlocutors. Merely by posing the question of desire, Socrates opens readers to the possibility of an unsettling truth. And his formulation of the question—Is desire anything more than a desire for desire itself? Is love, to recall Augustine, anything but the love of loving?[4]—gestures at an uncomfortable answer. Yet in order to see the game that is very much afoot, one must pay close attention not only to what is being said but also to how it is being said, who it is being said to, who is saying it, where and when it is being said, and often what is not being said, what is merely being hinted at, or even concealed behind what is being said.[5] It is by learning to notice the subtleties of the text, by learning to read Plato not as a logician but rather as an incredibly subtle poet, that one begins to recognize the ideas hidden in plain view.[6] And this is especially true when it comes to trying to untangle the enigma of desire, an enigma that, as we shall see, stands at the foundation of the *polis*, of civilization, and thus is the key to interpreting the construction of the city "in speech" (*Republic*, 369a) that accounts for the majority of the *Republic*.

The Desiring Animal: A Privilege and a Curse

In *Life Against Death*, Brown observes "man is distinguished from other animals by the privilege of being sick . . . there is an essential connection between being sick and being civilized . . . neurosis is the privilege of the uniquely social animal."[7] And Freud similarly suggests that "the whole of mankind," through the process of socialization, has "become neurotic."[8] But what accounts for the malady of man, the malady that man himself is? Why is social living a sickness? What is it about civilization that nauseates all who reside therein? The answer that the *Republic* offers is *desire*—desire as distinguished from need.[9] Whereas need arises out of lack and is therefore necessary, desire is humanity's *beyond-need*, our longing for unnecessary pleasures. An example may help to illustrate the point. I said earlier that when we are hungry, we desire a good meal. But strictly speaking, that is not the case. As anyone who has gone a day without eating can tell you, when you are hungry, truly hungry, in need of food, what you want is not a *good* meal but *a meal*, any meal; so long as it is edible, it will do. Your need compels you to seek sustenance from whatever will fill the lack. When the Nazis besieged Leningrad and attempted to starve its population into submission, the helpless citizens barricaded within turned to eating wallpaper and sawdust and anything that might satiate their hunger.

It was need, not desire—empty animal bellies, not cultivated human longing—that pushed them to such extremes.

Now should a *polis* dedicate itself to meeting man's needs—should it strive to become what it was originally intended to be (*Republic*, 369b), that which Socrates so aptly calls "the city of utmost necessity" (*Republic*, 369d)—it will necessarily have to rid itself of a great many excesses. It will have to work to no longer be "gorged with a bulky mass of things, which are not in cities because of necessity," things that aim at satisfying our desires, not at meeting our needs (*Republic*, 373b). It will have to eliminate the things that make civilization civilized—the ingredients that turn nourishment into cuisine, the trimmings that turn clothes from functional to fashionable, the philosophy, poetry, music, and art that make men cultured, the leisure and luxuries that move us beyond *mere life* and make our lives valuable, human, worth living (cf. *Republic*, 372e–373e). That is because, contrary to the commonplace understanding of desire as arising out of need or lack—an image of desire which, at times, Plato seems to endorse (cf. *Symposium* 200a–201c)—the *Republic* introduces a distinction between need and desire. Need, as we have said, is that which truly comes from lack. But desire is born of surplus.

Only when it is possible to have more than is necessary, only when we have transcended the level of the need and moved into the realm of the unnecessary, the *beyond-need*, do we have desire. Desire is a longing for more and evermore. It is an insatiable appetite for excess. (One is tempted to call it "lust" to emphasize its sexual origins.) The things we desire we desire not because they are useful but precisely because they are useless; their value resides in the fact that they are beyond use. Consider man's relation to his animal ancestors. Like animals, we eat, sleep, seek shelter and warmth, reproduce. Yet while the animal eats what it needs to survive, I eat what tastes good, what looks good, what I can post a picture of online. I eat when I'm not hungry, because I'm not hungry, because I have nothing to do, because I'm being useless and desire nothing more than to intensify my own feeling of uselessness. Examples abound. I sleep when I'm not tired and waste whole days in bed. I stay up when I should be sleeping so I can drink and watch TV. I wear the same three shirts again and again for no practical purpose but because they're the only ones that look just right. I read pointless books that offer no edification. I show up late for work because I have been sitting in my car listening to sports talk radio.

I refuse to even consider moving into a house that doesn't feel like the type I would live in.[10]

Think about sex. In the sphere of sexuality, animals are staunch teleologists. Every sexual act has its aim or purpose. But how low, how degraded does human sexuality become when it limits itself to being a mere means to end, a tool in the service of reproduction? Or, similarly, how much is lost when sex is seen as the equivalent of scratching an itch? The brilliance of Freud is that he recognizes the oddity of human sexuality, the many strange and startling things we bring to it. What is the aim of a fetish? What is the purpose of a kiss? (For Freud, the two are connected.)[11] Why do we dress up and play pretend? What is foreplay? And not merely the acts that fall under that moniker, but the perfumes, the makeup, the ribbons and the ties, the music, the dancing, the fruits and wines and lavish meals? Why the performance? Why the show? Such useless and unnecessary add-ons are so integral to human sexuality that to eliminate them is to eliminate the human element altogether. (This, incidentally, is what the city being constructed by Socrates and his pals seeks to do.)[12]

The same can be said of all forms of love. Love is and must be a love of the useless. Any love that does not transcend transaction is no love at all. I had a student once who took issue with me for insisting that my children are useless. He said that no matter what challenges childrearing poses, kids more than make up for them with chores and yard work as they grow. Leaving aside that such a perspective could only be offered by someone who has experienced the yard work end of that bargain and not the raising and being responsible for another human person end, it is revealing all the same. What it shows is that we are used to thinking in terms of use. We are accustomed to assessing people—others and ourselves—in terms of how productive they are, what they do for work, what they offer to society, how much they benefit us. But I do not want to be loved for my use. Nor can I be. I am not my job. I am not my societal role. I am more than what I am good for. We love our iPhones because they benefit us and when they break, we throw them away. But I do not want to be thrown away when I am no longer useful. (That we do, as a society, throw people away when they no longer conform to the uses we ascribe them is obvious to anyone who has spent time in a nursing home.) I want to be loved simply because I am, independent of whatever benefit I have to offer. If I loved my children because they were useful, if I measured their worth by what chores they did around the house or even by how much happiness they brought me, I wouldn't love them at all.

Desire, then, is that which distinguishes us from the animal, that which makes us human by freeing us from the bonds of necessity and allowing us to step forth into the light of the useless. Only that which is useless can be valued, valued not in terms of what it does but what it is, valued in and of itself. Yet we said above that desire is that which makes us sick. The root of the uniquely human malady, the cause of our neurosis, is the fact that we exist beyond purpose, that, contrary to Angelus Silesius's oft-quoted poem, it is not the rose but the human being that blooms *without why*. Camus rightly insists that "the meaning of life is the most urgent of questions" and then goes on to conclude that life lacks meaning, that the best we human beings can do is fight on in the face of a sterile, meaningless existence.[13] And while much of his assessment is apt, the thing he fails to note is that it is precisely the ambivalent nature of desire that makes a meaningless existence both a blessing and a curse. Existing without meaning means existing without limitations. Unlike the animal or mineral, bare life or lifeless rock, I cannot be defined. I am beyond definition. Desire frees me from a meaning that is not my own. And yet what could be more painful than to lack purpose? Is there anything more degrading, anything more perverse, than living a life in the pursuit of nothing at all?[14]

The problem of desire, the problem posed by desire, is that desire is aimless and thus cannot be fulfilled. Unlike need, which can be satiated, which is done away with once one finds a means of providing for what one lacks, desire is insatiable. It only wants *more*. It is, to return to Socrates' question in *Charmides*, a desire for desire itself. One of the fundamental problems of politics—a problem which each successive generation seems less equipped even to recognize, let alone address—is rooted in the conflation of need with desire. The Marxist revolutionary and the neoliberal capitalist suffer from the same deficient understanding of the human person, an understanding that Dostoevsky's underground man disposed of more than a century and a half ago. (Of course, who has time to read Russian literature when there are ideological adversaries to tar?) According to the underground man, no amount of material comfort will do. Even if the social programmers were able to build for me a crystal palace in which all my needs could be met, still, he insists, I would choose "destruction and chaos" and even "suffering" over living therein, simply because "that is my desire."[15]

> [M]an is a frivolous and unaccountable creature, and perhaps, like a chess-player, he is only fond of the process of achieving his aim, but not of the aim itself. And who knows (it is impossible to be absolutely sure about it), perhaps the whole aim mankind is striving to achieve on earth merely lies in this incessant process of achievement, or (to put it differently) in life itself, and not really in the attainment of any goal, which, needless to say, can be nothing else but twice-two-makes-four, that is to say, a formula; but twice-two-makes-four is not life, gentlemen. It is the beginning of death.[16]

Of course, desire, too, is the beginning of death and the underground man—who is himself plagued by that uniquely human disease[17]—knows it. It is no accident that he pairs destruction, chaos, and suffering with his image of human life. As Socrates notes, the "feverish city"—that is, the city in which we find ourselves, civilization, rife as it is with the ills of social living—arises out of desire, is born of our lust for unnecessary pleasures (*Republic*, 372e). It is, he says, our futile attempts to satiate our insatiable appetites that cause strife within our cities by causing factions that feud with one another (*Republic*, 470b–e). It is our greed for "unlimited acquisition," our willingness to overstep "the boundary of the necessary" in pursuit of unnecessary desires, that causes us to take up arms and go to war with our neighbors (*Republic*, 373d–e). To quote Camus, "the plague is born of excess. It is excess itself, and has no limits."[18] And, as recent commentators on the pandemic we currently face have observed, the plague is the sickness of the city, the uniquely human disease.[19]

Desire, then, is both that which humanizes and, at the very same time, that which dehumanizes. Look to the examples offered earlier. Each of the useless pleasures that distinguishes me from my animal counterpart is also a form of vice. Gluttony, sloth, lust, greed—which deadly sin isn't connected with desire, which isn't just another guise for desire itself? Elsewhere I have argued that the Eros of Freud is simply Thanatos by another name. Desire is the death-drive.[20] My insatiable appetite for *more* cannot but lead to destruction—be it the destruction of others who stand between me and my desires or the self-destruction that comes from me giving myself over to my desires. The danger of desire, then, for both society and the individual is *the* political problem. All other problems stem from it. But how should we address this danger? What does it mean for the human person to attempt to address desire? Can desire be reined in, can it be managed, without sacrificing the human person thereby?

City of Man: Limiting the Limitless

The construction of the city in the *Republic* has as its stated aim the purgation of everything luxurious, all that is unnecessary (*Republic*, 399e). Desire, we have seen, is that which makes us human by allowing us to move above our bare needs into the realm of the unnecessary. But human beings are sick, dangerous creatures whose competing desires pose continuous threats to their own security and the security of others. Thus, it should come as no surprise that Socrates' program for achieving social stability and cohesion is to purge the city of desire by bringing its citizenry back down to the level of need. In the pages of the *Republic*, we witness a radical reduction of the human being, a systematic reversion that brings the human person back to the state and status of the animal. (It is not accidental that Socrates and his interlocutors continuously refer to the citizens of their *polis* as cattle, sheep, swine, dogs, etc.) Step by step, the *Republic*'s regime carves from man the very things that make him human.[21] Yet before we criticize such a move—and, indeed, there is much to criticize—we must first understand it. Only once we have identified both *why* and *how* Socrates offers such prescriptions for the ills of the city can we assess whether the *polis* of the *Republic* represents an ideal city—one to be hoped for—or makes plain civilization as it actually is.[22]

Now the *why* is easy enough to address. As our foregoing discussion has shown, desire is the disease. It is, to use Kierkegaard's language, the sickness unto death, a sickness that festers, that makes foul everything it touches, even when it fails to kill. And, paradoxically, the very thing in need of remedy—society—is itself both the cause and the symptom of its ailment. If desire is the neurosis of the city, the city is to blame. If civilization makes man sick, it is the very sickness with which he is infected. Allow me to elaborate. Anyone who wishes to understand social life will inevitably find himself confronted by the question, *Why society?* Why do human beings live and work together? There is, of course, one answer that jumps readily to mind. A city "comes into being because each of us isn't self-sufficient but is in need of much.... Since many things are needed, many men gather in one settlement as partners and helpers" (*Republic*,

369b). Need, then, is the catalyst behind social living. Lack is the reason we form communities. By remaining within the confines of society, I ensure (or at least attempt to) that my needs will be met, that I will have a means of confronting my lack.

But human beings are resourceful animals. We are good at devising ways of meeting our needs. So good, in fact, that when we work together, we soon find that we have more than met our needs. Society, then, is the overcoming of society. A partnership that was established in order to address lack not only addresses but eradicates it. Society transcends need. It is the self-overcoming of need, the transformation of need into abundance.[23] And once we have provided for our necessities, we find ourselves wanting *more*. Abundance proves lacking. Enough is never enough. Civilization is discontented precisely because it is civilized. Society is sick because it meets our needs and thus points a way beyond them. In the *Republic*, "the city of utmost necessity" devolves into the "feverish city" (or, as Freud would have it, the neurotic city) as a matter of course. From the moment the city is founded, it harbors within itself the seeds of its own destruction. Its citizens will soon have enough and more than enough and will subsequently demand more and more and evermore (see *Republic*, 373d–373e).

How can society address the problem that society has created? What remedy can society offer to the illness that society is? This, I would argue, is the chief concern of the *Republic*, the task that Plato sets out to answer. At first glance, there seems to be no way out of this quagmire. Civilization appears of necessity to entail its own ruin. But further consideration reveals that the illness and the remedy are one. The very city that makes men sick by raising them above the level of need cures them by reducing them back to it. It is by implementing a regime that prevents people—if not all, then certainly most—from moving into the realm of desire that society secures its own foundations. This is why Socrates famously defines justice as each citizen doing his one job. For, so long as everyone focuses on fulfilling just "one of the functions in the city" and nothing more, everyone will do only what is necessary (*Republic*, 433a). No one will desire what another has or want to do what another does because each will embody justice as "the practice of minding one's own business" (*Republic*, 433b).

Of course, this reduction of the human being back to the animal comes at a price. But that price is paid by individual persons, not the city. (As one ardent defender of civilized society so eloquently put it, better that the individual die than the nation perish.) The question, then, is not whether society should treat its citizens like swine (*Republic*, 372d)—it already does and, indeed, must if it is going to survive (cf. *Republic*, 343b–d; 459a–e; etc.)—the question is how society can accomplish so great and difficult a task. By what means can it secure itself against the threat posed by the desire of its citizens? How can it get the genie back into the bottle? And here the *Republic* offers a startling answer—startling, in part, because of how thoroughly misread the text has been on this very point, the most fundamental point in the book. Reason. Reason, the *Republic* tells us, is the tool by which civilization reduces man to beast. Reason, logic, the rational faculty.

In *Against Method*, Feyerabend writes:

> Just as a well-trained pet will obey his master no matter how great the confusion in which he finds himself, and no matter how urgent the need to adopt new patterns of behaviour, so in the very same way a well-trained rationalist will obey the mental image of his master, he will conform to the standards of argumentation he has learned, he will adhere to these standards no matter how great the confusion in which he finds himself, and he will be quite incapable of realizing that what he regards as the 'voice of reason' is but a causal after-effect of the training he had received. He will be quite unable to discover that the appeal to reason to which he succumbs so readily is nothing but a political manoeuvre.[24]

Feyerabend is a good reader of Plato. Revisit the last line in particular. There you will find, in a single sentence, the clearest, most concise articulation of the central thesis of Plato's masterwork. Reason is a political maneuver, a means of restricting the desires, restricting them because they are dangerous . . . to the state. And it does so, as Feyerabend aptly observes, by reducing man to a rational animal, a well-trained pet.

Consider the education of the guardian class in the *Republic*. Book IV, in particular, details at length the rearing of the guardian souls, souls that, we are told, have been trained to obey the dictates of reason: "as a dog is called back by a shepherd, [so the soul of the guardian] is called back by the reason within and calmed" (*Republic*, 440d).[25] Strikingly, Glaucon responds to this assertion by noting that the guardians themselves have, throughout the conversation, been likened to "dogs obedient to the rulers, who are like shepherds of a city," and Socrates replies, "You have a fine understanding of what I want to say" (404d). What Socrates wants to say is that while some souls are "trimmed in earliest childhood" (*Republic*, 519a), "maimed," as it were, by their indoctrination into the cult of reason (the noble lie of education) which turns man into "a swinish beast" (*Republic*, 535e), others—the rulers—are allowed to leave their desire fully intact. But more on this in the pages to come. For now, let us emphasize that it is the "calculating part" of the soul—reason—that is introduced as a means of constraining and restricting desire (*Republic*, 441e) and that the chief goal of training people to be rational is to protect society from the desires of its citizenry.

Indeed, what can be trusted more than a well-trained dog (cf. *Republic*, 442e–443c)? But even an untrained dog is predictable and thus preferable to a human being. In spite of the traditional definition—a definition that, our argument now leads us to suspect, may have been offered in bad faith—man is not distinguished from his animal brethren by reason. No, every animal is a rational animal. Rational self-interest is the driving force behind all life. What distinguishes man, as we have said, is not his ability to follow necessary means to a necessary end (Spinoza's dictates of reason). What distinguishes man is *desire*—the drive to follow unnecessary means to no end at all. And, while Socrates is convinced—and convinces us—that by cultivating reason as a safeguard against desire we will live "according to nature" (*Republic*, 444d), human beings, we must admit, are the most unnatural of animals—and that is precisely the thing that sets us apart.

The Female Drama: Desire Returns to the City

The city as we have described it is, we must admit, a thoroughly masculine affair. The old Augustinian moniker *city of man* can be understood in its narrowest sense to describe a *polis* so constructed, a city that prizes reason over desire—reason to the exclusion of desire—necessity over caprice, order over life itself. In some ways, that is to be expected. The *Republic* is, after all, a dialogue authored by a man in which eleven male interlocutors from a thoroughly patriarchal society discuss politics. What is more, it is no secret that the history of philosophy has often neglected the feminine, feared it, suppressed it, relegated it to the realm of the irrational and untrue. Yet in Book V, Socrates makes a striking admission. Everything described prior to that point, he says, has merely been a "male drama." And "having completely finished the male drama," the time has come "to complete the female" (*Republic*, 451c).

When I teach the *Republic*, my students—who, like all of us, are products of the age and thus assume its ideals—gravitate to Book V. Socrates, they say, is laudably progressive. His call for the education of women, his recognition of the natural equality of the sexes, his belief that women too can and should take part in matters of state, make him an almost unheralded pioneer of the women's rights movement. His only fault is that he comes too soon, arrives on the scene two and a half millennia too early. If we today have yet to fully realize his revolutionary vision that is because we still fail to see that society as it is structured is "against nature" (*Republic*, 456c), that our roles are merely constructs, that we have been trained to see difference where no essential difference lies.

Such readings, while in many ways valid, bring more to the text than they take from it. Remember, for Socrates, returning us to our natural state is returning us to the level of the animal. It is precisely the *unnatural* that makes us human. Thus, to educate female guardians alongside their male counterparts is not to emancipate them but to reduce them along with the men to useful tools, predictable animals that can be trusted to do society's bidding.

> "Do we believe the females of the guardian dogs must guard the things the males guard along with them and hunt with them, and do the rest in common; or must they stay indoors as though they were incapacitated as a result of bearing and rearing the puppies, while the males work and have all the care of the flock?"
>
> "Everything in common," he said. . . .
>
> "Is it possible," I said, "to use any animal for the same things if you don't assign it the same rearing and education?"
>
> "No, it's not possible."
>
> "If, then, we use the women for the same things as the men, they must also be taught the same things."
>
> (*Republic*, 451d–e)

Men and women—"both animals" (*Republic*, 455d)—are, according to Socrates, equally capable of contributing to society and securing its foundations. Neither, then, ought to be neglected. Both can be put to use; both become pawns in the hands of a civilized regime. What is more, if we fail to educate women, then we fail to educate the desire out of them. Men cannot be allowed to have a monopoly on reason because female desire is as dangerous to the social order as male desire—perhaps even more.[26] No, everyone must be stripped of *his or her* humanity, a stripping made explicit when we are told that the women in Socrates' ideal city will be made to exercise "naked with the men in the palaestras" (*Republic*, 452b).

We said earlier that Book V is where the male drama gives way to the female, and now we find not an affirmation of female desire but a degrading of the female to the same hyper-rational, quasi-animal state of men in the *polis*. In what way, then, does Book V represent a transition away from the masculine structure that came before? What shift allows us to call this a "female" drama? The answer, I think, lies in an insult leveled against Plato's Socrates by Alcibiades: "You're quite a flute-player, aren't you?" (*Symposium*, 215b). Anyone who reads enough of the dialogues will begin to notice certain recurring themes, themes that never seem to be mentioned in the traditional readings of the texts. One, for instance, is how vitally important it is to both be handsome and to surround oneself with other handsome people (*Republic*, 494c; *Symposium*, 194d; *Charmides*, 154b–e; *Meno*. 67b–c; 80c; etc.). Another is how immoral it is to play the flute (*Republic*, 561c; *Protagoras*, 347c–e; *Philebus*, 56a; *Alcibiades*, 106e).[27] The *Symposium*, you will remember, begins with the expulsion of the flute girl (*Symposium*, 176e), an expulsion that, I have argued elsewhere, signals the exclusion of female desire from the conversation on Eros at the all-male drinking party. In the *Republic*, both the flute makers and flute players find themselves banished from the city (*Republic*, 399d). Why such animus? Why such hostility? What did flute playing do to deserve Plato's ire?

The flute, Socrates tells us, is "panharmonic"—that is, not simple, orderly, and harmonious in the way that, say, a lyre is, but rather unruly, improvisational, Dionysian (to use Nietzsche's language). It is "the most many-stringed" instrument (*Republic*, 399d), capable of captivating its listeners, enflaming their unconscious desires, encouraging them to give themselves over to it and be led by it like a marionette dangling from its strings (cf. *Republic*, 411a–b). It is dangerous because it is the instrument of Marsyas, not Apollo (*Republic*, 399e), the instrument of revelry, drunkenness, and excess, not modesty, orderliness, and moderation. Well then, what are we to make of the fact that Socrates—that stoical old moralizer—is accused of playing the flute? What are we to make of it that Alcibiades compares him to Marsyas himself (*Symposium*, 215c)? Is Socrates not, if we are being honest, very much like a pied piper, charming the youths of Athens with his charming little tune (cf. *Phaedo*, 60d–61c; 77e–78b)?[28]

Book V is the central book of the *Republic* both literally—coming precisely at the center of the ten-book work—and metaphorically—containing the work's most central idea: the rule of the philosopher-king. It is a turning point where the dialogue's focus shifts from a conversation on the nature of justice to a conversation on the nature of philosophy and, more to the point, the philosopher *herself*. I change pronouns here intentionally because, if from Book V on the *Republic* becomes a female drama, it does so with the philosopher as its leading lady. Unlike the other citizens of the *polis*—those thoroughly masculine rationalists who, as we have seen, are robbed of their desire and thus reduced to a more natural, animal state—the philosopher—who is "erotic," "insatiable," "a desirer of wisdom" (*Republic*, 475a–d)—the philosopher alone is allowed to be "unnatural" (*Symposium*, 219c). She alone can be a flute girl, indulging her passions, pursuing her desire, pursuing it in the extreme, enjoying that sweet human lust for more and, evermore, that truly erotic impulse to never have enough.[29]

The Multiplicity of Man

Justice in the city is, according to Socrates, nothing more than each person doing his one job, each fulfilling the role assigned to him for the benefit of all (*Republic*, 433a). And if we look honestly at the demands of society—the demands that we social creatures place upon one another—we will have to admit that justice understood as such is the law of all social living. When students enter my classroom, they do not want me to be Matthew Clemente the lover or friend, the sufferer, the worrier, the man with a short temper who resembles (to an unsettling degree) his father, the adult child who still feels and acts like a little boy, the self-possessed writer who is desperate for the admiration of others, the frustrated parent who can't seem to get parenting right, the anxious control freak who lies awake all night with tightness in his chest and wonders if he is finally dying or just having another panic attack. No, what they expect—what they demand— is that I be Professor Clemente. What they want is for me to be my job.

To students—and even more so to the university that employs me—I am an expert in my field, someone who has spent a lot of time reading books and thus knows what they say, someone who can articulate clearly what it means to fulfill the core requirement the university has forced on students and perhaps can show why the university has forced it on them. The secret, of course, is that what they expect me to be is not what I am. What they expect me to be is the opposite of what I am. Anyone who has read enough to be an expert knows that he is no expert. Anyone who has attempted to understand a book knows that he has no clue what it says. Anyone who has cared enough about philosophy to dedicate his life to it knows that it is utterly useless, cannot benefit students, not in the way they want it to, not in the way they expect it to, pay for it to—not in the way he once thought it could. And anyone who has asked himself *who am I?* knows that he is not one but many, not a static, definable thing but a multitude of urges and impulses, drives and desires coursing and colliding under the skin.

In *Being and Nothingness*, Sartre offers his famous example of the waiter who is not actually a waiter—not actually anything at all—but becomes one simply by showing up and playing the part. The would-be waiter is not his one job, is not limited to the role it assigns him. He only becomes a waiter when he starts to act like one. Once he begins putting on his show, once the patrons in the café see him dressed up in a waiter's attire, moving hurriedly from table to table, taking down their orders, walking back and forth to the kitchen, carrying their food around the room on his arms—then he is a waiter. It is only by pretending that he becomes what he is. It is by going along with the game, by forgetting that it is a game and, like a good method actor, refusing to give up the part, that he placates society and justifies himself.[30]

Now, each of us is a waiter in a café. Each spends his days convincing others that he is defined by and confined to his one job. (Is it an accident that when we meet someone for the first time, we introduce ourselves by saying what it is we *do*?) But in order to deceive others, we must first deceive ourselves. So we play our parts, claim for ourselves the roles that society forces upon us. Before the *polis* has the chance to tell me that I must limit myself to my function, that I must exist as an object to be used by others for the benefit of society itself, I volunteer. I am eager to exist at the level of necessity. I want to be definable, knowable, limited to my use. I want to be rid, once and for all, of the desire to be anything *more*, anything ambiguous, elusive, not a human *being* but a human *becoming*, a transitional creature that cannot be nailed down. That is why I like being a professor, why I liked being called "Professor" (so much so that when some hapless student begins an email with the accurate yet imprecise greeting "Dear Mr. Clemente"—or, horror of horrors, "Dear Matthew"— it has the ability to prejudice me against him forever). Being a professor gives me an identity, a meaning, a way of understanding myself. It rids me of the burden of indeterminacy, chaos, change—the burden of human existence.

For Socrates, there is no greater threat to the social order than for individuals to want to be more than the one thing they are. The "destruction of the city," he says, comes about when citizens desire to step beyond their narrowly defined roles (*Republic*, 434b). Anyone who wants to do another man's job or have another man's things—"covetousness" it used to be called, although today the cheerful neoliberal calls it ambition—anyone who wants to live another man's life, to be another man, other than what he already is, is guilty of committing the most "extreme evil-doing" (*Republic*, 434c).[31] Of course, Socrates is not unaware that every man is already another man, each of us always already double. Just as the doctor is both healer and poisoner (*Republic*, 332d), the poet both liar and truth teller (*Republic*, 377a), the philosopher-king both just ruler and unjust tyrant, so, too, does each of us harbor within himself a "double man" (*Republic*, 397e); so, too, does each of us possess a Gyges-like ability to reveal or conceal our secret interiorities, our manifold desires, the multiplicity hidden within.

In Book VIII, where Socrates lays out the devolution of the city from aristocratic to tyrannic, he criticizes democracy for encouraging citizens to pursue their desires without distinguishing good from bad, necessary from unnecessary, useful from harmful (*Republic*, 561c). The democratic man, he says,

> lives alone day by day, gratifying the desire that occurs to him, at one time drinking and listening to the flute, at another downing water and reducing; now practicing gymnastic, and again idling and neglecting everything; and sometimes spending his time as though he were occupied with philosophy. Often he engages in politics and, jumping up, says and does whatever chances to come to him. . . . And there is neither order nor necessity in his life, but calling this life sweet, free, and blessed, he follows it throughout.
>
> (*Republic*, 561c–d)

The dangers associated with encouraging citizens to live thusly have been established at length earlier. What is of particular interest, however, is how Socrates describes the inner life of this singular man, singular not because he is just one thing but because his many desires belong to him and him "alone" (*Republic*, 561c). "'Well,' I said, 'I suppose that this man is all-various and full of the greatest number of dispositions, the fair and many-colored man'" (*Republic*, 561e).

This all-various man is what each of us is, though none of us seems to know it. (Who among us can resist the pleasures of "drinking and *listening to the flute*"?) He is human, truly human, free from the bonds of necessity, able to pursue his "insatiable desire" without end (*Republic*, 562c). Desire is that which distinguishes him, that which sets him apart. Anyone who has bought into the Socratic ideal—civilized society's ideal—of *one man, one job* only to lose his job has had to face the fact that he has always been replaceable.[32] Contrary to what we tend to believe, it is not what we do that makes us who we are but what we want. Desire differentiates. A cow is a cow, and one is as good as any other. If my cow fails to do its job, if it stops producing milk, I will go to the cow store and buy myself a new cow. (Admittedly, I know very little about how one acquires a cow.) And, just as one cow can replicate the output of another and thus be used to do the work of its equal, so, too, are there countless others who can do my job as well, if not better, than me. When it comes to work, I can be replaced.

Thus to define myself as my job is to become one of the herd, a faceless unit in an all-consuming crowd. To find my identity in the work I do is to reject my singularity, to refuse to be what I already am: a multiplicity, an array of desires living and breathing together in one unrepeatable, utterly singular human being. That "our body is but a social structure composed of many souls" is the secret of the philosopher,[33] a secret she must guard and prevent others from finding out (hence, the perpetual need in the history of philosophy to *prove* the unity of the soul). That is because, as Socrates asserts in the *Apology*, philosophy depends on the *polis*. Without the city structure, the philosopher cannot exist. Society makes desire possible. It allows us to transcend the level of need, to live above brute animal reason. But desire is always the competition of desires, the fight to see who will get to enjoy the fruits of desire and who will be forced to work to make it possible for the one who enjoys them. The philosopher is the desirer *par excellence*. She desires knowledge and the power that comes from knowledge, and she can never have enough.[34]

Is it surprising, then, to find philosophers advocating for philosophy and political power to coincide in the same place (*Republic*, 473d)? Is it surprising that Lady Philosophy should declare that "the greatest and most beautiful part of wisdom deals with the proper ordering of cities" (*Symposium*, 209a)? Or might we suggest that if there really is a rift between philosophy and poetry (*Republic*, 607b) that is because the philosopher and the poet are in competition to see who gets to enjoy her manifold desires and the philosopher, quite shrewdly, has aligned herself with politics—knowing as she does that "politics is the death of art"?[35]

Art Is Justice: Plato's Joke on the World

Politics is the death of art? Perhaps. Yet in Book VIII, Socrates makes a startling admission. Returning to the question of what role the poets play in his ideal regime, the would-be philosopher-king reiterates his earlier claim that most ought to be banished. Now, however, his reason for sending "those children of the gods who have become poets" (*Republic*, 366b) into exile has changed. It is no longer because they peddle untruths but rather because they proclaim the truth too liberally, reveal it to the uninitiated, let the rabble in on the secret wisdom reserved only for the few.

> "It's not for nothing," I said, "that tragedy in general has the reputation of being wise and, within it, Euripides of being particularly so."
> "Why is that?"
> "Because, among other things, he uttered this phrase, the product of shrewd thought, 'tyrants are wise from intercourse with the wise.' And he plainly meant that these men we just spoke of are the wise with whom a tyrant has intercourse."
> "And he and the other poets," he said, "extol tyranny as a condition 'equal to that of a god' and add much else, too."
> "Therefore," I said, "Because the tragic poets are wise, they pardon us, and all those who have regimes resembling ours, for not admitting them into the regime on the ground that they make hymns to tyranny."
> "I suppose," he said, "they pardon us, at least all the subtle ones among them."
>
> (*Republic*, 568a–c)

Art, it seems, is the death of politics. For it reveals the nearness of the tyrant and the philosopher, the learned king who becomes wise through intercourse with the wise and the lover of wisdom who desires intercourse for its own sake. Anyone who makes plain the aspirations of the philosopher, who states publicly that the philosopher is on the side of desire and not reason, that the philosopher is the desirer *par excellence*, is liable to expulsion. And rightly so. For it is to the advantage of the philosopher to be able to "soothe and gently persuade" (*Republic*, 476e) those who are sick with desire that health resides in the letting go of desire, that well-being can only be achieved by renouncing that which makes them human. After all, not everyone can enjoy his humanity to the same degree. The pursuit of desire is a war over who gets to pursue his desire. And if that insatiable pursuit is reserved only for the few, then it is up to those few to make sure that others know nothing of it. How then can the philosopher not resent the poet, the one who reveals the philosopher's deceit?[36]

Well, not every poet reveals the philosopher's deceit. There are, as Adeimantus observes, a subtle few—rare, to be sure—who see the benefit of the deception and learn to play the game. There are those who know the most beautiful dithyrambs are sung through the mask of justice (cf. *Republic*, 361a). But where to find such subtle poets? Where are the clever imitators composing their hymns to Apollo? Where—if not hidden in works of philosophy? For, it is the rare artistic genius who understands that the pleasure of the greatest jokes resides in the fact that few people get them. And where better for the playful philosopher-poet to hide himself and have his fun than in a book whose intended audience has proved time and again to be "the source of laughter" for many (*Republic*, 517a), whose readers have earned a "reputation of buffoonery" (*Republic*, 606c) in spite of their red-faced insistence that philosophic "truth must be taken seriously" (*Republic*, 389b)? Why not end the "old quarrel between philosophy and poetry" (*Republic*, 607b) by making the philosopher the unwitting butt of an inside joke (cf. *Republic*, 396d)?

An example will help illustrate the point. One would expect readers to be wary of an author who publishes under multiple names. Yet that Kierkegaard, master of Socratic irony and poetic misdirection, might offer an argument in jest is a gag too obvious for most readers to get. Take the following passage from *Fear and Trembling*:

> If a human being did not have an eternal consciousness, if underlying everything there were only a wild, fermenting power that writhing in dark passions produced everything, be it significant or insignificant, if a vast, never appeased emptiness hid beneath everything, what would life be then but despair? If such were the situation, if there were no sacred bond that knit humankind together, if one generation emerged after another like forest foliage, if one generation succeeded another like the singing of birds in the forest, if a generation passed through the world as a ship through the sea, as wind through the desert, an unthinking and unproductive performance, if an eternal oblivion, perpetually hungry, lurked for its prey and there were no power strong enough to wrench that away from it—how empty and devoid of consolation life would be! But precisely for this reason it is not so.[37]

Now the typical reader of philosophy, being a member of the world's most humorless lot, fails to see beneath the surface of a text like this and thus takes its author at his word. (Kierkegaard, after all, is a Christian and no Christian could believe in a bleak and meaningless world bordering on nonexistence and perpetual dark.)[38] Taking for granted the sincerity of this philosophical word wizard, the reader goes on to accept the distinction offered in the pages that follow between the poet and the hero, the one who writes and the one who fights, and, in so doing, misses the punchline and misreads the text. What such readers fail to grasp is that Kierkegaard's knight of faith—like the errant knight Don Quixote, after whom he's modeled—is both hero and poet, Cervantes to himself, author of his deeds, one who lives out the adventures he writes with the story of his life.[39] And failing to understand that, they fail to understand the philosophy altogether.

Similarly, the jokes of Plato are missed by the many and perhaps even the few who don't know that the joke is on them. Returning once more to the banishment of the poets, consider the style of writing Socrates finds most repugnant: "when someone takes out the poet's connections between the speeches and leaves the exchanges" (*Republic*, 394b)—that is, dialogue. But not just any kind of dialogue; the kind that also "proceeds wholly by imitation" (*Republic*, 394c)—that is, fictional dialogue, especially fictional dialogue that brings together "two kinds of imitation that seem close to one another, like writing comedy and tragedy . . . at the same time" (*Republic*, 395a)—that is, the fictional dialogues of Plato (see *Symposium*, 223d). And what is worse? Fictional dialogues that depict such shameful things as a woman "who's abusing her husband" (*Republic*, 395d; cf. *Phaedo*, 60a) or "one who's caught in the grip of misfortune, mourning and wailing" (*Republic*, 395e; cf. *Phaedo*, 117d–e) or "one who's striving with the gods and boasting because she supposes herself happy" (*Republic*, 395d–e; cf. *Symposium*, 203b–212c) or "one who's sick or in love or in labor" (*Republic*, 395e; cf. *Symposium*, 206a–208b). And, of course, no true poet would "imitate slaves" (*Republic*, 395e; cf. *Meno* 82b–85b).

> Nor, as it seems, bad men [cf. *Alcibiades, Charmides, Critias, Meno*, etc.] who are cowards and . . . insulting and making fun of one another [cf. Socrates' conversations with Thrasymachus, Callicles, etc.] and using shameful language [cf. *Gorgias*, 494e, to cite the first instance that comes to mind], drunk or sober [cf. *Symposium*, 212e], or committing the other faults that such men commit against themselves and others in speeches and deeds. Nor do I suppose they should be accustomed to likening themselves to madmen in speeches or in deeds [cf. *Symposium*, 173e; *Phaedrus*, 244a–245c]. For, although they must know both mad and worthless men and women, they must neither do nor imitate anything of theirs.
>
> (*Republic*, 395e–396a)

The works of Plato, in short, would be banned in Socrates' proposed *polis* and their author sent "to another city" (*Republic*, 398a). For, although such a subtle poet—"able by wisdom to become every sort of thing and to imitate all things"—is "a man sacred, wonderful, and pleasing" (*Republic*, 398a), so, too, is he an all-various man, an insatiable desirer, and thus a threat to the social order. He is, on closer examination, a tyrant—a "manifold" (*Republic*, 588e), "many-headed" (*Republic*, 589a), "many-formed beast" (*Republic*, 590a). He is "*Eros* incarnate" as Strauss calls him.[40] A wolf who is ready to cull his own.

And yet, this is Plato's great joke—that no one knows it. Rather, he "seems to have discovered an art which he has disguised very well" (*Phaedrus*, 273c). For he is "such an artful speaker," so able to "escape detection" as he shifts "from one thing to its opposite," that he can "toy with his audience and mislead them" (*Phaedrus*, 261d-262d), say one thing to "those with understanding" and another to "those who have no business" reading his works (*Phaedrus*, 275e), earn for himself "immortal fame as a speech writer" (*Phaedrus*, 258c), make himself "equal to the gods while he is still alive" and convince "those who live in later times [to] believe the same about him when they behold his writings" (*Phaedrus*, 258c). Contrary to Strauss's insistence that the poets are banished from the *Republic* because "philosophy as quest for truth is the highest activity of man and poetry is not concerned with truth,"[41] we now find that the philosopher-tyrant expels the poets with his art. His art is his justice, to borrow another line from Strauss, because if justice is doing one job and minding one's business (cf. *Republic*, 433a) and the philosopher-poet's job is "to become every sort of thing and to imitate all things" (*Republic*, 398a) while at the same time "tast[ing] every kind of learning with gusto" (*Republic*, 475c) and organizing and leading a city (*Republic*, 474c)—that is, doing every job and minding everyone's business—then the philosopher-poet-tyrant-king becomes just precisely by being unjust and replacing the artists, the lawgivers, the priests, the statesmen—with himself.

To put it most simply, such a man is a greater artist than his rivals, capable of making "everyone who has ever attempted to compose a speech seem like a child in comparison" (*Phaedrus*, 279a). And yet with time, he comes to see his own writing as beneath him, a means of "amusing himself" and nothing more (*Phaedrus*, 276d). With his pen, he outdoes his competition, undermines their authority, damages their reputations (see, *Apology*, 21b–23a; *Republic*, 599b–601a; *Symposium*, 199d–201c; etc.). He continues to do so "until he purges the city" of their presence (*Republic*, 567c) and crowns himself the victor (cf. *Symposium*, 213e). But he doesn't stop there. "A higher, divine impulse leads him to more important things" (*Phaedrus*, 279a). That impulse is called *desire*. And those strivings will form in him a new and noble ideal, the creation of a previously unimagined art, an art that points us, if we let it, beyond the postmodern, toward that which creates the world anew (cf. *Letter II*, 314c; *Cratylus*, 432b–c).

Notes

1 Nietzsche goes so far as to call Emerson the author with the "richest ideas" of the nineteenth century and speaks of being "at home"—"and in *my* home"—in his work. As quoted in Kaufmann's introduction to Nietzsche, *The Gay Science*, 12.
2 Lyotard, *The Postmodern Condition*, 79.
3 Strauss, *The City and Man*, 53.
4 See Augustine, *Confessions* (3.1.1).
5 See Strauss, *The City and Man*, 50–138; Derrida, "Plato's Pharmacy" in *Dissemination*, 67–186.
6 As Nietzsche—one of those rare readers of Plato who not only picked up on the game but also actually joined in—observes, "[e]very philosophy also conceals a philosophy; every opinion is also a hideout, every word also a mask." Nietzsche, *Beyond Good and Evil*, (§290).
7 Brown, *Life Against Death*, 82–83.
8 Freud, *Civilization and Its Discontents*, 110.
9 Interestingly, Freud also asserts that desire (Eros) is the root cause of civilization and thus the root cause of its illness. See ibid., 81.
10 If this sounds like privilege, it is. One of the most pernicious things about privilege is that it allows some people to exist at the level of desire by forcing others down to the level of need. Those who lack opportunity must work slavishly to feed themselves and their families in order to meet their immediate needs while those in positions of privilege are free to pursue their useless desires.
11 See "For Freud . . . the kiss is the first perversion. It is the prelude to all other perversions, since it is a use of erogenous zones with the aim of pure pleasure, separated from the goal of reproduction." Miller, *Literature as Conduct*, 33. For my treatment of the kiss as a perversion in Freud and elsewhere, see my *Eros Crucified*, 62–66.
12 See "But, next, Glaucon, to have irregular intercourse with one another, or to do anything else of the sort, isn't holy in a city of happy men nor will the rulers allow it" (*Republic*, 458d). Indeed, only "erotic necessities" are permitted to take place within the confines of the ideal city; that is, sex that looks very much like animal husbandry.
13 Camus, *The Myth of Sisyphus*, 4
14 Freud correctly defines *perversion* as the desire that exists beyond function, beyond *telos*, that which seeks no end or aim other than itself. See "the abandonment of the reproductive function is the common feature of all perversions. We actually describe a sexual activity as perverse if it has given up the aim of reproduction and pursues the attainment of pleasure as an aim independent of it." Freud, *Introductory Lectures on Psychoanalysis*, 316.
15 Dostoevsky, *Notes from the Underground*, 224–225.
16 Ibid., 222–223.
17 See the work's famed opening: "I am a sick man"; ibid., 193.
18 Camus, "Les Cahiers de la Pléiade."

19 See "Of course, a plague is not just any disease: it is an infectious disease—that is a disease that manifests itself not on the body of the individual but through a communal infection. Plague, for Sophocles as later for Camus, does not affect so much the individual *qua* individual as their relationships—insofar as one belongs to a community and precisely *on account of* that community.... The plague is a sickness of the community, of the city, of the *polis*. In fact, one could say that the plague is a *political* disease." Manoussakis, "The City Is Sick."
20 See my "Thanatos: Descent into the Id" in *Eros Crucified*, 143–159.
21 See, among countless passages, 403b–d, where the guardians have their desires for sex, drunkenness, elaborate meals, and every other unnecessary pleasure educated right out of them.
22 For Strauss, "the *Republic* does not bring to light the best possible regime but rather the nature of political things—the nature of the city." Strauss, *The City and Man*, 138.
23 Abundance, of course, does not mean abundance for all. The absurdity of human affairs is never more apparent than when one considers how a society with the means of meeting its citizenry's needs invents ways not to meet them because the desires of some trump the needs of others. Think, for example, of the Agricultural Adjustment Act passed during the Great Depression, which, at a time when people were literally starving to death, paid farmers to slaughter their cattle and not plant crops. Such insanities, it goes without saying, persist to this day.
24 Feyerabend, *Against Method*, 25. I am thankful to Andrew J. Zeppa for pointing me to this citation.
25 Here I rely on the 1903 Adams rendition of the text because it conveys more clearly the meaning intended. For future citations, I return to Bloom unless otherwise stated.
26 See Lacan, *Encore: Seminar XX*; Clemente, *Eros Crucified*.
27 Nietzsche, who, as I noted earlier, understood Plato and the games he played well enough to want to get in on the joke, also has some derogatory things to say about flute playing. See *Beyond Good and Evil* (§186).
28 What's more, as he himself acknowledges, those drawn to his flute playing are those who live not at the level of animal need but of human desire, the privileged few who have the requisite money and thus leisure to indulge their lust for excesses. See "The young men who follow me around of their own free will, those who have most leisure, the sons of the very rich, take pleasure in hearing people questioned" (*Apology*, 23c).
29 Flute girls were young prostitutes who would attend male banquets in ancient Athens in order to provide musical entertainment and sexual pleasure for the guests. See Aristotle, *The Athenian Constitution*, (L,2) and Aristophanes, *Wasps*, lines 1342–1365. I am indebted to John Panteleimon Manoussakis, a talented flute player in his own right, for first bringing this to my attention.
30 Sartre, *Being and Nothingness*, 100–104

31 Cf. Kierkegaard, *The Sickness Unto Death*, 17–21. Kierkegaard, it would seem, is not as immune to the charms of Socratism as he would have us believe.
32 Bill Belichick—head coach of the New England Patriots, the football team for which I root—has built the single most impressive dynasty in the history of sport (I may be biased) around this very principle. For twenty years, he has convinced players that in order to be successful, each must "Do your job" and has subsequently relieved even the most talented of players of their jobs when cheaper alternatives could be found.
33 Nietzsche, *Beyond Good and Evil* (§19).
34 See "the one who is willing to taste every kind of learning with gusto, and who approaches learning with delight, and is insatiable, we shall justly assert to be a philosopher, won't we?" (*Republic*, 475c).
35 Beauchard, *The Mask of Memnon*, 35.
36 See, for example, the following passage from Thomas Mann's *The Magic Mountain*. "Illness was supremely human, Naphta immediately rebutted, because to be human was to be ill. Indeed, man was ill by nature, his illness was what made him human, and whoever sought to make him healthy and attempted to get him to make peace with nature, to 'return to nature' (whereas he had never been natural), that whole pack of Rousseauian prophets—regenerators, vegetarians, fresh-air-freaks, sunbath apostles, and so forth—wanted nothing more than to dehumanize man and turn him into an animal. Humanity? Nobility? The Spirit was what distinguished man—a creature set very much apart from nature, with feelings very much contrary to nature—from the rest of organic life. Therefore, the dignity and nobility of man was based in the Spirit, in illness. In a word, the more ill a man was the more highly human he was, and the genius of illness was more human than that of health." Mann, *The Magic Mountain*, 456.
37 Kierkegaard, *Fear and Trembling*, 15.
38 Cf. Augustine, *Confessions* (12.7.7).
39 Compare Kierkegaard, *Sickness Unto Death*, 74, with Clemente, *Eros Crucified*, 129–134.
40 Strauss, *The City and Man*, 133.
41 Ibid., 134.

Bibliography

Augustine, *Confessions*, trans. Maria Boulding (New York: Vintage, 1998)

Beauchard, Jean-Luc, *The Mask of Memnon: Meaning and the Novel* (Eugene, OR: Cascade Books, 2022)

Brown, Norman, *Life Against Death: The Psychoanalytical Meaning of History* (Middletown, CT: Wesleyan University Press, 1985)

Camus, Albert, *Les Cahiers de la Pléiade*, trans. Sandra Smith, www.penguin.co.uk/articles/2020/may/albert-camus-the-plague-an-appeal-to doctors.html

Camus, Albert, *The Myth of Sisyphus*, trans. Justin O'Brien (New York: Vintage, 1991)

Clemente, Matthew, *Eros Crucified: Death, Desire, and the Divine in Psychoanalysis and Philosophy of Religion* (London: Routledge, 2019)

Derrida, Jacques, *Dissemination*, trans. Barbara Johnson (Chicago, IL: University of Chicago, 2010)

Dostoevsky, Fyodor, *Notes From Underground*, trans. Jessie Coulson (New York: Penguin, 1972)

Emerson, Ralph Waldo, *Self-Reliance and Other Essays* (Nashville, TN: American Renaissance Books, 2010)

Feyerabend, Paul, *Against Method* (New York: Verso Books, 2010)

Freud, Sigmund, *Civilization and Its Discontents*, trans. James Strachey (New York: W.W. Norton, 1962)

Freud, Sigmund, *Introductory Lectures on Psychoanalysis*, trans. James Strachey (New York: W.W. Norton, 1977)

Kierkegaard, Søren, *Fear and Trembling*, trans. Howard Hong and Edna Hong (Princeton, NJ: Princeton University Press, 1983)

Kierkegaard, Søren, *The Sickness unto Death*, trans. Howard Hong and Edna Hong (Princeton, NJ: Princeton University Press, 1983)

Lacan, Jacques, *Encore: The Seminar of Jacques Lacan Book XX: On Feminine Sexuality, the Limits of Love and Knowledge*, trans. Bruce Fink (New York: WW Norton, 1999).

Lyotard, Jean-Francois, *The Postmodern Condition: A Report on Knowledge*, trans. Brian Massumi and Geoffrey Bennington (Minneapolis, MN: University of Minnesota Press, 1984)

Mann, Thomas, *The Magic Mountain*, trans. John E. Woods (New York: Vintage, 1996)

Manoussakis, John, "The City Is Sick," https://churchlifejournal.nd.edu/articles/the-city-is-sick/

Menard, Pierre, *Les problèmes d'un problème* (Paris: Éditions de la Nouvelle Revue Française, 1917)

Miller, J. Hillis, *Literature as Conduct: Speech Acts in Henry James* (New York: Fordham University Press, 2005)

Nietzsche, Friedrich, *Beyond Good and Evil*, trans. Walter Kaufmann (New York: Vintage, 1989)

Plato, *Charmides*, trans. Christopher Moore and Christopher Raymond (Indianapolis, IN: Hackett, 2019)

Plato, *Five Dialogues: Euthyphro, Apology, Crito, Meno, Phaedo*, trans. G. M. A. Grube (Indianapolis, IN: Hackett, 2002)

Plato, *Phaedrus*, trans. Alexander Nehamas and Paul Woodruff (Indianapolis, IN: Hackett, 1989)

Plato, *The Republic of Plato*, trans. Allan Bloom (New York: Basic Books, 2016)

Plato, *Symposium*, trans. Alexander Nehamas and Paul Woodruff (Indianapolis, IN: Hackett, 1989)

Sartre, Jean-Paul, *Being and Nothingness: An Essay on Phenomenological Ontology*, trans. Hazel Bames (New York: Simon and Schuster, 1992)

Strauss, Leo, *The City and Man* (Chicago, IL: University of Chicago Press, 1978)

Farrago

Mythos and Logos in Plato's *Phaedrus*

Bryan J. Cocchiara

Perspectives on Western Culture: A Prelude

Who am I? What do I know? These two questions have vexed me for as long as I can remember. At present, despite my immense dissatisfaction, I am afraid that I still do not have the answers to these questions, answers that could potentially bring about any semblance of equanimity. Yet my inability to produce substantive answers to these enduring questions has in no way yielded a flippant skepticism, the type of skepticism that Michel de Montaigne was renowned for. That type of skepticism, in my humble opinion, amounts to nothing more than a casual dismissal of the gravity of these questions and, as a result, would inevitably lead to further obfuscation. So I will continue to search for answers, without losing reverence for the questions themselves. With any luck, this search will bear fruit in the form of an "idea"; I suppose that would be a satisfactory outcome. In the absence of definitive answers, an idea is the best that I can hope for.

After all, there are few things in this world as powerful as an idea. Despite centuries of dense, oft-misunderstood philosophical analysis, I do not think it necessary to rely on the esoteric metaphysics of Kant or Descartes to make this point pellucid. Ideas have built empires and brought dynasties to ruination. Some ideas have cured devastating illnesses, and some have perpetuated oppressive socioeconomic modalities. Every soldier who enters the field of battle does so with their equipment on their back, their weapons in hand, and the idea of victory in their mind. Every politician, bloviating from the bully pulpit, in an attempt to seduce the body politic, uses the most grandiose and hopeful of ideas to beguile the public. An idea made Oppenheimer's Manhattan Project a reality, thrusting the world into the "Atomic Age," allowing the specter of death to loom larger than at any other point in human history. Conversely, it has been the persistence of a few ideas about a certain Nazarene that have allowed some to set aside their own existential dread and aspire to triumph over death itself. Indeed, ideas are powerful things.

An idea, much like a seed, can become implanted in the mind, using an individual's experiential pattern and proclivities for the causes of germination, growth, and eventual reproduction. If we are willing to entertain the analogy that attempts to juxtapose the botanical with the epistemological, then careful attention must be paid to the following biological observation: when a seed is planted, before any nascent plant life emerges from the ground, roots will sprout and embed the seed. Why is this observation so significant? Precisely because this is the unfortunate predicament that is often seen taking place with the adoption or acceptance of a *new* idea.

How many of us truly change our positions when prompted with novel information that challenges what we hold dear? How many of us critically assess the things that we claim to know on a regular basis? How many of us vet our ideas rigorously, ensuring that only the best among them remain? If we are answering any of these questions in earnest, then the response put forth ought to be, "very few of us, if any." To press the point, in undertaking an honest reflection in the form of a personal epistemological inventory, I would argue, that many of us would find that the ideas that we have in our possession, our very basis for knowledge, resembles an epistemic structure that rests on an unstable foundation. That is to say, much of what we claim to "know" in actuality resembles "belief" more closely than it does any sort of unassailable apodictic knowledge. And if it is indeed the case that these ideas truly take root in the mind well before any epistemological pruning can alter a fully sprouted and matured idea, then it would appear that our ideas are just as stubborn as they are powerful.

I suppose the question that must be posed at this point is whether all this epistemological uncertainty poses any threat? The unfortunate answer, which may seem obvious at this point, is yes. Yet perhaps the most pernicious feature of this predicament is the way in which these deeply held but unsubstantiated beliefs ultimately propagate. This propagation model seems to be most clearly explicated in the memetic theory originating in the early work of evolutionary biologist Richard Dawkins. Dawkins not only coins the term *meme*, a term that has far more academic significance than participants in contemporary internet culture would have one believe, but he also describes with stunning accuracy the way in which a unit of culture, or *meme*, is transmitted. In this sense, an idea is a type of *meme*, although every *meme* is not necessarily an idea. Dawkins states that "[i]f the idea catches on, it can be said to propagate itself, spreading from brain to brain . . . memes should be regarded as living structures, not just metaphorically but technically."[1] As such, these *memes* take on a life of their own, spreading at will. The problem then is that communicability is not based on veracity or merit but rather on the tenacity of the meme itself. As Dawkins goes on to say, "when you plant a fertile meme in [the] mind you literally parasitize [the] brain, turning it into a vehicle for the meme's propagation in just the way that a virus may parasitize the genetic mechanism of a host cell."[2] Who among us is doing the planting? Who would go out of their way to ensure the spread of a particular meme, and more importantly why? One need only look towards Fredrich Nietzsche's "hermeneutics of suspicion" to find the answers to these questions:

> There exists neither "spirit," nor reason, nor thinking, nor consciousness, nor soul, nor will, nor truth: all are fictions that are of no use. There is no question of "subject and object," but of a particular species of an animal that can prosper only through a certain relative rightness; above all, regularity of its perceptions (so that it can accumulate experience)—Knowledge works as a tool of power. Hence it is plain that it increases with every increase of power—The meaning of "knowledge": here, as in the case of "good" or "beautiful," the concept is to be regarded in a strict and narrow anthropocentric and biological sense. In order for a particular species to maintain itself and increase its power, its conception of reality must comprehend enough of the calculable and constant for it to base a scheme of behavior on it. The utility of preservation—not some abstract-theoretical need not to be deceived—stands as the motive behind the development of the organs of knowledge—they develop in such a way that their observations suffice for our preservation. In other words: the measure of the desire for knowledge depends upon the measure to which the will to power grows in a species: a species grasps a certain amount of reality in order to become master of it, in order to press it into service.[3]

It stands to reason then, as Herr Nietzsche so assiduously points out, there are those who would take advantage of these "viruses of the mind," using them only as tools of power, allowing them to spread their programs of deception unabated, regardless of the level of virulence, for their own ends. It is in this way that these powerful and stubborn ideas of ours can also be quite dangerous.

Given this epistemological nightmare, how are we to proceed? Turning again to Herr Nietzsche, perhaps we ought to take him seriously when he states that "facts is precisely what there is not, only interpretations."[4] But is Nietzsche encouraging a wholesale adoption of subjectivism, a veritable epistemological free-for-all? Quite the contrary, he is instead imploring us all to take seriously what one is actually claiming when they claim to know something and, by extension, when they intend to act on that supposed knowledge. In that regard, are Nietzsche's words really all that different from the lessons on offer in the writings of Plato?

γνῶθι σεαυτόν.[5] These words, inscribed in the pronaos of the Temple of Apollo at Delphi, were not merely decorative but rather a concretization of the maxim emblazoned on the very souls of all who dwelled in Attica. This divine imposition to "know thyself" was so foundational to the spirit of Hellenism that it was the inspiration for the Socratic teaching that "the unexamined life is not worth living" (*Apology*, 38a). At what point then did it become acceptable practice to ignore this wisdom and treat the Platonic dialogues as if they were something that could be learned by rote? When did it become appropriate to treat the popular interpretations offered by Platonists and Neoplatonists as if they are the definitive readings of Plato? Most important, when did it become commonplace to ignore the obvious and vibrant artistry on display in Plato, instead treating his corpus like some festering corpse?

I do not think I can really answer any of these questions in any meaningful way with the space that remains in this brief preamble. Instead, what I can do is offer my own reading as we move throughout this chapter. Perhaps some will label it as a misreading, but if it is done in the spirit of Plato and Nietzsche, then that is of no consequence because it will be mine and not theirs. What follows then is an imposition to uproot ourselves in an intellectual sense; it is a call to awaken from certain dogmatic slumbers that have left us committed to certain readings and interpretations, specifically those that have the audacity to masquerade as definitive and factual, while actually only being positions advanced in service of some other agenda. This (mis)reading hopes to represent the *pharmakon* that can save us from those Platonic *memes* that have plagued us for so long; it hopes to be a solution for those viruses of the mind. Will this particular *pharmakon* be seen as a cure or as a poison? That question remains to be answered.

Introduction

Quite early on in the text of Plato's *Phaedo*, we are introduced to a rather interesting portrayal of Socrates. As a man awaiting his inevitable fate, he seems fairly comfortable taking philosophical liberties that were curiously never before articulated in the earlier Platonic dialogues. In particular, one of the most interesting liberties that Socrates seems to take concerns his treatment of myth. When questioned by Cebes as to why he is now in the habit of making myths and music, Socrates is adamant that this is a new development in his life. He states:

> So first I made a poem to the god whose day of sacrifice was at hand. And taking note that a poet, if he's to be a poet, has to make stories, not arguments, and that I myself was not a storyteller, therefore after the god I turned to the stories of Aesop, the ones I had at hand and knew—whichever I chanced on first—and made them into poetry.
> (*Phaedo*, 61b)

Thus, Socrates seems to suggest that he was never before a storyteller, never a mythologizer. Second, he seems to be drawing a comparison between his usual habit of crafting arguments (*logoi*) as opposed to the telling of stories (*mythoi*).

When taken in conjunction with the well-known diatribes levied against poets, poetry, and myth found in Books IV and X of the *Republic*, it is not uncommon then that many feel as if *mythos* is not only inferior to *logos* but that it also has no legitimate philosophical application. In the *Republic*, Plato writes that some myths go about "using the written word to give a distorted image of the nature of the gods and heroes, just as a painter might produce a portrait which completely fails to capture the likeness of the original" (*Republic*, 377e). Indeed, one can say that this is certainly not Plato's project, as he is very much committed to truth, especially the divine truth. Therefore, the role of myth seems to be negative when approached from this narrow perspective. Yet, in the larger scheme of Plato's corpus, this is simply not the case.

The treatment of myth in Plato's work is far more complex than one would glean from a cursory reading. His use of myth seems to have a varied, even layered approach across different dialogues. Yet one thing remains certain; in analyzing the dialogues of Plato, myth should not be neglected or taken for granted. In support of the importance of myth in relation to Plato, taking a look at Plato's *Phaedrus* becomes absolutely necessary. The *Phaedrus* is, on the surface, a simple dialogue concerning the merits of the lover as opposed to the nonlover in terms of their role in pedagogy, but to take this as the only purpose of this dialogue would be to ignore the richness and depth that so famously characterizes the works of Plato. It is within this dialogue, and specifically the palinode, that Plato characterizes the importance of myth by establishing a complementary relationship between the concepts of *mythos* and *logos* as related to the soul. In looking at this relationship, we can begin to grasp the complexities of *mythos*, its relationship to *logos*, and its ultimate relevance in the realm of philosophy.

Mythos and Logos

To attempt to articulate the complexities and nuances which characterize the relationship between *mythos* and *logos* in their entirety, especially as found in the Platonic dialogues, is a nearly impossible task. It is one that would require an intimate knowledge of ancient Greek culture, language, and intended audiences. Additionally, the playful manner in which Plato sometimes addresses *mythos* and *logos* can become confusing since he sometimes uses the terms interchangeably.[6] For example, Socrates refers to his first speech in the *Phaedrus* as both "my argument" and a way in which he is "telling the tale" (*Phaedrus*, 237a). Why is this playful? A *logos* is commonly considered to be an argument, while a *mythos* would be the literal telling of some tale. In this instance then, Socrates would consider his first speech both a *mythos* and a *logos*. It would be very peculiar for him then to find one of these terms subordinate to the other, especially if he is willing to equate them in certain instances. This is just one of the many examples that illustrate the dynamism that characterizes the relationship between *mythos* and *logos*. Therefore, it goes without saying that to attempt to accomplish such a feat in this brief section would be ludicrous. Rather, it would prove more prudent to provide a basic outline of the terms *mythos* and *logos* and the way in which they interact in the Platonic dialogues.

What then can we say of *logos*? It is apparent, almost in an obvious sense, that *logos* is an essential dimension of the Platonic dialogues. It would appear then that in terms of popular opinion, "the more specific sense we tend to construe in terms of the post-Platonic understanding of *logos* as something like 'rational' or theoretic' discourse."[7] Evidently, there is a desire to immediately understand *logos* as a type of definition or rational discourse, thus making it the most important and most truthful component of the dialogues. Yet, this would be an understanding more indicative of post-Platonic scholars, and to understand *logos* in such a way would be a disservice to Plato. This is not to say that *logos* cannot approach a rational element, but to understand it as merely such would be imprecise. A proper understanding of *logos* requires a much broader understanding of the term. "In the loosest sense [*logos*] is the dimension of the speeches presented in the dialogues."[8] This "loose" understanding is taken from the basic translation of the word *logos* itself.[9] If we take this understanding seriously, then we can truly begin to understand in full the richness and variety that Plato intends in using the term *logos*. As such, *logos* is anything that is said. It can be an argument, it can be a speech, it can be an *apodeixis*, it can be an analogy, and so on. What is important is that the *logoi*, or what is said, inspire further thought and ultimately a solution to a posed problem. This proper understanding of *logos* will be instrumental in articulating an appropriate idea of *mythos*.

The dimension of *mythos* itself plays an integral role in the Platonic dialogues. It ought not be brushed aside without serious consideration. First off, the appearance of and reference to various types of myth within the dialogues is undeniable. Additionally, all those who would suggest that Socrates is a demythologizer need only turn to the introduction of the *Phaedrus* to see an indication of the contrary:

> Anyone who does not believe in [myths], who wants to explain them away and make them plausible by means of some sort of rough ingenuity, will need a great deal of time. But I have no time for such things; and the reason, my friend, is this. I am still unable, as the Delphic inscription orders, to know myself. . . . I accept what is generally believed, and, as I was just saying, I look not into them but into my own self.
>
> (229e–230a)

This is a clear indication that not only is it futile to attempt to deconstruct myths, but it also seems to suggest that *mythoi* have a role to play in the acquisition of knowledge, even if it is only in terms of the Delphic imposition for self-knowledge. The role of *mythos* becomes clearer as we investigate the types of myth that appear in the dialogues.

Plato makes use of three types of myth: traditional, state-regulated, and self-generated.[10] The use of, or reference to, traditional Greek myths is commonplace enough to the point where we see Plato using or referencing Homer, Hesiod, and the like in numerous dialogues (e.g., the Boreas passage in the *Phaedrus* at 229c). The state-regulated myths are those mentioned in the *Republic*. Whether they are censored versions of traditional myths, or ones created by the rulers, these myths are used for educational purposes within the *polis*. Finally, and most important, we have the myths which Plato creates himself. These Platonic myths are of particular interest because they are the myths that can be said to be most relevant to philosophy.

While it would be irresponsible to look at specific excerpts from various Platonic dialogues and make a global statement akin to "Plato does not care for traditional Greek myth," it would be completely incorrect to state that Plato has no use for any myth at all. Although traditional and state-regulated myths do have their own particular functions, Platonic myths in particular undermine this claim of irrelevance. The Platonic myth serves a very important purpose. "It is presumably through its mythical dimension that a dialogue has something corresponding to the feet of a living being, that it has within itself a link to the earth, a bond to something opaque."[11] *Mythos* may not have the clarity present in other forms of discourse, but it remains a valuable tool for articulating concepts in terms of relation. This is to say that *mythos* bears a resemblance to the truth, even if the imagery used in the myth is fantastical. *Mythos* shows us what something is like, rather than what it is, and so it has the benefit of discussing nearly any topic by way of a maintained distance.

The remaining question follows quite naturally: What then is the relationship between *mythos* and *logos*? It is easy to misinterpret this complex relationship, especially if one is still confined to a post-Platonic understanding of these terms. In this regard, if *logos* is to be understood as merely a rational discourse, then it would follow quite nicely that *mythos* is subordinated in every way by *logos*, after all the purpose of rational discourse is to arrive at the truth. Yet a proper understanding of *mythos* and *logos* makes it quite clear that "the contrast between logos and mythos is not a contrast between a perfected and an imperfect discourse."[12] *Mythos* is not the "handmaiden" of *logos*. In fact, the two are interconnected. We must remember that in the loosest sense, *logos* is "that which is said." Thus, the connection lies in the fact that

> a *mythos* is itself something spoken, and the contrast is, to that degree, a contrast within *logos* itself, or, perhaps more fundamentally, a

contrast which is to be understood as determined from out of a prior domain in which *logos* and *mythos* are the same.[13]

Mythos and *logos* are not opposites but rather complements. This similarity would seem to suggest that despite differences in usage, both derive a certain "sameness" from their nature as "spoken," as well as their objective of an approach to a deeper sense of reality or ultimacy. With this basic understanding, we can now turn to one of the best examples of this relationship in the dialogues: the palinode of Socrates as found in the *Phaedrus*.

Palinode: *Logos* of the Soul

In Socrates' second speech, the palinode, he attempts to rectify the blasphemous content of his first speech regarding the notion of the lover. In many ways, this speech as a whole is a recantation of the *logoi* used in Socrates' first speech. As a result, we can see already the way in which a *logos* can be used to either compliment, expand, or refute another *logos*. Socrates is very clear that before the merits of love can be seen, "we must first understand the truth about the nature of the soul, divine or human, by examining what it does and what is done to it" (*Phaedrus*, 245c). Thus, in order to show the possibility of the divine madness of love, Socrates starts with a discussion of the soul. It is in this discussion where a true understanding of human knowledge and its limitations begins to develop.

The beginning of the palinode is widely regarded as providing a *logos* for the soul. This *logos* is an attempt to illustrate that soul itself is immortal. Yet, for one to assume that this *logos* is a rational discourse to be taken at face value is to make an assumption in line with post-Platonic interpretations of the text. Rather, we can accept the argument for the immortality of the soul as a *logos* precisely because it is something that is "said." Objections may lie in the fact that Socrates says, "[I]t will be a proof that convinces the wise if not the clever" (*Phaedrus*, 245c). However, the sense in which the term *proof* is used is poorly served by our modern language. Plato did not intend any modern connotation of the word, namely, one that would imply undertaking some sort of logical deduction.[14] Rather, he uses the term *apodeixis*. In the original Greek, "'apodeixis' means a showing forth, an exhibiting of something about something, a making manifest of something so that it might be seen in its manifestness."[15] This discussion of the soul's immortality then is a showing of something, from something else. It is in this sense that it also represents a *logos*, as "apodeixis."

This "showing forth" begins with a very simple assertion, "every soul is immortal" (*Phaedrus*, 245c). This claim is then further illustrated by another suggestion, "that is because whatever is always in motion is immortal, while what moves, and is moved by, something else stops living when it stops moving" (*Phaedrus*, 245c). Finally, Socrates shows that "it is only what moves itself that never desists from motion" (*Phaedrus*, 245c). The whole structure of the "apodeixis" is clear and present in three parts. First, all souls are said to be immortal. Next, something that is immortal is shown to never stop moving. Finally, Socrates shows that something that is in never-ending motion is a self-moving object. What remains as the basic premise of the argument is that there is a deep connection between life and motion, and what is even more apparent is that the latter is a mark of the former.[16] The implication of these words illustrates the way in which a soul trapped within a body would be responsible for the motion of that body:

> In fact, this self-mover is also the source and spring of motion in everything else that moves; and a source has no beginning. That is because anything that has a beginning comes from some source, but there is no source for this.... Since it cannot have a beginning, then necessarily it cannot be destroyed.
>
> (*Phaedrus*, 245c–245d)

There is a sense in which this "apodeixis" is not necessarily complete in itself. If this were to be taken literally as a logical proof, then we could indeed find this problematic. However, since is to be understood as a showing of something, from something, there can be no true quibbles as to the soundness of this "proof," because Socrates did demonstrate effectively how the three principles of immortality, perpetual motion, and self-motion are related in this showing forth. He has shown a possible (and frankly plausible), albeit untested, nature of the soul—"that whatever moves itself is essentially a soul—then it follows necessarily that soul should have neither birth nor death" (*Phaedrus*, 245e). Yet the specific application of this motion and its legitimacy remain to be seen. It will require another mode of discourse in order to complement what has already been shown forth. It will require a *mythos*.

Palinode: *Mythos* of the Soul

Socrates himself states that "to describe what the soul actually is would require a very long account, altogether a task for a god in every way" (*Phaedrus*, 246a). This knowledge of the soul would be an understanding of *being that is what it really is—ousia ontôs ousa* or *Being being beingly*. This is true being, and it is achievable by the intellect (*nous*) alone. As such, this type of knowledge is left almost exclusively to the gods. Therefore, in order to discuss the soul as such, in conjunction with the nature of the soul as previously "shown forth," we should supplement the "apodeixis" with the use of *mythos*. Socrates' motivation for doing this revolves around the notion that "to say what [the soul] is like is humanly possible and takes less time" (*Phaedrus*, 246a). By stating "what it is like" and not "what it is," Socrates is attempting to move past the previous "apodeixis," which described the nature of the soul, as well as the limitations of language, and gain some insight into the soul by means of *mythos*. Socrates states that in terms of language, "we are in accord with one another about some of the things we discourse about and in discord about others" (*Phaedrus*, 263a). Language, as such, is limited in its ability to convey the truth. As a result, the language we would employ to attempt to articulate a *logos* of the soul as *ousia ontôs ousa* is prone to imprecision that could potentially lead to falsities. Therefore, *logos*, in the post-Platonic sense (as a rational discourse), is unsuitable for investigating the *ousia ontôs ousa* of the soul. However, *mythos*, as something that is spoken, is, in fact, a form of *logos*. This is precisely why Socrates makes use of an elaborate *mythos* in order to try to explain what the *ousia ontôs ousa* of the soul is like through representation and relation. *Mythos*, as a type of distinct *logos*, has the potential as a discourse to create a sense of wholeness to human experience through distance. This allows for knowledge to progress by moving past the limitations of language, as well as arrive at novel solutions to distinct problems in the form of a unique type of *logos*. This understanding of the whole is unencumbered with particularities and differences; rather, what it seeks is to relate to the truth without purporting to be the truth.

Mythos will never say what the soul is, but by constructing a whole within a framework, it can attempt to articulate what the truth is like. This *mythos* of the soul attempts to "liken the soul to the natural union of a team of winged horses and their charioteer" (*Phaedrus*, 246a). This is a natural image that seamlessly corresponds to the "apodeixis," which previously likened the nature of the soul to ceaseless self-motion. The notion of this *mytho*s is integral to Plato's notion of true being (*ousia ontôs ousa*). Socrates states that "the gods have horses and charioteers that are themselves all good and come from good stock besides, while everyone else has a mixture" (*Phaedrus*, 246a–246b). As a result, we can see that the divine motion of the soul is immediately that which is highest and in accordance with true being. This notion of true being results from a dualism established from the *mythos* itself, rooted in knowledge as opposed to opinion and being as opposed to becoming. The gods themselves are the only ones capable of seeing into this plane of true being consistently, because the charioteers of their souls are driven by a perfect sense of *nous* and the chariots themselves are led by two flawless winged horses (one representing temperance, and the other justice). These godly souls can perceive the "real" quite easily, in as far as they are perfect beings, and these perceptions give them "the knowledge of that really is what it is" (*Phaedrus*, 247e). Their movements are able to keep them as close to the "divine banquet" as possible. "These movements as a whole, the movement pertaining to the divine banquet, is the most significant movement of all."[17] It is at this divine banquet where souls are able to "feast" on true being itself. Human beings do not have perfect *nous*. Human beings are not guided by two perfect winged horses. As a result, "this means that chariot-driving in our case is inevitably a painfully difficult business" (*Phaedrus*, 246b). However, despite the fact that we are imperfect, there are times when we can muster enough virtue to overcome our flawed winged horses and our imperfect charioteers. This allows us to ascend, with or without a daimon, and "although distracted by the horses, this soul does have a view of reality, just barely" (*Phaedrus*, 248a).

Yet this is a rare occurrence, especially for the human being who is not a lover of wisdom. Only a lover of wisdom can control the reigns of his horses enough to feast at the divine banquet, to gain a glimpse at the really real, the *ousia ontôs ousa*. Most people are left in the mere world of becoming, led by furious horses whose wings have long since fallen off. These individuals are incompetent and uninitiated, and they live entirely in the world of opinion. If a lover of wisdom is able to pursue this reality in accordance with virtue and eros, then his soul shall return to the realm of true being in a fraction of the time it would take for an incompetent human soul to accomplish the same feat. Thus, we see how mythos is integral to knowledge both in its presence and its execution. In terms of Socrates himself, he does not claim to know the truth about matters that are beyond him. For he does not yet know the truth about himself. He recognizes that only the gods have access to ultimate Truth. Only the gods are wise. He is content with simply being "wisdom's lover—a philosopher" (*Phaedrus*, 278d). For it is the philosopher whose soul, in its motion, can come close to attaining the purest, divine knowledge of the True, Holy, Beautiful, and Good.

Philosophical Implications: Collection and Division

Thus far, we have seen that Plato illustrates how it is necessary to use all manners of *logoi*, including *mythos*, in order to arrive upon the closest approximation to the divine truth. This becomes crucial in the second half of the *Phaedrus*, because it is Plato who seems to suggest that discourse, be it speech making or writing, which is indifferent to the truth is useless, if not dangerous. Socrates states that "the art of a speaker who doesn't know the truth and chases opinions instead is likely to be a ridiculous thing—not an art at all!" (*Phaedrus*, 262c). This is the concern with Lysias or any other rhetorician not committed to the truth. Their words are hollow; they lack substance and gravity. They are empty *logoi* with a desire to win an argument rather than pursue wisdom's divine path. In word, it is sophistry, and as such, these empty *logoi* are prone to falsities, and they can only take us so far. Socrates insists that the limits of language apply to writings as well. He states that

> the same is true of written words. You'd think they were speaking as if they had some understanding, but if you question anything that has been said because you want to learn more, it continues to signify just that very same thing forever.
>
> (*Phaedrus*, 275d–275e)

Thus, we see that any discourse that focuses on language or the strength of arguments, rather than on substance, virtue, and knowledge, is suspect at best. Socrates concludes by describing the discourse that is expectable and capable of transcending the limits of language. That discourse is the method of collection and division, or dialectic. Socrates proclaims:

> Well, Phaedrus, I am myself a lover of these divisions and collections, so that I may be able to think and to speak; and if I believe that

someone else is capable of discerning a single thing that is also by nature capable of encompassing many, I follow "straight behind, in his tracks, as if he were a god."

(*Phaedrus*, 266b)

In this way, collection and division (dialectic) are the discourses that are capable of best approximating the truth. It is the discourse that makes it most possible for the human soul to once again partake in the divine banquet.

Understood properly, dialectic "is a discourse written down, with knowledge, in the soul of the listener; it can defend itself" (*Phaedrus*, 276a). By establishing collection and division, and with a firm commitment to the divine truth, rooted in *eros*, dialectic is a discourse that can approach the real, the *ousia ontôs ousa*, and aid the lover of wisdom in returning to the realm of true being. It is capable of this because Dialectic is not concerned with one particular argument, proof, or story but rather all of the above. Through the use of dialectic (collection and division), we get a unity of various parts of the truth, which are represented by various *logoi*. The collection would be gathering up various individual *logoi* (be it "apodeixis," *mythos*, or any other form of spoken discourse). The division aspect of dialectic would be the distinction between these various components, and the way in which they all aid in approaching the truth of the matter. It is in this way that dialectic is "the living, breathing discourse . . . of which the written one can be fairly called an image" (*Phaedrus*, 276a).

There is one further distinction that needs to be made in terms of the method of collection and division. There is a sense in which the discourse of dialectic itself is not just a collection of *logoi* differentiated from each other, but it is also itself a *logos*. Of course, one could make the natural connection that has been made up until this point, and understand quite clearly, that as something that itself is spoken, the discourse of dialectic is a *logos*. However, if we probe further, we can see that the tertiary definition of *logos* can be understood as "to lay in the sense of bringing things to lie together, collecting them, gathering them together."[18] This is precisely the project of dialectic: to gather up as many potential solutions to a posed problem as possible. In this way, it can be said, without a doubt, that the discourse of dialectic is the paramount mode of discourse, ideal for reaching the divine truth. Thus, the conclusion drawn by the end of the second half of the *Phaedrus* is clear as day:

once the necessity of the reference to what is spoken about is thought through, it becomes evident that perfected speech takes the form of collection and division, that is, of dialectic. This is the kind of *logos* which Socrates, the lover of *logoi*, loves preeminently.[19]

Returning to the Palinode: Aesthetics as First Philosophy

If we are to take the Platonic project seriously, then there is no way in which one could possibly dismiss *mythos* as some sort of deceptive fallacy or inferior mode of discourse. In fact, the argument put forth here seems to suggest that *mythos* is an indispensable discourse. Loosely defining *logos* as "that which is said" (which a proper translation of ancient Greek would yield) indicates that although *mythos* is its own distinct discourse, it is also a type of *logos*. Similarly, Socrates indicates that the discourse of dialectic, a collection and division of various *logoi*, is itself the greatest type of *logos*. The complexity at play here warrants a return to the very text that illustrated it: the palinode. Indeed, the palinode contains a *mythos* and a rather clever one at that. Yet, it also contains various other *logoi*. All these *logoi* are gathered together to arrive at the truths of the soul and knowledge. This gathering is clearly an example of collection and division, and as a result, the palinode must also be an example of dialectic. As dialectic then, the palinode is a *logos*, composed of *logoi*, aimed at discovering the truth. It follows naturally then that what is truly at play here is a written deed (*ergon*),[20] a literal example of the *logoi* articulated on the page. The *Phaedrus*'s great second speech of Socrates, the palinode, is no less than a *mythos*, *logos*, and *ergon* working synergistically in order to arrive at the truth. It is in this understanding that we can put the issue to rest. There is no hierarchy between *mythos* and *logos*, there is no opposition. They are at the very least complements, and in a very interesting way, they are one and the same.

If we can accept that Plato does not intend for any petty hierarchies to separate *mythos* and *logos* in terms of their significance, then perhaps we can also take more seriously his treatment of art and the artist. Despite layered language and shallow critique, it is very clear to any reader of Plato just how significant art is to him in both principle and practice. Indeed, it can be argued that Plato's understanding of Beauty as the deepest reality—or, as he terms it, *ousia ontôs ousa*, Being being beingly—cements the importance of aesthetics not only in his work but also in the annals of Western thought.[21] As illustrated in the aforementioned Platonic discussion of *The Good, The Beautiful, The Holy, and The True*, it becomes clear that any process of dialectic (collection and division) is going to be working toward a sense of reality and ultimacy that is not only in possession of these constituent elements but instead one that also treats them as an unattainable unity to strive toward.[22] What is Good is Beautiful, what is Beautiful is Holy, what is Holy is True, and so on. Thus, any lover of wisdom, on a quest for the *Good* and the *True*, must necessarily be searching for Beauty as well, as there is no distinction; they are all subsumed by *being that is what it really is* or "true being."[23]

Is it any wonder then why Plato reviles those artists that he so harshly criticizes, or why he might advance positions that restrict or prohibit art and censor artists? Could it not be said that an inauthentic artist peddling their degenerative work is just as much of a threat to lover of wisdom's quest toward *ousia ontôs ousa* as the sophist who seeks to make the weaker argument the stronger, solely for their own profit?[24] Is it not painfully clear then that bad art can damage our collective ability to receive the *Beautiful* just as much as the sophist's rhetoric can damage our ability to perceive the *Good* or the *True*? Are we really to believe that Socrates the fighter, the lover, the father, the sculptor, the poet, and the mythologizer would advocate for any of his disciples to turn away from the *Beautiful* to exclusively trade in a sterile and lifeless discourse, guided by instrumentalized reason? I do not think he would. Instead, I contend that this is the work of the Platonizers and not of Plato. This is the position advanced by those who have their own designs of how philosophy ought to be done and, in turn, how Plato ought to be read. As Nietzsche says, "[w]hen these honorable idolaters of concepts worship something, they kill it and stuff it; they threaten the life of everything they worship."[25] Clearly then, they have their *pharmakon*, and I have mine. The questions remain: Which is the cure, and which is the poison? That, my dear reader, is for you to decide.

Notes

1 Dawkins, *The Selfish Gene*, 192.
2 Ibid.

3 Nietzsche, *The Will to Power*, §480.
4 Ibid., §481.
5 Transliterated as *gnōthi seauton*.
6 The connection between the terms is a complicated one, but this suggestion calls on basic linguistic analysis and definition—Werner, *Myth and Philosophy in Plato's Phaedrus*, 8.
7 Sallis, *Being and Logos*, 14.
8 Ibid.
9 If we take a look at the verb form *legein*, we see how this understanding comes about. This verbal form can be translated as "to say," "to speak," and "to lay." Therefore, a loose definition of "that which is said" can be assigned to *logos* without objection. The implications of the tertiary definition, "to lay," will be drawn out for our purposes later (Sallis, 7).
10 Werner, *Myth and Philosophy*, 7.
11 Sallis, *Being and Logos*, 16.
12 Ibid., 16.
13 Ibid.
14 It is important to remember that Plato precedes the historical foundations of formal logic, which were started by his student Aristotle.
15 Sallis, *Being and Logos*, 139.
16 Werner, *Myth and Philosophy*, 51.
17 Sallis, *Being and Logos*, 144.
18 Ibid., 7.
19 Ibid., 171.
20 *Ergon* is the third essential dimension of a Platonic dialogue. Its relationship to both *mythos* and *logos* is inseparable. Sallis, *Being and Logos*, 17–18.
21 Again, as mentioned previously, take a look at *Phaedrus*, 247e, for a discussion of this concept.
22 A thorough discussion of this unified concept can be found in *Republic* 507c–508e.
23 Ibid.
24 Perhaps it is Joseph Campbell (whose own modern commentary on myth is essential for anyone interested in the topic) that most clearly explicates the Platonic connection between myth and art in simple terms. Look no further than this exchange from *The Power of Myth*:
"Moyers: Who interprets the divinity inherent in nature for us today? Who are our shamans? Who interprets unseen things for us?
Campbell: It is the function of the artist to do this. The artist is the one who communicates myth for today. But he has to be an artist who understands mythology and humanity and isn't simply a sociologist with a program for you." Here we can see that Campbell, much like Nietzsche and Plato, has a very clear idea as to what type of art is essential. *The Power of Myth*, 122.
25 Nietzsche, *Twilight of the Idols*, "Reason" in Philosophy, §1.

Bibliography

Campbell, Joseph and Bill Moyers, *The Power of Myth*, ed. Betty Sue Flowers (New York: Anchor Books, 1988)

Dawkins, Richard, *The Selfish Gene* (Oxford: Oxford University Press, 1976)

Nietzsche, Friedrich, *Twilight of the Idols* in *The Portable Nietzsche*, trans. Walter Kaufmann (New York: Penguin Books, 1976)

Nietzsche, Friedrich, *The Will to Power*, trans. Walter Kaufmann (New York: Vintage Books, 1968)

Plato, *Phaedo*, trans. E. Brann, P. Kalkavage, and E. Salem (Newburyport, MA: Focus Classical Library, 1998)

Plato, *Phaedrus*, trans. Alexander Nehamas and Paul Woodruff (Indianapolis, IN: Hackett, 1995)

Plato, *Republic*, trans. Robin Waterfield (Oxford: Oxford University Press, 2008)

Sallis, John, *Being and Logos: Reading the Platonic Dialogues*, 3rd ed. (Indianapolis, IN: Indiana University Press, 1996)

Werner, Daniel S., *Myth and Philosophy in Plato's Phaedrus* (Cambridge: Cambridge University Press, 2012)

Plato at the Opera
The Sounds of Philosophia

Elisabeth Lasch-Quinn

In a sparsely furnished Parisian garret, an aspiring poet hurries to finish a piece of writing so he can join his roommates for revelry in a nearby tavern. Searching in vain to find inspiration and words, he hears a knock on the door. Rather than one of the other young men with whom he shares the hardships as well as the joys of the bohemian life, he discovers a woman whose candle has gone out. After some false starts involving candles getting lit and going out again, intentionally or not, and keys getting lost and found and lost again, accidentally or not, a conversation slowly blooms. The man gives his guest a taste of his life as a poet, poor but happy. She answers with a bit of the story of her own life making cloth flowers to sell at market. But. . .

Rarely does the word *but* accomplish as much as it does here. Given all that follows the word serves as a bridge opening onto a new vista. The word, the softer *ma* in Italian, lingers and thus postpones. We have no idea for a moment what will come next. We sense that the woman has something to say that will somehow complete the picture she has just drawn of an existence so humble that it borders on bleak. Maybe some missing detail will provide color. The seamstress eats dinner by herself, does not attend church often yet does pray, and lives alone in a small white room looking beyond the roofs of the city into the sky. "Ma. . .," she sings, "quando vien lo sgelo il primo sole è mio, il primo bacio dell'aprile è mio! Il primo sole è mio!" (But when the thaw comes, the first sunshine is mine—the first kiss of April is mine. The first sunshine is mine!)

This is the "Mi chiamano Mimi" ("My Name Is Mimi") aria from Giacomo Puccini's *La Bohème*, one of the most famous vocal centerpieces in all of opera. It follows the aria "Che gelida manina" (What an Icy Little Hand) aria sung by Rodolfo. Over the course of these two arias in the

DOI: 10.4324/9781003201472-4

opera's first act, Mimi and Rodolfo introduce their lives to one another and fall in love. But depending on which performance we hear and view, something more might be happening if we are attuned to what is communicated philosophically as well as vocally.

Perhaps it is not immediately clear what Plato might have to do with an opera such as Puccini's *La Bohème*, first performed in Turin in 1896. While he did have much to say about love, he also said a great deal about music and not all of it good. In fact, he had such serious reservations about the arts, or at least he put such reservations in the voice of Socrates (a crucial distinction), that a common misreading of Plato is that he despised poetry, music, theater, and the other arts. If he had his way, he would, according to these critics, restrict artistic expression and banish poets from his ideal city. But we must look further to grasp his real point. Doing so can show more clearly his views on not just poetry and music but also the philosophy of life embedded in those art forms, as in all aspects of our life.

To modern ears, Plato's discussion of music in the *Republic* seems to advocate nothing short of censorship, and this gives critics cause to dismiss his views of the arts and of much else. In times of community fragmentation and division, one thing those of different political stripes agree on today is the importance of liberty. Americans disagree on policy yet constantly enlist freedom for their reasoning. They defend everything from speech on social media and explicit scenes of sex or violence in the movies to bearing arms on the grounds of freedom. Any argument for censorship is bound to hit a brick wall before even revving its engines. An overly hasty reading of Plato based on points made by one of the speakers in the *Republic* without attention to the context of the larger arguments, or, worse, a general impression abstracted from the text, take them on face value and suggest them as a reason Plato should be dismissed entirely not only because of his assumed elitism, as a benighted and disgruntled philosopher of the aristocratic class, but also as a laughable killjoy. How could someone who rejects music, even if only to censor what he did not think belonged in the ideal state, be anything but irrelevant in our own age, in which the combination of personal liberation, the expansion of consumerism and niche marketing, and technologies of mechanical recording, reproduction, and dissemination have made music omnipresent and helped make individual expression not just a right but an imperative as well?

In *After Virtue*, Alasdair MacIntyre explores the ramifications of our contemporary ethic of emotivism, a philosophical disposition whereby only the individual's emotional preference can arbitrate disagreements and generate judgments about the world. In the absence of any intact and coherent moral framework from the past, all that remains are shards of past philosophies. Amid these ruins, nothing remains to harken to when making or justifying an act or argument except individual inclination. Philip Rieff explored the emergence of this state of affairs in *The Triumph of the Therapeutic* as a long-term result of the deep structural change from religion to psychology as a worldview. Communities devoted to a shared understanding of the sacred have been replaced by societies guided by the unleashed wants and needs of the individual. Since a culture centers on what it allows and disallows—its "interdictions and permissions," in Rieff's words—their abandonment leaves an "anti-culture" in their wake. However, this ethical vacuum threatens to yield a new culture whose new allowance is unlimited expression and its new disallowance is restraint. Without valorization of self-discipline, a necessary condition for the inner life, the resources for the cultivation of the moral self cannot be marshaled, and a fundamental bulwark against not only temptations but also external power relations fall away. Both MacIntyre and Rieff saw this as a crisis for the individual as well as the community and culture. An overemphasis on personal expression in the absence of shared ethical commitments provides a blueprint for psychological chaos within and social and cultural chaos beyond, as private considerations pervade the world once thought to be external to the individual. The public realm collapses as the quest for self-interest ends, overshadowing any other reason for its existence.

Eric Voegelin, in *Science, Politics, and Gnosticism* and other works, conveyed the high stakes of what he saw a resurgent Gnosticism cutting across a range of ideologically driven movements of modernity, each emboldened by the belief that they possessed insider knowledge or *gnosis* of how the world really worked and thus had a special, self-sanctioned role in remaking it. That late antique movement rejected the created world as an illusion and the creator God as evil, teaching that an elite few possessed fragments of divinity within and thus had the capacity to reunite with the ultimate divinity, a spiritual force beyond God. All other humans, in this view, are left in the darkness of ignorance. Desire becomes a replacement metaphysics and epistemology combined, determining what is real and known, recasting it as that which is yearned after and sought in the personal quest for liberation from the bondage of mundane existence.

MacIntyre, Rieff, Voegelin, and others have drawn on still other ideas and intellectual influences to understand the reflexive individualism of modern life and tribalist offshoots that defend one or another version of individualism, as connected to the assertion of personal affect as the only basis of assumed and imagined truths, impenetrable to logic and evidence. While critics warn of the prevalence of the manipulation of self and others possible in the absence of firmer philosophical moorings, given the multitudinous modes at the ready in the reign of marketing, advertising, consumerism, elite-consolidation, political demagoguery, social media, and self-serving behavior of many other kinds, many embrace this credo as liberating. In this context, reading the signs and references to earlier philosophical traditions can be vital for resistance to dominant ways of thinking or even for the retrieval of options to what Rieff suspected was an anti-culture on the way to becoming the dominant culture even as early as the mid-twentieth century when he was writing. Examining the ideas, inchoate or crafted, in everything from everyday thoughts and experiences or the manipulation and construction of our physical world to our cultural expressions and artifacts reveals alternative philosophies of life even—perhaps especially—in their subtlest shadings.

Contrary to the most monolithic renderings of his views, Plato actually discusses music in different registers. At times, the status of the arts in Plato is dubious; at times, they are vital. The first line of Iris Murdoch's nuanced meditation on the question, *The Fire and the Sun: Why Plato Banished the Artists*, completes her subtitle: "To begin with, of course, Plato did not banish all the artists or always suggest banishing any." She conceded some points while adding her voice to those who questioned the wholesale charge against Plato that he had no use for the arts. She points to Tolstoy, for instance, who thought that in the case of the arts, as with all things, Plato had use only for those forms and expressions that kept goodness ever in mind. It was not a question of poetry or music *per se* but of what moral valence particular poems or pieces possessed if they were to serve higher ideals.

Going beyond prevalent impressions to the precise interworkings of Plato's ideals, positions, and ideas about music, we can hear reverberations of Platonic motifs still with us today. Tuning our ears can help us recognize different philosophies audible in modernity and winnow out the timbre of Platonism. This chapter juxtaposes different interpretations of the same piece, a single operatic aria, to hear the timbre of different schools of thought and reach toward the often elusive intersection between music and philosophy.

Plato has been dismissed and condemned for allegedly wanting to banish all poetry and drama, and by implication all music and the other arts, from the ideal city. The portrait of Plato as belittling the importance of the arts could not be further from the truth. Scholars have attempted to put to rest this tendency, yet it persists. In one summary of some twentieth-century scholarship on Plato, Danielle Allen pointed to varied schools of thought that, based on nuanced readings of the *Republic* and his larger oeuvre, guarded against simplistic conclusions about Plato's views. In this case, what is at stake is not only a misunderstanding of the particulars of Plato's perspective on the music of interest to specialists. If so, that might be a matter of arcane detail. Instead, this view of music also obscures the rest of his philosophy, since other fundamental aspects of it are tied to music. It perpetuates a false notion that Plato did not recognize the importance of music when the truth is that he thought it possessed nearly unrivaled importance. Grasping the nuances in his thinking causes us to take music more, not less, seriously.

Let us first turn to one of the passages in the *Republic* to see what ideas about music actually appear. But rather than scour them for answers to the question of whether Plato did or did not advocate censorship, let us identify the precise grounds of his concern. Examining this passage, we can grasp some of the precise standards Plato was suggesting for looking at poetry and music. Then we can try these out in an unusual way, by applying them to two different renderings of the "Mi chiamano Mimi" aria. Doing so not only helps us understand what forms and qualities Plato recommended and why but also helps us see the persistence of Platonic approaches closer to our own time, however unconscious or inchoate. This can show us the philosophy that underlies a particular artistic rendering and point to a Platonism we can find, in this case, in opera.

Focusing on one particular section of one aria in one opera gives us a method and amount of time and space necessary to grasp the subtle nuances of interpretation that shape how the passage is communicated and how we, in turn, might experience it. Just like each artistic expression, cultural artifact, or attempted human communication, each performance of this passage has an elaborate backstory. Before Puccini imagined and recorded the first notes that became the full score of *La Bohème*, the author of the novel on which the opera was based conceived of and wrote the story of the lives of Mimi and Rodolfo, as well as their friends, in the bohemian social milieu of Paris around 1830. Next the authors of the Italian libretto, Luigi Illica and Giuseppe Giacosa, adapted Henri Murger's *Scènes de la vie de Bohème* (*Scenes of the Bohemian Life*) from the French, an act of interpretation, invention, and translation. In the 1840s, Murger had published a set of stories in the small literary magazine *Le Corsaire*, coauthored a play based on them that was first performed in 1849, and gathered them together as a book that came out in 1851. Since Puccini's opera opened in 1896, it has been recorded innumerable times and performed throughout the world. It has also inspired other works, such as Jonathan Larson's 1989 rock musical *Rent*. Each performance of the opera is, if not an act of invention in the sense of adding new material or a literal act of translation (it is nearly always performed in Italian), an act of interpretation. Better yet, it is an act of *interpretations* running in the millions, some so minute they are hard to discern and some so large they noticeably affect the entire performance. From the precise pacing and volume of notes sounded by a particular instrument to the appearance of the set, all decisions great and small come bearing their own backstories—training and ability, sensibility, aspirations for abstraction or realism, to name just a few factors that converge in the moment. Whether major or minor, conscious or unconscious, these acts of interpretation, like all of our thoughts and actions, cannot help but be shaped by and speak of our philosophies. Taking a page from my most recent book, *Ars Vitae*, I hope to gesture here to places where we can glimpse such philosophies—appearing in widely varying degrees of fragmentation, conflict, and clarity and sometimes barely apparent or more notable for their absence—in our cultural forms and expressions. It can be not just fascinating but at times vitally important to do so, as Plato would agree.

Turning to some of the passages in the *Republic* cited as proof that Plato wants a rational regime that rules out music and poetry, we can see what they really say. Book III of the *Republic*, a key place where Plato discusses music, continues the theme from the previous book of how the members of the governing or guardian class should be brought up. It is interesting that Socrates phrases the problem to be what those "who are to honor the gods and their parents and who value friendship" should "listen to, or not listen to, from earliest childhood" (*Republic*, 386a). Caring about what we should *listen to* signals right off the importance, not triviality, of poetry (at that time recited aloud) and music—basically, *all things heard*.

In his discussion of poetic analysis, because of poetry's aurality often applying equally to music, Socrates argues in favor of some treatments over others for specific reasons. One reason is because of the emotional reaction certain scenes can arouse, as well as the long-term effects those reactions can have on the human person. Socrates begins with a critique of some lines in Homer, citing passages from the *Iliad* and the *Odyssey* that portray Hades in a harsh light. In the *Iliad*, Homer describes Patroclus after he was killed by Hector: "The soul flew from its limbs and went to Hades/Bewailing its fate, leaving behind manhood and youth" (*Republic*, 386d). To describe the underworld as "real and terrifying" will instill fear among those who will need the courage to die in battle. (It is difficult not to think this one of Plato's playful moments, even while taking seriously the passage's invitation to weigh the good and bad in our imaginative life.) Those who risk their lives to fight off enemies to defend the state against subjugation should not hear "fables" and "fearful names like Cocytus and Styx and 'those below' and 'corpses'" that could lessen their resolve (*Republic*, 386b–387c).

In this second reason, it is not just that scenes of the horrors that might await after death will frighten children and impinge on the formation of the character traits that they will need but that such renderings are untrue. Poets should avoid displaying the "lamentations and pitiful wailing of famous men," as Homer does when he describes Achilles, "son of a goddess," mourning Patroclus: we find him rolling on the ground and then "weaving around distraught along the shore of the barren sea" (see *Iliad*, 24.10–12; quoted in *Republic*, 388b). It does not help "those whom we say we are bringing up to guard our country" to imagine Achilles "crying and complaining about things to the extent and in the way the poet has described" or his mother, Thetis, complaining, "Oh what a wretch I am, unhappy mother of the noblest son" (see *Iliad*, 18.54; quoted in *Republic*, 388d). Hearing that a hero and goddess acted in this way, the listener, if unable to see the absurdity in this depiction, would also go on to "sing many dirges and laments at the least sufferings without shame or restraint" (*Republic*, 388d).

Socrates' main objection is that such renderings do not ring true. Making death and the underworld so terrifying not only makes the future guardians "more feverish and softer" (*Republic*, 387c) than they should be but also "would not be relating what is true or helpful for those who are destined to be warriors" (*Republic*, 386c). Depicting the hero as losing his capacity for reason and given over to prostrate grieving does not accurately capture reality if a good man is one who "does not consider death fearful for the good man, even if he is his comrade-in-arms" (*Republic*, 386d). And if a good man is also someone who is independent of others and "particularly self-reliant with regard to living well" (*Republic*, 387d), then he should "bear it as resignedly as possible whenever such a disaster befalls him" (*Republic*, 387e). Socrates finds more praiseworthy—and realistic—Homer's portrait of Odysseus. Unlike Homer's Achilles, who implausibly loses all control, showing "contempt for gods and men," in the vicious deeds he committed upon Patroclus's death, the hero of the *Odyssey* instead shows "perseverance in the face of everything" when, for instance, "[h]e struck his breast and rebuked his heart / Be patient, my heart, you have endured things even more horrific than this" (see *Odyssey*, 20.17–18, quoted in *Republic*, 390d).

This kind of inner moral truth—given the integrity and coherence only to be found in moral truth—matters in the next discussion in the *Republic* as well. Socrates unveils the stories of disgraceful deeds on the part of heroes or gods as just that, *stories* that "are neither sanctioned nor true." These myths amount to false accusations that "are harmful to those who hear them" and give others excuses to follow in the footsteps of the miscreants. Instead of perpetuating these falsehoods, Socrates beseeches,

> let us compel our poets either not to say that these are their deeds, or say that they are not the sons of gods, but not to say both, and not to try to persuade our young that the gods bring about evil and our heroes are no better than men.
>
> (*Republic*, 391d–e)

If myths continue to depict gods as immoral, they foster "an indifference to vice among our young" (*Republic*, 392a). This has a direct bearing on the larger pursuit of the foundation for justice in the *Republic*. When it comes to mere mortals, he insists that there is a common view that injustice can be personally rewarding—"if you can get away with it, justice is the good of someone else, but a dead loss for oneself." Dispelling this requires taking care not to recite, and by doing so glorify, deeds such as seduction, plunder, and violence on the part of the gods (*Republic*, 392b). Here as in other key passages in Plato and the Neoplatonists, divinity as goodness is the formative principle for a coherent vision of moral truth.

Socrates follows this, after his discussion of imitation in the arts, or *mimesis*, which we will not go into here, except to say it, too, involves literary style and not the wholesale condemnation of theater as sometimes assumed (see also *Republic*, II and X), with a discussion of music itself. In the case of lyric verse, he identifies three fundamental elements: "words, melody, and rhythm" (*Republic*, 398d). As with his section on *mimesis*, his concern is with subtle shadings of style. For instance, in alluding to a trend at the time, Socrates argued that rather than the words following the melody and rhythm, those two elements should follow the words (*Republic*, 400a). He refers to the ideas of Damon, a fifth-century BC Athenian musicologist, matching particular rhythmical movements to different ways of living but says he does not know what those are. He asks his interlocutor to ponder a more accessible question: "But can you at least distinguish the fact that the element of elegance and that of inelegance [or of "grace and gracelessness," as in the Grube translation in Cooper, ed.] match what is good rhythm and bad rhythm respectively?" (*Republic*, 400c). After receiving an affirmative answer, Socrates proceeds:

> "And another aspect of what is good and bad rhythm and what isn't: the first resembles and matches fine language, the other does the opposite, and the same applies to what is melodious and what isn't, if rhythm and melody match the words, as was said just now, and not the other way round."
>
> "Yes indeed," he said, "these must match the words."
>
> "What about the style of language and the content?" I said; "don't they match the character of the soul?"
>
> "Of course."
>
> "And everything else matches the language?"
>
> "Yes."

> "Fine language then, melodiousness, elegance and good rhythm match goodness of character, not in the sense of simplicity that we say by way of endearment, but the quality of mind equipped with a truly good and fine character."
>
> "I agree in every way," he said.
>
> "So shouldn't our youngsters pursue these goals everywhere, if they are going to manage their own affairs?"
>
> "Yes, they must."
>
> (*Republic*, 400c–e)

Music is thus nothing less than a path to self-sufficiency. Imagination can (or can fail to) bring resources for the coherence required by sturdy selfhood and required for recognition of the sublime. Moral truth thus becomes a required category of aesthetic analysis.

We know from some of his most enduring passages that Plato thought it a human possibility to sense a self-transcendent higher reality through reason and wisdom, the sole avenue to participation in the divine. Socrates' recitation of Diotima's speech in the *Symposium* (206a–212a) described the rigors of self-cultivation that led up the rungs of the "ladder of love," whereby one began with loving one individual, went on to love whole practices and principles and ended up seeing a glorious vista of the good, the true, and the "divine Beauty" (*Symposium*, 212a). In the *Phaedrus* (246a–254e), Plato offers his striking simile that likens the soul to a charioteer guiding a team of winged horses toward the truth. This driver, our intellect, has to use reason to balance the good horse on his right, rational and moral impulse, with the unruly horse on his left, irrational appetite. Successful journeying on this course of struggle leads to the rarified beauty of sacred love. These and the other transformative experiences in the dialogues hold out real possibilities for human beings (most famously, intellectual illumination as an allegory of emerging from the cave to see reality in the light of the sun in *Republic*, 514a–520a), signaling the literal infinity to be grasped through this moral, intellectual, and spiritual discipline.

The passage we have been exploring from Book III in the *Republic* helps us envision what hinges on the content and style of a particular artistic expression: *everything*. It can either rule a universe of wondrous insight out of bounds for the human person or provide a bridge to it. To make the truth of the soul obscure or inaccessible was Plato's grave concern regarding artistic endeavors. Plato encouraged an understanding of art and craft that took into account the intellectual, moral, and spiritual dimensions of creative activity and wed them to everyday demands. The arts helped most when they made people independent and resilient by providing a vision of grace, elegance, and inner beauty that could be attained (or not) through any human activity, depending on how it was done, from painting to "weaving and embroidery, house building and every trade concerned with household artifacts in general, and again the physical nature of animals and plants as well." All such activities have the capacity for "elegance or gracelessness" through decisions about style and content for expressing "poor language and poor character" or "good sense and good character" (*Republic*, 401a). Those subject to "images of baseness" do not realize they are "accumulating great evil in their souls." Instead, Socrates asks,

> but must we search out those craftsmen who have the innate ability to track down a natural goodness and beauty in order that our youngsters, living in a healthy place as it were, may benefit from everything, wherever it may come from, which brings to their eyes or ears something resulting from fine works of art, like a breeze bringing health from wholesome places and leading them unawares from their earliest childhood into resembling, being friendly toward and in harmony with the beauty of reason?
>
> (*Republic*, 401b–d)

Once Glaucon agrees, Socrates concludes by asking him,

> Isn't an education in the arts most essential for these reasons, in that rhythm and melody above all penetrate to the innermost part of the soul and most powerfully affect it, bringing gracefulness, and, if one is brought up correctly, make one graceful; if not, isn't the result the opposite?
>
> (*Republic*, 401d)

Our fine-grained understanding of this discussion prepares us to examine the two versions of the section of the Puccini aria in *La Bohème*. Our opening two paragraphs of this chapter provide the bare bones of the scene.

If we had sketched the outline of someone's face, we would now seek to fill it in with texture and shading, color and light—whether it will be light from within, without, or both, it remains to be seen. As mentioned earlier, an accumulation of the results of a vast number of decisions precedes the performance: the details of the original musical composition, vocal line, and orchestration; choice of vocalists, set designer, lighting coordinator, conductor, and everyone else involved; costume design, makeup, staging, and all the rest. Here we are at last. The curtain goes up. The opera begins. There comes the knock on the door. Much to Rodolfo's surprise, it is a woman. He confides that he is a poet, she confides that she is a seamstress. Then begins the aria in question: "Mi chiamano Mimi / il mio nomè è Lucia" (They call me Mimi / but my name is Lucia). After Mimi describes her simple and lonely sounding existence, there arrives the lingering, "Ma. . .," and we anticipate the long-awaited predicate to the unstated subject of this thought. The words are staggeringly simple, which makes the intricacy of the inflections possible in different interpretations of these lines all the more mysterious and remarkable.

For our first interpretation of this aria fragment, let us turn to the more recent 2008 performance and then go back about thirty years to a 1977 performance for our *comparandum*. Both Metropolitan Opera performances were recorded on both audio and video, which lends them perfectly to our analysis for some of the small details of interpretation that shed light on an almost intangible yet observable philosophical difference in both content and style. Both versions begin with Mimi answering Rodolfo "Si" to the question of whether she will tell him who she is now that he has divulged a bit about himself.

In the 2008 performance of the aria, Angela Gheorghiu, who plays Mimi, readjusts herself noticeably to face forward from where she had been leaning over a table to look closely at Ramón Vargas as Rodolfo across a table. It is evening, and the pair are surrounded by the trappings of the bohemian life—well-worn chairs, canvases stowed against the wall, an empty wine bottle. Mimi wears a floor-length dress that is blue gray with a subtle leaf pattern on the main fabric and a striped apron, lace encircling her wrists where the long sleeves of her dress meet her fingerless mesh gloves and more lace lying as a collar along a low-cut neck. Mimi's hair is long, glistening, and jet black against her pale skin. From the initial adjustment on, Gheorghiu carries her body with great formality, even when striving for intimacy, and this overstated intention calls attention to her every movement. From the start, the choreography telegraphs that we should pay attention to the physical interaction between Mimi and Rodolfo. As she says that her real name is Lucia, she holds her palm before her as if to prepare to push him away, although he has merely stood, not made a motion toward her. He sits back down to listen, turning a chair around to straddle it. She sets the stage for the rest of the aria by letting him know that she embroiders lilies and roses in silk and satin and has a simple but happy life. She delivers an expressive, physically active rendering, illustrating the content of the words as she goes along, her dark eyes and each muscle of her cheeks and forehead strenuously enlisted in the task of forming the words and notes and projecting each emotional gradation. She raises and lowers her hands slowly and dramatically as she sings; closes her eyes, squints, and then opens them wide by raising her eyebrows; alternates smiles with intense looks. Gheorghiu's voice brings a virtuoso's ability to the task of conveying the sweetness of Mimi, but the sweetness is an open question. The stilted gestures and hyperbole make it difficult to forget that this is a performance of an aria rather than a glimpse of an exchange between two people in a private moment. She shows a lovely smile not only to Rodolfo but also to the audience, as if posing for a picture. She stands and moves closer to where he sits and then steps back abruptly.

As the scene goes on, we see more of the room, as it receives more light to accent her aria. It turns out it is not as spartan as it looked when it was in darkness in their meeting scene and adding physical clutter to the excess of physical and emotional micro-movements. Now we see a sculpture of a Greek female nude, pitchers and canisters, candles, a satiny curtain, and various textiles. Rodolfo wears a tie, plaid pants, and what looks like a velvet jacket.

On the question of whether there is real sweetness here, time will tell, even if it is just a few measures away. It is the delivery of the lines quoted at the start of this piece that we are after. Mimi moves closer to Rodolfo, singing playfully about living alone in her little white room looking over the rooftops into the sky, then drawing out the last word, in Italian *cielo*, while leaning back to full stature with a pose unidentifiable in meaning, almost as if either sanctimonious or as if mocking the sweetness of Mimi while (it is assumed) not intending to. Attempting to convey purity—her athletic voice, achieving stunning variations of volume, now so quiet as to be barely audible—Gheorghiu looks off into the distance and poses with her hand lightly touching the front of her dress just below where her long hair falls in waves over one breast her "Ma . . ." lingers in the air. Then she draws both hands up, which makes her arms especially thin, with sharp elbows angling outward in an awkward geometrical shape. She stands over Rodolfo as she delivers the next lines, looking down into his eyes then back into the distance, then inward as she closes her eyes, and finally, after a couple of sharp, flitting steps, off toward the right as she turns her back on him, looking back to see if his eyes are following her: "Ma quando vien lo sgelo il primo sole è mio, il primo bacio dell'aprile è mio! Il primo sole è mio!" (But when the thaw comes, the first sunshine is mine—the first kiss of April is mine. The first sunshine is mine!)

The most telling details come during the final "Il primo sole è mio!" Right after "dell'aprile," she becomes somber and then pained, which fits the changed tone of the music, from the lush orchestration, which had become *fortissimo* over "il primo bacio," and then subdued over "dell'aprile è mio," which becomes calmer and slower and quieter. This is supposed to foreshadow the pathos of what will occur in the opera's final act. But the real essence of the emotional inflection, gestures, and staging has been hard to pin down until Mimi repeats the final phrase. Here we realize that in this interpretation the scene is first and foremost a flirtation. With the final "Il primo sole," she touches her hair, bends her ear to her shoulder, bends at the waist. Her posture melts, becoming less rigid, as she turns intensely toward him, eyes glistening and face beaming, and then turns away, in what is not entirely modesty, although it is definitely intended as a display of modesty. As she sings "è mio!" she emphasizes *mio* by extending her arms fully in front of her, hands up as in the gesture again of pushing him away. Her head tilts to the side as her hand reaches up to touch her face, as if the hand of someone else is touching her cheek endearingly. She glances back behind her in his direction, touching her bare skin above her breast, suggesting more caressing. And the next lines begin, ending that moment and that musical and vocal statement.

Now that the groundwork for the scene has been laid, the details of our second example of an interpretation of this aria can be filled in more quickly. In our 1977 version, the character of Mimi was sung by Renata Scotto as Mimi and Luciano Pavarotti as Rodolfo. At the start of the aria, Scotto is already facing front, sitting on a stool. She wears a high-necked gray frock, with simple lines, just a slight gathering at the shoulders and dark trim down the front and around the wrists. Her brown hair is in a bun, with slight wisps of bangs framing her face. While Angela Gheorghiu, who is tall and thin, alternated between stiff and lithe as she continually moved around the stage, Scotto's body is petite, softly rounded, and held perfectly still, hands folded in her lap. As she sings, it is mostly only her mouth that moves, although her eyes speak quietly of depths that remain mysterious. Rodolfo is at her back and to her right, sitting on the edge of a table, listening with rapt attention. Mimi moves her head the slightest bit, frequently looking into her lap or the very near distance, almost a new close-in spatial dimension created by her thoughts, rarely looking at him, turning only once to meet his eyes momentarily. Dramatic only in its understatement, her entire being seems not to represent but to *be* sweetness. As she draws out the word *cielo* that leads us to the pivotal "Ma. . .," she separates her entwined fingers and raises one arm slowly and then raises her fingers delicately at the end of her arm in an exquisite pose. She looks into the distance, for the first time looking up and beyond the personal space she has defined as completely private, enchantingly so. Her gaze is riveting. We want to know what she is looking at. She sustains this gaze as she slowly rises from her perch and takes slow steps forward and away from Rodolfo. She is like someone seized by a vision of comparable beauty—no, once again, she *is* someone seized by that vision. Pavarotti stands from his own perch and walks slowly toward her, drawn irresistibly yet simultaneously catapulted into abject reverence. Scotto clasps her hands before her ample bosom, suggesting restrained passion as her voice yields the notes at the greatest volume to "il primo bacio" (Pavarotti steps away as if in physical pain at the sheer majesty and allure of her voice and the meaning of the words); then she becomes rightly subdued over "dell'aprile è mio," as the music asks. She completes this thought in the final "Il primo sole è mio!" that she delivers with the utmost seriousness, hinting at the agony to come for her and Rodolfo.

    In this interpretation of the aria, we do not just hear technically superior singing and orchestration. Instead, in Scotto's version, over the course of the song, something *happens*. We are witnesses to a transformation. "Ma . . ." turns out to be a bridge to somewhere new. The building of the music, the slow opening of her body and voice, all these come together but not to fuel a primarily physical attraction as in the first interpretation, although longing and desire are part of it. The force of her newfound stature, as if all-embracing, is all the more powerful because it is unexpected, hardly imaginable given her initially closed demeanor. What is conveyed is suspension in the unfolding of a moment that is both fading already and permanent. By singing in this way, Mimi reveals that she, too, has fallen in love with Rodolfo, as he has made it clear that he has with her. They have conveyed this not by saying so and demonstrating it physically but by communicating the details of their lives to one another. Yet even further, the aria in Scotto's version conveys a kind of independence she gained through her own direct encounter with the real world, with its hardships as well as joys, that makes sharing her intimate world with Rodolfo the event of meaning and moment and weight that it is. In this Platonic interpretation, it is the sacred and otherworldly space of the soul, with room for someone of this world and at the same time a transcendent love for the world beyond this one.

While Scotto's Mimi (alongside Pavarotti's Rodolfo) fulfills what Plato described, Gheorghiu's bears traces of what is wrong with the emotivist and therapeutic culture of our times. In trying to convey sweetness, it overdramatizes it into familiar over-emoting that can thus be disregarded as just more of the kind of expression that is self- and not other-oriented. It speaks not of a world in which it is the greatest gift to allow another human being into our private existence but a world in which the private has become quickly and commonly shared to the point where it no longer exists. This is in no way a criticism of the superb musicality of Angela Gheorghiu. It is unclear what she was able to contribute to the particular interpretation. In a different performance altogether, the result of a different backstory of decisions, her rendering of Mimi hewed much closer to that of Scotto. There are other performances starring other sopranos that represent to a much greater degree the premium on subjective emotional experience of therapeutic emotivism we see here. Choosing one identifiable only through attention to the subtlest cues allows us to see the almost imperceptible presence of philosophy in our endeavors, expressions, performances, and inhabitations. It is wildly apparent in some instances, but the intrigue of locating it when it is almost invisible or inaudible is a discipline worth cultivating. The point here in comparing our two versions is that we can identify in a production as a whole or in part, as in our lives, with all the decisions that inform what we think or do at every given moment, traces of particular philosophical leanings that might be vital for us to know about. They could be just a matter of whether we do or do not experience something like a moment of spiritual exhilaration, and that could seem like mere entertainment, dispensable and discretionary. Or they could make for a life worth living.

Plato guides us toward the possibilities for art and craft in all fields in a way that speaks of a world beyond the self. He stresses unity of style and content; in opera that would mean words and music. Scotto's Mimi goes beyond imitating sweetness. It *is* sweet. It speaks to a truth that is real and, miraculously, even attainable for us. But that attainability comes only for those not bombarded with "images of baseness" into becoming hardened by "gracelessness"—those prepared by an education in the moral arts as our bridge to the beyond—to listen for their very opposite.

Bibliography

Allen, Danielle, "Platonic Quandaries: Recent Scholarship on Plato," *Annual Review of Political Science*, 9 (2006), 127–141.

Annas, Julia, *An Introduction to Plato's Republic* (Oxford: Oxford University Press, 1981)

Borges, Jorge Luis, "Pierre Menard, Author of the *Quixote*," in *Collected Fictions*, trans. Andrew Hurley (New York: Penguin, 1999)

Lasch-Quinn, Elisabeth, *Ars Vitae: The Fate of Inwardness and the Return of the Ancient Arts of Living* (South Bend, IN: University of Notre Dame Press, 2020)

MacIntyre, Alasdair, *After Virtue: A Study in Moral Theory* (South Bend, IN: University of Notre Dame Press, 2007)

Murdoch, Iris, *The Fire and the Sun: Why Plato Banished the Artists* (Oxford: Clarendon Press, 1977)

Plato, *Complete Works*, ed. John M. Cooper (Indianapolis, IN: Hackett, 1997)

Plato, *Phaedrus*, trans. Harold North Fowler (Cambridge, MA: Harvard University Press, 1914)

Plato, *Republic*, trans. Chris Emlyn-Jones and William Reddy (Cambridge, MA: Harvard University Press, 2013)

Plato, *Symposium*, trans. W. R. M. Lamb (Cambridge, MA: Harvard University Press, 1925)

Puccini, Giacomo, *La Bohème* in *Complete Italian Libretto*, trans. Ellen H. Bleiler (New York: Dover, 1984) Dual-Language Edition (Italian and English).

Puccini, Giacomo, *La Bohème* in *Full Score* (New York: Dover Publications, 1987)

Puccini, Giacomo, *La Bohème*, Metropolitan Opera Conducted by James Levine. Performed March 15, 1977. Production by Fabrizio Melano. Renata Scotto as Mimi. Luciano Pavarotti as Rodolfo.

Puccini, Giacomo, *La Bohème*, Metropolitan Opera Conducted by Nicola Luisotti. Performed April 5, 2008. Production by Franco Zeffirelli. Angela Gheorghiu as Mimi. Ramón Vargas as Rodolfo.

Rieff, Philip, *The Triumph of the Therapeutic: Uses of Faith after Freud* (Wilmington, DE: ISI Books, 2006)

Voegelin, Eric, *Science, Politics, and Gnosticism* (Wilmington, DE: ISI Books, 2004)

True Lies

A Defense of the Sophists[1]

Simon Critchley

An Introduction to the Sophists

The discursive invention that we call philosophy and that begins with Plato is premised on two exclusions that are linked: the expulsion of the tragic poets and the opposition between philosophy and sophistry. This opposition continues to this day, both in very general terms, that is, sophistry is deemed a bad, unworthy thing, and philosophy is a good, worthy thing, and in more specific terms, as with, say, Alain Badiou's reassertion of Platonism against the alleged relativism of the Sophists or alleged contemporary neo-Sophists. The standard narrative is that the Sophists were itinerant, rather flashy, usually foreign teachers, who taught the arts of rhetoric, oratory, and persuasion to people who could pay their large, indeed sometimes exorbitant, fees. But, so the story goes, they weren't concerned about the truth. Socrates, by contrast, is meant to be our hero because he was interested in the truth and he didn't get paid. So, in a way, anyone (such as myself) who gets paid to teach philosophy is really a Sophist, and if someone wants a salary for teaching philosophy (such as some possible readers of this book), then they want to be Sophists too.

Sophistry, I argue in *Tragedy, the Greeks, and Us*, exploits the concept of *antilogia*, or contradiction, as an argumentative procedure. Consider, for instance, the antithetical nature of sophistical thought found in the following fragment from the Greek sophist Gorgias: "Tragedy, by means of legends and emotions, creates a deception in which the deceiver is more honest than the non-deceiver, and the deceived is wiser than the non-deceived."[2] Gorgias's contradictory thought is that tragedy is a deception or an act of fraud or trickery that reveals the truth to those whom it deceives. What Gorgias seems to describe, then, perhaps even celebrate, is precisely that which Socrates/Plato sees as the great danger of tragedy, the

DOI: 10.4324/9781003201472-5

danger of deception, the power of persuasion to induce the affective effects of imitation, of *mimesis*.

I'd like to give a more complex and sympathetic picture of the Sophists than one gets from philosophers. The Greek word *sophistes* originally meant "skilled craftsman" or "wise man" but was used to describe traveling teachers who visited Athens from the mid-fifth century BCE and acquired a negative connotation in the comedies of Aristophanes, like *The Clouds*, and then in the writings of Plato and, later, Aristotle. The word *sophistes* means something like an expert or pundit, one who is wise, *sophos*. Ever since and for us still, the name *Sophist* is a term of abuse, meaning someone who uses a bad argument deliberately to deceive the audience. A Sophist, then, is a fraud. In the *Sophist*, Plato argues that the Sophist is a "mercenary hunter after the young and rich . . . a wholesaler of learning. . . [and] a salesman of his own products of learning" (231d). Aristotle says the same thing in *On Sophistical Refutations*, describing the Sophist as "a money-maker" (165a). Xenophon in the *Memorabilia* calls those who sell wisdom for money "Sophists, just like prostitutes" (I, 1, 11). This brings to mind Cassin's suggestive proposal of looking at the history of philosophy from the standpoint of the prostitute rather than the client, as is usually the case.[3] Of course, it is rather intriguing that Aristophanes, who was a good deal closer to the context than we are, simply lumped Socrates together with the Sophists in his "thinkery" in *The Clouds*. Aristophanes didn't see Socrates through the rose-colored spectacles provided by Plato. Aristides, a Greek orator who lived during Roman times in the second century CE, polemically suggested that the reason for Plato's revulsion at the Sophists "is both his contempt for the masses and for his contemporaries."[4] This doubtless goes too far, but we have to take seriously the question of the relation between Socrates' contestation of sophistry and his critique of Athenian democracy.

Thanks to the reforms of Pericles from around the 460s BCE, Athenian democracy, limited as it was, was still remarkable and placed a high value on oratory, the ability to speak persuasively in public. It might be noted that Thucydides, in the most famous speech that has come down to us from antiquity, Pericles's Funeral Oration, which some claim was inspired by new learning provided by the Sophists, claims that the virtue of the Athenians in part consists in the capacity of being instructed through speeches (*logoi*). At the same time as the democratic reforms, there was a spectacular rise in lawsuits generated through the popular courts, which, it should be remembered, consisted of large panels of up to 501 citizens. Athens was also a society without lawyers, where citizens had to defend themselves if they were accused, as Socrates does in the *Apology*.

Following the defeat of the Persians and the formation of the Delian League, Athens had become very powerful and very wealthy in a relatively short space of time, and—*plus ça change*—the city attracted foreigners, "professors" of a kind, like Protagoras from Abdera on the Thracian coast, Prodicus from the Aegean island of Ceos, and Gorgias from Leontini in Sicily. They converged on Athens to give dazzling set-piece public orations and apparently very expensive private tutoring to those who could pay. If a suitably wealthy young man wanted to get on in public life, then he hired a Sophist to train him to speak persuasively. The Sophists apparently made an awful lot of money instructing the wealthy young men of Athens and elsewhere (and, like contemporary star academics, they were constantly traveling).

Almost nothing survives of the voluminous writings of the original or older Sophists, particularly with the first and most famous of them, Protagoras. Three doctrines are associated with Protagoras, although evidence here is scanty and skewed by Plato:

1. Man is the measure of all things. Protagoras's fragment, which displays his use of *antilogia*, reads, "Of all things the measure is man, of the things that are, that they are, and of the things that are not, that they are not."[5] In Plato's hands, this leads to what we would now call subjectivism in relation to knowledge and relativism in relation to virtue. Each man judges what is true for him, but this is not true for all. It is a question of virtue as that which is advantageous. This view is attacked in the *Theaetetus* and the *Protagoras* where the image of the philosopher is constantly presented as not being concerned with the human measure but with the divine measure and the possibility of *ho bios theois*, the life of the gods. Obviously, the key question is whether virtue can be taught. For the Sophists, apparently it can. For Plato, it cannot. But there is no evidence that Sophists like Gorgias claimed to teach virtue. I want to defend the sophistical emphasis on the human measure as opposed to the philosophical preoccupation with the divine measure. Linked to this, I see the entire problematic of relativism as

a by-product of philosophy's obsession with universalism. Once that universalist obsession is pushed to one side, then the problem of relativism also disappears in a puff of smoke and we might finally be able to engage in a more realistic and plausible account of the life of virtue and its relation to place and, indeed, other places.

2. Skepticism about the gods: "Concerning the Gods, I am not in a position to know either that they exist, or that they do not exist, for there are many obstacles in the way of such knowledge, notably the intrinsic obscurity of the subject and the shortness of human life."[6] This seems an eminently reasonable approach to the question, as opposed to Socrates, who, in the *Phaedo, Republic*, and *Gorgias*, is consistently arguing for the immortality of the soul and the afterlife as the reward for the philosophical life of virtue. Given the evident limitedness of human intelligence and the brevity of life, perhaps we should just put the question of God or the gods to one side.

3. The view that everything can be contradicted, the technique of *antilogia*, which was taught as a rhetorical skill. This linked to the use of double arguments *dissoi logoi*, which meant looking at both sides of a case, in order to make the weaker argument stronger and vice versa.[7] A fragment of Protagoras reads, "To make the weaker cause the stronger."[8] This is taken to an absurd conclusion by Aristophanes in *The Clouds*, who has two characters, one called "Stronger Argument" and the other called "Weaker Argument."

Gorgiasm

But, in my view, the greatest of the Sophists, for whom we have a lot more precious textual evidence, is Gorgias, and I would like to focus on him. There is an amusing book called *Lives of the Sophists* from the third century CE by Philostratus, which is short of absolutely any intellectual merit but full of nice anecdotes. When Protagoras introduced a fee for his lectures, Philostratus quips that we prize those things we spend money on more than those we don't. Gorgias apparently charged incredibly high fees and was the wealthiest of the Sophists. Philostratus adds that there was even a verb in Greek, "to Gorgianize," *gorgiazein*, meaning to engage in oratory of a grand and florid style, or to speak in an excessive manner, to speak like Gorgias. Philostratus reports that Gorgias was praised for his great eloquence, his daring and unusual expressions, and the sudden transitions in his discourse.[9]

Gorgias probably lived circa 483 to 375 BCE, which means that he lived to be 108 years old. Philostratus confirms this, although there is no way of knowing if it is true (Diogenes Laertius often claims that pre-Socratic thinkers enjoyed extraordinary longevity). He arrived in Athens in 427 BCE, when he was already in his mid-fifties, as an ambassador for his native city, Leontini, after the outbreak of the Peloponnesian Wars. Gorgias delivered a number of show speeches to the Athenian assembly with great success, displaying what was seen as the new Sicilian form of rhythmic prose. He was acquainted with and on some reports (the *Suda*) the student of Empedocles and knew of Parmenides, as he ridiculed the latter's type of being-talk in his own spoof, "On Not-Being," to which we will turn presently (if it is indeed a spoof, which is unclear). We are fortunate to have two versions of reports of "On Not-Being" and two short, brilliant examples of the set-piece speech, or *epideixis*, the stunningly beautiful text "The Encomium of Helen" and the rather less beautiful "The Defense of Palamedes."

There are many odd, ancient anecdotes connected with Gorgias. According to the satirist Lucian, he died by abstaining from food with all his faculties intact. According to the wonderfully dull Diogenes Laertius, Gorgias was the father of the sophistic arts, as Aeschylus was the father of tragedy. Diodorus of Sicily reports that Gorgias's eloquence astonished the Athenians, winning them over to support an alliance against Syracuse, which had attacked his hometown of Leontini. This would all end badly for Athens, with the military disaster of the Sicilian Expedition, reported in detail by Thucydides. Gorgias's speeches are repeatedly described in testimonies as highly poetic. Pausanias describes a statue of Gorgias at Olympia as "undistinguished." There was also a gilded statue of Gorgias (in some reports, it was made of solid gold) in the temple to Apollo at Delphi that he dedicated himself. He was very wealthy and clearly a little vain. Amazingly, in 1876, the inscribed base of the statue was found during excavation. It finishes with the words "His statue stands too in the vale of Apollo / Not as a show of his wealth, but of the piety of his ways."

No doubt in order to parade his piety, there are also reports that Gorgias went about in purple clothes, the royal or imperial color (the same is said of Empedocles). This is a good example of sophistical bling. The Sophists are widely reported as dressing well, as opposed to Socrates, who usually went barefoot, wore an old cloak, and—as Nietzsche enthusiastically reports—was ugly. In Plato's *Meno*, it is said that Gorgias allowed any Greek to question him on any topic and he would improvise a response. On the topic of his teaching and methods, Gorgias did not teach any set of doctrines but a method, a *hodos*, which was, in his view, value-free. He gave the highest status to the power of rhetoric, and elsewhere I have summarized and interpreted the three main extant texts by Gorgias: the first—*To me on*, "the not-being," "the nonexistent," "what is not"—a setpiece example of sophistic *antilogia*, or contradiction, characterized by the technique of *elenkos*, refutation; the other two—"The Encomium of Helen" and "The Defense of Palamedes"—examples of how antithetical language can be used in order to show how the weaker can always become the stronger and how the seemingly indefensible (namely, Helen, the cause and object of the Trojan War) can be rationally defended and exonerated of any guilt.[10] Let us now consider how these views conflict the philosophical idealism of Plato and his teacher Socrates.

Plato's Sophist

What picture of the Sophist emerges in Plato's dialogues? This would appear to be an easy question to answer. It is clearly a negative image. Socrates relentlessly opposed the Sophists, and most of what we know about them comes from the caricatures we get in a large number of Plato's dialogues. Think of the many dialogues devoted to Socrates' debates with various leading Sophists (*Protagoras, Gorgias, Hippias Major, Hippias Minor, Euthydemus*, and the *Sophist*, of course). Sometimes, indeed very often, Plato reduced the enemy to the level of flat caricature. Elsewhere, as in the *Sophist*, in which the philosophical authority is given to the Stranger from Elea and Socrates is present but silent after some opening remarks, the final—rather abstruse—definition of *sophistry* runs as follows: "Sophistry is a productive art, human, of the imitation kind, copy-making, of the appearance-making kind, uninformed and insincere in the form of contrary-speech-producing art" (268c–d). The contrary-speech-producing art refers to the sophistical practice of *antilogia*, which proceeds by antithesis. We find a cruder definition in the *Protagoras*: "a Sophist is really a merchant or peddler of goods by which a soul is nourished" (313c). Once again, we go back to the idea of the Sophist as a wisdom whore turning cheap rhetorical tricks for rich young men that gives them the patina of virtue without any real knowledge.

For Socrates, by contrast, virtue cannot be taught. It cannot be sold in a neat financial parcel. A similar view can be found in Aristotle's *On Sophistical Refutations*. The point of this short, polemical text is to show that the arguments provided by the Sophist, of the kind found in Gorgias's fragments, *appear* to be refutations, but they are merely superficial fallacies. Aristotle claims, "The art of the sophist is the semblance of wisdom without the reality" (165a). Such an art is an excellent acquisition for people who want to appear to be wise without being so. In other words, sophistry is bullshit, and we dearly love declaring that things are bullshit.

But there is a more interesting and complex way of answering the question about the relation of Socratic dialogue to sophistry. I'd briefly like to consider two dialogues: the *Phaedrus* and the *Gorgias*. These dialogues are strongly related in that they deal with the same topic, broadly speaking the relation between philosophy and rhetoric, as exemplified in sophistical practice. But they deal with the topic in surprisingly contrary ways, in which one dialogue is a stunning success and the other is arguably an abject failure. We proceed, then, in the manner of *antilogia*, balancing affirmation and negation, success and failure. Let's begin with the success.

The *Phaedrus*, a Philosophical Success

There appears to be something enigmatic about Plato's *Phaedrus*. It seems to discuss two distinct topics, rather than one: *eros* and rhetoric. The first half of the dialogue culminates with Socrates' Second Speech on *eros*, which many readers appear to like and find memorable. But it is followed by a long forensic discussion of rhetoric that readers tend to find rather dull and forget about. But this is a profoundly mistaken impression of the *Phaedrus*: the twin themes of *eros* and rhetoric are really one.

The purpose of the *Phaedrus* is to induce a philosophical *eros* in the rather unphilosophical Phaedrus. Phaedrus is not the kind of feisty, angry, and highly intelligent opponent that Socrates finds in the Gorgiastic Callicles, or even in Thrasymachus in the *Republic*, let alone the superior intellect of the Stranger from the *Sophist*. Phaedrus is a simpler soul. We might define him as a being who lives in order to receive pleasure from listening to speeches, sophistical speeches. So Socrates gives him that pleasure in order both to please and to persuade him. Not just once but twice. Indeed, the sheer length of the Second Speech on *eros* might arouse our suspicion, for we will see in the *Gorgias* that Socrates hates long speeches, even delivered by the most eloquent of Sophists. Why is Socrates doing what he hates?

He is doing it in order to engender philosophical *eros* in Phaedrus. And this requires rhetoric. That is, rhetoric is the art by which the philosopher persuades the nonphilosopher to assume philosophical *eros*, to incline their soul toward truth. But to do this does not entail abandoning the art of rhetoric or indeed sophistry, which teaches that art, although it does so falsely, according to Socrates. Philosophy uses true rhetoric against false rhetoric. The philosopher is not just the anti-Sophist but the *true* Sophist as well. This is a terribly important point. There is no philosophy without rhetoric and thus without the passage through sophistry. Does philosophy pass beyond what it sees as sophistry? Such is the question.

I am not suggesting that Phaedrus is stupid, but he's perhaps not the brightest spark in Athens, which was a city with many bright sparks. He keeps forgetting Socrates' argument and needs constant reminders: "So it seemed," he says late in the dialogue, "but remind me again how we did it" (277b). And this is during a discussion of recollection versus reminding. Phaedrus forgets the argument during a discussion of memory! Much of Socrates' rather obvious and extended passages of irony in the dialogue also seem to pass him by completely. Occasionally, Phaedrus will burst out with something like, "Socrates, you're very good at making up stories from Egypt or wherever else you want" (275b). Phaedrus is nice but a little dim.

Rehearsing a definition itself given by Gorgias in Plato's dialogue (*Gorgias*, 452e—it would appear that the *Gorgias* was written prior to the *Phaedrus*), *rhetoric* is defined as inducing persuasion in the soul of the listener. Socrates goes further and defines *rhetoric* as a *techne psychagogia*, an art of leading or directing the soul, a kind of bewitchment that holds the listener's soul spellbound (*Phaedrus*, 261a). Of course, the irony here is that it is precisely in these terms that Socrates criticizes the effects of tragic poetry in the *Republic*, which is why all forms of poetic *mimesis* cannot be admitted into a philosophically well-ordered city.

We have to keep this irony in mind because Socrates' speeches in the *Phaedrus* are precisely the kind of *psychagogia* of which he is apparently so suspicious in the *Gorgias*. Phaedrus, who loves speeches, is completely entranced. His soul is conjured by Socrates with complete success. The dialogue brings Phaedrus to love philosophy by loving philosophically. It might appear on a superficial reading that the question of *eros* disappears in the second half of the *Phaedrus*. But this is deceptive, for the forensic discussion of Lysias's speech on *eros* leads to a definition of artful or true speech that we will see presently. The dialogue culminates in a definition of the philosopher as the true lover or lover of truth (278d), by which point Phaedrus is completely persuaded by Socrates.

The intention of the *Phaedrus* is thus to persuade Phaedrus. Nothing more. Someone like Phaedrus. Someone not supersmart. The purpose of the dialogue, as Alexander Nehamas has persuasively suggested, is to enflame a philosophical *eros* in him that gives him the ability to distinguish bad rhetoric, of the kinds found in Lysias's speech and in Socrates' First Speech (and, by implication, in Sophists like Gorgias), from true rhetoric, of the kind found in the Second Speech and then analyzed in the second half of the dialogue, using the techniques of division and collection that are extended in intricate detail in the labyrinthine discussions of the *Sophist*. True rhetoric passes over into dialectic. Sophistry becomes philosophy.

The sheer reflexivity of the *Phaedrus* is astonishing. It is not only a piece of the most beautiful writing that, in the concluding pages, denounces writing. It is also an enactment of the very conditions of the true philosophical rhetoric theorized in the dialogue. It is the enactment of theory as practice. The opposite of self-contradiction, the *Phaedrus* is a performative self-enactment of philosophy. The subject matter of the *Phaedrus* is rhetoric, true rhetoric. Its intention is to show that true *eros*, as opposed to the kind of vulgar pederasty that Socrates criticizes and that was the Athenian specialty of the time, is both subject *to* true rhetoric and the subject *of* true rhetoric. Philosophical *eros* is the effect of rhetoric, of language used persuasively.

Consider Socrates' conclusion about the nature of true or artful speech, which allows an interesting and possibly troubling question to be raised about the relation between philosophy and sophistry. Socrates says, toward the end of the *Phaedrus*, in an anticipation of the description of the method of division and collection,

> No one will ever possess the art of speaking, to the extent that any human being can, unless he acquires the ability to enumerate the sorts of characters to be found in any audience, to divide everything according to its kinds, and to grasp each single thing firmly by means of one form (*idea*). And no one can acquire these abilities without great effort—a laborious effort a sensible man will make not in order to speak and act among human beings, but so as to be able to speak and act in a way that pleases the gods (*theois*).
>
> (Phaedrus, 273e–74a)

To this the ever-so-slightly-dull Phaedrus exclaims, "What you've said is wonderful, Socrates—if only it could be done" (274a). But what needs to be emphasized here is that the huge effort involved in speaking well is not made, as it is with Sophists or with people who speak in a law court or public assembly, in order to please human beings, but in order to please those who are truly wise, namely, the gods.

We are here brought face-to-face with a persistent theme in Plato, which also appears elsewhere in ancient Greek philosophy (Empedocles), the Hellenistic schools (Epicurus), Neoplatonism (Plotinus), and which could be said to resurface in modernity in Spinoza and when Hegel defines Spirit in the *Phenomenology of Spirit* as "God manifested in the midst of those who know themselves in the form of pure knowledge."[11] Against Protagoras, man is not the measure of all things. Such is sophistry. The philosophical measure—that is, the measure *of* philosophy—is divine. Philosophy's highest ambition is the life of the gods or the divine life. Such is what Aristotle calls at the end of the *Nicomachean Ethics* (1177b–78a) *ho bios theois*, the life of the gods. In the famously enigmatic "digression" in the *Theaetetus*, Socrates says that the philosopher's body alone dwells within the city's walls. In thought, they are elsewhere. The philosopher lives by another measure, what Plato calls a divine measure, the life of the gods (172c–78c).

I am making this point in order to underline an essential distinction between philosophy and sophistry. If philosophy promises the life of the gods or some kind of blessedness that is more than human, then sophistry is resolutely human, all too human; confines itself to human affairs; and expresses not disbelief but simply skepticism about the gods. The choice between philosophy and sophistry is a choice between the divine and the human. Which should one choose? It's hardly for me to say. The point is that one has to make a decision.

The *Gorgias*, a Philosophical Failure

If the *Phaedrus* is a glorious success as a dialogue, then the *Gorgias* is an abject failure. Socrates is peculiarly irritating throughout this dialogue. Before the action of the dialogue begins, Gorgias has been declaiming eloquently and extremely effectively in the house of Callicles. But Socrates doesn't want to go and hear Gorgias's speech, because he hates long speeches unless he gives them himself, as he often does, for example, in the *Phaedrus*, at the end of the *Gorgias* itself and with the myth of Er at the end of the *Republic*. Instead, Socrates catches Gorgias at the end of his speech when he is already tired. He then begins to badger him with questions.

Socrates stubbornly persists in asking what it is that Gorgias teaches. What is his art? Gorgias says he teaches the art of rhetoric, and he offers to make other people rhetoricians too. Rhetoric is the art of persuasive speech. If someone is taught rhetoric, then they possess a powerful weapon that can be used to persuade judges in the law courts and citizens in the assembly (*Gorgias*, 452e). Led on a little deceptively by Socrates, Gorgias claims that rhetoric is not a particular art but embraces all the other arts and is more powerful than medicine (*Gorgias*, 456a–c).

Then something entirely predictable happens. When Gorgias says that this prodigious art of rhetoric must be used justly, Socrates seizes on the opportunity to interrogate him about the nature of justice and the good. Can rhetoric teach virtue? Gorgias declines to accept that virtue or excellence is anything in itself as distinct from the displays of excellence in specific practices. In the *Meno*, Socrates calls this position "a swarm of excellences" and demands, as ever, a single definition, a unique *eidos* or *idea* (*Meno*, 72a). Incidentally, Aristotle, in the *Politics*, sees things differently and opposes those who seek a single, general definition of excellence, saying, "Far better . . . is the simple enumeration of the different forms of excellence, as followed by Gorgias" (1260a). Unlike Protagoras, Gorgias did not claim to be able to teach virtue. Rhetoric must be used justly and judiciously, but the teaching of the art of rhetoric does not make people good.

Socrates is having none of this, and while Gorgias is sidelined in the dialogue, his place as interlocutor is taken by his acolyte Polus, and things begin to take a turn for the worse. Socrates refuses to accept that rhetoric is an art and calls it instead a knack and then insists that it is the knack of flattery that is itself a branch of politics. Socrates says, "I call it [i.e., rhetoric] foul, as I do all ugly things" (*Gorgias*, 463d). Matters deteriorate even further when Polus's place is taken by the tough and unforgiving Callicles. Now, I find Callicles very funny, a kind of fifth-century version of Nietzsche. Whereas most of Socrates' opponents, like Thrasymachus, eventually roll over and play along with his endless questions, Callicles refuses to play the game. Philosophy, Callicles insists, is nice enough to engage in when you're young, "[b]ut if one grows up and becomes a man and still continues in the same subject, why, the whole thing becomes ridiculous, Socrates" (*Gorgias*, 485c). Philosophy is unmanly, "skulking in corners, whispering with two or three little lads, never pronouncing any large, liberal or meaningful utterance" (485d). "Such a man," Callicles goes on, "is one you can slap in the face with impunity" (486c). Socrates doesn't forget this insult. He can clearly bear a grudge. When the philosopher is fully grown, he should abandon his childish ways and take up "the fine art of business" (486c), make some money, and contribute to the life and upkeep of the city. Callicles sounds rather like my dad—God rest his soul.

For Callicles, justice is merely the set of conventions and customs that keep the strongest in check. Instead, we should follow what is naturally good, namely, that which accords with power and strength. In other words, morality is the consequence of a slave revolt and is a consequence of *ressentiment* as Nietzsche will argue in *The Genealogy of Morals*. The only moral code is that which corresponds to our desire, and "[a] man who is going to live a full life must allow his desires to become as mighty as may be and never repress them" (*Gorgias*, 491e–492a). Callicles is not just the progenitor of Nietzsche; he is also the precursor of Spinoza, Deleuze, and, on a certain reading, Lacan, where the ethical demand of psychoanalysis is not to give way to one's desire.

What is so fascinating about this dialogue is that Socrates can get no grip on Callicles because he refuses to share any common ground with him. At one extraordinary moment, Callicles simply refuses to answer Socrates' endless and, for him, endlessly piffling questions, at which point, after the final intervention of Gorgias himself (who is a model of decorum and even manners throughout the dialogue), Socrates simply starts to speak to himself and answer his own questions. Indeed, this goes on for several pages (see *Gorgias*, 506–509). Callicles quips to Socrates, "Go on and finish up by yourself, friend" (506c). Socrates talks to himself like a crazy person in the street.

The *Gorgias* perhaps shows the limits of Socratic dialogue, which makes one wonder what Plato was up to in writing it in the first place. What is the point of the dialogue? It is unclear. At the very least, in stark opposition to the *Phaedrus*, the *Gorgias* is a powerful example of how philosophy can go wrong when rhetoric is not used effectively or persuasively. Rather than bringing his interlocutor around to his point of view, all that Socrates does in the *Gorgias* is alienate his audience and show what a painful irritant he can be. Happily or unhappily, Callicles does not punch Socrates in the face but allows him to drone on until he is finally done. The *Gorgias* is a fascinating failure. But what does it reveal?

The usual way the exchange between Callicles and Socrates is discussed in philosophy classes is to say that the example of Callicles shows how difficult it is to refute a determined immoralist. But it is not clear to me that Callicles is the immoralist in the *Gorgias*. This becomes clear, I think, in the final stages of the dialogue, when Callicles rejoins the discussion and matters turn to politics. Socrates asks Callicles whether there are any good statesmen in Athens. Callicles thinks for a moment and says that while there are none that he knows of who are still living, there are the examples of Themistocles, Cimon, and, most interesting, Pericles, who is said by Callicles to have died "only recently" (*Gorgias*, 503c), which means that the dramatic date of the dialogue could be around 425 BCE, as Pericles died from the effects of the plague in 429 BCE.

Socrates vigorously denounces Pericles and his democratic reforms in Athens with the words "Pericles made the Athenians idle and cowardly and loquacious and greedy by instituting the system of public fees" (*Gorgias*, 515e). To be clear, these were the fees provided to working citizens that enabled them not only to engage in the democratic practices of Athens, such as the assembly and council but also to participate in the theater of the City Dionysia through the "Theoric Fund," which was given as a dole to enable citizens to pay the theater entrance fee. For Socrates, Pericles was a bad man and a pernicious influence in political life. And the same goes for Themistocles and Cimon: "Men say that they made our city great not recognizing that it is swollen and ulcerous" (*Gorgias*, 518e). The inference is clear: Periclean democracy has corrupted the virtue of Athens, and this corruption has been aided and abetted by "those who call themselves Sophists" (*Gorgias*, 519c).

Two striking things happen before the end of the dialogue, both of them very revealing. First, Plato exploits the *anachronism* of a dialogue that is staged nearly thirty years before Socrates' trial and execution but is written long after it, to anticipate Socrates' condemnation by the city of Athens. If Attic tragedy uses the anachronism of Mycenaean Bronze Age past by juxtaposing it with the present of the Athenian *polis*, then Platonic dialogue exploits the more minimal, but still significant, time lapse between the date of the staging of the dialogue and the moment of its literary composition by Plato (it is a little like writing a dialogue now that is set in the 1960s, when everyone knows that the main protagonist was put to death by the state in the late 1980s). In response to Callicles's teasing that Socrates might well end up being dragged into court for his heretical views, Socrates grows morally indignant and wildly arrogant. He defensively declaims, "In my opinion I am one of the few Athenians (not to say the only one) who has attempted the true art of politics, and the only one alive to put it into practice" (*Gorgias*, 521d).

Socrates thinks he is entitled to this view because he does not have his eyes on personal gratification but only on "the highest good, not on that which is merely pleasant" (*Gorgias*, 521e). At this moment, in my view, Socrates is revealed as a moral absolutist whereas Plato anachronistically exploits the foreknowledge of Socrates' demise at the hands of the Athenians in order to justify the dogmatism of his position. And if politics is the life of the city's institutions, like the assembly and the council, then it is clear that the true art of politics is antipolitical.

Not only that. What is going on here is a massive idealization of the figure of the morally righteous but death-bound and solitary philosopher. This view finds its final vindication in a second feature, namely, a story about the afterlife, which is how the *Gorgias* ends. Socrates recounts the myth of the judgment of souls in the afterlife in Hades by King Minos, who holds the urn of doom. At this moment of the last judgment, the final reckoning, "the philosopher, who has kept his own business and has not meddled with others' affairs during his lifetime" (*Gorgias*, 526b), will be judged well and granted immortal life, Socrates says. By contrast, when Callicles—and, by implication, Gorgias—awaits the judgment on the state of his soul, he will be judged severely: "You will stand there with gaping mouth and reeling head no less than I here; and it will be you, perhaps, whom they will shamefully slap in the face and mistreat with every indignity" (*Gorgias*, 527a). The Sophist may well slap the philosopher's face here in the city, but the Sophist's face will be slapped in the afterlife for eternity. Here, then, is the final refutation of sophistry, in the afterlife when all are judged according to their merits. From the standpoint of eternity, philosophy will finally be vindicated. From the standpoint of the divine life, the immortal life that is the philosopher's goal, the Sophist will appear to be the fool and the philosopher will be judged to be wise. As to the wisdom or folly of Socrates' case against Gorgias, I suppose we will find out the truth in the hereafter, if there is anything after here.

Notes

1 An earlier version of this essay appears in my *Tragedy, the Greeks, and Us*.
2 Freeman, *Ancilla to the Pre-Socratic Philosophers*, 138.
3 Cassin, *Sophistical Practice*, 3–4.
4 Quoted in Diels, *The Older Sophists*, 1.
5 Freeman, *Ancilla to the Pre-Socratic Philosophers*, 125.
6 Ibid., 126.
7 Ibid., 162.
8 Ibid., 126.
9 Ibid., 29–31. I follow closely the excellent and helpful presentation of Gorgias in John Dillon and Tania Gergel, *The Greek Sophists*, 43–97.
10 See Critchley, *Tragedy, the Greeks, and Us*, 101–120.
11 Hegel, *Phenomenology of Spirit*, 409.

Bibliography

Aristotle, *On Sophistical Refutations*, trans. E. S. Forster (Cambridge, MA: Harvard University Press, 1955)

Badiou, Alain, *Plato's Republic: A Dialogue in Sixteen Chapters*, trans. Susan Spitzer (New York: Columbia University Press, 2012)

Cassin, Barbara, *Sophistical Practice: Toward a Consistent Relativism* (New York: Fordham University Press, 2014)

Critchley, Simon, *Tragedy, the Greeks, and Us* (New York: Pantheon, 2019)

Diels, Hermann, *The Older Sophists*, ed. Rosamond Kent Sprague (Indianapolis, IN: Hackett Publishing Company, 1972)

Dillon, John and Tania Gergel, *The Greek Sophists* (London: Penguin Books, 2003)

Freeman, Kathleen, *Ancilla to the Pre-Socratic Philosophers* (Cambridge, MA: Harvard University Press, 1983)

Hegel, G. W. F., *Phenomenology of Spirit*, trans. A. V. Miller (Oxford: Oxford University Press, 1977)

Philostratus and Eunapius, *The Lives of the Sophists*, trans. Wilmer Cave Wright (New York: G. P. Putnam's Sons, 1922)

Plato, *Complete Works*, ed. John M. Cooper (Indianapolis, IN: Hackett, 1997)

Plato, *Gorgias*, trans. W. C. Helmbold (Upper Saddle River, NJ: Prentice Hall, 1997)

Plato, *Phaedrus*, trans. Alexander Nehamas and Paul Woodruff (Indianapolis, IN: Hackett Publishing, 1995)

Xenophon, *Memorabilia*, trans. Amy L. Bonnette (Ithaca, NY: Cornell University Press, 2014)

Part II

The Ethics of Desire

5

Blinded by Desire

Self-Deception and the Possibility of the True Lie in Plato's *Republic*

Stephen Mendelsohn

Introduction

What a human being would hate the most and would find to be the most unacceptable prospect would neither be a life lived at the mercy of the arbitrary whims of a tyrant nor even perhaps the threat of an eternity of torment in Hades but rather the discovery of a lie in the place that for each individual is supposedly the most transparent and intimately well known—the soul itself.

According to Socrates, it is the true lie, "the ignorance in the soul of the man who has been lied to," which would be the most hateful and unbearable thing for a human to have to endure (*Republic*, 382b). But why is this so? The final pages of Book II of the *Republic* are the only places in which Socrates mentions the true lie. So, given what we are told about the possibility of true lie in these passages, we are left to wonder what would even constitute a true lie and how it might come to arise or to find safe harbor within the soul of the one who holds it.

Again, given what little Socrates actually says about the prospect of the true lie, apart from the fact that it is most hateful to both humans and to the gods, what follows first and foremost is an attempt to explicate and interpret what Socrates could possibly mean in these few brief passages. Having accomplished this, I then go on to offer some reflections on the effects of the true lie on the life of the individual soul and the broader consequences it may facilitate at the level of the political—the life of the *polis*. I argue that the true lie is a facilitator of a certain kind of *blindness* to *oneself* that is at the same time manufactured in, by, and ultimately for the self as a justification for the things that one does and the pursuit of those things that one desires. The true lie is at once one of the most commonplace, mundane, and everyday things that human beings partake in. While, at the same time, it is one of the potentially most dangerous things—especially in the arena of the *polis*. The true lie is that which makes possible the tyranny of the tyrant in this life, and the most horrific fate imaginable for the individual soul in the afterlife. This is what Socrates imagines it in the "Myth of Er." As such, the true lie lays the foundation for the ultimate betrayal of others at the level of the *polis*—namely, tyranny—and it can come to constitute the worst kind of betrayal of the self *by* the self at the level of the soul.

The Possibility of the True Lie

What would it mean for a lie to be true? On its surface, even the term, *true lie* (ὡς ἀληθῶς ψεῦδος), seems like an obvious contradiction in terms—an absolute impossibility. But Socrates marks a distinction between the true lie and the lie in *logos* (τό εν τοῖς λόγοις ψεῦδος), and this distinction provides some essential clues regarding the nature of the true lie. According to Socrates, "the lie in [*logos*] is a kind of imitation of the affection in the soul, a phantom of it that comes into being after it, and not quite an unadulterated lie" (*Republic*, 382b–c). The lie in *logos* therefore is something of an *image* of the true lie—an impure and adulterated reflection of the "truth" of the true lie.[1] While Socrates has yet to elaborate on what he even means by the lie in *logos*, this much at least is clear: the lie, when it is cast in *logos*, is somehow a distortion of the lie in its true and unadulterated state. The lie in *logos* exists at a remove from the paradoxical space inhabited by the true lie.

Socrates goes on to ask:

> What about the [lie in *logos*]? When and for whom is it also useful, so as not to deserve hatred? Isn't it useful [χρήσιμον] against enemies, and, as a preventative, like a drug [ὡς φάρμακον] for so-called friends when from madness or some folly they attempt to do something bad? And, in the telling of the tales we were just now speaking about—those told because we don't know where the truth about the ancient things lies—likening the lie to the truth as best we can, don't we also make it useful?
>
> (*Republic*, 382c–d)

Here Socrates seems to have forgotten his objection to Polemarchus's formulation of justice located in Book I that justice consists in "doing good to friends and harm to enemies" (*Republic*, 332d). Socrates resisted Polemarchus there on the basis that human beings often make mistakes in discerning who their friends and who their enemies really are. Here he introduces the distinction between *seeming* and *being*, and he concludes that it would be safer to avoid doing harm altogether (*Republic*, 335d). So the friend/enemy distinction is banished. I believe this is pertinent to the consideration of the nature of the true lie and the lie in *logos* for two reasons. First, someone's enemy might make themselves *seem* or *appear* to be a friend by telling a lie. The true nature of an enemy masquerading as a friend is brought to light as a result of their having been caught in a lie—actively manipulating the boundary between being and seeming. Second, looking ahead to the discussion of the possibility and the power of the true lie, it is worth noting that the earlier prohibition of doing harm to anyone seems to vanish here. We often mistake friends for enemies. Now it seems, in the face of the perceived utility offered by the lie in *logos*, namely, the potential to do harm to one's enemies and to benefit one's friends, the friend–enemy distinction is back in full force, and the prospect of potentially doing harm is back on the table. It is quite the reversal from Book I to Book II. And, I argue, this illustrates that we are all prone to sometimes forget ourselves and the principles that we subscribe to in the face of some perceived good or benefit. What marks the distinction between the true lie and the lie in *logos* is, first and foremost, that the lie in *logos* is the kind of lie that we *tell*. In this regard, it is something very commonplace and seemingly mundane indeed. This kind of lie is *useful*, and therefore, it is not deserving of the hatred that is reserved for the true lie.

Socrates provides three examples of its utility. First, telling a lie in *logos* can be an expedient way to gain an advantage over an enemy. Furthermore, second, they can be used as a preventative measure or a prophylactic in the event that a friend is about to do something bad out of ignorance or madness. And this example, too, harks back to Book I, namely, Socrates' rebuttal to Cephalus's view that justice consists in telling "the truth and giving back what a man has taken from another" (*Republic*, 331c). In response to this prospect, Socrates offers up the example that

> everyone would surely say that if a man takes weapons from a friend when the latter is of sound mind, and the friend demands them back when he is mad, one shouldn't give back such things, and the man who gave them back would not be just, and moreover, one should not be willing to tell someone in this state the whole truth.
>
> (*Republic*, 331c)

In other words, the one holding onto the weapons owes *a lie* (not the weapons) to the friend who has gone mad. The other friend, having gone mad, cannot *recognize* the harm they might do with weapons in their hands. The example raises the question as to whether it is ever possible for someone who has gone mad to recognize their own madness. And the same could potentially be said regarding ignorance. It is up to the one who is holding onto the weapons to recognize the madness or the ignorance in the other and to then make use of the lie in *logos* in order to prevent some greater evil or injustice from occurring, should the weapons fall into the wrong hands. In this case, rather strangely for a Socratic dialogue, it is *better* for the one requesting the return of the weapons to remain ignorant of the truth.

Finally, third, according to Socrates, the lie in *logos* serves as a kind of *supplement* to our knowledge (or lack thereof) when it comes to the tales that we tell to one another when speaking about the "ancient things." Here of course Socrates is referring to the poetry of Homer and Hesiod, whose stories about the gods and the origins of various other "ancient things" artificially fill an essential yet collective blind spot in human knowledge: in our accounts of how and why things are the way that they are and where we ourselves fit into the story. Such attempts to fill these gaps in our accounts of ourselves and the origins of our communities represent our best approximations of whatever the truth might really be, and yet by nature, such attempts seem doomed to fail.

There is a common thread that runs through each of these instances of the lie in *logos* that, I believe, allows us to recognize them for what they are and at the same time marks them off as distinct from the true lie. In fact, the very matter of *recognition* will prove to be central to the distinction. On one hand, if we look to the various uses to which the lie in *logos* may be put—in each case, it seems that the lie is recognized for what it is, at least by the one who is telling it. In the first two cases, the lie's usefulness in potentially harming enemies and benefiting friends, the teller of the lie is presumably in possession of the truth and actively seeks to distort it. In the final instance, the case in which poets like Homer and Hesiod tell tales in order to account for the "ancient things" which lie beyond our collective memory, the teller of the tale at the very least recognizes their own ignorance. Interestingly, in the third case, the telling of the lie in *logos* represents an attempt to approximate the truth rather than to distort it—as in the first two instances. Again, what is common to all three cases is that the teller of the lie in *logos* knows that they are telling a lie. They are in control of the boundary that marks the distinction between the lie and the truth that they are either actively trying to distort or to approximate. They are therefore able to recognize the lie for what it is even if the one on the receiving end of the lie is not always able to mark the distinction between the lie and the truth.

On the other hand, I argue that what seems to constitute the "truth" of the true lie, that which makes it most "truly" a lie, is precisely a *lack* of recognition of it on the part of the one who holds it in their soul. As Socrates says, the true lie consists in "the *ignorance* in the soul of the man who has been *lied to*" (*Republic*, 382b, my emphasis). Moreover, he says that it is something of an involuntary lie that one tells oneself "about the most sovereign things *to* what is most sovereign in himself," namely, the soul (*Republic*, 382a, my emphasis). So the true lie is *like* the lie in *logos* insofar as it is a lie that is told *by* someone *to* someone; however, what is unique about the true lie is that the *someone* in each instance here is the self-same self. The true lie is the lie that we tell *ourselves*. Furthermore, the "truth" of the true lie seems to consist not in the lie itself, but rather in the "*ignorance* in the soul of the [one] who has been lied to" (*Republic*, 382b, my emphasis). And this ignorance seems to be twofold in nature. On one hand, in a very straightforward and commonplace sort of way, the one who holds the true lie in their soul is ignorant simply insofar as they are ignorant of the truth. On the other hand, this simple kind of ignorance is compounded, redoubled so to speak, insofar as the holder of the true lie, the one who has ignorance in their soul, must at the same time be *ignorant* of that very *ignorance*. That is, unlike the teller of tales about "ancient things," who creates such tales precisely because they are *aware* of their ignorance, the possessor of the true lie is entirely unable to recognize the lie as a lie. Rather, they *believe* that the lie is indeed true—hence the "true" lie.[2]

It is with this in mind that I, in the spirit of *mis*reading Plato, would like to go ahead and offer some extended reflections on some of the potential ramifications of the true lie within the context of the Platonic dialogues in general but especially in the treatment of the soul and the *polis* in the *Republic*. As I mentioned in the introduction, with this interpretation of the true lie in hand, I make the case that, on one hand, it is something exceedingly mundane and everyday—the kind of thing that we human beings tell ourselves all the time in order to make our way through our lives. On the other hand, *potentially* at least, the true lie can be the source of the *tyranny* of the tyrant at the level of the city and that which makes possible the most terrifying prospect for the afterlife, or better yet the after*lives*, of the individual soul according to the "Myth of Er." Both of these possibilities, I argue, will result from the individual not merely possessing or holding onto the true lie within their soul but, rather, somehow *desiring* the true lie as well—something akin to a willful sort of ignorance. By way of such desire, the individual, effectively, will be blinded *by* desire, and in many ways will become blind to themselves. This will all run the risk of a *mis*reading precisely because Socrates himself has offered so little within the context of the *Republic* to elaborate upon his claim that a human being "fears holding a [true] lie there [(in their soul)] more than anything" (*Republic* 382a). So, for that reason, much of what I have to say is speculative in nature, but I hope to show within the context of the Platonic text that the dangers engendered by the true lie are a real and frightening possibility that lurk both behind and within the text itself. They simply need to be brought to light.

The True Lie in Its Everyday Aspect

Usually, the true lie manifests itself in a way that is non-threatening and rather inconsequential. I look to two examples from the Platonic corpus in order to elucidate this point. First, it will be helpful to reexamine Socrates' example of the friend who goes mad in his response to Cephalus's view of justice in Book I of the *Republic*. Then, in order to demonstrate the way in which desire enters the picture when it comes to the true lie, I look very briefly at Socrates' initial encounter with the character Euthyphro in the dialogue that bears his name. This sets into relief some of the more potentially pernicious and nefarious consequences of the true lie—when it moves beyond the mundane and becomes pathological.

The case of the mad friend and the weapons bears repeating just so we have it clearly in view. Socrates says that

> everyone would surely say that if a man takes weapons from a friend when the latter is of sound mind, and the friend demands them back when he is mad, one shouldn't give back such things, and the man who gave them back would not be just, and moreover, one should not be willing to tell someone in this state the whole truth.
>
> (*Republic* 331c)

The point seems simple and straightforward enough. On one hand, the friend who is holding the weapons may indeed "owe" them back to the friend who has gone mad under Cephalus's strictly transactional view of justice. But clearly the friend holding the weapons, being a real friend, owes the one who has gone mad something more than a simple transaction given the potential harm that could be done. In this case—without further elaboration—Socrates suggests that the friend holding the weapons should withhold not only the weapons themselves but also some portion of the truth. So, presumably, the friend holding the weapons simply does not tell the whole truth to the other, or they may even go so far as to tell a lie in *logos* to the friend who has gone mad. Perhaps the friend with the weapons lies and says that the weapons have been lost or something to that effect.

The friend who has gone mad, and who has additionally been lied to or shielded from the whole of the truth, is in possession of something like the true lie—a bit of ignorance lodged in the soul. The mad friend believes whatever the other friend tells them about the whereabouts of the weapons, and disaster is averted. But say that the friend who had gone mad comes to their senses later on and is informed by the other friend about what happened—about the judgment that had to be made and the lie that had to be told. Presumably the formerly mad friend would now be grateful to the other, for the benefit that was done and the potential harm that had been averted through keeping the mad friend in a state of ignorance. And although not usually regarding weapons and going mad, I think it is safe to say that this *sort* of thing happens all the time. Sometimes friends tell lies to friends in order to prevent them from doing bad things.

To see where the issue of *desire* can enter the picture of these everyday sorts of examples, it is helpful to look at the opening sequence of Plato's

Euthyphro, where the question of piety and the pious is first broached. Euthyphro is "said to be a professional priest who considers himself an expert on ritual and on piety generally, and, it seems, is generally so considered."[3] This is how Euthyphro sees himself. When Socrates runs into him, Euthyphro is making his way to the office of the king-archon of Athens in order to bring formal charges of murder against his own father for the death of a servant who was in his father's care. And while Socrates expresses traditional shock and alarm at such a prospect—given that doing harm to one's father is traditionally the pinnacle of impiety in ancient Greek culture—Euthyphro is very self-assured regarding his chosen course of action. Indeed, he claims that it is due to his knowledge of piety itself that he believes he has no choice but to prosecute his father (*Euthyphro*, 3e–5d).

What is most curious is Euthyphro's initial response to Socrates' inquiry to him regarding the nature of the pious and the impious—Euthyphro regards himself as an expert in such matters after all. Socrates asks Euthyphro: "Tell me then, what is the pious, and what [is] the impious, do you say?" Euthyphro responds: "I say that the pious is *to do what I am doing now*," and he goes on to further qualify this with some justification about "persecute[ing] the wrongdoer" in all cases, even if the wrongdoer is one's own mother or father (*Euthyphro*, 5d–e, my emphasis). I would like to bracket Euthyphro's qualification here and focus just on his initial response that "the pious is to do what I am doing now." He could have gone on to say almost anything and call it "the pious." He could just as well have been on his way to court in order to *defend* his father in the face of the very same murder charge because it is impious to harm one's parents according to ancient Greek custom. The point is that Euthyphro regards himself as the expert in piety; he is therefore in a sense the arbiter of what is pious and what is not. So it seems like in his estimation the pious is *always* going to be "to do what I am doing now," whatever that may be. The pious is whatever he says it is, whatever he *wants* it to be, whatever he *desires* it to be, so long as it serves as a justification for his actions.

Of course, as the remainder of the dialogue plays out, Euthyphro appears to be ignorant about that which he claims to be an expert in—namely, piety and the pious; however, this does not seem to change his own estimation of himself as the judge of what is pious and what is not. In the end, he continues along his way to the office of the king-archon as though his interaction with Socrates never occurred (*Euthyphro*, 15e). My point in highlighting the Euthyphro example is this: by the end of the dialogue, it is clear that Euthyphro is indeed ignorant when it comes to what piety is, and yet he still *believes* or at least he *wants* to believe that he knows what is pious—namely, whatever he as an expert happens to be doing at any given moment. So in an odd way, he seems to be a person who is "voluntarily. . . [lying] about the most sovereign things to what is most sovereign in himself" (*Republic*, 382a). That is, he willfully deceives himself regarding his ignorance and *acts* on the basis of that self-deception. He seems to willingly accept, albeit unreflectively, the true lie in his soul as it allows him to justify his actions by way of his act of self-deception: in this case deception about his very ignorance. And this is something that Socrates has said would be the most fearful and most hateful thing for a human being to do. And yet here is Euthyphro doing just that: unreflectively embracing the true lie. Yet Euthyphro is decidedly unable to *recognize* the operation he is carrying out despite Socrates' vain attempt to bring it to light for him. At least in the case of Euthyphro, the very worst that can happen is that his father gets convicted of a murder that, according to Euthyphro, he seems to be guilty of. And this is regardless of whether Euthyphro really desires justice in this case or he just desires to persecute his father for some reason. We can leave those issues for the courts and for the analysts.

The Tyranny of the Tyrant

Turning our attention back to Plato's *Republic*, having linked the notion of the true lie to a kind of self-deception on the basis of one's desires, I would like to use this notion of the true lie in relation to yet another paradoxical idea from the *Republic*, namely, perfect injustice. It is a frightening prospect that receives two separate treatments within the narrative of the *Republic*, so it is essential to get clear about how the two might be related. The first iteration of perfect injustice comes from Thrasymachus in Book I, and he simply conflates the idea of perfect injustice with that of tyranny. He says that it is

> the most perfect injustice, which makes the one who does injustice most happy, and those who suffer it and who would not be willing to do

injustice, most wretched. And that is *tyranny*, which by stealth and force takes away what belongs to others, both what is sacred and profane, private and public, not bit by bit, but all at once. . . . [W]hen someone, in addition to the money of the citizens, kidnaps and enslaves them too, instead of . . . shameful names, he gets called happy and blessed, not only by the citizens but whomever else hears that he has done injustice entire.

(*Republic*, 344a–c, my emphasis)

Thrasymachus seems to be a bit confused here. For, on one hand, he has said that the most perfect injustice is tyranny, which, according to him, is carried out "by stealth and force." And yet, on the other hand, for him what seems to mark its perfection is that it (tyranny) will be able to parade around in broad daylight and be praised by those who see it. Presumably this is because the tyrant is strong enough to do in broad daylight all the injustices that we secretly all wish that we could do. This conception of perfect injustice—as conflated with outright tyranny—is very different from the more extreme version of it that is articulated by Glaucon in Book II. For Thrasymachus, it seems that the tyranny of the tyrant is very much on display and recognizable to all—the tyrant included. For Thrasymachus, the appeal of tyranny is that the tyrant can parade injustice out in the open. In contrast, for Glaucon, perfect injustice masquerades as its opposite, namely, justice—it is unrecognizable.

Glaucon provides his extreme conception of perfect injustice in Book II. He says:

[L]et the unjust man also attempt unjust deeds correctly, and get away with them, if he is going to be extremely unjust. The man who is caught must be considered a poor chap. For the extreme of injustice is to seem to be just when one is not. So the perfectly unjust man must be given the most perfect injustice, and nothing must be taken away; he must be allowed to do the greatest injustices *while having provided himself* with the greatest reputation for justice. And if, after all, he should trip up in anything, he has the power to set himself aright; if any of his unjust deeds should come to light, he is capable both of speaking persuasively and of using force, to the extent that force is needed. . .

(*Republic*, 361a–b, my emphasis)

This extreme conception of perfect injustice, I argue, is a much more terrifying prospect than simple tyranny precisely because it is unrecognizable. Not only that; it is also recognized as its opposite, as justice. Even worse still, should any of its injustice come to light, it has the powers of persuasion and force at its disposal to keep its injustice hidden and in the dark.

Now, what is essential to Thrasymachus's notion of perfect injustice is a kind of recognition, at least on the part of those tyrannized, that the good of the tyrant, the open and unabashed fulfillment of the tyrant's desires, is something that they, too, would all want to aspire to if only they had the power. So there is in a strange sense a conflation of the good of the tyrant with everyone else's notion of the good according to Thrasymachus—namely, the complete and open fulfillment of desire; however, in such a case, presumably, those who are tyrannized also *recognize* that the tyrant's pursuit of their own personal good, their own desires, comes at the *expense* of the common good—hence the potential for resistance. And this is consistent with the explication of the tyrant as it appears in Book IX of the *Republic*, as someone who pathologically pursues their own desires without limit or restraint, takes control of a *polis* in order to do so, and ultimately ends up being miserable and afraid (*Republic*, 587a). This is precisely why, in Book IX, the tyrant who rules over a *polis* is likened to a master in a house full of bondsmen carried out by some gods into the middle of "a desert place" (*Republic*, 578e). There is never any sort of security for the tyrant in this sort of tyranny. The tyrant will always be afraid of, suspicious of, and ultimately subservient to those over whom they pretend to rule.

But what about the extreme of perfect injustice that is offered up by Glaucon in Book II? What would this look like? Injustice that is ultimate and without recognition or distinction able to parade around as the just? This, I argue, would constitute the most *extreme* form of tyranny, in which the good of the tyrant, the tyrant's pursuit of their own desires, is not just conflated but also *equated* with the common good. And this not just by the tyrant themselves but also by the subjects of the tyrant. They would somehow be convinced to recognize the good of the tyrant as being equivalent to their own collective good. In fact, they wouldn't recognize the tyranny of the tyrant at all. Furthermore, if the perfection of this sort of perfect injustice lies in its utter lack of recognition, then presumably the perfectly unjust individual, too, must be blind to one's own injustice. One, too, must equate one's own good, the pursuit of one's own desires, with the common good. One must be convinced that, much like Euthyphro is with respect to the pious, whatever one does is just—is consistent with *the* just, with justice itself. This would be the most dangerous and most extreme manifestation of the true lie: the ability to persuade oneself and others that the unjust and tyrannical pursuit of one's desires is, in fact, what is just. To truly believe, and to make others believe, that what is just is "to do what I am doing now," whatever that may be (*Euthyphro*, 5d). Whatever it is I so happen to desire is coincidental with what is just.

Plato on the Eternal Recurrence of the Different

Turning now, by way of conclusion, to the "Myth of Er" in Book X of the *Republic*, one might justifiably wonder what lies in store for such a perfectly unjust individual in the afterlife. Or, given that according to the myth, we live, die, forget, and then choose our subsequent lives on the basis of our ignorance of the life we just lived, the after*lives*. On one hand, there are the outright tyrants, the ones the likes of whom Thrasymachus would praise. They seem, according to Socrates, to become permanently trapped in Tartarus. Unlike the other souls that are able to move on and to choose their next lives, having ten times the punishment relative to the injustice they have committed in life, those who are truly tyrants are trapped in an eternal and unescapable punishment (*Republic*, 615d). At least, however, such individuals may be able to take the same kind of solace in eternity that Camus suggests Sisyphus is able to find.[4] They could potentially take responsibility for their fate and thereby take ownership of it in their own way. Somehow, this might make their fate more acceptable to them.

But what happens to the souls modeled after Glaucon's vision of perfect injustice, those who are self-convinced and have managed to convince others that they have lived lives of justice? In the "Myth of Er," we see the consequences that individuals such as these might face in their afterlives. Having been able to convince themselves, their peers, and perhaps maybe even the gods that they have lived the life of justice, they are treated to the reward of a thousand-year journey through the heavens; however, upon their making the selection of their next lives, they immediately choose the life of the tyrant, and in the next afterlife they will receive a one-thousand-year trip through Tartarus as punishment (*Republic*, 614d–615c). Without any memory of their experiences from the previous lives and bound by the fate and necessity that they have chosen from out of their self-forgetting, it seems impossible that this cycle could ever be stopped. For these individuals, the Myth of Er presents a nightmarish vision of the afterlife indeed. The souls bound to its cycles of rewards and punishments, self-forgetting and self-condemnation, are like people trapped on a roller coaster of life and death, cycling through lives of tyranny and perfect injustice that they can never ever escape.[5] Forever unable to mark the difference between the two lives, forever condemned to choose one and then the other. The curse of the true lie.

Notes

1. It is worth noting that the language that Socrates uses here to describe the true lie and its phantom imitation in the lie in *logos* also mirrors that which is used to describe the relationship between the original and image of *ideas*—the very measure of truth—later on in Book X of the *Republic*.
2. It is interesting to note that, if indeed this interpretation of the true lie is correct, it bears a nearly identical structure to Sartre's notion of "bad faith," as it is outlined in chapter 2 of *Being and Nothingness*.
3. Plato, "Euthyphro," G.M.A. Grube trans., as it appears in *Five Dialogues*, (Indianapolis: Hackett Publishing Company, Inc., 2002), p. 2n1.
4. Albert Camus, *The Myth of Sisyphus and Other Essays*, 123.
5. Cf. Marina McCoy, *Image and Argument*, 274. "The sharing of stories about the lives and experiences of the just and unjust alike are central to the process by which these imperfect souls become better prepared to choose their subsequent lives. Indeed, such narratives expand the range of moral scenarios available to the moral actor. Those who have heard others' accounts of the consequences of particular good or bad choices are less likely to come unprepared to situations like those they have heard. In other words, they learn how to discern through considering and reflecting upon others' narratives."

Bibliography

Camus, Albert, *The Myth of Sisyphus and other Essays* (New York: Vintage Books, 1983)

McCoy, Marina, *Image and Argument in Plato's* Republic (Albany, NY: SUNY Press, 2020)

Plato, *Five Dialogues*, trans. G. M. A. Grube (Indianapolis, IN: Hackett Publishing Company, Inc., 2002)

Plato, *The Republic of Plato*, trans. Allan Bloom (Philadelphia, PA: Basic Books, 2016)

Sartre, Jean-Paul, *Being and Nothingness*, trans. Hazel E. Barnes (New York: Washington Square Press, 1984)

Philosophical "Descent"

Between the Philosopher and the Other

Melissa Fitzpatrick

In Books V and VI of the *Republic*, Adeimantus challenges Socrates' twin claims that the philosopher is, in fact, the one who should rule and that until the philosopher rules, there will be no freedom from evils (*Republic*, 473d). Adeimantus perhaps rightly points out those who start out in philosophy "become quite queer, not to say completely vicious; while the ones who seems perfectly decent, do nevertheless suffer at least one consequence of the practice you are praising—they become useless to the cities" (*Republic*, 487d). Socrates responds with a striking image of a captain steering a ship of oblivious, power-hungry sailors, who want nothing more than the power that the pilot has: the sailors are, as Socrates puts it, *statesmen as they are now* (*Republic*, 489c).

One of the crucial questions raised within this discussion in the *Republic* is, *Why can't people recognize the benefits that the philosopher brings?* In Paul Neiman's article "The Practicality of Plato's Statesman," he stresses that one of the chief preoccupations in the *Statesman* is whether non-philosophical citizens are capable of recognizing the *true* statesman when they arise—a worry similar to that of the middle books of the *Republic*.[1] As Neiman points out, the question of whether people can recognize the philosopher or the true statesman critically relates to the *milieu* in the *Apology*: the philosopher is mistakenly interpreted to be a threat to society because he is unorthodox, an outcast of sorts, reiterating Adeimantus's point.

What I hope to address here is whether the philosopher needs to be interpreted this way. If "the cave" is, at least as Socrates seems to suggest, our human condition, is the inability to recognize the philosopher the non-philosopher's fault? And what is to be said about the philosopher? Must they be apolitical? And beyond this, linking the dialogic hunt that

DOI: 10.4324/9781003201472-8

commences in the *Sophist* for the sophist, the statesman, and the philosopher (and deciphering whether they are three kinds or one kind with three different names), if the philosopher were not apolitical, what *kind* would they be? Would they still be a philosopher? Given Adeimantus's observation, it seems worth considering to what extent the philosopher might be responsible for most people's misinterpretation of who they are, what benefits they bring, and how that (mis)interpretation relates to the distinction between the philosopher and the statesman.[2]

My overarching claim is that the middle books of the *Republic*—particularly the conversation concerning the plausibility of philosophers as kings—could provide a subtle critique of the philosopher *qua* lover of the sight of truth, as it becomes clear that the philosopher should not stay too far "removed" from the community in the cave and thus should resist the temptation to preserve their own happiness in the light of the sun at the expense of the community. The *true* statesman is, therefore, perhaps distinct from the philosopher in the sense that they unquestionably fulfill their responsibility to the community: *hearing* and *heeding to* the call of the other, compelled, by care, to weave and gift light into the community.

I ultimately hope to show that in distinguishing the philosopher-king from the philosopher in the middle books of the *Republic*, Socrates gives us tools to better understand the difference between the philosopher and the true statesman and that this distinction might provide a critique of a strictly apolitical variety of philosophy, serving as an *ethical* call to action for those who practice philosophy.

Philosophers as Kings? Who Is the Philosopher Anyway?

In Book V of the *Republic*, Socrates addresses the third and perhaps largest wave of criticism he receives from Adeimantus and Glaucon regarding the city they are constructing in speech: that philosophers should rule as kings (*Republic*, 473d–e). Underscoring Socrates' hesitation to proceed and Glaucon's response (*Republic*, 474a), Allan Bloom notes that the coincidence of politics and philosophy is precisely this: *a coincidence, an accident*. Philosophy and kingship, by Bloom's account, are two separated, if not mutually exclusive functions.[3] Socrates continues nonetheless, invested in the inquiry and well-being of his friends, and explains that the first thing he needs to do to adequately address this wave of criticism is to distinguish philosophers from non-philosophers.

Philosophers, as Socrates explains, are those with an insatiable love of learning—a desirer of the *whole of wisdom*, rather than just one part (*Republic*, 475b). Glaucon retorts that Socrates' description of philosophic natures would include a handful of strange people:

> For all the lovers of sight are in my opinion what they are because they enjoy learning; and the lovers of hearing would be some of the strangest to include among philosophers, those who would never be willing to go voluntarily to a discussion and such occupation who—just as though they had hired out their ears for hearing—run around to every chorus at the Dionysia, missing none in the cities or the villages. Will we say that all these men and other learners of such things and the petty arts are philosophic?
>
> (*Republic*, 475d)

Socrates corrects Glaucon and says that these people are certainly *like* philosophers, but rather than being lovers of sights and sounds, philosophers, "the true ones," are lovers of the sight of truth (*Republic*, 475e). He continues by further distinguishing the philosopher as the one who delights in the fair itself, rather than the many fair sounds, colors, and shapes, and then beyond this, as the one who delights in what *is*, rather than what participates in *both "to be* and *not to be"* (*Republic*, 478e). He presents Glaucon with an image of a spectrum of light, anticipatory of the cave image in Book VII, in which light corresponds to knowledge or what is (to be), darkness corresponds to ignorance or what is not (not to be), and opinion falls in between these two extremes: "darker than knowledge" but "brighter than ignorance" (*Republic*, 478c). The philosopher is associated with the light of knowledge, while non-philosophers (particularly the lovers *and masters* of opinion) dwell somewhere between light and darkness—uncompelled to acknowledge the light itself.

After an extensive list of the qualities characteristic of the philosopher (*Republic*, 486b–e), Socrates asks, when such men "are perfected by education and age, wouldn't you turn the city over to them alone?" (*Republic*, 487a). Adeimantus quickly interjects, reminding Socrates that non-philosophers do not interpret philosophers this way and that those who start out in philosophy are thought to be quite queer, useless, and even vicious (*Republic*, 487d), provoking Socrates' image of the philosopher as the pilot of a ship. Key in Socrates' image is that although the seamen consider the pilot useless—vying for the power he has over the ship, assuming that the only reason he has that power is because he is the cleverest—the pilot, in fact, possesses the most comprehensive knowledge, paying "careful attention to year, seasons, stars, winds, and everything that's proper to the art, if he is really going to skilled at ruling a ship" (*Republic*, 488d–e). As John Sallis points out, "the image is an 'apology' intended to show that if the philosopher is useless the blame lies on those who fail to make use of him."[4] As Socrates puts it,

> however, bid him blame their uselessness on those who don't use them and not on the decent men. For it is not natural that a pilot beg his sailors to be ruled by him, nor that the wise go to the doors of the rich . . . the truth naturally is that it is necessary for a man who is sick, whether rich or poor, to go to the doors of doctors, and every man who needs to be ruled to the doors of the man who is able to rule, not for the ruler who is truly of any use to beg the ruled to be ruled. You'll make no mistake in imagining the statesmen now ruling to be the sailors we were just not speaking of, and of those who are said by them to be useless and gossipers about what's above to be the true pilots.
> (*Republic*, 489b–c)

The striking part of Socrates' response is what is implicit in the last sentence. The true pilot—presumably, the true statesman—is the one who is, in fact, most useful, understanding and safeguarding the well-being of the ship, its sailors, and the voyage as a whole. Just like a doctor, the true statesman is the one who people come to when they need to be ruled, and, just like a doctor, they are able to tend to their subjects by appropriately applying the knowledge they have of the whole to each specific case. This *naturally* does not involve the doctor seeking out his patients but rather the opposite: the patients seek out the doctor. The trouble with the analogy, to reiterate Neiman's point, is that while it is perhaps obvious who the doctor is to most people, the true pilot remains completely concealed—revealed only in conversation, by way of Socrates' "apology" against the third wave.

The conclusion of the ship image marks the important shift in the discussion from the philosopher to the sophist: the man who "learns by heart the angers and desires of a great, strong beast he is rearing" (*Republic*, 493a–c)—that "beast" presumably being the *polis*, the people. The sophists are depicted as those who begin with the same propensity for learning as the philosophers do but become vicious—not because of philosophy but because of their thirst for power and their desire to enslave the masses. Thus, the sophist, although at first indistinguishable from the philosopher, emerges as distinct from the philosopher in the sense that they are an educator who corrupts. The sophist is paid for counsel in the art of persuasion, "schooled" in argumentation and the convictions of the many and, again, dwells in and feasts on opinion without reference to the light of being—no regard for the souls they move.

Nature and Necessity

Returning to the paradoxical notion of philosophers as kings, Socrates reiterates that neither city nor regime will ever become perfect "before some necessity chances to constrain those few philosophers who aren't vicious, those now called useless, to take charge of a city, whether want to or not" (*Republic*, 499b–c), and that even though the coincidence of philosophy and political power is *unnatural*, it is by no means *impossible*. As Socrates puts it,

> therefore, if, in the endless time that has gone by, there has been some necessity for those who are on the peaks of philosophy to take charge of a city, or there even now is such a necessity in some barbaric place somewhere far outside of our range of vision, or will be later, in this case we are ready to do battle for the argument that regime spoken of has been, is, and will be when this Muse has become master of a city. For it's not impossible that it come to pass nor are we speaking of impossibilities. That it's hard, we too agree.
>
> (*Republic*, 499d)

Socrates continues by somewhat shockingly defending the many—freeing them from the responsibility of fostering the alleged impossibility of a philosopher-king. After getting Adeimantus to agree that the many could be to blame for their misunderstanding of philosopher and the philosopher, Socrates responds:

> You blessed man . . . don't make such a severe accusation against the many. They will no doubt have another sort of opinion, *if instead of indulging yourself in them, you soothe them and do away with the slander against the lover of learning by pointing out whom you*

> *mean by philosophers, and by distinguishing, as was just done, their nature and the character of their practice so the many won't believe you mean those whom they suppose to be philosophers.* And if they see it this way, doubtless you'll say that they will take on another sort of opinion and answer differently. Or do you suppose anyone of an ungrudging and gentle character is harsh with the man who is not harsh or bears grudges against the man who bears none? I shall anticipate you and say that I believe that so hard a nature is in the few but not the multitude.
>
> (Republic, 500a, emphasis mine)

Socrates insinuates that the many non-philosophers are not necessarily to blame for philosophy's reputation. It is, at least in one sense, the vicious natures that start out in philosophy that give her a bad name. But in another sense, the onus is on those who know what demarcates the philosopher to appropriately disseminate that information: soothing the many and doing away with slander by way of distinction and gentle conversation. Thus, it is clear that Socrates is well aware of the fact that there is an obligation for those who know (the philosophers and his friends) to set the record straight and free philosophy from slander. Although philosophers, faithful lovers of the sight of truth, are wrapped up in and obsessed with keeping company with the divine with "no leisure to look down toward the affairs of human beings" as they imitate the things that are (e.g., justice itself and beauty itself), Socrates mentions another crucial possibility: "If some necessity arises . . . for [the philosopher] to practice putting what he sees there into the dispositions of men, both in private and in public, instead of forming only in himself (*Republic*, 500d).

It seems that Socrates wants to illuminate the possibility of a necessity that challenges the natural order of things. This necessity would at least in part involve the seemingly useless philosopher assuming his role as the "true pilot." I want to suggest that in this discussion about nature, possibility, and impossibility, Socrates is instilling a sense of hope in his interlocutors who, since the beginning of the dialogue, have not lost hope in their pursuit of justice itself, even after particularly convincing arguments and images depicting justice as nothing more than injustice in drag. This hope is twofold: (1) hope in the possibility of non-philosophers to understand the benefits the philosopher brings and (2) hope in the possibility of a philosopher recognizing and assuming their unnatural, albeit necessary role as pilot of the ship, that is, *acknowledging their duty to and responsibility for the others*.

There is no explicit talk about the "true statesmen" in the *Republic* but rather a careful delineation among the philosopher, the sophist, and perhaps non-philosophers in general. What I want to suggest, however, is given what has been established thus far as implicit in the conversation in middle books of text, the true statesman would be the philosopher who, out of some *unnatural* and thus *unerotic* necessity, takes charge of the city and finds a way to make the city obey. This might seem tyrannical at first glance, but Socrates' emphasis on the gentle disposition that should guide the many suggests something more like *care*.

Before turning to the description of the statesman in the *Statesman*, I want to address a crucial point that Sallis makes regarding the distinction in the *Republic* between the lovers of sights and sounds and the lovers of the sight of truth, that is, the philosopher.[5] In addition to hearing and the love of sounds being notably absent in the description of the philosopher, Sallis goes on to emphasize that the lover of the sight of truth *sees* beautiful things and the beautiful itself but that this whole is not a whole in any complete or final sense, nor is it explicitly *a love of the whole*.[6] The philosopher then, *loves* the beautiful itself, but merely *sees* the beautiful things, thus loving only a part of the whole (again, forsaking hearing and sounds altogether) rather than the whole itself, that is, the things that are *and* the images of those things in their manifestations.[7]

So, how does this discussion relate to the distinction between the philosopher and the statesman? While it seems that at least in some sense the philosopher *is* the true pilot or statesman, as Noburu Notomi points out:

> Thus, the single project of the *Sophist* and the *Statesman* suggests a sophisticated idea of the philosopher-rule, originally proposed in the *Republic*. The genuine statesman turns out to be in the very epistemological states of the philosopher. . . . On the other hand, it is also important that the philosopher and the statesman are not explicitly united, as suggested in the *Republic*. Is there any gap between the two?[8]

With this question posed by Notomi and the clues from the extensive discussion about who the philosopher is in the middle books of the *Republic*, we can turn to the stranger and young Socrates' pursuit for the statesman in the *Statesman* to attempt to determine what in particular might constitute the "gap" between the two.

Who Is the Statesman?

After various unsuccessful attempts at defining the statesmen by way of *diaeresis*, in the final third of the *Statesman*, the stranger and young Socrates decide to stick with the paradigm of weaving as the most illuminating of what is meant by the art of statesmanship, which is "a knowledge of the rule of human beings, pretty nearly the hardest and greatest to acquire" (*Statesman*, 292b). The statesman does not merely know the art of legislation, that is, building "rigid and unchangeable laws," but also has the strength necessary to exercise and appropriate their knowledge in the *polis*.[9] This is to say that in addition to knowing and preserving order by way of good legislation, the statesman is attuned to the particularities of human existence, able to appropriately act and react to the various changes that inevitably occur within the community. The statesman is, therefore, the one who exercises and implements *phronesis* in the *polis*.

The stranger points out that this type of rule is at least in some sense implausible (*Statesman*, 295a–b). But, as is the case with physicians and the distribution of medicine, a vital part of any practical science is the ability to suggest things that are contrary to the laws, based on specific circumstances (*Statesman*, 295d–e). Similarly relying on the image of the statesman as the captain of a ship, the stranger explains:

> And just as the captain always maintains the advantage of the ship and sailors, not by laying down writing but by supplying his art as law, and keeps his fellow sailors safe and sound, so too, in accordance with this same manner, would a right regime issue from those who are capable of ruling in this way, supplying the strength of the art that's mightier than the laws? And there is no mistake in everything intelligent rulers do, as long as they maintain one big thing—as long as they always distribute to those in the city that which with mind and art is most just, and can keep them safe and make them better from worse as far as possible.
>
> (*Statesman*, 296e–297b)

Thus, distinct to the statesman and the art of kingship is the forte that enables both application and supersession of the law in praxis (*Statesman*, 300d). The statesman is the one who truly possesses this practical knowledge, whereas the tyrant or the sophist, for example, merely *imitates* the knowledge of the statesman by ruling "neither in conformity with the laws nor in conformity with the usages," ignorant to everything just or holy, harming "whichever one of us he wants to on each and every occasion" (*Statesman*, 301c–e).

Echoing Socrates' challenges to the proposed definition of justice in Book I of the *Republic*, doing harm cannot be part of justice, and intrinsic to the stranger's conception of the statesman is justice embodied. As Socrates says to Polemarchus, harming is not "the work of the good but of its opposite . . . it is not the work of the just man to harm either a friend or anyone else, Polemarchus, but of his opposite, the unjust man" (*Republic*, 335d–e). Beyond this, the doing of harm and general abuse of power by those who rule is at least in some sense to blame for the general lack of trust by most people, i.e., the many, thus contributing to the non-philosophers' inability to recognize the true statesmen, as addressed in the *Statesman* (*Statesman*, 298a–301e), or the benefits the philosopher brings, as addressed in the *Republic*. Sophistic distortion and tyrannical oppression are what give statesmanship a bad name—notably mirroring the *statesmen as they are now* giving philosophy a bad name—and not only render the practical knowledge of the statesman untrustworthy but also make the rhetorical art or the science of persuasive speaking, vital to the power of the statesman; that is, the statesman must be surrounded by those skilled in persuasion and the artful dissemination of information (*Statesman*, 304a). This is to say that the art of rhetoric or the science "with the capacity to persuade the multitude and the crowd through mythology" must be subservient to the art of rule, as the ruler should above all decide when persuasion is appropriate (*Statesman*, 304d).

To return to the paradigm of weaving, the statesman is defined as the one who "rules over all of these and the law, cares for all things throughout the city, and weaves them all together most correctly" (*Statesman*, 305e). The statesman, guided by what is good, beautiful, and true, thus weaves together the quick and courageous and the gentle and moderate in "unanimity and friendship," completing the "best and most magnificent of all webs—the extent that this can hold of a common web—and by wrapping everyone else in the cities it . . . hold them together by this plaiting, and to the extent that it's suitable for a city to become happy" (*Statesman*, 311c). One of the chief ways in which this virtuous web is woven (in addition to rhetoric by those who know and have been instructed by the things that are) is education (308e)—the educators tasked by the statesmen to inculcate virtuous dispositions into the souls of the people. Through education, the statesman can actualize his care for the community: seeing, hearing, and, most important, healing the disorder; focusing on the betterment of both the whole and the parts of the *polis*; and imposing law and order on the flux and flow of life (by way of education, rhetoric, etc.), weaving together harmony and conflict, sameness and difference.

How, then, is the statesman distinct from the philosopher? Linking the stranger's description of the statesman to the middle books of the *Republic*, I want to suggest that the statesman, unlike the erotic lover of the sight of truth, not only sees the whole in the complete sense—weaving the many, disparate parts of the community together so as to constitute a unified city—but, unlike the lover of the sight of truth, also hears the discord to which he can respond with his godlike art and that this attuned listening to the needs of the *polis* is characteristic of care.

To be a statesman, therefore, is to care for, and thus listen to or hear, the call and suffering of the others. That being said, as Stanley Rosen notes, "there is no mention of Eros in the statesman. The word literally appears once in the dialogue, at 307e6, where it refers to an excessive desire for peace, not to sexuality or love of the beautiful."[10] While it is without question a stretch to say that the statesman *loves* to listen, especially as there is no mention of *eros* in the stranger's description of care, I think it is safe to assume that the care endemic to statesmanship implies an unerotic, albeit earnest commitment to (commitment being a component to or a variation of love) and concern for the various parts of the city that should to be woven, rather than assimilated, together. While the parts that are woven together are natural in themselves, the weaving itself is unnatural—it, the unified city, is the *unnatural* result of the art of statesmanship.[11] Law (*nomos*) modifies nature (*phusis*). As Rosen points out, "human nature is such that it must be modified by *techne* if it is to survive and prosper."[12] The statesman thus sees and, most important, listens to difference and the particularities of human existence and weaves accordingly, healing disorder and suffering by way of both theory and praxis, navigating back and forth between opinion and the things that are.

Learning as Suffering

To return to the main guiding questions here, (1) Must the philosopher be interpreted as useless? and (2) What is the difference between the philosopher and statesman? I want to first turn to Socrates' challenge to Thrasymachus's definition of justice in Book I of the *Republic*. By Socrates' account, the one who rules ultimately does so not by nature but out of *necessity* (*Republic*, 346e–347e). Linking this to the stranger's account of the statesman, the statesman is distinct in his understanding of and commitment to the flourishing of the other. This commitment to the other, as least as Socrates construes it, is not the object of erotic desire but a responsibility, a duty. The statesman, therefore, recognizes that, whether they like it or not, they have been called and have no choice but to hear and heed to that call. As *phronesis* embodied, the statesman listens, prescribes, and weaves, heals, educates, and informs. The statesman, formerly a philosopher, insatiably obsessed with the sight of truth, surrenders to his obligation to the other (at the expense of exclusively keeping company with the divine), living for the other by striving to gift harmony to the *polis*.

To link the image of weaving to the allegory of the cave of Book VII of the *Republic*, the statesman, like the philosopher-king, is inevitably tasked with dealing with the "disturbance of the eyes" that occurs "when they have been transferred from light to darkness" and weaving the divine light of the sun into the community that inevitably resides in darkness (*Republic*, 518a). Thus, as tempting as it is for the one who has seen the light of the sun to "remain there" and "not be willing to go down again among those prisoners or share their labors and honors, whether they be slighter or more serious," that dwelling in the light of the sun—ascent without descent—is not justice (*Republic*, 519b). Glaucon's awe at Socrates' claim is again a testimony of the paradox built into the notion of a philosopher-king: Why would the philosopher, reveling in the brilliant light of the sun, ever come back down? Socrates stresses:

> Well, then, Glaucon . . . consider that we won't be doing injustice to the philosophers who come to be among us, but rather that we will say just things to them while compelling them besides to care for and guard the others. . . . But we have begotten for yourselves and for the rest of the city like leaders and kings in hives; you have been better and more perfectly educated and are more able to participate in both

> lives. So you must go down, each in his turn, into the common dwellings of others and get habituated along with them to seeing the dark things. And, in getting habituated to it, you will see ten thousand times better than the men there, and you'll know what each of the phantoms is, and of what it is a phantom, because you have seen the truth about fair, just, and good things. And thus, the city will be governed by us and by you waking, not in a dream as the many cities nowadays are governed by men who fight over shadows with one another and form factions for the sake of ruling, as though it were some great good. But the truth is surely this: that city in which those who are going to rule are least eager to rule is necessarily governed in the way that is best and freest from faction, while the one that gets the opposite kind of rulers is governed in the opposite way.
>
> (*Republic*, 520b–d)

Thus, the knowledge of and desire for what is good, true, and just, is something the statesman and the philosopher share. But listening to, understanding, and responding to the call and suffering of the others seem to be something distinct to the statesman. The statesman, then, appears to be a philosopher who, out of necessity, commits themselves to a somewhat selfless life of care for the other—substituting, at least in a sense, their obsessive, utterly channeled erotic desire for the divine for the flourishing of the other. And again, as Socrates reiterates throughout the *Republic*, the true pilot cannot be the one who desires and fights for power, yearning to rule for his own advantage, but instead the one who steers the ship because they care about the welfare of the passengers—acknowledging the need to secure the safety of the voyage, *preserving and fostering life*. While the philosopher prioritizes their steadfast pursuit to keep company with the divine—the true lover of the sight of truth—the statesman, though still informed by the divine, prioritizes care. Care can perhaps be understood as a different form of desire.

That said, the description we get of the true statesman in both the *Statesman* and the *Republic* is a tall order. It seems that the statesman, perhaps even more so than the philosopher, is described as a sort of god among humans. A philosopher who knows the good, just, and true; sees and loves the whole (the one, the many, and the relation between the two); and acknowledges and actualizes their duty to others through care of the need to govern is perhaps nothing short of idealistic and "optimistic." As Rosen claims at the conclusive of his extensive commentary on the *Statesman*, there is no such person.[13]

So, what, then, are we to make of, and take away from, this paradigm of the true pilot or genuine statesman that, although seemingly paradoxical, is nonetheless a possibility? And how does this relate to most people's interpretation of the philosopher as useless?

It seems appropriate to conclude with Socrates, the philosopher *par excellence*, who, in discourse, always holds open the possibility for something more—extends the invitation to challenge alleged impossibilities. Perhaps the preservation of the invitation is what demarcates or defines the philosopher, whereas the true statesman is the one who in acknowledging this invitation accepts the challenge to care in the name of the good, just, and true *not out of erotic desire but out of the necessity of care*. The statesman is perhaps the one who is most able to show that philosophy is not something useless but the condition for the possibility of peace: the philosopher who is able to detach himself ever so slightly from keeping company with the divine so as to "descend" and devote himself to care for the others. This is not to say that the philosopher fails to care for the other but that the statesman prioritizes the duty that derives from care.

Thus, it seems that we can interpret Socrates' description of the philosopher *qua* lover of the sight of truth as a subtle call to action: a call to listen and heed to the necessity of care. If we take this call to action seriously, it seems that part of our task as those who study philosophy and strive to become philosophers should be to not only to hold the door open to possibility but to, like Socrates, also make philosophy a way of life—fully embodied and fully entangled in the web that is our social and political reality. This is to say that in the wake of Socrates, our task is *to learn how to descend*: to learn how to communicate and educate in the name of the love of wisdom and to show that philosophy and politics need not be at odds. Beyond this, our task as philosophers is to understand that nonphilosophers are not to blame for their misunderstanding of the philosopher and philosophy but instead that the onus is on us, the philosophers, to refuse to forsake the community.

Notes

1 Paul Neiman, "The Practicality of Plato's Statesman."
2 As Noburu Notomi notes in "Reconsidering the Relations between the Sophist, the Statesman, and the Philosopher," presented on November 20, 2014, at

the *Plato's Statesman Conference* at Boston College, some scholars assume that Plato intended to write a dialogue, the *Philosopher*, while others suggest that the *Sophist* and the *Statesman* already show the philosopher in defining the other two (2–3). I hope to build on Notomi's thesis by looking to clues in the *Republic*, in which we get the infamous image of a seemingly impossible philosopher-king *qua* distinct from the sophist.
3 See Allan Bloom's commentary, *Republic*, 460–461.
4 John Sallis, *Being and Logos: Reading the Platonic Dialogues*, 399.
5 Ibid., 382.
6 Ibid.
7 Ibid., 387–388.
8 Notomi, "Reconsidering the Relations between the Sophist, the Statesman, and the Philosopher," 12. This at least in some sense challenges Stanley Rosen's last word in *Plato's Statesman: The Web of Politics*, "The highest form of political existence, ironically enough, turns out to be the transpolitical existence of *phronesis* or, in other words, philosophy" (190).
9 Neiman, "The Practicality of Plato's Statesman," 407 (in reference to *Statesman*, 294b).
10 Rosen, *Plato's Statesman: The Web of Politics*, 154.
11 Ibid., 185.
12 Ibid., 188.
13 Ibid., 155.

Bibliography

Neiman, Paul, "The Practicality of Plato's Statesman," *History of Political Thought*, 28, no. 3 (2007), 402–418

Notomi, Noburu, "Reconsidering the Relations between the Sophist, the Statesman, and the Philosopher," Presented on November 20, 2014 at the *Plato's Statesman Conference* at Boston College

Plato, *The Being of the Beautiful: Plato's Theaetetus, Sophist, and Statesman*, trans. Seth Benardete (Chicago: University of Chicago Press, 1984)

Plato, *Republic*, trans. Allan Bloom (New York: Basic Books, 1968)

Rosen, Stanley, *Plato's Statesman: The Web of Politics* (New Haven, CT: Yale University Press, 1995)

Sallis, John, *Being and Logos: Reading the Platonic Dialogues* (Indianapolis, IN: Indiana University Press, 1995)

7

"Halt!"
Socrates, Levinas, and the Divine Sign

Eric R. Severson

> My friend, as I was about to cross the stream my usual divine sign occurred, which occasionally arrests me before I complete an action. In that spot I seemed to hear the voice forbidding me to leave until I made atonement, since I've committed some offense against the divine.[1]
>
> —Socrates in Plato's *Phaedrus*, 242b

Introduction

The landscape of Western philosophy is littered with the ruins of attempts to transcend, critique, circumvent, or otherwise go beyond Plato. The work of Plato continues to exert truly unparalleled gravitational force in Western thinking. One cannot attempt a *new* idea without contending with Plato, whose thinking continues to age without getting old. Plato's significance is such that, beyond the nearly innumerable explicit engagements of his extant dialogues, his specter continues to haunt and influence even philosophy that neglects to mention his name. Plato is perhaps misread as often as he is read well. This chapter, which engages one idea in the relationship between Plato and Emmanuel Levinas, does not presume to have cornered the correct or proper reading of Plato—as if such an achievement is even possible. Neither is it conceivable in one chapter to assess the way Levinas reads Plato, who appears in his work hundreds of times.[2] What I attempt is a close look at Levinas's critique of the "voice"—the "divine sign" (δαιμόνιον) which occasionally stops Socrates in his tracks. By correcting Levinas's reading of Plato, and offering a more Levinasian interpretation than Levinas himself, I hope to offer a clearer view of both Plato and Levinas on the "Halt!" that plays an underappreciated role for Socrates.

This chapter proceeds in two parts. In the first, I locate Levinas's work as it relates to the "beyond being" invoked by Socrates in *The Republic*.

DOI: 10.4324/9781003201472-9

Levinas latches onto this opening in Plato's most famous work and presses the questions it evokes relentlessly. In so doing, I argue, Levinas finds himself working on a singularly Platonic problem for his entire career. In the second section, I explore Plato's *Phaedrus*, Levinas's favorite and most-quoted dialogue.[3] I then identify a misreading of Plato in Levinas's work, on the question of Socrates' "divine voice," and seek ways to understand both Plato and Levinas better through any analysis of the "Halt!" that plays a prominent role for both.

Being's Yonder

Levinas is an inconsistent but often insightful reader of Plato. He is propelled by the urgent need to say something *new* about philosophy, particularly as it relates to the other person, and he knows from the beginning that this work will require an ongoing and contentious conversation with Plato. References to Plato are scattered throughout his work, often in pivotal places, and the very structure of his main ideas are perhaps best understood in light of Platonic terminology and concepts. Within the orbit of Levinas scholarship, much has been written about this relationship. Rather than look backward into Levinas's work for evidence that he was a good or bad reader of Plato—he was demonstrably both—my efforts here are directed at a tension in Levinas's reading of Plato that remains productive. Jacques Derrida commented that Levinas's writing "proceeds with the infinite insistence of waves on a beach."[4] With each publication, and many times within each work, Levinas further pressures Western philosophy to contend with its egocentrism. Levinas argues that a fundamental egoism has become endemic to Western language, philosophy, and culture; he blames Plato more than anyone else. By Levinas's reading, Plato is the godfather of an egoic structure for "European humanity"—from the kernel of Socrates' dictum to "know thyself," an entire universe was built "in the mode of self-consciousness."[5] Levinas understands his project, which replaces the ego with the *other person* as philosophy's principal concern, as an attack on the foundations of Western philosophy. No wonder he likes to pick on Plato.

At the same time, there is a remarkable and ongoing affinity to Plato in the work of Levinas, particularly inasmuch as Plato's "know thyself" was troubled by the idea of that which transcends being, the "beyond being" (ἐπέκεινα τῆς οὐσίας) invoked by Socrates in the closing lines of the sixth book of Plato's *Republic*. The *Good*, Socrates argues there, can be the cause or source of knowledge, the way the sun provides growth and nourishment to things on earth (*Republic*, 509a–c). The Good itself is not some component of "essence" or "being," but radically transcends it all (*ἐπέκεινα τῆς οὐσίας*, "on the yonder side of being"). It would be foolish to look for the sun beneath a rock it has warmed; for Socrates, the Good cannot be found in being but must "surpass" it. This, for Levinas, is an incredible spark within the *Republic* and within the philosophy of Plato overall. When Glaucon hears Socrates declare that "[t]he good is not being, but something far surpassing being in rank and power," he is stunned and brings the party to laughter by declaring, "Ye gods! . . . What a miraculous transcendence."[6] This appeal to the beyond being is a puzzle, and it occurs at a pivotal point in the *Republic*. When all that is known is tethered to *οὐσία*, the essence, to the word *to be*, how can anything be spoken of otherwise? Glaucon has pushed Socrates to ground his political philosophy on the highest Good, and their line of questioning has led him to declare that the entire republic is to be structured according to a goodness that *is not*, but lies outside of, *οὐσία*. Levinas may, in fact, be reading Plato *well* when he points to these lines as the heart of the *Republic*. And so, in Plato, Levinas finds his friendliest ally and fiercest foe. He accuses Plato of the "bad conscience" of a fundamental egoism that locates the adventure of philosophy in self-consciousness. Then, in almost the same breath, Levinas clings to a component of Platonic philosophy that locates the Good outside of the enterprises of knowledge, truth, and reason—on which Western philosophy is founded.

There is no consensus among scholars of Plato regarding the meaning of this theme in Book 6, which is perhaps the way Plato would have wanted it.[7] "Barrels of ink have been spilled" in attempts to understand these lines, and the spilling continues unabated.[8] Neither can we say definitively that the unsettling of the ontological structure of Plato's world by the introduction of its *otherwise*, its yonder, should be centralized as Levinas has arranged it. Still, Levinas has drawn profound attention to an undeniable problem within Plato's *Republic* that continues to vex modern scholars. After attempting to resolve the question of being's "beyond" with a proof from formal logic, Rafael Ferber and Gregor Damschen conclude that "Plato seems serious, but not completely serious, about the hyperbolic status of the Good."[9] If the Good is a *chimera*, how might ethics or politics ever be founded on it?[10]

Levinas provides some fresh tools for considering the "otherwise than being"; his second major work carries that phrase as its title. In *Otherwise than Being or Beyond Essence*, Levinas explores options for thinking about the Good that arises from experiences other than hermeneutics, knowledge, thinking, and thematizing. These ventures, as Socrates noted in the *Republic*, pertain to being, which Socrates delimits as "things which are known" (*Republic*, 309b). Ferber and Damschen conclude that there can be no resolution to what the "beyond" might indicate and seem to be resigned to an aporia on this matter; a "Good" beyond being, when all we have for consideration is οὐσία, is comparable to the concept of a "square circle."[11] And perhaps this is why Glaucon—Plato's brother—chuckles when he replies with "What a miraculous transcendence!" Ferber and Damschen, and many other scholars of Plato's work, hope that Socrates was not entirely serious when he appealed to something beyond οὐσία. Levinas hopes the opposite.

By dwelling at great length with the ἐπέκεινα τῆς οὐσίας, it may be that Levinas expresses here a faithfulness to Plato that is rare even among Platonists. He is determined to dwell at this point where modal logic grinds to a halt and asks plainly: Is there some other way that this "beyond being" is made known to us? What if being's otherwise is encountered in a manner other than cognition, thematization, understanding, and knowledge? Levinas suggests that the encounter with the other person, particularly the suffering other, is an event of this register, an existential and phenomenological happening that bears traces of something *beyond* (or, as he increasingly suggests, *prior to*) the scope of being. The other person, obviously, appears to me *in being*, as a being among beings. Elsewhere I have argued that he uses innovative thinking about time to express this apparently simultaneous experience of οὐσία and its otherwise.[12] I experience the other person, and in that encounter, I discover that in time-before-the-present I have already been summoned to responsibility for her (their/his) suffering. The experience of the ἐπέκεινα τῆς οὐσίας is better understood, for Levinas, as an experience of that which does not fall to "presence." It is for this reason that the word *otherwise* is preferred to the term *beyond*; one might imagine that something beyond is just a few steps farther down the line. Levinas's "otherwise" takes on a temporal connotation. Socrates evokes spatial imagery to indicate the "beyond" being, using the analogy of the sun and its externality to the "being" of things on the earth below. Levinas tries an alternative, positioning the yonder of "being" as a manifestation of nonsynchronous temporality. The prime example of this nonsynchrony, of diachrony, is language. Specifically, Levinas detects the ἐπέκεινα τῆς οὐσίας in the escape of the "Saying" from the "Said." This is not the place for an extended treatment of Levinas's various attempts to articulate the "beyond" indicated by Socrates in Book 6 of the *Republic*. I hope this brief summary accomplishes two things: (a) to demonstrate the proximity to Plato at the very core of Levinas's most radical ideas and (b) to indicate an important watchfulness for the "beyond" in Levinas's reading of Plato.

Levinas might be best understood as a philosopher of vigilance. Since humans are *beings*, we cannot detect the "beyond being" with conventional epistemology. The beyond appears as trace, as *glory*, as guilt, as the diachronic experience of language, as responsibility. The swift current of being moves toward self-interest and survival (Levinas uses the term *conatus essendi*) and obscures the subtle appearance of the beyond.[13] To encounter the other person as a *mere* being is to miss "what is better than being, that is, the Good."[14] Since it is in the suffering of the other that the beyond breaks into being, for Levinas, it is a responsibility that precedes and supersedes knowledge. Thus, "morality is not a branch of philosophy, but first philosophy."[15] This very obviously opposes a long Western tradition that turns to ethics as an application of other first-order philosophical claims. Levinas takes Socrates as his point of departure, and the question on which his ethical philosophy hinges is the trace of the ethical origins of philosophy as it becomes manifest in being. For this reason, I turn in the second section of this chapter to the appearance of another apparent outside voice in Plato's work, the "divine voice" that plays a crucial role in several dialogues.

The Summons of the Other(wise)[16]

The *Phaedrus* is a lengthy and complex dialogue, often considered among Plato's finest literary works. I have selected this text, among the many works of Plato important to Levinas, because of the privileged role it plays in the evolution of Levinas's own philosophy. Levinas refers to the *Phaedrus* more than any other Platonic work, and the core ideas of the *Phaedrus*—love, *logos*, language, rhetoric, and the danger of the written word—are central to his project and particularly his later work. These themes are all opportunities, for Levinas, to attempt to speak of the nonthematizable glimpse of the ἐπέκεινα within being. In his efforts to express a radical and new configuration of human responsibility, Levinas turns both toward and against the voice of Plato. What I propose in this second half of my chapter is a *more* Levinasian reading than the one provided by Levinas himself. My argument is that Socrates displays the kind of vigilance that is so important to Levinas's project in his attention to a "divine voice" that stops him in his tracks at critical moments.

Socrates is wandering the countryside around Athens, Plato reports, when he encounters Phaedrus. They begin to walk together, and Phaedrus divulges that he has recently been at the home of Lysias, where Phaedrus heard Lysias give a speech in praise of pederastic love. Socrates expresses a deep desire to hear this speech, which becomes the first context for their conversation as they wander together. They stroll for a time before settling beneath the cool shade of a sycamore (plane) tree, probably close to the banks of the Ilisos River, and spend the day in conversation concerning the quality of Lysias's argument, the nature of love, and the danger of rhetoric and writing. The dialogue is difficult to summarize; two scholars rarely agree on what the "central" topic of the discourse might be. Nevertheless, the *Phaedrus* is widely considered to be among Plato's finest and most influential dialogues. Among the striking literary aspects of this text is the style Plato chooses for its composition. In the roughly contemporary dialogue the *Symposium*, Plato utilizes rhetorical maneuvers to underscore the powerful intervention of the narrator in the story. The *Symposium* is delivered as a fifth-hand account of a dialogue that took place many days before its narration. In the *Phaedrus*, where the conversation will dwell for some time on the problems of writing and narration, there is no narrator. The conversation proceeds with no framing that is not offered in the discourse, no third party describing an interlocution between these acquaintances, nothing but the presentation of a firsthand account of two human beings in conversation. To read the *Phaedrus* is to observe a conversation in action, to be made into a witness of a discussion beneath a sycamore that has long since died and rotted away. The words, because Plato wrote them down, reverberate today. It is clear that Plato wanted readers to have an experience of proximity to this conversation but perhaps also to be aware of the chasm between the written word and the utterance of this dialogue so many centuries ago. When I assign the *Phaedrus* in philosophy courses, I always encourage my students to read the text with their back against a tree. This text urges us to attend to a conversation that has both slipped irrevocably into the past and remained as vibrant and relevant as the shady trees that shade readers, and dialogue partners, still today.

The conversation first explores the speech of Lysias, which is critiqued by Socrates for many failings. Phaedrus wants to hear Socrates provide an alternative speech and swears on the tree they lean against that he will never form another speech again himself until he hears one.[17] Socrates proceeds with his first—a speech about the dangers of love and the perils of *eros*. At the conclusion of his scathing speech, Socrates prepares to leave the shade of the tree and cross the river back toward Athens. He is "stopped" in his tracks, however, by a voice that he hears from time to time—an internal, divine voice that sounds an alarm when he is about to do something wrong. Plato inserts this feature into several dialogues; Socrates hears a voice that does not give him *answers* but alerts him to the need for more contemplation or to revisit that which he has said. He is about to err, to walk away from a speech attacking *eros*, when this voice alerts him to his folly. He is arrested and settles back down beneath the sycamore tree to try again. Here, in fact, begins the dialogue in earnest. Love is more complicated than both the farcical version praised by Lysias and the narrow eroticism attacked in Socrates' first speech. This interruptive event is a pivotal point in the conversation and plays an underappreciated role in the dialogue and its themes.

Levinas does not think highly of Socrates' divine sign, only briefly mentioning it as a voice that "speaks in the depths of the I" and guides Socrates' words and behavior.[18] According to Levinas, the voice of the daimon is internal to Socrates, a deep-seated "muse" or "genius" to which Socrates attends in an expression of faithfulness to an "I profiling itself behind the I."[19] To read the divine sign as a voice *internal* to Socrates, or as a rhetorical trick utilized by Socrates to add gravitas to his ensuing speech, is consistent with a trend in modern philosophy to be somewhat embarrassed by the appearance of anything resembling theology in Plato. Hegel, paradigmatically, specifies that this is an *inner voice*, and therefore the exemplification of Hegelian dual-consciousness. By Hegel's misreading of the δαιμόνιον, this voice is both internal and *constructive*.

Hegel writes that Socrates "had a *daimon* within him, which counseled him what to do, and revealed to him what was advantageous to his friends."[20]

As common as such interpretations may be, they do not square with a straightforward reading of both the source and operation of the δαιμόνιον according to Socrates. First of all, there is consensus on at least this: Socrates never receives guidance from the divine sign. As Nickolas Pappas puts it, "Plato consistently presents an inhibiting divine agent."[21] Second, the sign *comes*—or does not come—to Socrates.[22] We learn the most about the divine sign in the *Apology*, although what Socrates says about its appearance in his life is consistent across brief mentions in the *Euthydemus*, the *Euthyphro*, the *Phaedrus*, the *Republic*, and the *Theaetetus*. Socrates alters his behavior and discourse according to its appearance and according to its nonappearance. In the *Apology*, he waits for the sign to alert him to problems with his defense against his accusers and draws confidence from the silence of the voice. In the *Phaedrus*, Plato picks the word γίγνομαι to refer to the arrival of the sign, a word that implies the arrival of something genuinely new. We can know the mind neither of Socrates nor of Plato on the question of the δαιμόνιον. We *can* know that Plato took pains to articulate the appearance of this voice as something that happened *to* Socrates. This directionality is crucial for Socrates' self-defense in the *Apology*; how can they impugn him for responding faithfully to a divine voice? Luc Brisson argues that the δαιμόνιον is, for Socrates, essentially *involuntary*. If the divine sign resided "within him," this is never stated by Socrates and is seemingly opposed by the phrase "came to me" (*Phaedrus*, 242b). Socrates is consistent and persistent in the way he presents this voice: it is always explained as an external interruption. The word δαιμόνιον is not a noun, here, but functions as an adjective applying to σημεῖον—"sign."[23] There are signs, and then there are *divine* signs. To parrot Glaucon's declaration in the *Republic*, "By God! What a marvelous transcendence!" (*Republic*, 509c).

It would seem that Hegel, and the modern philosophical disposition he exemplifies, is therefore wrong about the δαιμόνιον on at least two counts: Socrates' voice never told him what to do, and Socrates receives the voice as an intrusion. Levinas follows Hegel's misreading, placing the δαιμόνιον within Socrates and suggesting that the divine voice provides some kind of direction or guidance. It should be noted that Levinas and Hegel are joined by some contemporary scholars of Plato in locating the divine sign within Socrates. Plato scholar Gerd Van Riel argues that the δαιμόνιον should be considered an internal voice.[24] Mark McPherran suggests that the δαιμόνιον should be seen as a component of Socrates' philosophical project, a way to deliver an "anti-hubristic" message to human beings.[25] In appealing to a mysterious and godly voice, Socrates performs an act of piety, even if some who heard him speak of this voice may have questioned its source. Ultimately, philosophers today struggle to interpret the "sign," and most commentaries and monographs expend little energy on the topic.[26] Since Socrates never names the deity whose voice he hears, Plato invites ambiguity. Is this a new deity? Does the "divine sign" perform a fundamentally religious function? Is this a private voice, unique to Socrates, or something we should all listen for?

There is certainly nothing close to a consensus on the nature or source of this voice. Levinas spends considerable energy encouraging his reader to consider the voice of the other person, the voice that arrests and stuns the ego from beyond being. Socrates' δαιμόνιον is counted among the voices that do not qualify. Levinas places this δαιμόνιον alongside the character of Mephistopheles in the legend of Faust, based on the historical Johann Georg Faust (ca. 1480–1540). After a failed attempt at suicide, the legend goes, Faust strikes a deal with the devil in order to enjoy the pleasures of the world he failed to escape. The devil sends a representative, Mephistopheles, who resides *within* Faust and offers magical powers for several years. The deal Faust strikes is the forfeiture of his soul and eternal enslavement. Faust carries Mephistopheles within him, a voice and a power that enable him to seduce beautiful and innocent women. In the early versions of the story, including the one dramatized by sixteenth-century playwright Benjamin Marlowe, Faust's deal leads to damnation.[27] "Socrates' *daemon*, Faust's Mephistopheles, speak in the depths of the I and guide it," writes Levinas.[28] When Levinas, in *Totality and Infinity*, aligns Mephistopheles with the δαιμόνιον, he misreads Plato, at least if we take Socrates at his word regarding its external appearance. Socrates positions the voice from without, an involuntary and unbidden interruption in his progress. The δαιμόνιον does not guide Socrates—it stops and warns him. The mark of his piety is not his capacity to summon this voice but to listen for it. Commentator Harvey Yunis puts it this way: "Other than the command of prohibition the divine sign gives Socrates no information about what is wrong in his intended actions. Socrates is responsible for figuring that out himself."[29]

In *Euthyphro*, the title character vocalizes a popular view that Socrates can use the δαιμόνιον to predict the future; he scoffs, claiming that "the outcome is not clear except to you prophets" (*Euthyphro*, 3d). Socrates declares, in the *Apology*, "It is a voice, and whenever it speaks it turns me away from something I am about to do, but it never encourages me to do anything" (*Apology*, 31d). It appears that Meletus, one of Socrates' accusers at trial, included the δαιμόνιον in his indictment of Socrates, mocking him in the process.[30] The lack of attention to the voice in Platonic scholarship is particularly problematic given the importance Socrates places on the voice: "You have heard me give the reason for this in many places," he tells the jury at his trial (*Apology*, 31d). Socrates insists, repeatedly, that he plays no part in the conversation with this voice. His is a work of waiting, listening, speaking, proceeding, with an openness to an external interruption, an interruption that does not guide but blocks. The arresting voice is apotreptic: it just says "no."[31] To minimize this enigmatic feature of Plato's Socrates is to ignore a substantial, explicit part of his philosophical labors.

Socrates notes that the arrival of this voice is a familiar one. He has grown accustomed to being accosted when he is about to do or say something wrong. In the *Phaedrus*, he was about to walk away from a conversation with Phaedrus, having provided a lopsided and overly negative view on love. Arrested by a *divine* voice, Socrates stops, reports his experience to Phaedrus, and then begins to compose his *palinode*—a speech of retraction. The next steps are not scripted but left up to Socrates. The voice doesn't stop him and then guide him; it grinds him to a halt and leaves him to consider why it appeared and how he might address its interruption.

It is no coincidence, I suggest, that readers of Plato reach aporia at the two junctures of his work featured in this chapter. Both the "divine voice" and the "beyond being" are quasi-theological limits to philosophy as Plato frames the discipline. Both cases involve some manner of irony and leave Socrates vulnerable to mockery. Both the δαιμόνιον and the ἐπέκεινα indicate a hard stop for the important work of truth as it is revealed in "being." There is, within this literary character Socrates, a tension that we are wise to hold as we read Plato's work. To collapse it by dismissing the *beyond* of the voice, of the Good, is to be a mis-reader of Plato. This would be an adequate conclusion for my work here and a fine place to stop if my only concern was to indicate a manner in which Levinas helps us better understand a vital tension within Plato's dialogues. The hard stop indicated by the δαιμόνιον, and the aporia that results when Socrates attempts to explain the ἐπέκεινα, it may indicate that Plato quite intends the trouble these phrases cause his readers.

However, Levinas gets to work on these very problems, searching for ways to articulate events outside the vernacular of οὐσίας. In his effort to articulate the outsideness of the voice of the other, Levinas joins Socrates in an appeal to religious imagery if not theology. In *Otherwise than Being*, Levinas points to a passage in the biblical book of Isaiah and to the summoning of Isaiah to serve as God's prophet. Here, the encounter with the arresting voice occurs amid a despairing and self-referential lamentation. Before referencing some of Levinas's appeals to the voice of the Hebrew God in biblical passages, it is important to clarify: I am not suggesting any correlation between the voice heard by Socrates and the voice heard by Abraham and Isaiah. It would be more accurate to say this: Levinas finds Plato asking a question about philosophy that cannot be answered from within its conventional logical boundaries. When Plato has Socrates pause, humbly listening for a voice to "Halt!" him before immoral behavior, Plato indicates a *need* in philosophy for a discourse of another register. As I reflect briefly on Levinas's invocation of the voice of God from his Jewish tradition, I am not attempting any new insight on Plato's texts or the mind of Socrates or the appearance of the δαιμόνιον. These, I think, pose a philosophical question, and Levinas sees in the Hebrew tradition something that amounts to an answer. Isaiah cries, "Woe is me! I am lost, for I am a man of unclean lips, and I live among a people of unclean lips."[32] His despairing cries are interrupted, stopped in their tracks, and his attention redirected to the suffering people of Israel. Isaiah hears the question from God: "Whom shall I send? And who will go for us?" When he speaks again, he has pivoted, turned: "*Heneni*" or "Here I am."[33] For Levinas, the "here I am" indicates the event whereby the ego is stripped of its "scornful and imperialist subjectivity."[34] The voice that speaks here is the voice of the Infinite; Levinas writes, the "here I am" is a witness to the glory of the Infinite that is beyond being.[35] The voice stops Isaiah in his tracks, and turns his attention toward the suffering other.

Levinas detects this voice, again, in the famous account of Abraham's near sacrifice of Isaac in Genesis 22. Contesting the famous philosophical account of this passage by Søren Kierkegaard, in *Fear and Trembling*, Levinas writes, "Abraham's attentiveness to the voice that led him back to the ethical order, in forbidding him to perform a human sacrifice, is the highest point in the drama."[36] Here, perhaps, Levinas articulates the "Halt!" of the divine sign in the clearest of terms. On the precipice of carrying out his mission, Abraham is stopped from *without*, from beyond obedience. Levinas scolds Kierkegaard for supposing that this "Halt!" represents a suspension of the "ethical." Although he contests any such suspension of ethics, Levinas is perhaps closer to Kierkegaard than he realizes. The ethical, in *Fear and Trembling*, is precisely the good derived from reason; Levinas would surely agree that rationality must be held loosely for the voice to be heard. For Levinas, the appearance of the voice that says "stop" coincides with the gaze of Abraham onto the face of Isaac. It is in the face of the other, Levinas writes elsewhere, that "God comes to mind."[37] In Levinas's reading of Genesis 22, he emphasizes that Abraham does not "look up" until after hearing the voice; he was, necessarily, looking at Isaac when the voice called out, "Stop!"[38] For Levinas, the encounter with the other person is the context for the divine voice, a voice that first says, "Stop," and then binds the arrested person to the suffering and precarity of the other person. After his lips are touched by hot coals, arresting his speech, Isaiah hears: "[W]hom shall I send?"[39]

Conclusion

Levinas's consistent attempts to critique the Western philosophical tradition lead him back, over and again, to Plato. For Levinas, and he seems right in this, any possible road to new expressions of philosophy runs through ancient Athens and through Plato, in particular. At times, we find Levinas offering only sweeping dismissal of Plato, using Plato as a figurehead for a Western tradition Levinas wants to unsettle and usurp. At other times, Levinas writes like a man inspired by Socrates to pull at the seams of a problem with virtue and knowledge that Plato stubbornly includes in his dialogues. The problem of the Good beyond being is literally and figuratively at the center of the *Republic*, and Levinas's diligent attention to similar ruptures in Plato's work is a consistent component of his analysis. He does not credit Plato with inserting a voice from outside-being in the *Phaedrus*, but it is worth considering whether this is not the most Levinasian moment in the Platonic dialogues. Face-to-face with Phaedrus, and just before disappointing and misleading Phaedrus concerning *love*, the divine voice calls Socrates to revoke his words, to reconsider, to try again in the endless attempt to put words on what cannot be languaged. The function of the interruptive divine voice is to return Socrates to his one-on-one, face-to-face conversation with *this* person, just one person, just Phaedrus. Plato offers the dialogue for all who would have conversations, for all who would attempt to ossify the event of *speaking* into writing. In this venture, Socrates models humble openness to the failure of words and ideas; in the *Phaedrus*, as in the *Republic*, the Good from which all speaking arises is subject to that which cannot find ontological expression.

Socrates sometimes seeks to provide this "Halt!" himself. This is, in fact, a key feature in several dialogues, perhaps most obviously in the *Euthyphro* and the *Meno*. In both of those cases, Socrates has an encounter and conversation with men on a mission, with momentum and confidence at their back. He offers little wisdom in these dialogues beyond the "Halt!" and offers to share a conversation that might pivot their lives. Meno comes to Socrates to talk about virtue, probably as a side quest in his mission to gather troops and resources for a mercenary mission. Socrates asks him a series of questions about his ideas and leaves Meno stunned, stopped in his tracks. He accuses Socrates of being a "torpedo fish," a Mediterranean stingray that stuns and paralyzes its attackers (*Meno*, 84b). I have elsewhere argued for an interpretation of the *Meno* informed by the report of Xenophon, who records that Meno died shortly after this visit to Athens, in ignominy, in a foolish and ill-conceived pursuit of fame and fortune.[40] If Plato's readers knew about Meno's fate, which is likely, then the "sting" or "stun" of the Socratic voice could be read as an attempt to save Meno's life and reputation. The "Halt!" in Plato's writings is an underappreciated opening in thematic arguments. The following is worth exploring at further length, given this Levinasian reading of the δαιμόνιον: when Socrates "stuns" his interlocutors, is he trying to offer the "divine voice" to others? This question exceeds the parameters of this chapter.

The next steps in understanding what is at stake in the "beyond being" almost certainly involve a revisiting of the concept of οὐσίας. This term, in Plato and throughout ancient Greek philosophy, is laden with *monetary* connotations.[41] The term might be more closely translated to "sum" rather than the common English rendering "being." For this reason, to grapple with the ἐπέκεινα τῆς οὐσίας will require a consideration of the influence of money and commodification on the imagination of Plato. Greek philosophy, like capitalistic economics, often involves a strategic investment and return. The voice that arrests Socrates catches him in the act of doing philosophy in this conventional way, wagering on ideas and strategies and watching them bear fruit. The voice is a full stop to this progression, which is what makes the modern interpretation utilized by Hegel and Levinas so problematic. The voice doesn't guide the next investment but shames and questions the economic engine that produced it. There is a clash between a Socrates that *exemplifies* a philosophy of the "sum" (οὐσίας) and a Socrates who seems to be attuned to something *otherwise* than being. Perhaps it is in this gap between two Socrateses that the "Halt!" appears.

The entire philosophical project of Levinas is structured to facilitate the work of waiting for a voice, speaking and seeking truth with an ear for the unraveling of this venture. There is, in both Levinas and Socrates, a summons to unrelenting vigilance. Levinas refers to the voice as something to which one can *bear witness* but never thematize.[42] In Levinas, the appearance of the voice operates at the register of responsibility, the literal and material obligation to care for the one whose voice has arrested me. For Levinas, this responsibility irrupts amid being. Socrates can only testify to the irruption, nothing more. Scholars have struggled in vain to map this δαιμόνιον onto Platonic ontology, parallel to the search for a meaningful interpretation of the *beyond being*. In both cases, perhaps Levinas can help contemporary scholars better understand a baffling but perhaps crucial aspect of Plato's work.

Notes

1 This new translation of Plato's *Phaedrus* 242b–c was completed with the generous assistance of Yancy Dominick, with special gratitude to Franklin Dominick.
2 For a book-length review of Levinas's readings and uses of Plato, see Tanja Staehler's excellent monograph: *Plato and Levinas: The Ambiguous Out-Side of Ethics* (Routledge: New York, 2010).
3 Staehler claims that "[t]he Phaedrus occupies a special place in Levinas's philosophy. Firstly, Levinas alludes to the Phaedrus more than to any other Platonic dialogue." *Plato and Levinas*, 7.
4 Jacques Derrida, *Writing and Difference*, 312, n. 7.
5 Levinas, *Entre Nous: Thinking of the Other*, 191–192.
6 Literally, "By Apollo!" Plato, *The Republic*, trans. Tom Griffith (Cambridge: Cambridge University Press, 2000), 216 n.29: "In the Greek Glaucon exclaims: 'By Apollo!', a god associated with the sun, although in Plato's day primary by philosophers rather than in official cult."
7 See, for instance, Rafael Ferber, "Ist die Idee des Guten nicht transzendent oder ist sie es doch? Nochmals Platons *epekeina tes ousias*," in Damir Barbarić,

ed., *Platon über das Gute und die Gerechtigkeit / Plato on Goodness and Justice* (Würzburg: Giustizia, 2005), 149–174.
8 This line is from Ferber and Damschen, "Is the Idea of the Good Beyond Being? Plato's 'epekeina tês ousias' revisited," 197.
9 Ibid., 203.
10 Of the attempt to consider the "beyond being" in the terms of formal logic, Levinas writes: "When stated in propositions, the unsayable (or the an-archical) espouses the forms of formal logic; the beyond being is posited in doxic theses, and glimmers in the amphibology of being and beings—in which beings dissimulate being. The otherwise than being is stated in a saying that must also be unsaid in order to thus extract the otherwise than being from the said in which it already comes to signify but a being otherwise. Does the beyond being which philosophy states, and states by reason of the very transcendence of the beyond, fall unavoidably into the forms of the ancillary statement?" Levinas, *Otherwise than Being: Or Beyond Essence*, 7.
11 Ferber and Damschen, "Is the Idea of the Good Beyond Being? Plato's 'epekeina tês ousias' Revisited," 202.
12 Eric R. Severson, *Levinas's Philosophy of Time*.
13 Levinas, *Otherwise than Being*, 139. Levinas often simply writes "conatus."
14 Ibid., 19.
15 Levinas, *Totality and Infinity*, 304.
16 See "The true essence of man is presented in his face, in which he is infinitely other than a violence like unto mine, opposed to mine and hostile, already at grips with mine in a historical world where we participate in the same system. He arrests and paralyzes my violence by his call, which does not do violence, and comes from on high." Levinas, *Totality and Infinity*, 290–291.
17 Harvey Yunis points out that Phaedrus uses the language and rhetoric of a solemn oath, "reminiscent of Achilles great oath." However, by swearing on the plane tree, Phaedrus indicates that he does not take himself very seriously and invites a playful response from Socrates. Harvey Yunis, *Plato: Phaedrus*, 110.
18 Levinas, *Totality and Infinity*, 272. Levinas does not clarify in this his only mention of the Socrates δαιμόνιον, which instance he has in mind, although Socrates is remarkably consistent in his description of its operation in a number of dialogues.
19 Ibid.
20 Hegel, *Lectures on the Philosophy of History*, 246.
21 Nickolas Pappas, review of "Socrates' Divine Sign: Religion, Practice and Value in Socratic Philosophy."
22 γίγνομαι insinuates the arrival of a new state of being. Liddell and Scott, *A Greek-English Lexicon*: "γείνομαι:—come into a new state of being."
23 In this regard, the common practice of using the term δαιμόνιον as a noun is potentially misleading; the noun is σημεῖον. Still, this common practice is

not without merit, for it underscores that which differentiates *this* sign from others. I repeat this practice with the preposition ἐπέκεινα in this chapter. The word, as "beyond" or "otherwise," is prepositional or, perhaps, adverbial. Using ἐπέκεινα as a noun (the beyond, the otherwise) underscores the importance of this departure from the language and thematic structure of οὐσίας. For helpful grammatical analysis of the *Phaedrus*, see Havey Yunis, *Plato: Phaedrus*, 122.

24 Gerd Van Riel, "Introducing a New God: Socrates and His Daimonion," 31–42.
25 Mark McPherran, *The Religion of Socrates*.
26 In one exception, a volume of collected essays edited by Pierre Destrée and Nicholas D. Smith (*Socrates' Divine Sign: Religion, Practice and Value in Socratic Philosophy*), the diversity of opinions on the matter is striking.
27 Goethe's version of the tale, however, provides hope for people who have made similar deals with the devil. Goethe's Faust is endlessly pursued by a loving God whose constant striving leads to salvation. Johann Wolfgang von Goethe, *Faust: A Tragedy*.
28 Levinas, *Totality and Infinity*, 272.
29 Havey Yunis, *Plato: Phaedrus*, 123.
30 "I have a divine or spiritual sign which Meletus has ridiculed in his deposition" (*Apology*, 31d).
31 Destrée and Smith, *Socrates' Divine Sign: Religion, Practice and Value in Socratic Philosophy*, ix.
32 *New Revised Standard Version Bible* (Oxford: Oxford University Press, 1990), Isaiah 6:5.
33 Levinas explores this connection in *Otherwise than Being*, 146.
34 Ibid.
35 Ibid.
36 Levinas, *Proper Names*, 74.
37 Levinas, *Of God Who Comes to Mind*.
38 Levinas, *Proper Names*, 74.
39 *New Revised Standard Version Bible*, Isaiah 6:8.
40 Debra Nails, *The People of Plato: A Prosopography of Plato and Other Socratics*, 204–205. I explore the significance of Meno's fate in relationship to Socrates' efforts to convince him to stay in Athens in Eric R. Severson, *Before Ethics* (Dubuque: Kendall Hunt, 2021).
41 The role of money in ancient Greece, and its relationship to the foundations of philosophy, is explored insightfully by Richard Seaford, *Money and the Early Greek Mind* (Cambridge: Cambridge University Press, 2004).
42 Levinas, *Otherwise than Being*, 146.

Bibliography

Derrida, Jacques, *Writing and Difference*, trans. Alan Bass (Chicago, IL: The University of Chicago Press, 1978)

Ferber, Rafael, and Gregor Damschen, "Is the Idea of the Good Beyond Being? Plato's 'epekeina tês ousias' revisited," in *Second Sailing: Alternative Perspectives on Plato*, ed. Debra Nails and Harold Tarrant (Espoo, Finland: Wellprint, 2015)

von Goethe, Johann Wolfgang, *Faust: A Tragedy*, trans. Martin Greenberg (New Haven, CT: Yale University Press, 2014)

Hegel, Georg Wilhelm Friedrich, *Lectures on the Philosophy of History*, trans. Ruben Alvarado (Aalten, Netherlands: Wordbridge, 2011)

Levinas, Emmanuel, *Entre Nous: Thinking of the Other*, trans. Michael B. Smith and Barbara Harshav (New York: Columbia University Press, 1998)

Levinas, Emmanuel, *Of God Who Comes to Mind*, trans. Bettina Bergo (Stanford, CA: Stanford University Press, 1998)

Levinas, Emmanuel, *Otherwise than Being: Or Beyond Essence*, trans. Alphonso Lingis (Pittsburgh: Duquesne University Press, 1998)

Levinas, Emmanuel, *Proper Names*, trans. Michael B. Smith (Stanford, CA: Stanford University Press, 1996)

Levinas, Emmanuel, *Totality and Infinity: An Essay on Exteriority*, trans. Alphonso Lingis (Pittsburgh, PA: Duquesne University Press, 1969)

Liddell, Henry George and Robert Scott, *A Greek-English Lexicon* (Oxford: Clarendon Press, 1940)

McPherran, Mark, *The Religion of Socrates* (University Park, PA: Pennsylvania State University Press, 1999)

Nails, Debra, *The People of Plato: A Prosopography of Plato and Other Socratics* (Indianapolis, IN: Hackett, 2002)

New Revised Standard Version Bible (Oxford: Oxford University Press, 1990)

Pappas, Nickolas, Review of "Socrates' Divine Sign: Religion, Practice and Value in Socratic Philosophy," *Notre Dame Philosophical Reviews* (2005), https://ndpr.nd.edu/reviews/socrates-divine-sign-religion-practice-and-value-in-socratic-philosophy/, accessed April 2021

Plato, *Five Dialogues: Euthyphro, Apology, Crito, Meno, Phaedo*, trans. G. M. A. Grube (Indianapolis, IN: Hackett, 2002)

Plato, *Phaedrus*, trans. Robin Waterfield (Oxford: Oxford University Press, 2002)

Plato, *Republic*, trans. Tom Griffith (Cambridge: Cambridge University Press, 2000)

Severson, Eric, *Levinas's Philosophy of Time* (Pittsburgh, PA: Duquesne University Press, 2013)

Smith, Nicholas D. and Pierre Destrée, *Socrates' Divine Sign: Religion, Practice and Value in Socratic Philosophy* (Kelowna, BC: Academic Printing and Publishing, 2005)

Van Riel, Gerd, "Introducing a New God: Socrates and His Daimonion," in *Socrates' Divine Sign: Religion, Practice and Value in Socratic Philosophy* (Kelowna, BC: Academic Printing and Publishing, 2005)

Yunis, Harvey, *Plato: Phaedrus* (Cambridge: Cambridge University Press, 2011)

8

Ignorance, Flattery, and Dialectic

Philosophical Rhetoric in Plato's *Gorgias*

Christine Rojcewicz

Introduction

Haunting the background of Plato's *Gorgias* is a contradiction. On one hand, Socrates never lets the *logos* stray from its natural, presumably truthful, path, and on the other hand, he always cares for the moral improvement of his interlocutor. He tailors the conversation, and no two *logoi* are ever the same. This appears contradictory, for, if Socrates is always abiding by the truth of the *logos* itself, and truth is stable and unchanging, then any external influences, like the needs or sensibilities of the interlocutor, would jeopardize the purity of the *logos*. Likewise, if Socrates cares wholeheartedly for the well-being and the improvement of his various interlocutors, then surely each *logos* would compromise its adherence to the truth for the sake of the interlocutor. Of course, only the truth and never falsity could possibly improve the interlocutor, yet each individual person takes up a unique path to moral virtue.

In the *Gorgias*, this contradiction is particularly apparent because Socrates converses with three separate interlocutors, namely, Gorgias, Polus, and Callicles, and each conversation takes place in front of a large audience. Additionally, the content of the *logoi* themselves concerns rhetoric and whether rhetoric can at all be truthful. Thus, the *Gorgias* is the perfect place for a discussion of Socrates' philosophical method. In this chapter, I resolve this apparent contradiction by arguing that Socratic rhetoric is both truthful and directed toward the interlocutor because of (1) Socrates' claims to ignorance, (2) his refusal to flatter, and (3) his adherence to dialectic. I argue that these three moments define the philosophical rhetoric that Socrates embodies. It is a truthful rhetoric directed outward—toward the moral improvement of others. Rather than resulting in contradiction, truth and soul-leading develop alongside each other. Additionally, these three moments are reflected in the myth at the end of the dialogue—they make up the three changes Zeus makes to improve the method of deciding the fates of the dead.

Truth as Goal for Socrates

To say that Socrates has no concern for the truth would simply be a mistake. He devotes his life to the pursuit of truth, and he would never willingly assert anything untruthful. For example, when Socrates and Gorgias first begin to engage in dialogue, Socrates makes clear that his goal in the conversation is to finally know the nature of rhetoric. He tells Gorgias, "not on account of you, but on account of the argument, in order that it may go forward so as to make what is being talked about as manifest as possible to us" (ὡς μάλιστ' ἂν ἡμῖν καταφανὲς ποιοῖ περὶ ὅτου λέγεται; *Gorgias*, 453c). It is the *logos* Socrates is after, not Gorgias' opinions. Furthermore, Socrates affirms that he is not going to pay special attention to whether he is hurting Gorgias' feelings or being rude; rather, he and Gorgias will follow the course of the *logos* as it leads them. The point is that Socrates, first, is not trying to disrespect Gorgias or give him undue deference. And second, Socrates hopes to keep the discussion away from personal affronts. Rather, the *logos* itself will determine the correct course of action. The discussion will be successful if it remains impartial.

If Socrates and Gorgias succeed, then the truth of the matter, that is, the definition of rhetoric, will reveal itself to them. If they stray from the *logos*, they will miss the definition. According to Socrates,

> I ask for the sake of the argument's being brought to a conclusion in a consequential manner, not on account of you but so that we may not become accustomed to guessing and hastily snatching up each other's words, but so that you may bring your own views to a conclusion in accord with what you sent down.
>
> (*Gorgias*, 454c)

The point of following the *logos* naturally is to avoid making any leaps in the line of thought or state any conclusions that do not follow. Rather, for Socrates, proceeding slowly, consequentially, and impartially will reveal the truth.

Additionally, the truth that philosophy reveals is permanent and enduring. In a long speech during his conversation with Callicles, Socrates states that "philosophy always says what you now hear from me and is much less capricious with me . . . for [Callicles] presents various speeches at various times, whereas philosophy always presents the same" (ἡ δὲ φιλοσοφία ἀεὶ τῶν αὐτῶν; *Gorgias*, 482a–b). The aim of philosophy—truth—is eternal and fixed, so presumably the practice of doing philosophy should be too.

The question then becomes, how does Socrates fulfill the aim of philosophy, namely, stable and unchanging truth? To answer, we have to look at the way in which Socrates philosophizes. Socrates engages in dialectic for the sake of removing false opinions. He would rather endure the shame and embarrassment of being refuted than defend a position that he knows to be untrue. Socrates states that there are two kinds of people: "those who are refuted with pleasure if I say something not true, and those who refute with pleasure if someone should say something not true—and indeed not with less pleasure to be refuted than to refute" (*Gorgias*, 458a). Some people prefer to point out the flaws in the *logoi* of others and are themselves ashamed when they are refuted. Others, according to Socrates, prefer to be refuted because then their own false belief is removed. They are brought closer to the truth through the removal of the falsehood. These people do not feel ashamed but are rather glad and relieved when they are refuted. Socrates, of course, belongs in the second category.

> For I consider it a greater good, to the extent that it is a greater good to be released oneself from the greatest evil than to release another. For I think that nothing is so great an evil for a human being as false opinion about the things that our argument now happens to be about.
> (*Gorgias*, 458a–b)

Socrates cares even less about looking like a fool than he does about winning "arguments." Rather, for him, the truth itself is the aim of all conversation, and if one loses sight of that for the sake of one's honor, then one is committing a great misdeed.

The key, however, is that in order to prefer to be refuted than to refute, Socrates must first assume that he does not know the truth for certain. He begins in ignorance, and through the *logos* itself truth will come about.

Truth is the *telos*, not the starting point, of philosophy, for Socrates. According to Marina McCoy, Socrates' method does not guarantee

> that one will arrive at the truth if one is only willing to submit oneself to his questions. First, the starting points of the discussion are beliefs that are not independently argued for in advance of the argument and perhaps cannot be independently argued for. Socrates' approach is decidedly non-foundationalist.[1]

Merely engaging in dialogue with Socrates does not guarantee that one will emerge with a greater knowledge of the truth. Rather, truth is reached if there is either a change in attitude or a confirmation of the initial belief. Furthermore, most Platonic dialogues end aporetically—the initial belief is shown to be false, but nothing is set in its place as the truth. There is no guarantee of truth, but that should not stop one from trying to attain it.

We see evidence of this phenomenon in *Gorgias*. Gorgias is a highly respected person in the ancient world, but Socrates is not intimidated by his fame. He disapproves of what Gorgias has spent his entire life pursuing, namely, the "art" of rhetoric and flattery, and he is not afraid to say so for the sake of the *logos* at hand. That is to say, Socrates attends to the truth of the matter at all costs in his dialogue with others. Often Socrates needs to constrain Callicles[2] to speak his true opinion so as not to contradict what was said earlier or to stray from the true path of the *logos*.

Socrates' Care for His Interlocutors

Nevertheless, Socrates also cares wholeheartedly for the well-being of his interlocutors. He has the virtue of others in mind, and almost every conversation is undertaken for someone else's sake. In the *Apology*, Socrates defends his way of life by claiming that he does not care at all for himself but only for others. He goes so far as to concern himself with others at the cost of harming himself:

> it does not seem like human nature for me to have neglected all my own affairs and to have tolerated this neglect now for so many years while I was always concerned with you, approaching each one of you like a father or an elder brother to persuade you to care for virtue.
>
> (*Apology*, 31b)

Socrates is aware of how odd and unusual it is for someone to only care for others at the expense of himself. Socrates is poor, for he refuses to take payment for any learning that might occur from him. Even in his defense speech itself he aims to make his audience more virtuous:

> I am far from making a defense now on my own behalf, as might be thought, but on yours, to prevent you from wrongdoing by mistreating the god's gift to you by condemning me; for if you kill me you will not easily find another like me.
>
> (*Apology*, 30d)

Here we see Socrates caring for not only one or two interlocutors individually but a large audience of 501 as well. Socrates, notoriously, refuses to ingratiate himself at the feet of the jurors and lament and call out for his family. Rather, he seeks to educate the jurors, even in his own defense, not to pander to them. That is to say, Socrates does not seem to practice philosophy, engage in dialectic, or speak rhetorically *for the sake of himself*. Rather, Socrates always has the virtue of his interlocutor, or in the case of the *Apology* and of the audience in the *Gorgias*, for the sake of the many. For McCoy, Socrates'

> questions are guided by a sense of *kairos*, knowing when and how to speak to his interlocutors in particular circumstances. Socrates makes choices as to how to question those with whom he is speaking, but those choices cannot be exhausted by a limited set of universal principles.[3]

Socrates' care for his interlocutors exceeds any universal, static, and rigid principles set down before the beginning of the dialogue. But does that make his *logos* any less truthful?

For Socrates, each conversation with each interlocutor could take any direction. According to McCoy, "perhaps it is for this reason that Plato presents Socrates in dramatic dialogues, where we can see how his questioning is guided by attention to *kairos* and his ubiquitous individualized care for the souls of those to whom he speaks."[4] This is why Socrates prefers dialogues with individuals rather than speeches before large audiences—dialogue requires that one stray from what one has rehearsed beforehand and what one has memorized; a dialogue with prepared speeches would be stilted and artificial. In the *Apology*, Socrates trusts himself to speak the truth in this spontaneous way of speaking rather than using a predetermined and rehearsed speech. He claims that we will hear from him the whole truth "spoken at random and expressed in the first words that come to mind, for I put my trust in the justice of what I say, and let none of you expect anything else" (*Apology*, 17c). Premeditated speech runs the risk of carefully crafted lies and misleading speech, but if one speaks from the heart without rehearsing or writing down one's speech, then there is a greater chance that one will tell the truth.

In the *Gorgias*, we can see clearly the ways in which Socrates can speak to different souls in different ways. In each of his three conversations with Gorgias, Polus, and Callicles, respectively, the topic remains the name, namely, rhetoric, but Socrates' method and the outcome of each conversation are radically different. All the characters are present for the whole meeting, but each conversation takes on a dramatically different appearance. The reason is that each of the interlocutors, including Socrates, represents an extreme position: Gorgias and Polus care only for the form and not the meaning of what they say; Callicles cares only for the utility of rhetoric, that is, the power one gets from rhetorical skill; and Socrates represents an extreme care only for the soul, virtue, goodness abstracted from life, and contemplation.[5] A "one-size-fits-all" method of refutation would fail with such a diverse grouping of views, so Socrates must attend to each interlocutor individually while still addressing himself to the crowd surrounding them as well. The philosophical rhetor must be attuned to the different kinds of souls and the different ways souls can be persuaded. For example, when conversing with Gorgias, Socrates takes a more rational, level-headed approach. In contrast, in his conversation with Callicles, Socrates appeals to Callicles' sense of outrage, and his *logoi* carry a certain shock value.

Philosophical Rhetoric: Resolving the Contradiction

As a result, it seems as though one could either ignore the well-being of one's interlocutor in order not to stray from the truth or cater to each interlocutor without abiding as strongly to the truth. I argue that this dichotomy between care for interlocutor and adherence to the truth is in fact a false dichotomy. To make this point, I want to use the example of a strange moment in the *Gorgias* in which Socrates briefly lets Polus completely control the conversation, and it results in utter confusion. After the interlocutors have been shocked and left in complete disbelief at Socrates' equating rhetoric with flattery (κολακεία), Socrates asserts that "rhetoric according to my argument is a phantom [εἴδωλον] of a part of politics" (*Gorgias*, 463d). Rather than asking what exactly Socrates means by this, as it is undoubtedly a cryptic answer, Polus immediately asks, impatiently, the same question he has been trying to get Socrates to answer the whole time: Is rhetoric noble or shameful (*Gorgias*, 463d)? Here Socrates relaxes some of the control that he has over the conversation. Polus has asked whether Socrates thinks rhetoric is shameful or not multiple times by now, and earlier, Socrates had refused to give an answer before they determine exactly what rhetoric is. For how could he pass judgment without yet knowing what it is? Yet, curiously, Socrates lets Polus lead the discussion and answers Polus' question here, even though they are nowhere near ready to pass judgment on rhetoric. The ensuing lines are telling:

SOC: I say [rhetoric is] shameful—for I call bad things shameful—since I must answer you as if you already knew what I'm saying. Gor: But by Zeus, Socrates, even I myself do not comprehend what you're saying! Soc: Quite likely, Gorgias, for I am not yet saying anything clear, but Polus here is young and swift. Gor: Well, leave him be, and tell me. . . (463d–e)

Then Socrates and Gorgias spend some uninterrupted time conversing together. Obviously, Polus cannot comprehend the answer Socrates gives, and even Gorgias steps in to show that he and the rest of the crowd cannot follow either.

Why does Socrates indulge and humor Polus here? I claim that it is part of Socrates' rhetorical method of teaching Polus not to get ahead of himself. It seems as though Socrates is simply exasperated by Polus' pestering him with the same question, but in indulging him for a moment, Socrates accomplishes two things. First, he, at least temporarily, lets Gorgias step into the conversation. After all, conversing with Gorgias was Socrates' initial reason for his and Chaerephon's visit (*Gorgias*, 477b). Second, he shows how going through the *logos* too quickly is detrimental to the truth of the matter. Socrates is aware that Polus will never realize that he is rushing too fast through the *logos* if he is not *shown* the ridiculous result of that rushing. For McCoy,

> the rhetorician must know when to speak but also when not to say anything for the sake of his interlocutor's wellbeing. Socrates is not interested only, then, in intellectual knowledge of soul and subject matter but also in practical knowledge that consists of how to apply this knowledge in particular contexts.[6]

The preceding interaction with Polus is an example of Socrates not saying anything. It seems as though Socrates is placing the needs and desires of his interlocutor over and above his adherence to the truth—Socrates lets the *logos* fall into confusion when he remains silent and does not constrain Polus in the proper way. Yet I argue that this is merely a way in which Socrates lets his interlocutor learn firsthand the ways in which a *logos* can be misled. Here we see how Socrates is able to both care for his interlocutor and remain steadfast in his *logos* without straying from the intended topic.

I also want to call into question the dichotomy between philosophy and rhetoric traditionally understood. I argue, following Roochnik (1995), McCoy (2008), and others, that there exists a practice of philosophical rhetoric that does not fall prey to these two dichotomies, namely, between truth and care of interlocutors and between philosophy and rhetoric. This is the proper philosophical rhetoric that Socrates practices. For McCoy, philosophy is

> intertwined with rhetoric. Socrates prefers to ask questions when possible, for questioning is a way for both speakers and audiences to express many of the virtues of being a philosopher, including knowledge of one's own ignorance, a sense of wonder about the world, responsibility for one's speech (*parrêsia*), goodwill, and love of those with whom one speaks.[7]

Philosophy and rhetoric are not equivalent to each other, but they must be intertwined in the right way and for the right reasons. For McCoy, wisdom, goodwill (*eunoian*), and frank speech (*parrêsian*) are what separate Socrates' *logos* apart from that of his interlocutors.[8] I agree with this assessment entirely, but I do think these previous commentators of philosophical rhetoric fail to explain in concrete terms of exactly what this philosophical rhetoric consists. They fail to articulate adequately specific characteristics of what they call philosophical rhetoric. Therefore, in the remainder of this chapter, I argue that philosophical rhetoric must occur in three distinct moments: (1) it must begin in ignorance, not with presupposed knowledge; (2) it must avoid flattering the audience; and (3) it must be dialogical. In these three ways, philosophical rhetoric can best attempt to attain the truth and make others more virtuous. These also constitute the three changes to the old system of the judgment of the dead that Zeus makes in the myth that concludes the *Gorgias*.

Philosophical Rhetoric: Essential Moments

Socrates notoriously admits in the *Apology* that he has no wisdom. Philosophy, for Socrates, is not a matter of confirming an already held true belief but about discovering the truth for oneself. In addition to foreshadowing Socrates' trial at the close of the dialogue, the opening scene of the *Gorgias* brings the reader in direct contact with the *Apology*—Socrates missed Gorgias' performance because Chaerephon held him up in the *agora*, and in the *Apology*, we learn that Chaerephon was the man who asked the oracle if Socrates was the wisest (*Apology*, 21a). And, of course, Socrates spends his life trying to figure out what the oracle meant, since Socrates himself does not think he has any wisdom, and he finally reaches the conclusion that another person might "think he knows something when he does not, whereas when I do not know, neither do I think I know; so I am likely to be wiser than he to this small extent, that I do not think I know what I do not know" (*Apology*, 21d). Socrates knows he does not know, whereas other folks think that they know. Gorgias claims to be able to speak about anything and answer any questions, yet neither he nor Callicles and Polus can give an accurate and proper definition of rhetoric, so they are reduced to failure. Socrates, on the other hand, is actually able to speak about anything because he begins with a lack and hopes to be filled (with wisdom). The goal of the conversation is always truth, and all presuppositions or previously held beliefs should be suspended before engaging in philosophical rhetoric (*Gorgias*, 487e).

This is reflected in the myth in the *Gorgias* (523a–527a) as well. Socrates concludes his *logos* with a *mythos* that helps illustrate why it is always better to suffer injustice than to do injustice, a key point in which

Socrates departs from Polus and Callicles. The myth is about the judgment of the fate of the souls in the time of Cronos. People used to be judged on the day of their death while still alive, and the judges themselves were alive and embodied too. As a result, just souls were occasionally sent to Tartarus and unjust souls sent to the island of the blessed. To solve this problem, Zeus implemented a series of changes that I argue correspond to these three essential moments of philosophical rhetoric (beginning in ignorance, removal of flattery, and dialectic). The first change that Zeus makes is to remove the element of foreknowledge from the soul that is undergoing judgment (*Gorgias*, 523d–e). Such foreknowledge could have the effect of corrupting the soul, only to make amends right at the end of one's life. Rather, without this foreknowledge, one is encouraged to act virtuously and truthfully throughout one's life, for death could come at any time. Likewise with philosophical rhetoric, if one begins in ignorance, then one will not be weighed down with biases and presuppositions that would mar the truthfulness of the path of the *logos*.

One could object, however, that in the *Phaedrus*, in which Socrates and Phaedrus discuss proper rhetoric at length, Socrates *does* assert that knowledge is necessary for doing philosophy. Socrates states that

> the person who's seen the truth always knows best how to find these similarities [to the truth]. . . . Unless a person can distinguish the natures of those who are listening and can divide the things that exist in accordance with their forms and comprehend each individual thing in terms of a single form, *one will never be as artful in one's speeches as a person can be.*
>
> (*Phaedrus*, 273d–e)[9]

Someone who knows the truth will speak about it better than someone who does not. This would be an odd thing to deny, and Socrates certainly does not deny it. Accordingly, it seems as though knowledge of the Truth and the Good are necessary in order to speak philosophically, and beginning in ignorance is detrimental for philosophical rhetoric.

In order to make sense of this passage, however, one must keep in mind the myth in the *Phaedrus*—before one's soul becomes embodied, it did have knowledge, although not complete knowledge, of the Good, and philosophy is a mere recollection of that godlike knowledge. Complete recollection, however, is impossible. So while it is true that someone who has knowledge of the truth would speak best, it is impossible to obtain that knowledge here on Earth, and holding a false belief is worse than merely suspending judgment until one can know for certain, for Socrates. Hence at the end of the *Phaedrus*, Socrates states that "to call them 'wise' seems excessive to me, Phaedrus, that's appropriate only for a god, but to call them a 'friend of wisdom' or something of that sort would be both more fitting for them and more harmonious" (*Phaedrus*, 278d). Philosophical rhetoric *aims* at the truth; it does not possess the truth. In the *Gorgias*, Socrates says essentially the same thing to Callicles:

> If I happened to have a golden soul, Callicles, would you not think I'd be pleased to find one of those stones with which they test gold—the best such stone, so that when I had applied the soul to it, if that stone agreed with me that the soul had been finely taken care of, I would at last be on the point of knowing well that I am in sufficiently good condition and have no further need for another touchstone?
> (*Gorgias*, 486d)

Socrates wishes for a touchstone that would tell if his beliefs were true or false. Yet, Socrates would rather know he were wrong than not know if he had the truth, because clinging to a false belief is much more dangerous than not being sure one has a true belief.

The second essential element of philosophical rhetoric is the removal of all flattery (κολακεία) from one's speech, for flattery, while it does appease the interlocutor, will either detract from the truth of the *logos* or cloak a lying *logos*. Socrates claims that flattery "hunts after folly with what is ever most pleasant, and deceives, so as to seem to be worth very much" (*Gorgias*, 464d). Blandishment is pleasant, but it is deceptive, and it tricks the listener into thinking that the speaker is being truthful. Socrates states that it is also shameful because "it guesses at the pleasant without the best," and it "cannot state the cause of each thing," so it is not a *technê* (*Gorgias*, 465a). Like the cook, the rhetor who uses adulating speech does not care about the wellbeing of the audience but merely aims to please and gratify the audience. Flattery is a useful tool for the rhetorician, for one is much more likely to be convinced when one is praised for being wise, beautiful, noble, and so on.

Socrates claims that the practice of flattery is shameful, however, because it disregards what is best for the sake of what is pleasant, and it has no knowledge of causes, and it is not a *technê*. David Roochnik makes a crucial distinction here. He argues that "the various branches of flattery are not *technai* because they cannot give a *logos* of the *aitia*. Does this inability make rhetoric shameful? Not in itself, for that would imply that anything that is not a *technê* is shameful."[10] Many things that are not *technai* are also not shameful, for example, babies taking their first steps. The baby does not have the *technê*, but no one would call the baby walking shameful.[11] Rather, it is the deceitful character that makes flattery shameful. It tricks the audience, rather than offering truthful and good *logoi* to the audience.

In contrast, Socratic rhetoric seeks to unnerve the interlocutor, not make him or her more comfortable and charmed. For McCoy, "Socrates refuses to flatter the crowd, while the rhetoricians, like cooks, seek to please their audiences. Instead, Socrates seeks to make his interlocutors uncomfortable with themselves and their own ideas."[12] The goal of Socratic rhetoric is to make interlocutors realize that they do not know what they first thought. This often leads to anger and pain, rather than pleasant and comforting flattery, but Socrates does this because he always has the best interests of the interlocutor's soul in mind.

In the myth, the second change that Zeus makes is to strip the souls being judged from all finery. Before, those

> who have base souls are clothed in fine bodies, ancestry, and wealth, and when the trial takes place, many witnesses go with them to bear witness that they have lived justly; the judges, then, are driven out of their senses by these men, and at the same time they themselves pass judgement clothed as well, with eyes and ears and the whole body, like a screen, covering over their soul.
>
> (*Gorgias*, 523c–d)

Humans are judged while they are still alive, embodied, and surrounded by earthly possessions such as wealth, friends, and so on, which leads to the judges becoming distracted and persuaded by the finery rather than the virtue or baseness of the soul. An undeserving king might be ushered into the island of the blessed because his or her splendor has dazzled and hoodwinked the judge. To make sure the judging process is more impartial, Zeus declares that "one must try them naked, without all these things; for they must be tried when they are dead" (*Gorgias*, 523e). Now the soul is stripped of all flattery and false finery. The true nature of the soul is laid bare, and in this way, it can be judged accurately. Flattery in a speech covers over and obscures the truth or falsity of the words, and a decorated, embodied soul distracts from the virtue or baseness of that soul. Thus, it is necessary to remove all flattery in order to even have a chance at being truthful.

The judges also must be stripped of their finery because that, too, affects their judgment, and this corresponds to the third essential moment of philosophical and Socratic rhetoric, namely, its dialogical form. In *Gorgias*, Socrates insists that he and the interlocutors speak as briefly as possible in order to avoid long speeches, and his initial request to Gorgias was not for a demonstration but for a discussion. Callicles offers to host Socrates and Chaerephon so that Gorgias can make a display, and Socrates responds:

> what you say is good, Callicles. But then, would he be willing to talk with us? For I wish to learn from him what the power of the man's art is, and what it is that he professes and teaches. As for the other thing, the display, let him put it off until afterwards.
>
> (*Gorgias*, 447b–c)

Socrates cares more about the dialogue than the display for which Gorgias is famous, because he knows that he will not hear the truth from Gorgias as long as he is making a speech. But if he and Gorgias converse, there is a chance that they will obtain knowledge of the truth. If Gorgias were to make a speech, then he would be the superior professing his wisdom to the inferior. Dialogue, in contrast, takes place among equals. The interlocutors are on the same level, conversing together about the same topic, and one does not claim to be wiser or more intelligent than the other.

For McCoy, the conversational nature of Socratic rhetoric is related to Socrates' claims to ignorance. She argues that

> philosophy is not the art of discovering the truth, to be followed by a distinct art of rhetorical persuasion. For Socrates, the philosopher by his nature is always incomplete in knowledge and continues to learn about the truth through conversation. The philosopher's soul is drawn closer to the truth through speeches, particularly through speeches between friends.[13]

Equality is crucial for proper philosophical dialogue. Persuasion and truth-seeking occur together, that is, truth is discovered *during* the actual conversation itself. In a display of speech, in contrast, the speakers decide the truth that they are going to tell the audience beforehand and then, subsequently, impart this wisdom onto others. The object of Socratic philosophy is directed outward. That is, one does not philosophize for the sake of oneself but rather for the sake of making others better and more virtuous. Truth is reached together in a dialogue between equals.

This notion of equality embodied by dialogue corresponds to the third change that Zeus implements in the myth of the judgment of souls. Not only must souls on trial be judged once they are dead and stripped naked, but the judges themselves must be dead and naked as well. The judge must "with his soul itself contemplate the soul itself of each man" (*Gorgias*, 523e). It is imperative for the judges not to be adorned in finery as well, for true judgment must take place among equals. Of course, the judges are gods, not humans, but the part doing the judging is the soul itself judging another soul itself.

Conclusion

The pursuit of knowledge of the truth and care for the interlocutors are not contradictory but make up true Socratic, philosophical rhetoric. This proper type of rhetoric is defined by three essential moments: it begins in ignorance, it avoids flattery, and it is necessarily dialogical. These correspond to the three changes that Zeus makes to the process of the judgment of souls in the concluding myth. At the conclusion of the dialogue, Socrates gives Callicles a final word of advice:

> one must flee from all flattery, concerning both oneself and others, and concerning both few men and many; and one must use rhetoric thus, always aiming at what is just, and so for every other action. Be persuaded, then, and follow me there where, having arrived, you will be happy both living and when you have come to your end, as the argument indicates.
>
> (*Gorgias*, 257c)

Remove flattery from your speech, and be aware when others are trying to ingratiate you. One's rhetoric should always aim toward the true, the just, the good, and the virtuous. If one succeeds in this philosophical rhetoric, according to Socrates, one will be happy both in this life and the next. That is, philosophical rhetoric is not the correct practice merely for life here on earth. Socrates refuses to ingratiate himself to his audience in the *Apology*, and he is put to death for it, but he knows that he can approach the judges in the afterlife with confidence that they will see clearly the virtue in his soul. As the *logos* indicates, abiding by the truth and caring for others will lead to the happiest life and, ultimately, the most persuasive speech.

Notes

1 McCoy, *Plato on the Rhetoric*, 95.
2 Examples occur at 495a, 515b, and elsewhere.
3 McCoy, *Plato on the Rhetoric*, 194.
4 Ibid.
5 Arieti, "Plato's Philosophical *Antiope:* The *Gorgias*," 199–200.
6 McCoy, *Plato on the Rhetoric*, 174.
7 Ibid., 194.
8 Ibid., 103.
9 Emphasis mine. For the sake of keeping this chapter focused and concise, I am not going to engage in the debate about whether rhetoric is a *technê*. It is not my primary concern here, and it has been discussed at length by McCoy, Roochnik et al.
10 Roochnik, "Socrates' Rhetorical Attack on Rhetoric," 85.
11 Ibid.
12 McCoy, *Plato on the Rhetoric*, 92.
13 Ibid., 175.

Bibliography

Arieti, James, "Plato's Philosophical *Antiope:* The *Gorgias*," in *Plato's Dialogues*, ed. Gerald A. Press (Lanham, MD: Rowman & Littlefield Publishers, 1993), 197–214

McCoy, Marina, *Plato on the Rhetoric of Philosophers and Sophists* (Cambridge: Cambridge University Press, 2008)

Nichols, James H. Jr., "Introduction: Rhetoric, Philosophy, and Politics" and "The Rhetoric of Justice in Plato's *Gorgias*," in *Gorgias* (Ithaca, NY: Cornell University Press, 1998)

Plato, *The Apology*, in *The Trial and Death of Socrates*, trans. G. M. A. Grube (Indianapolis, IN: Hackett Publishing Company, 2000)

Plato, *Gorgias*, trans. James H. Nichols Jr. (Ithaca, NY: Cornell University Press, 1998)

Plato, *Phaedrus*, in *Plato's Erotic Dialogues*, trans. William S. Cobb (New York: SUNY Press, 1993)

Roochnik, David, "Socrates' Rhetorical Attack on Rhetoric," in *The Third Way*, ed. Francisco Gonzalez (Lanham, MD: Rowman & Littlefield Publishers, 1995), 81–94

Scott, Gary Alan, *Plato's Socrates as Educator* (New York: SUNY Press, 2000)

Seeskin, Kenneth, "Is the *Apology of Socrates* a Parody?" *Philosophy and Literature*, 6 (1982), 94–105

Part III

The Desire of Ethics

Being and Seeming
On Socrates' Ontological Humiliation of the Sophists

William J. Hendel

> "I think you would agree, if you did not have to go away before the mysteries as you told me yesterday, but could remain and be initiated."
> —Plato, *Meno*, 76e

If it's an overstatement to call Socrates' tangles with the sophists great dramas (after all, the outcome is never really in doubt), they are, nonetheless, tremendously compelling. The *Gorgias* and the first book of the *Republic*, in particular, deliver a level of entertainment not often achieved in philosophy. The prophet of the good and the beautiful and the immortal soul comes wit to wit with a few of the most brazen will-to-power types imaginable—and the blows between them are thrown with bad intentions. Instead of receiving the recumbent affirmations of his young admirers ("of course," "necessarily," "what you say is fine"), Socrates is repeatedly insulted ("It's not shameful to practice philosophy while you're a boy, but when you do it after you've grown older and become a man, the thing gets to be ridiculous, Socrates!" [*Gorgias*, 485a]; "Tell me, Socrates, do you have a wet nurse?" [*Republic*, 343a]). He responds, in turn, with irony at the highest pitch of impudence ("Most admirable Polus, it's not for nothing that we get ourselves companions and sons. It's so that, when we ourselves have grown older and stumble, you younger men might be on hand to straighten our lives up again" [*Gorgias*, 461c]). As can be expected, in the end, Socrates dispatches each of his opponents methodically, with evident and infectious pleasure. He walks off with their most prized, most flaunted, most jealously guarded possession; he takes their *logoi*. He takes the wind right out of their bag.

Obscured in these delights is the puzzling realization that Socrates' arguments are almost uniformly bad, or better yet, they're failures—if an argument is ultimately judged by its power of persuasion. That's not

DOI: 10.4324/9781003201472-12

what one would expect given the gravity of these encounters. The sophists generally, and these sophists in particular, represent everything that Socrates is trying to finally defeat and discredit. They are concerned only with the pursuit of power, and they are pleased enough with their command of *logos* not to bother to hide that fact; indeed, they often boast of it. By their reckoning, power is very obviously the greatest good because it is the means to all other goods. It matters little, practically speaking, if the wielder of power is the wisest or the most knowledgeable. The sophists teach the ability to move judges, councilors, and assemblymen; in short, theirs is the art of making other men slaves.[1] Socrates eventually defeats them all, but the denouements are more like split decisions than knockouts: the losers are neutralized, not flattened. Callicles sums up Socrates' triumphs aptly: "I don't know, Socrates—in a way you seem to me to be right, but the thing that happens to most people has happened to me; I'm not really persuaded by you" (*Gorgias*, 513c). Socrates does not refute these skeptics; he embarrasses them, which is not quite the same thing.

If the reader glides over this subtlety, the texts helpfully draw his attention to it on several occasions. Socrates' opponents keenly and repeatedly identify his gambits. It is, indeed, easier to ask questions than answer them, as Thrasymachus alleges.[2] He does, in fact, have a penchant for invoking the aid of inapposite analogies. Callicles yells in exasperation, "You keep talking of food and drink and doctors and such nonsense. That's not what I mean!" (*Gorgias*, 490d). And he, no doubt, enjoys walking his victims right into a contradiction, as Polus complains.[3] After each one of his victories over Gorgias, Polus, Callicles, and Thrasymachus, Socrates is accused, not without merit, that he has won on a technicality or some kind of underhanded trick. Adeimantus describes Socrates' method unimprovably when he relates an (allegedly) common criticism of philosophy:

> [H]ere is how those who hear what you are now saying are affected on each occasion. They believe that because of inexperience at questioning and answering, they are at each question misled a little by the argument; and when the littles are collected at the end of the arguments, the slip turns out to be great and contrary to the first assertions. And just as those who aren't clever at playing draughts are finally checked by those who are and don't know where to move, so they too are finally

checked by this other kind of draughts, played not with counters but speeches, and they don't know what to say. However, the truth isn't in any way affected by this.

(*Republic*, 487b)

As we shall soon see, this assessment just about captures it, but the last remark requires a slight modification: the truth does not *seem* to be in any way affected. With Socrates, nothing is quite as it seems.[4] So often he says one thing while obviously meaning another and less obviously meaning still another—even his ironies are ironical. In these particular mischiefs at the expense of the sophists, he means to make a profound observation, which affects the truth (and its pursuit) in every way. There is substance in the subterfuge, and it kicks at the foundation of every rational choice.

Three-Card Socrates

To understand why the opinion that Adeimantus relates is ultimately wrong, we must first understand how it is right. Let's start with a careful evaluation of Socrates' showdown with Gorgias. It is easy to overlook this exchange, given its brevity and the drama that follows, but it provides a surprisingly comprehensive illustration of Socrates' alleged sins as a debate partner—and even more significantly, it is the conversation that Socrates is seeking. Polus and Callicles (and, in the *Republic*, Thrasymachus) insert themselves into the dialogue, but Gorgias is pulled in by Socrates. "I'd much rather ask you," he says to Gorgias, brushing aside Polus's early interruption (*Gorgias*, 448d). As an esteemed instructor, flanked by young, eager admirers, Gorgias is, at least in theory, a counterpart to Socrates, even a rival. Gorgias, like Socrates, is taking souls into his care. Socrates explains the stakes to a young pupil who is seeking out the instruction of another famed sophist, although the young man is not quite sure what the sophist teaches:

> Do you see what kind of danger you are about to put your soul in? If you had to entrust your body to someone and risk its becoming healthy or ill, you would consider carefully whether you should entrust it or not, and you would confer with your family and friends for days on end. But when it comes to something you value more than your body,

namely your soul, and when everything concerning whether you do well or ill in your life depends on whether it becomes worthy or worthless, I don't see you getting together with your father or brother or a single one of your friends to consider whether or not to entrust your soul to this recently arrived foreigner.

(Protagoras, 313a–b)

Polus and Callicles are mere students of Gorgias, which is to say that they are derivations, examples, in different degrees, of his cultivation; they are the fruits, he is the root. All the subsequent battles in the dialogue merely continue and amplify the initial conflict between Socrates and Gorgias in both substance and form. (The dialogue is not named for Gorgias in error.) It is Gorgias and his philosophy that Socrates is after, even when the renowned orator has been embarrassed and chased from the foreground.

The encounter begins in earnest with a harmless question: "Gorgias, why don't you tell us yourself what the craft you're knowledgeable in is, and hence what we're supposed to call you?" (*Gorgias*, 449a). Gorgias responds that he is an orator, "and a good one" (*Gorgias*, 449a). Socrates then pretends that he has no understanding of this craft called oratory. Like an experienced cross-examiner, Socrates hides the pursuit of a carefully chosen end under performative curiosity. He wonders obtusely why doctors and physical trainers aren't considered orators even though their crafts, like so many others, require *logos*. He is, of course, not confused at all and is here only subtly introducing what he will make more explicit later on (in fact, what his questions will force Gorgias to admit)—what distinguishes the orator from the craftsman who also uses *logos* is that the orator has no underlying knowledge of what he speaks:

Oratory doesn't need to have any knowledge of the state of their subject matters; it only needs to have discovered some device to produce persuasion in order to make itself appear to those who don't have knowledge that it knows more than those who actually do have it.

(Gorgias, 459c)

Gorgias, however, has a remarkable rejoinder for Socrates: so what? "Well, Socrates, aren't things made very easy when you come off no worse than the craftsmen even though you haven't learned any other craft than this one?" (*Gorgias*, 459c). The orator can tame crowds and arrogate power to himself; he can, thereby, negate his knowledge deficit to anyone, no matter how immense the gap might be. Isn't it, then, quite plainly better to be strong than right?

A spectator unfamiliar with Socrates' methods, but only aware of his reputation as a friend of the good and the wise, might expect this to be the moment of decisive action. Here he would give the lie to Gorgias's shameless fetishization of power. That, after all, must have been the point of all the ironic questions, all the digressions about doctors and physical trainers: he needed to draw Gorgias out, to force him to state his real opinion openly—so it could be summarily crushed.

Instead, Socrates dodges the question altogether: "Whether the orator does or does not come off worse than the others because of his being so, we'll examine in a moment if it has any bearing on our argument" (*Gorgias*, 459d). It's an odd pivot given the fact that this question is more than pertinent; it's essentially the entire argument. Socrates has been subtly (and not so subtly) suggesting that oratory is no better and no different than carnival barking. Gorgias is saying it's better to be a con artist than an impotent knower.

But rather than pursuing the issue further, Socrates asks Gorgias if orators are as ignorant about the just and the unjust as they are about everything else. That, of course, is a leading question meant to elicit the response Gorgias gives: if one of his students doesn't already know about justice and injustice, Gorgias will teach him. Socrates continues with more puzzling questions:

SOCRATES: A man who has learned carpentry is a carpenter, isn't he?
GORGIAS: Yes.
SOCRATES: And isn't a man who has learned music a musician?
GORGIAS: Yes.
SOCRATES: And a man who has learned medicine a medical doctor? And isn't this so too, by the same reasoning, with the other crafts? Isn't a man who has learned a particular subject the sort of man his knowledge makes him?
GORGIAS: Yes, he is.
SOCRATES: And, by this line of reasoning, isn't a man who has learned what's just a just man too?

GORGIAS: Yes, absolutely.
SOCRATES: And a just man does just things, I take it.
GORGIAS: Yes.
SOCRATES: Now isn't an orator necessarily just, and doesn't a just man necessarily want to do just things?
GORGIAS: Apparently so.
SOCRATES: Therefore an orator will never want to do what's unjust.
GORGIAS: No, apparently not.

(*Gorgias*, 460a–c)

Although you would hardly guess it, if you are not familiar with the dialogue, Socrates has just defeated Gorgias. To be precise, he's caught him in a contradiction. A little earlier in the debate, after suffering several not-so-thinly-veiled attacks on oratory and a final ironic barb ("[oratory] seems to me," says Socrates with wonder, "to be something supernatural in scope" [*Gorgias*, 456a]), Gorgias launched an extended defense of his craft, boasting that many times he has proven more persuasive to the sick than doctors—such is the formidable power of oratory. Perhaps sensing that Socrates had baited him into too much candor, or hoping to preempt a possible line of attack, he hastily qualified his remarks by disclaiming any responsibility for the actions of his pupils; instructors of oratory are like boxing trainers—they're not to blame for the sins of those they teach. But now Socrates has got him to admit that an orator could never use oratory unjustly because whoever learns what justice is must be just, and Gorgias agreed that all his students already learned that knowledge, either from him or someone else.

What we have here, beyond an anticlimax, is a brief tutorial in the efficacy of Socrates' ungallant tactics. The not-so-obviously germane references (this time to carpenters, musicians, and doctors) lure Gorgias to happily assent to his own undoing. There is nothing immediately objectionable in the claim that a man who has learned carpentry is a carpenter or that a man who has learned music is a musician. But this is just an essential prelude for the sleight of hand signaled by the equally innocuous "by this line of reasoning." Indeed, "by this line of reasoning," a man who has learned what is just is "absolutely" just, as Gorgias gladly agrees. "This line of reasoning," however, ignores that justice really isn't at all like medicine or music or carpentry. All the censure that attaches to being unjust comes from the implicit expectation that the actor knew what he should have done and failed to do it; there's no coherent concept of injustice without some knowledge of justice. And, come to think of it, it's not knowledge of carpentry alone that makes one a carpenter but the act of carpentry. A carpenter who has never swung a hammer (or never will again) can hardly be called a carpenter.

None of that matters now, however. The specious nature of the questions has already achieved the necessary agreement. This was what Adeimantus was talking about: "when the littles are collected at the end of the arguments, the slip turns out to be great." There's no going back for Gorgias. You can, if you look closely, watch defeat wash over him. His answers degrade from "Yes, absolutely" (blithe unawareness) to "Yes" (a fugitive sense of danger) to "Apparently so" (oh, no). He's been checked by a superior—a master—draughts player.

But has he been refuted? Adeimantus claimed, most damningly, "that the truth isn't in any way affected" by Socrates' methods. Here, the primary question, "the heart of the matter," as Socrates will call it a little later, has been left untouched; namely, is the happy man powerful—or is he something else?[5]

Polus, Gorgias's young admirer, won't let Socrates off on a technicality. He makes Socrates face the question head-on: How can you deny, Socrates, that you are not envious of those with the ultimate power, who can rob and kill and imprison whomever they please?[6] Socrates replies, unironically, for a change, that being unjust is the worst possible fate. An incredulous Polus responds with a hypothetical:

> What do you mean? Take a man who's caught doing something unjust, say, plotting to set himself as tyrant. Suppose that he's caught, put on the rack, castrated, and has his eyes burned out. Suppose that he's subjected to a host of other abuses of all sorts, and then made to witness his wife and children undergo the same. In the end he's impaled or tarred. Will he be happier than if he hadn't got caught, had set himself up as tyrant, and lived out his life ruling in his city and doing whatever he liked, a person envied and counted happy by fellow citizens and aliens alike?
>
> (*Gorgias*, 473c)

It's a good, if colorfully rendered, question. Here again, the uninitiated might be drawing in a deep breath of anticipation: surely, Socrates cannot wriggle out of this one. The charge has been starkly made; he, in turn, must now make the case for the just and the good. Well, not quite.

Socrates responds with questions, and Polus answers by asserting that it is worse to suffer injustice and more shameful to commit it (which the implicit thrust of his hypothetical for Socrates already made plain). They then proceed to agree that admirable things are pleasant and beneficial; if one admirable thing is more admirable than another, it's because the more admirable thing surpasses the other in either pleasure or benefit. The shameful is the opposite of the admirable, and therefore, if one shameful thing is more shameful than the other it's because it surpasses the other in either pain or in badness. "Of course it is," Polus confidently affirms (*Gorgias*, 475b). Nothing so far is obviously amiss, or obviously relevant, but after leaping to the aid of Gorgias's supine form, Polus probably should have been a little warier. Like Gorgias before him, he's been struck with such a brutally efficient blow that he doesn't even know he's falling yet. Socrates continues by asking if committing injustice is more shameful than suffering injustice because it surpasses in pain or badness, and then says triumphantly, "Submit yourself nobly to the argument, as you would a doctor, and answer me" (*Gorgias*, 475d). Polus realizes where he has been unwittingly led: committing injustice isn't more painful, so it must be more bad, that is, worse. Committing injustice, it has now been proved, is worse than suffering it.

It's hardly necessary to say that if it is true that it is better to suffer injustice than be unjust, this isn't the way to prove it. All Socrates has done is execute one of his magic tricks of performative density. Here, he is pretending that he does not understand the difference between public and private interest, or more specifically, the indissoluble tension at the point where an individual's well-being conflicts with that of the community. There's little rational debate about the fact that it's in a community's interest that its citizens are just or that it's in an individual's interest that his neighbors are just. There really isn't even a question about whether it's in an individual's interest to appear just. But the real question of ethics, and of the *Gorgias* as a whole, is if it is in the individual's interest that he actually be just.[7] Polus's hypothetical tries to show the indisputable answer. When push comes to shove, says Polus, it's better for the community that

I become eunuch than a tyrant, but it's far better for me to tyrannize and hang on to my privy parts.

Socrates knows well what Polus is after, but his entire line of questioning, and its resolution, appears as though he does not. Admiration and shame are always from the perspective of the community; to be proud or ashamed of yourself without an other (real or imagined) is an incoherent concept. Furthermore, things aren't more admirable because they are pleasant, but because they are beneficial—specifically, because they are beneficial to the community. Nor are things more shameful because of their badness. That's a tautology. Something is shameful because the community has judged it to be something bad. Now, conversely, pleasantness (pleasure) and pain are private feelings; that is, they are felt by the individual; they have considerable influence over the judgment of the subject who experiences them. But they are not relevant to admiration or shame or, if they are, only inversely (e.g., the amount of pain endured might increase admiration or the amount of pleasure might increase shame). Socrates, in effect, has loaded the dice. All he needed to do was to get Polus to play with them. Whichever way he shakes it, it's coming up justice, because admiration and shame are community judgments, and it's always in the community's interest that individuals are just.

Polus, like Gorgias before him, allowed Socrates to escape because he allowed himself to be lured in by the ostensible harmlessness of Socrates' preliminary questions. He did not see anything in them that warranted further investigation and he assented readily, without appreciating what he was assenting to. Before he knew it, he was embarrassed and Socrates was gone, unrefuted and essentially unchallenged. And he's not the last to treat Socrates so accommodatingly.

Callicles storms to the fore with a magnificent speech in favor of the unchecked dominion of the strong and the exceptional that would bring a tear to Nietzsche's eye. He warns Socrates, almost prophetically, of his mortal danger at the hands of tribunals, and he mocks the effeminacy and immaturity of philosophy. And then he is summarily unhorsed. The decisive blow is, as we can now reliably expect, a fair distance from the substance of Callicles' claims and entirely banal, at least in appearance: "So we find things that a man both gets rid of and keeps at the same time, it's clear that these things wouldn't be what's good and what's bad?" To give him a chance, Socrates even follows up with this admonition: "Are we agreed on that? Think very carefully and tell me." But like his predecessors, Callicles greets his end with comical innocence. "Yes, I agree most emphatically," he says, as the lance shatters his breastplate (*Gorgias*, 496c).

The great irony is that these sophists certainly would not consider themselves naïve by any measure. In fact, both Polus and Callicles blame the defeat of their immediate predecessors on each's failure to state his clear-eyed, rational appraisal of things: Gorgias was too ashamed to say that the instructor of oratory does not teach his students about justice,[8] and Polus was too ashamed to say that suffering an injustice is actually more shameful than committing it.[9] They are true cynics, and if they had only acted so, they wouldn't have allowed the weaker argument to win.

It seems reasonable, in the way that all specious arguments initially do, but the truth is quite to the contrary. Socrates gives the lie to their consoling interpretation with this witheringly ironic response to Callicles: "[Gorgias and Polus have] come to such a depth of shame that, because they are ashamed, each of them dares to contradict himself, face to face with many people, and on topics of the greatest importance" (*Gorgias*, 487b). Or in other words, it hardly seems plausible that Gorgias or Polus would be willing to shatter their reputations before any norms—particularly when one considers that the dialogue begins with Gorgias boasting that he will answer anyone's question and that "no one has asked me anything new in many a year" (*Gorgias*, 447c). What's more, neither Gorgias nor Polus is particularly coy about their affection for power, and Callicles, for all his supposed courage of conviction, doesn't enjoy any more success than his more delicate predecessors. To ensure that this fact is not lost Callicles, Socrates needles him with warnings that he be careful to not "get caught being ashamed" (*Gorgias*, 489a).

In fact, it's the innocence—the credulousness—of Gorgias, Polus, and Callicles that seals their fates. Adeimantus criticized Socrates' tactics because they relied on his opponent's "inexperience at question and answering." We have now seen precisely in what that inexperience consists: the uncritical acceptance of what is apparently true (a man who has learned music is a musician; what is good can't also be bad). In a masterly turn, Socrates has exposed these amoral power fetishists—who are satisfied above all with their cynicism—as almost pitifully guileless. It's not the philosopher, it seems, who still needs a wet nurse.[10]

Must We Imagine Archelaus Happy?

Even for the master of irony, it's a delicious bit of irony. But is it more than that? We have seen the merit in the bulk of Adeimantus's critique, but now we are faced with the last and most significant part: has Socrates neglected the truth? So far, it appears so. In fact, an unsympathetic observer might even say that Socrates deliberately obscures the truth so he can avoid arguments that he cannot answer—otherwise, why doesn't he respond with substance?

Once Callicles realizes that he has been cornered, he complains to Gorgias about this exact feature of Socrates' gamesmanship: "He keeps questioning people on matters that are trivial, hardly worthwhile, and refutes them!" Socrates responds cleverly and, I think, significantly: "You're a happy man, Callicles, in that you've been initiated into the greater mysteries before the lesser. I didn't think that was permitted" (*Gorgias*, 497c).

It's easy enough to pass by this remark, but I believe that it offers more than just a wry smile. Socrates is inordinately fond of mysteries and hierarchies. The divided line, the allegory of the cave, and Diotima's ladder are all epistemological and ontological ascents, from the love of a body to the love of the beautiful, from gaping at shadows to catching a glance of the Good. Each one begins with a first tier, a lesser mystery. At this initial stage, there is some kind of distortion; shadows are not yet recognized as shadows, ones are scattered in manys. The first step up, on the way out, is the recognition of something beyond seeming. For Diotima, it's the realization that the beauty of all bodies is the same and, therefore, that love cannot be limited to one body alone but must be extended to all beautiful bodies. For the cave dwellers, it's their turning to see the operations of their artificial world in its artificiality. In either case, ascent is not possible without first losing the inherent and incautious faith in what, at one time, was self-evident.

Socrates is not just playing three-card monte with these sophists. He's making as substantive a critique of their will-to-power philosophies as he can make. As anyone who has endured more than a few arguments well knows, the point of contention is rarely one of faulty reasoning. Almost everyone can move from the premises and on to the conclusion without falling over or getting lost.[11] The problem is the premises themselves, especially the first premises. They are often unstated or unknown (even to the reasoner) and thus frustratingly inaccessible, even though they determine every argument.[12]

If we look at the syllogism, the simplest species of deductive logic, we can begin to appreciate the problem. Take the paradigmatic example: all men are mortal; Socrates is a man; therefore, Socrates is mortal. The conclusion is merely a rearranging (or we might be tempted to say, a "recollecting") of the major and minor premises (absent the middle term) into subject and predicate. When one agrees to a premise, one is also agreeing, consciously or not, to the conclusion. And that's not only the case for a simple syllogism but all logic as well, as Socrates never tires of teaching. Once you have agreed, for example, that a man who has learned a particular subject is the sort of man his knowledge makes him (e.g., a man who has learned carpentry is a carpenter, a man who has learned music is a musician, a man who has learned justice is just) and that you teach your students justice, you must either agree that your students are just (any other conclusion would contradict the premises) or confess that one of your premises is false and start over again. Premises delimit, and thereby determine, the outcome of all logical reasoning.

Gorgias, Polus, and Callicles assume that things, more or less, are as they seem—that's what we learn from their humiliations at the hands of Socrates. They have a flawed, inexplicit, perhaps even unconscious, first premise.[13] And there are consequences for this initial misstep, both metaphysically and ethically. That's why it's obvious to them that it is better to be a tyrant than a martyr, and that's why Socrates will not waste his time arguing with them regarding the particulars.

As anyone who has had the misfortune of teaching a compulsory introduction to philosophy course can tell you, philosophy begins with wonder, or more often, ends without it. The questions of philosophy, most particularly metaphysics, are incomprehensible to the incurious because their answers are so obvious. What does it mean to be? Most people would be confident that a child could show you, but if some kind of definition must be provided, they would say that it simply means to be present in material reality (or rather, just reality), which can be charted by microscopes, telescopes, and other instruments that heighten our senses. What are we? We are mammals, as we learn in the earliest years of education, *Homo sapiens* to be precise, that are born, grow, decay, and die. There is, you see, an implicit ontology—or rather an anti-ontology—for those who are satisfied, like the sophists, with what is apparent. For these, the question of what it means to be is not a question at all.

But it is one's answer to this question that decides in substantial part one's answer to everything else and, most especially, one's ethics. All value judgments stand upon some factual judgments: if anyone ought to do anything it is only because something happens "to be." Imagine for a moment that you are the type of person who enjoys taking your work to a café. You have unfurled your effects (laptop, several impressively thick books, more than one pen) across a sticky, uneven table. The heftiest and most imposing volume is cracked open on your lap; your face is contracted in profound thought, and just as you raise your latte to your lips, a throat clears, and you hear at your back, "You know, you really ought to be leaving." You turn to meet the unfamiliar voice, which you learn quickly comes from an unfamiliar face. "What? But why?" you ask innocently. The injunction stands or falls on what follows. "Well, for one thing, the building is on fire," would be a good reason to leave. "I have a guitar, and in just a few moments I will be playing some contemporary pop ballads" would be another. In either case, or in any case, what "is"—a fire, an acoustic guitar—creates the conditions for what "ought" to be done. (An "ought" without an "is" is empty.)[14] Therefore, one's metaphysics—as the study of what is and can be—determines in significant measure what one will decide one ought to do.

A memorable episode in the *Gorgias* demonstrates the practical consequences of one's metaphysical orientation. Polus tells a brief anecdote about the rise of the Macedonian ruler Archelaus to refute Socrates' claim that the unjust are miserable people that ought to be pitied. Apparently, Archelaus ruthlessly connived and murdered his way to power, descending so low as to drown the seven-year-old heir to the throne in a well (while telling his mother that the boy fell in while chasing a goose).[15] And yet, despite all this depravity, Polus is entirely assured of the happiness of this man and cannot believe that Socrates or anyone else could claim otherwise. This assessment is a direct and inevitable consequence of his anti-ontology, his incurious materialism. Because Polus stops at what is apparent, he stops at the body. He can only conceive of sickness and health, well-being and misfortune, in terms of physical satisfactions and operations. What physical needs cannot be sated, what consequences could there be, for the King of Macedonia when his rivals are buried, his throne is secure, and there is no profound distinction between appearance and reality?

Polus cannot imagine Archelaus unhappy because he possesses no understanding of a ground for such a possibility. There is no "is" that could lead him to the conclusion that he ought to be the drowned prince or his ruined mother rather than the ruthless tyrant. Without that ground, there is no opportunity for Socrates to engage Polus or any of the other sophists in good faith. They have no capacity to understand what he is trying to say. When Callicles burst into the debate he says to Socrates:

> Tell me, Socrates, are we to take you as being in earnest now, or joking? For if you *are* in earnest, and these things you are saying are really true, won't this human life of ours be turned upside down, and won't everything we do be the opposite of what we should do?
> (*Gorgias*, 481c)

Indeed it would, in no small part because Socrates' first premise is the opposite of what now prevails. At the level appearance where we apprehend images—the lowest and foggiest level of the soul's operation—what *is* (the one) shows itself as what it is not (the many).[16] What *is* isn't what seems, or at least, it isn't how it seems. In fact, it is precisely the opposite. Without that fundamental insight, there is, for Socrates, no progression toward truth.[17]

But why doesn't Socrates expose the primary assumption of the sophists and explain their error? That is the thorny problem of first premises. Because they are first, they are not amenable to proof. They are prior to proof. They are the very measure of proof. And, in fact, all premises, not just the first ones, precede logical operations and are inaccessible in some way. Before any truths can be found, some truth must be taken for granted. The earlier syllogism, for example, does not prove that Socrates is a man or that all men are mortal but only what necessarily follows if those claims are true. (If it was more accurately rendered, it would read: if all men are mortal and Socrates is a man, it follows that Socrates is mortal.) One may, of course, subject premises to their own logical or empirical evaluation, but that evaluation, in turn, must take for granted its own premises and on and on. But it's not turtles all the way up. Eventually one must arrive at premises that cannot be evaluated but rather simply must be accepted in order for a proof to be possible.

Whether or not there is something beyond seeming, that is, whether Being can be completely comprehended by the senses or instruments accessible to the senses, is one of those first premises. The question is by definition beyond proof or disproof. To try to settle it one way or the other would be like trying to prove the existence of a snake by looking for its footprints. If you do not find them, that is hardly conclusive, because what is being sought is precisely that which has no feet (i.e., that which is beyond what is sensible). But if you do find them, you now have to explain how something can be revealed by what it is not (i.e., how a snake can have footprints or how the suprasensible can be sensed). In either case, the results will be inconclusive and unsatisfactory, as all of Socrates' attempts to prove the existence of the immortal soul ultimately are.[18]

And yet, we must choose. As we saw earlier, we cannot decide what we should do until we trace a boundary between what can and cannot be. In that determination, we are determining our ethics. If we decide that what is real is only what is present in some material sense, we are foreclosing the possibility of such things as a soul whose well-being is separate from the body's, a good beyond being, a true telos (and thereby, a true nature), eschatological judgment—namely, anything which could lead us to the conclusion that Archelaus is unhappy.

Perhaps now we can begin to appreciate the idiosyncratic methods of Socrates. If the question of ethics ("How should we live?") is merely the follow up to a metaphysical question ("What is, and what can be"), and if that metaphysical question is not susceptible to proof, Socrates cannot refute the sophists—but he can embarrass them. He can demonstrate that the anti-ontological are immature and unserious, that they can be tricked like small children, precisely because they start from the wrong assumption about the nature of Being. And that is precisely what he does.

Socrates Finds Some Bacchants

The beginning of the *Republic* bears out the singular importance of where one starts from. The second half of Book I is almost a *Gorgias* in miniature, where the same themes are taken up again but with a different outcome.[19] We pick up the action with Socrates trying to work out the definition of justice with Polemarchus when Thrasymachus comes roaring in like Cerberus.[20] He instantly decries Socrates' apparent talent of skirting the substance of his debates—the way he dexterously keeps the onus on everyone else by asking questions, his ironies, his clumsy analogies, his preternatural ability to make any argument absurd. Even more than

Callicles, Thrasymachus seems prepared to counter Socrates' skills, but just like Callicles, he'll end up leaving with his tail between his legs.

Thrasymachus argues that just men are fools because justice itself is only a benefit to the unscrupulously powerful. In the vertical, hierarchical orientation of society, what's called justice is only what ensures the bovine usefulness and passivity of the lower classes—justice is the advantage of the stronger.[21] In the horizontal orientation of society, the relations among equals, the just man is in every respect at disadvantage to his unregenerate counterpart—injustice is "good counsel" (*Republic*, 348c).

Socrates defeats these assertions, in part, by showing that the wage earner's art is separate from the art itself. A given art—medicine, horsemanship, shepherding—is not done for the benefit of the ruler of the art but, rather, what is ruled by that art—the body, the horse, the sheep. Those who rule do so with the best interest of the ruled as the greatest priority. Receiving wages has nothing to do with rule itself. If anything, it proves that ruling requires something for the effort. If ruling was its own reward, rulers would not need compensation.

In a catalogue of unpersuasive arguments, this one stands out as particularly unpersuasive, and for that reason, particularly ingenious. As he did when confounded Polus, Socrates is deliberately begging the essential question of what holds supremacy: the public or the private interest, the individual or the community concern.[22] One cannot plausibly separate a wage-earning art from its wage-earning aspect. It is, for example, in the doctor's best interest that he acts in his patient's best interest—or he will not be paid for his medical services for long. That is to say, one could make the opposite of Socrates' argument: in any wage-earning art, the concern for the ruled is incidental (and secondary) to the primary concern for one's self-interest. It doesn't mean it actually is, of course, but simply that the matter is not decided by facilely separating the competing interests and focusing on the one preferred.

For all his protestations at the outset, all his recalcitrance throughout the debate (which Socrates continually references[23]), Thrasymachus still is unable to see this ridiculous argument coming and, therefore, offer any resistance when it arrives—just as the other sophists before him. But in this case, the fatal reliance on seeming receives extra emphasis. When Thrasymachus makes his initial argument that justice is just the advantage of the stronger, Socrates asks about instances when rulers are mistaken about what is to their advantage; is justice obeying the ruler or disobeying him, in this circumstance? Cleitophon interjects and says Thrasymachus really means that justice is what the ruler believes to be in his best interest, or what seems to be, whether or not it actually is. In other words, Cleitophon's amendment "involves a total collapsing... of any distinction between seeming and being; what seems would simply determine what is."[24] Thrasymachus, surprisingly, rejects this suggestion and responds that a ruler is not ruling in the moment that he is mistaken: "the ruler, insofar as he is a ruler, does not make mistakes; and not making mistakes, he sets down what is best for himself. And this must be done by the man who is ruled" (*Republic*, 341a).

For a moment, it looks like Thrasymachus really does have Socrates' number. Unlike Gorgias, Polus, and Callicles, he is not going to make the fatal error of conflating seeming and being. And yet, as Socrates guides him to calamity on the art-versus-wage-earning distinction, he can only offer the same ingenuous assents: "'Yes,' he said, 'this is the way they differ'; 'Certainly'; 'Surely not . . .'" (*Republic*, 346a–b). That is to say, although he asserts the need for discernment, he cannot discern. In the end, he's indistinguishable from the other sophists felled by Socrates in the substance of his arguments, the cause of his downfall, and, most essentially, the moral of his story: to make the cynical argument, to say that justice is just the advantage of the stronger or that injustice is good counsel is to deny—despite any rhetorical claims to the contrary—any material difference between what seems to be and what is.

Thrasymachus has stumbled on the lowest rung of the ladder. "The beginning," Socrates tells Adeimantus, "is the most important part of every work" (*Republic*, 377b). One cannot grasp the greater mysteries before the lesser. And so Socrates assumes after he humbles Thrasymachus that he is "freed from argument" (*Republic*, 357a). Instead, he's stopped by Glaucon, who asks, "Socrates, do you want to seem to have persuaded us, or truly to persuade us, that it is in every way better to be just than unjust?" (*Republic*, 357a–b). When Socrates accepts the challenge, Glaucon, with the help of his brother Adeimantus, proceeds to take up Thrasymachus's argument. To settle the question, the brothers insist that the state of the perfectly just man must be compared to the perfectly unjust man. But it is essential that these men must be considered as having a reputation that is at odds with their actual character:

the just man must be reviled as an unjust man, and the unjust man must be admired as the most just of men. Adeimantus explains: "If you don't take the true reputation from each and attach the false one to it, we'll say you aren't praising the just but the seeming, nor blaming being unjust but the seeming" (*Republic*, 367b). Those who praise injustice over justice will tell you that the result will be obvious enough: the just man will be tortured and crucified and his agonies will teach him that it's much better to seem just than to be just, and the unjust man will enjoy every privilege, every victory, and every pleasure. If the sons of Ariston are to be brought to Socrates' cause, he must show by argument not only that justice is stronger than injustice but also that "what each does to the man who has it—whether it is noticed by gods and human beings or not—that makes the one bad and the other good" (*Republic*, 367d).

In a sense, Glaucon and Adeimantus are making a strange request. Glaucon has already described what justice and injustice will do to those who have them in the highest degrees. To ask the question, then, suggests a dissatisfaction with the apparent answer. They want to know what happens to the just and unjust men beyond what is immediately apprehended, even if gods and men do not notice it. In other words, Glaucon and Adeimantus have revealed themselves as the true apostates—the true cynics— that the sophists style themselves to be. In their nature, they are exposing a "directedness beyond nature," an "eruption of a certain monstrosity."[25] They don't trust their own eyes or even the turning of their stomach. The revulsion and the fear engendered by the protracted sufferings of the perfectly just man fail, unaccountably, to cow or convince them.

"That wasn't a bad beginning," says Socrates with pleasant surprise (*Republic*, 368a). The brothers have taken the first step in their ascent. Socrates can at last begin instruction in more the profound mysteries that are revealed over the ensuing nine books. It turns out that he has quite a lot to say about justice in the way of substance and subtlety; he's just been waiting for someone who might understand.

Notes

1 See *Gorgias*, 452e.
2 See *Republic*, 336c.
3 See *Gorgias*, 461b–c.
4 As Strauss notes, "nothing is accidental in a Platonic dialogue; everything is necessary at the place where it occurs. Everything which would be accidental outside of the dialogue becomes meaningful within the dialogue. In all

actual conversations chance plays a considerable role: all Platonic dialogues are radically fictitious. The Platonic dialogue is based on a fundamental falsehood, a beautiful or beautifying falsehood, viz. on the denial of chance" (Leo Strauss, *The City and Man*, 60). In the foregoing, I intend to treat the *Gorgias* in this way—as the work of master craftsman—but I acknowledge that this is not a universal approach to Plato or even this particular dialogue. According to A.E. Taylor, "the *Gorgias* . . . presents us with an exposition of the Socratic morality so charged with passionate feeling and expressed with such moving eloquence that it has always been a prime favourite with all lovers of great ethical literature. The moral fervor and splendour of the dialogue, however, ought not to blind us, as it has blinded most writers on Platonic chronology, to certain obvious indications that it is a youthful work. . . . Personally, I cannot also help feeling that, with all its moral splendour, the dialogue is too long: it 'drags'" (*Plato: The Man and His Work*, 103).

5 "For the heart of the matter is that of recognizing or failing to recognize who is happy and who is not" (*Gorgias*, 472c–d).
6 See *Gorgias*, 468e.
7 It is also the question of the *Republic*. At the beginning of Book II, Glaucon articulates the obvious utility of justice from the perspective of a community: "[The enemies of justice] say that doing injustice is naturally good, and suffering injustice bad, but that the bad in suffering injustice far exceeds the good in doing it; so that, when they do injustice to one another and suffer and taste both, it seems profitable—to those who are not able to escape the one and choose the other—to set down a compact among themselves neither to do injustice nor to suffer it. And from there they began to set down their own laws and compacts and to name what the law commands lawful and just" (*Republic*, 358e–359a).
8 See *Gorgias*, 461b.
9 See ibid., 482d.
10 See ibid., 485a–d; *Republic*, 343a.
11 To speak of premises is to introduce Aristotelian terminology where it does not strictly belong. But I do so anyway because, while Aristotle may have named and catalogued logical processes, he did not invent them, any more than the first students of anatomy invented breathing.
12 Aristotle makes this insight—the inaccessibility of first principles—central to his *Nicomachean Ethics*: "For neither in mathematics nor in moral matters does reasoning teach us the principles or the starting points; it is virtue, whether natural or habitual that inculcates right opinion about the principle or the first premise" (1151a17–20).
13 And so does Meno in his famous paradox. Specifically, he assumes that knowledge is fragmentary and "discontinuous" (see John Sallis, *Being and Logos*, 78). Considering that Meno is a student of Gorgias, it makes sense that their species of error is essentially the same. A false, implied first premise is a solecism endemic to the sophists.

14 See Alasdair Macintyre's chapter "Why the Enlightenment Project of Justifying Morality Had to Fail" for an explanation of the consequences of taking the Naturalistic Fallacy too seriously—namely, if we do, there is no discernable ground for ethics (*After Virtue*, 51–61); see also, Leo Strauss, *The City and Man*, 7.

15 See *Gorgias*, 470d–472d.

16 John Sallis, "Plato's *Republic* Lecture 8," Boston College, April 7, 2020 [emphasis added]: "A major consequence of what Socrates says [in Book V of the *Republic*] is that in both kinds of showings what shows itself is the same, namely, the εἶδος. In particular, in the showing in connection with actions and bodies, what shows itself is the εἶδος, not some thing distinct from, separated from, the εἶδος. In this mode of showing, the εἶδος shows itself as many, as dispersed. *It shows itself otherwise than it is*. In showing itself in this way, it is, as such, concealed. Bringing it, as one, out of the concealment effected by its own dispersion, by the many, requires the practice of truth."

17 A small textual detail that I believe underlines this point is the fact that when Socrates finally does provide a substantive defense for the virtuous soul (*Gorgias*, 506c–508a), he is talking only to himself. Callicles bows out of the argument just before, "Speak on, my good friend, and finish it up by yourself" (ibid., 506c). Socrates can only speak to himself because, among the present company, he is the only one with the proper foundation (the requisite ontology) to understand and appreciate the argument he is about to make. (We will see later that he will eventually discover some kindred spirits.)

18 Socrates is always apologizing for and qualifying his proofs of the immortal soul. In the *Meno*, right after he finishes his demonstration of the slave's ability to recollect geometry (and, thereby, the existence of the immortal soul), he says, "I do not insist that my argument is right in all other respects, but I would contend at all costs both in word and in deed as far as I could that we will be better men, braver and less idle, if we believe that one must search for the things one does not know, rather than if we believe that it is not possible to find out what we do not know and that we must look for it" (86b). In the *Phaedo*, where Socrates makes his most comprehensive defense of the immortal soul, he affixes several warnings to his arguments. In the first place, he has reinterpreted a recurring dream that he used to believe meant that he should practice philosophy to now mean that he should compose poems, and "a poet, if he is to be a poet, must compose fables, not arguments" (*Phaedo*, 61b). He also cautions Simmias and Cebes, "[T]ake care in my eagerness I do not deceive myself and you and, like a bee, leave my sting in you when I go" (ibid., 91b). At the conclusion of the dialogue, after his arresting account of the many levels of the earth and the different residences of the different kinds of souls, he admits: "No sensible man would insist that these things are as I have described them, but I think it is fitting for a man to risk the belief—for the risk is a noble one—that this, or something like this, is true about our souls and their dwelling places, since the soul is evidently immortal, and a man

should repeat this to himself as if it were an incantation, which is why I have been prolonging my tale" (ibid., 114d).
19. T.S. Eliot claimed that "we need to read all of the plays of Shakespeare in order to understand any of them" (*On Poetry and Poets*, 45). Plato is no different. Although there is some debate about the legitimacy of cross-reading the dialogues, I struggle to see the controversy. They are unified, at the very least, in the sense that they are the work of a single genius. There will inevitably be themes, echoes, resonances, developments, even contradictions that we cannot possibly appreciate if we treat the dialogues like encyclopedia entries. (See, Leo Strauss, *The City and Man*, 61–62.)
20. See John Sallis, *Being and Logos*, 334.
21. See *Republic*, 338c.
22. See *Being and Logos*, 340: "[I]t may be said that Socrates' introduction of this curious kind of art [the art of money making] amounts to a tacit admission of the seriousness of a problem which, at first glance, he might seem to merely pass over, namely the conflict between the private good and the public good."
23. "He finally agreed to this, too, although he tried to put up a fight about it" (*Republic*, 342d); "He assented with resistance" (ibid., 346b); "Now, Thrasymachus did not agree to all of this so easily as I tell it now, but he dragged his feet and resisted, and he produced a wonderful quality of sweat" (ibid., 350d).
24. *Being and Logos*, 338.
25. John Sallis, "Plato's *Republic* Lecture 9," Boston College, April 14, 2020: "Nature, it seems, can only have produced in the prisoner [of Book VII] a certain receptiveness to the teacher, a receptiveness that nonetheless does not lack resistance. The receptiveness would lie in a certain intimation of a 'beyond.' However ambivalent, the prisoner would, from within nature, have gained a certain directedness beyond nature. Within the prisoner the eruption of a certain monstrosity would have made him receptive—even though still resistant—to the Socratic teacher."

Bibliography

Aristotle, *Nicomachean Ethics* (Upper Saddle River, NJ: Prentice Hall, 1999)

Eliot, T. S., *On Poetry and Poets* (New York, NY: Farrar, Straus, and Giroux, 1957)

MacIntyre, Alasdair, *After Virtue* (Notre Dame, IN: University of Notre Dame, 2007)

Plato, *Five Dialogues: Euthyphro, Apology, Crito, Meno, Phaedo*, trans. G. M. A. Grube (Indianapolis, IN: Hackett, 2002)

Plato, *Gorgias*, trans. Donald J. Zeyl (Indianapolis, IN: Hackett, 1997)

Plato, *Protagoras*, trans. Stanley Lombardo and Karen Bell (Indianapolis, IN: Hackett, 1997)

Plato, *The Republic of Plato*, trans. Allan Bloom (New York, NY: Basic Books, 1968)

Sallis, John, *Being and Logos* (Bloomington, IN: Indiana University Press, 2019)

Strauss, Leo, *The City and Man* (Chicago, IL: University of Chicago Press, 1978)

Taylor, A. E., *Plato: The Man and His Work* (Mineola, NY: Dover Publications, 2001)

10

The Noble Taboo

Homoerotic Desire and
Philosophic Inquiry

Andrew J. Zeppa

What Is the Taboo?

In his 1905 adaptation of Oscar Wilde's *Salome*, Richard Strauss captures in sound the distinctive feeling of the taboo. His score is a sensual, decadent, polytonal cacophony, inspiring in the listener both exotic lust and nauseating disgust. In *Salome*'s climactic scene, the Princess of Judea dances erotically for her stepfather in exchange for the head of St. John the Baptist (Iokanaan) on a silver platter. As if to justify her actions, Salome declares that "the mystery of love is greater than the mystery of death" and that "love only should one consider."[1] She proceeds to kiss Iokanaan's lifeless lips, and the orchestra strikes what has been called "the most sickening chord in all of opera."[2] Horrified, Herod commands his soldiers to kill her, and they crush her to death beneath their shields.

Salome is shrouded in taboos. Not only does the plot hinge on the driving force of female desire (arguably a taboo in its own right), but it also represents a bastardization of its sacred source material. Wilde embellishes the biblical story of John's beheading to include several taboos—adultery, incest, suicide, necrophilia—and thereby embeds Émile Durkheim's archetypal sacred–profane dichotomy into the very essence of the play. That is, in addition to the taboo actions occurring onstage, *Salome*, as a work of art and by extension, as an idea, is itself taboo. What is fascinating about this realization is that it shifts the perspective away from the objective reality of the taboo, or the content that qualifies something as such, toward the formal reality of the taboo, or that which is inherent in the corresponding mode of thought. What, then, is the taboo in this abstracted sense, beyond an intuited moral compass about how to live? Why is it that Herod agrees to give Salome the head of John the Baptist and only *after* she has kissed it does he sentence her to death? Is not Iokanaan's beheading, which Herod himself has ordered, the real or, at least the more severe, wrongdoing?

In *Totem and Taboo*, Sigmund Freud attributes the origin of taboos to innate unconscious desires that, for one reason or another, become socially prohibited. Some such reasons are obvious, like the observable defects in the offspring of incest, whereas others are difficult to grasp, possibly irrational, or even nonexistent. Regardless, these prohibitions become assimilated through transgenerational social authority, creating what Freud describes as a psychological ambivalence toward certain acts or objects. When people obey taboos, "in their unconscious there is nothing they would like more than to violate them, but they are afraid to do so; they are afraid precisely because they would like to, and the fear is stronger than the desire."[3] This fear is based on "an internal certainty, a moral conviction, that any violation will lead to intolerable disaster"[4] rather than an external threat of punishment. Yet these internal certainties are clearly neither fixed nor universal. One needs to look no further than contemporary western attitudes toward gender, sexuality, and polyamory to witness the evolution of taboos. Words such as *nonbinary*, *heteroflexible*, and *throuple* reflect a zeitgeist that, at the very least, is more open to discussing, and thus less afraid of, such formerly taboo ideas.

While the social prohibitions and moral convictions involved in taboos may change, the underlying desires which inspire their emergence do not. Suppose that these desires have in common what they lack: taboo desires lack the possibility of utility. That is, they exist beyond any qualifying reasons, and engaging with them violates the rationality premise upon which democratic social life rests. In his *Reflections of a Nonpolitical Man*, Thomas Mann takes up the distinction between the terms *civilization* and *culture*, noting that while the two are often used interchangeably, they are "not only not the same, they are opposites."[5] Whereas civilization can be thought of as the culmination of rational thought and its applications to social life, culture is "the sublimation of the demonic."[6] Civilization lends itself to homogeny and universality. Culture lends itself to heterogeny and particularity. This is to say that civilization and culture necessarily belong to each other in the same way that mountains and valleys are conceptually inseparable. Nonutilitarian desires become taboo and stoke the fire of culture only in the stifling shadow of civilization. Similarly, entering into the social contracts of civilization demands certain concessions at the expense of nonutilitarian desires, which, in turn, prompts the sublimation of those desires into cultural expressions.

As an artist, Mann is in a similar camp to Wilde. In one of his most famous works, *Death in Venice*, Mann's protagonist is a widowed writer who becomes infatuated with the carefree beauty of a young boy, ultimately choosing to remain in cholera-ridden Venice and die rather than give up the pleasure of watching the boy from afar. Here is an embodiment of decadence not unlike that found in Wilde's *Salome*. Rather than try and fail to pinpoint its elusive subtleties, I will once again echo Salome's belief that "the mystery of love is greater than the mystery of death." Just as she is willing to kill to gaze into the depths of the mystery of love, so is Mann's protagonist willing to die for a similar cause. The irrationality of their desires transcends explanation. The taboo, I think, reflects precisely that which makes humans more than merely rational animals.

I have posited that while taboo prohibitions are context-dependent, the underlying compulsions remain constant. Epicureanism offers an alternative framework of understanding. In Epicurean psychological hedonism, what distinguishes natural from unnatural desires is not their telos but their cause. That is, natural desires arise from human nature, whereas unnatural desires arise from social conditions. Sexual appetite, therefore, is natural, but the desire for power in the context of civilization is unnatural. So long as the natural desires are sated in a way that maximizes pleasure and minimizes pain, they are permissible under this consequentialist ethical system. Not only does this presuppose an etiology of social conditions that is distinct from human nature (effectively arguing against the claim that social conditions are—intentional or not—the creations of humans), but it also ignores the crucial complexity of the so-called natural desires, which often involve the sublimation of the so-called unnatural desires. What, then, is the point of divergence?

It seems to me that the natural–unnatural distinction in Epicureanism hinges on a view of humanity as primarily driven by clear utilitarian motives or, to put it in a scientific context, evolutionary drives. Humans desire food, safety, shelter from extreme weather, sex—the natural desires—because, like the rest of the animal kingdom, humans are wired to survive and reproduce. The notion that unnatural desires arise only in the context of social living misses the point. It is not the origin of the desires that matters; it is their aim. For instance, one might desire food because one is hungry, but consumption may well surpass the point of satiety. Here it is clear that natural desires can compel one beyond immediate need. Furthermore, like the squirrel that stashes away nuts for the winter, humans too are inclined to prepare for potential, if not immediately present, need. Rather, it is when desires are aimless—not only beyond need but also beyond any practical use—that they become unnatural. These desires cannot be sated but lead to further and further desires in an endless cycle of uselessness.

Perhaps these irrational desires are manifestations of one primary underlying desire of irrationality: a desire for freedom from the tyranny of reason. This idea of the tyranny of reason emerges from a provocative reading of Plato's *Republic*, which takes his motives in designing the *politeia* to be somewhat pernicious.[7] For instance, his comparison of the auxiliaries to guard dogs reveals that educating them (read: training them to be obedient rational animals) is primarily aimed at protecting the regime and not the edification of the individuals themselves. I will return to (mis) reading Plato in this context, but first, it will be useful to take a closer look at one such manifestation of irrational desire—namely, homoerotic desire.

The Homosexuality Taboo

Homoerotic desire has always been irrational in the sense described earlier. It has no utilitarian ends and continues to resist adequate scientific explanation. Nevertheless, homosexual encounters, as in the context of pederasty, have not always been strictly forbidden. What makes homosexuality taboo, how does it relate to reason, and what role might it play in the ideal city as conceived in the *Republic*?

The distinction between the taboo form of the desires, or the idea of homoeroticism, and the content of the desires, which I will call "homosexuality," broadly construed, which is embodied by a class of behavioral, emotional, and psychological characteristics and constructed categorical identities, mirrors that between *Salome* as an abstract perversion of the sacred and the play's specific taboo plot elements. Thus, to understand the particularity of the homosexuality taboo, one must look not to the desires themselves, but to their typification. Consider, for example, that a heterosexual-presenting person might on occasion have a fleeting thought that involves some form of homoerotic desire. This thought may be taboo in the sense described in the previous section, but surely this individual has not become immersed in the homosexuality taboo by way of a single passive idea. They may experience internal strife and discomfort, but they have not abandoned their procreative utility. They have not assumed an identity that conflicts with the rational understanding of human sexuality. It is precisely that typification of homoerotic desires which requires further investigation. Tracing the etymological history of homosexuality provides a helpful starting point.

The emergence of the words *homosexuality* and *heterosexuality* in common vernacular is surprisingly recent. Heterosexuality first appeared in the late nineteenth century. Its 1901 *American Medical Dictionary* definition is "abnormal or perverted appetite toward the opposite sex."[8] Yes, heterosexuality in 1901 was considered abnormal or perverted, the idea being that common male–female sexual attraction needed distinction only from some extreme version of itself. This use of the word persisted for three decades, until the conception of heterosexuality as normal arose only in opposition to a new term in psychological discourse: homosexuality.[9] While sexual instincts and behaviors have, of course, existed in myriad forms throughout history, the differentiation and categorization of those instincts and behaviors, and the associated identities ascribed thusly to individuals, are historical phenomena. As queer theorist David Halperin put it, "sex has no history."[10] Sexuality, however, is a "cultural production."[11]

The logic of this transition in the American vernacular proceeds from the shift in the dominant normative position of a Judeo-Christian-Stoic sort to an increasingly secular-postmodern one. In the former, the concern about homosexual behavior was secondary to that of nonreproductive sexual behavior in general. That is, the reigning taboo was not sex between two men nor sex between two women, but all sex not in service of reproduction and the family structure at the foundation of society. Taboo sex was nonprocreative, extramarital, indulgent, and decadent rather than sacred and strictly teleological. This began to change, however, with increasing urbanization, industrialization, and the emergence of a new middle class. According to the historian Hanne Blank, the newfound anonymity in increasingly large cities lent itself to more visible and prevalent deviancy, including prostitution, promiscuity, and homosexual encounters. The rise in these behaviors, associated with the influx of the working class and poor into urban centers, became emblematic of the interwar decades. The city became a place where the wealthy and elite could engage in excess side by side with the uncivilized masses. Meanwhile, the middle class, finding its way out to the suburbs, sought to isolate itself "from aristocratic decadence on the one side and the horrors of the teeming city on the other."[12] As this demographic and geographical shift took place, the language evolved to reflect both a higher standard of tolerance and a more specific focus on the nature of sexual degeneracy. No longer hidden from view in the shadow of nonprocreative sex in general, heterosexuality and homosexuality emerged in opposition to one another, one, normal and the other, perverse.

To be clear, I do not mean to say that homoerotic desire is a result of the city, nor do I mean that homosexuality cannot or does not exist in any setting. I mean that the concept of homosexuality as understood today—that is, as a cultural production that is the opposite of heterosexuality—is intimately intertwined with the most basic defining qualities of civilization: necessity, utility, and desire.

The Freedom of Novelty (and the Novelty of Freedom)

Fundamentally, the modern city is built on human relationships: landlord and tenant, grocer and customer, teacher and student, neighbor and neighbor. More so than any infrastructure or political organization, the city consists of these relationships, and the mutual agreement to play certain roles is what keeps it intact. In contrast to ancient civilizations, the modern city is no longer physically and culturally centered on a temple honoring a particular deity. Just as the city becomes a metaphor for the soul in the *Republic*, so, too, do these relationships that make up the city come to represent the essence of one's own identity: My ideas of self and nonself hinge on how I relate to my various relationships. (Consider, in the extreme, how social media encourages its users to collect these relationships, if only superficially, without any recourse to who or what one is in the absence of this social network.) In this view, I am, in a sense, nothing more than my relationships to my relationships themselves. These relationships provide stability, or at least the illusion of it. But in exchange for that stability, and the many benefits begotten by civilization, I am obligated to sacrifice something of myself. When I am defined by my relationships to my relationships themselves, on one hand, I take part in a vast network of interconnected beings, each one touched by two degrees or a billion to every other. On the other hand, I cease to enjoy sufficient agency over my own individuality. In the modern city, people take part in the world like ants in a colony, serving some unknown queen. To partake in social life, it seems that one must sacrifice the ability to be truly novel—that is, the ability to create one's identity out of nothing but one's own intellectual and imaginative impulses. Indeed, it seems that one must sacrifice freedom itself.

Reading the *Republic* with some skepticism about Plato's true motives, it must be asked what distinguishes the philosopher-king from the auxiliaries and the otherwise uninitiated. In the *Symposium*, Alcibiades praises Socrates' novelty:

> There is a parallel for everyone—everyone else, that is. But this man here is so bizarre, his ways and his ideas are so unusual, that, search as you might, you'll never find anyone else, alive or dead, who's even remotely like him. The best you can do is not to compare him to anything human, but to liken him, as I do, to Silenus and the satyrs, and the same goes for his ideas and arguments. . . . If you are foolish, or simply unfamiliar with him, you'd find it impossible not to laugh at his arguments. But if you see them when they open up like the statues, if you go behind their surface, you'll realize that . . . they're truly worthy of a god, bursting with figures of virtue inside. . . . He has deceived us all; he presents himself as your lover, and, before you know it, you're in love with him yourself!
> (221d–222b)

Socrates, like the pregnant mind that gives birth in beauty to ideas, has given birth to a new kind of philosophy. Unlike his predecessors who studied the external objects of the natural world, Socrates places a premium on looking inward and challenges his interlocutors to do the same. And unlike the convincing, albeit rhetorical, arguments of the sophists, his arguments are laughable, at least on the surface. Socrates' method of questioning is deceptive in that he educates by not educating. He provides no answers, maintains that he knows nothing, and yet convinces his followers that he is truly the wisest man in Athens.

Socratic irony is on full display in the *Symposium*. The dialogue takes up the question of *eros*; seems to affirm various perspectives through the mouthpieces of Phaedrus, Pausanias, Eryximachus, Aristophanes, and

Agathon; and adheres to none. When Socrates questions Agathon, he demonstrates a difficulty that arises in the logical dialectic about the subject at hand. Love is a love of something beautiful and good. Since one would not desire what one already has (or in desiring the preservation of something already possessed, one still admits to desiring what one does not *necessarily* have in the future), *eros* must desire something that it lacks. But this contradicts Agathon's speech, because *eros* cannot then be beautiful and good. In his discourse with Diotima, Socrates concludes that *eros* must not be purely beautiful but rather lies somewhere between beauty and ugliness. This implies that Love is neither a god nor a mortal. Furthermore, just as "everything spiritual . . . is between mortal and immortal" (*Symposium*, 202e), philosophy is between being wise and being ignorant.

This idea of *eros* existing "in between" corresponds to that of the mirror of desire in John Panteleimon Manoussakis's Lacanian interpretation of Plato:

> The object of desire is not a terminus but an origin; it is not an object toward which desire moves but that object from which the very movement that we call desire originates. . . . Whom does he yearn for and by whom is he yearned for if not himself? Sure enough, that is a self which, like his reflection in the mirror, is reversed—he who sees himself is a subject and he who is seen is an object. What the beloved sees when he looks at his idol in the mirror is himself as an object in the lover and for the lover. Standing in front of the lover, the beloved can say to himself "thou art that." And what does the lover see in the beloved? Now things get a bit more complicated. For what is the lover's desire for the beloved if not the desire for himself? . . . As for Plato so, too, for Lacan, the mirror of desire does not reflect my body, it creates it and it is this creation that allows me to recognize that this is I.[13]

Only through the other is the self created. Lacan's mirror, which seemingly stands between the self and the other, acts as the "in-between" of *eros*, turning subject into object (for the beloved) and object into self (for the lover). Although Diotima's solution to the apparent riddle of Love succeeds well enough, an alternative interpretation arises in the context of Lacan's mirror: if *eros* itself is to be beautiful and good, then *eros* is one of those beautiful and good things that it itself loves. The deepest longing of *eros*, therefore, is a desire for the self: to enter the self, to self-penetrate, not just to see what is there (γνῶθι σαυτόν) but to inseminate the self with the seeds of that which it desires for itself. The desire for what the other has that the self does not have, then, is not a want of possession per se but a want to be or to become that thing—to create oneself willingly and completely.

If this is the case, then the philosopher in the *Symposium*, as a lover of wisdom, does not seek to gain nor transmit wisdom by means of sexual intercourse with his beloved; rather, he seeks to create wisdom itself. From this understanding emerges the realization that true philosophy cannot be taught or passed down to future generations by means of education. Rather, true philosophy is invented. Returning to Freud, the erotic love of the philosopher sublimated into a love of wisdom is, in a sense, parricidal. Through self-penetration and rebirth, it seeks to destroy a self that is defined by external factors—one's parents and upbringing, one's genetics, one's place in time and space, one's received culture—and replace it with pure novelty. Because this sort of disruptive individuality presents a threat to civilization in a democracy (or to the freedom of the philosopher-tyrant in Plato's regime), it is prohibited and, therefore, taboo.

The Function of Pederasty

In the speech of Diotima, pederasty from the perspective of the *erastes*, or lover, occupies a rung on the ladder of enlightenment that leads to knowledge of the ultimate form of beauty. But in the development of the philosopher, pederasty also plays a significant role for the *eromenos*, or beloved, who supposedly receives a moral education and mentorship from the *erastes*. Later in life, that same *eromenos* will himself become an *erastes*, and recognizing the beauty in a younger beloved, he takes the next step up the ladder of his own philosophical development. (It is important to note that in Athenian culture, the practice of pederasty was reserved for a particular class of male citizens. Specifically, it functioned as a sort of apprenticeship wherein the future leaders of society were groomed by those presently in power.) Since the discussion of pederasty in the *Symposium* contributes to the development of Plato's metaphysics of forms, one can draw a direct line of thought to the *Republic*, in which his metaphysics of forms is what grounds his political program. This connection between the *Symposium* and the *Republic* paints an incriminating picture of the real function of the pederastic relationship, suggesting that its educational component may play a coercive role in Plato's *politeia*.

Whereas Socrates, or at least the character of Socrates, seems to exalt same-sex *eros*, Plato seems to vilify it. In the *Laws*, Plato argues that citizens must obey laws willingly, and for this reason, he begins each section with a "preamble" to persuade the reader that the proceeding laws are indeed correct. He further implies that the fact the laws are written down is redundant when it comes to citizens avoiding wrongdoing, since the well-educated citizen will obey them on the basis that they are argumentatively sound alone. (The Athenian in *Laws* defines education as "a training which produces a keen desire to become a perfect citizen who knows how to rule and be ruled as justice demands" [644].) Of course, were this true, then why would he bother to write down the *Laws* at all? Plato's persuasive preambles fall under what is only the *guise* of reason. Consider the *Republic* in light of Paul Feyerabend's description of rational belief:

> Just as a well-trained pet will obey his master no matter how great the confusion in which he finds himself, and no matter how urgent the need to adopt new patterns of behaviour, so in the very same way a well-trained rationalist will obey the mental image of his master, he will conform to the standards of argumentation he has learned, he will adhere to these standards no matter how great the confusion in which he finds himself, and he will be quite incapable of realizing that what he regards as the 'voice of reason' is but a causal after-effect of the training he had received. He will be quite unable to discover that the appeal to reason to which he succumbs so readily is nothing but a political manoeuvre.[14]

Reading the Dialogues in this context resolves the apparent contradiction between the treatment of homoerotic desire in the *Symposium* and in the *Laws*. They are not incongruent if Plato means to coerce his readers.[15] Constraining pederasty to that elite class of men—the potential philosopher-kings—avoids the breakdown in the voice of reason within the minds of the masses that is so dangerous to civilization (and to the philosopher-king's power monopoly).

Within the pederastic model, the lover uses the beloved as a means to his homoerotic-philosophic ends, and pederasty's educational component acts as the apparent reason that covers up the irrationality of the underlying desire. Homoerotic desire in the *Symposium*, then, is a metaphor for the desire of the philosopher not to receive wisdom but to create it. Engaging with desire as such allows one to tear away the self from that interconnected network of relationships necessitated by society and to look inward—to philosophize in the Socratic sense. Without recourse to reason or received typification, one can give birth in beauty to new ideas.

Intuitive Knowing and Becoming

Mirroring the noble lie in the *Republic*, a prohibition of acting on homoerotic desire outside of pederasty serves to uphold the stability and rationality of the state in the same way that the myth of the metals keeps citizens compliant with their received roles. The *Republic*'s noble lie, therefore, is not only the myth of the metals but the myth of the voice of reason itself as well. The homosexuality taboo, as well as any taboo thusly construed, is noble in the sense of existing in service of society's greater good. Furthermore, since breaking a taboo—in this case acting on homoerotic desire—is reserved for those in the ruling class, it is also noble in the aristocratic sense of the word. But I propose that a taboo is noble in yet another way as well, that is, noble in the sense of being aspirational (at least to a certain degree), in that it is the ultimate expression of freedom.

There is a forbidden process in the taboo, one that proceeds from looking at what one is not supposed to see to knowing what one ought not to know to being what one should not be. This process, from looking to knowing to being, is precisely the philosopher's journey described by Diotima in the *Symposium*. But despite the apparent desirability of such a journey for those who lust after knowledge, it is also clear that engaging with taboos is a slippery slope. Surely, beheading the object of infatuation in order to kiss his lips is not the only means to peer into the depths of the mystery of love. One potential way to understand this process in practice is through the lens of Henri Bergson's concept of qualitative multiplicity.

For Bergson, human consciousness is purely temporal. To preserve free will, Bergson rejects a mechanistic philosophy by defining this temporality, or duration, as a qualitative multiplicity. While a *quantitative* multiplicity consists of distinct things separated spatially from one another, a *qualitative* multiplicity is a series of states that together constitute an indivisible whole. (The nuance required to adequately grasp qualitative multiplicity is too peripheral in scope to warrant further discussion here, but it is described fully in Bergson's *Time and Free Will*.) The key point is that quantitative multiplicity arises out of the practical needs of life. It ignores the space between things so that things, in turn, can be juxtaposed and symbolically represented, for example, numerically. A qualitative multiplicity still admits of difference, or change, and is therefore heterogeneous just like a quantitative multiplicity. But the different states are not separated by some underlying homogeneous space or time. Instead, a qualitative multiplicity is both heterogeneous and continuous. Moreover, the continuity is progressive. That is, it proceeds irreversibly, indivisibly, and uniquely: irreversibly because our consciousness accumulates only forward in time, indivisibly because no psychical state can ever be separated from those that preceded it and those that will follow it, and uniquely because the past is prolonged into the present through memory so that no present state is identical to a prior one.

Duration, this qualitative multiplicity, is the stuff of consciousness for Bergson. At its simplest, it can be thought of as a mixture of two seemingly disparate characteristics: unity and multiplicity. From this conception of consciousness, Bergson describes a process of intuition that can grasp absolute knowledge. Intuition exceeds the rational faculties that are involved in the analysis of things, the latter being a symbolic process leading to an intelligence of general concepts but never absolute knowledge of the things-in-themselves. This kind of intelligence comes from the habitual way of dealing with experience, wherein things are thought of as quantitative multiplicities for the purpose of practical utility.

Intuition, on the other hand, is a kind of sympathy, an entering into the essence of a thing, rather than experiencing something from various external perspectives and inferring generalities. To grasp absolute knowledge of the self, then, one must enter into the essence of the self, or self-penetrate. (As with the nuance of qualitative multiplicity, the process of intuition is out of scope and highly technical; it is treated at length in *The Creative Mind*.) Recall the earlier discussion of homoerotic desire in the context of Manoussakis's Lacanian mirror, in which the erotic desire is similarly oriented toward self-knowledge. Although Bergson criticizes Platonic metaphysics in his *Creative Evolution*, in the context of this (mis) reading, I believe Bergson teases out an intriguing epistemic proposition from Plato's corpus. This is that Socratic irony and dialectic point to the inadequacy of a purely analytic, external, extended, and spatialized approach to knowing.

Just so, human reasonings are drawn out into an endless chain, but are at once swallowed up in the truth seized by intuition, for their extension in space and time is only the distance, so to speak, between thought and truth. . . . The sensible forms . . . are for ever [*sic*] on the point of recovering themselves, for ever [*sic*] occupied in losing themselves. An inflexible law condemns them, like the rock of Sisyphus, to fall back when they are almost touching the summit.[16]

Here Bergson offers an explanation for the Socratic paradox. The arguments in the Dialogues inevitably fail just as they approach the summit of truth. Intuition, or encountering the qualitative multiplicity of duration, overcomes the tensions that otherwise seem to exist between unity and multiplicity, homogeneity and heterogeneity, universality and particularity, civilization and culture, utility and uselessness, and so forth.

Plato employs homoerotic desire within the pederastic framework to hint at this kind of knowledge that is beyond need. The role of the philosopher is to cultivate intuition to create for himself a body of absolute knowledge, ultimately coinciding with the reality of the self, or absolute becoming. That is, once again, absolute knowledge cannot be taught; it must be created. If this is the case, then the "pernicious Plato hypothesis" in setting up his *politeia* and educating its citizens by way of only the practical kind of "intelligent" knowledge is supported. Although perhaps this Bergsonian interpretation is grounds for a slight revision to the hypothesis instead. Perhaps it is not the threat to the philosopher-king's freedom but the potential harm to the inquiring individual that influences Plato's motives. Perhaps his motives are more protective than suppressive. After all, Salome's lust for knowledge leads her to carry out egregious acts and ultimately causes her own demise. The philosopher who dares to look at, to know, and to become in the absolute sense must proceed with caution. Engaging with the taboo is a noble pursuit of truth and freedom, but the path is one fraught with strange desires for the most sacred of beauties and the most repulsive of profanities.

Notes

1 Wilde, *Salome*, 84. See footnote 3: "Conspicuously, Douglas' translation omits the final line of this speech, which was later reintroduced into the script by Robert Ross: 'Il ne faut regarder que l'amour,' which Ross translates as 'Love only should one consider.' Literally: 'One must look only at love.'"

2 Johnston, "Salome's Grotesque Climax and Its Implications," 34.
3 Freud, *The Standard Edition of the Complete Psychological Works of Sigmund Freud, Volume XIII (1913–1914): Totem and Taboo and Other Works*, 31.
4 Ibid., 26–27.
5 Beha, "Thomas Mann on the Artist vs. the State."
6 Ibid.
7 See Clemente, "The Multiplicity of Man."
8 Dorland, *The American Illustrated Medical Dictionary*, 300.
9 Ambrosino, "The Invention of 'Heterosexuality.'"
10 Halperin, "Is There a History of Sexuality?," 257.
11 Ibid.
12 Blank, *Straight*, 13.
13 Manoussakis, "Dying to Desire," 125–127.
14 Feyerabend, *Against Method*, 9.
15 Taking up the puppet metaphor in *Laws*, could reason be the puppet of desire? That is, if education is merely persuasion—training the masses to think a certain way as part of a grand "political maneuver"—then might reason and argument be no more than means to desired ends? Going one step further, to what degree is Plato, as the student of Socrates, a puppet for Socratic philosophy, and to what degree is Socrates, as a character in Plato's Dialogues, a puppet for Platonic philosophy?
16 Bergson, *Creative Evolution*, 319.

Bibliography

Ambrosino, Brandon, "The Invention of 'Heterosexuality,'" *BBC News*, March 16, 2017. Accessed October 13, 2021. www.bbc.com/future/article/20170315-the-invention-of-heterosexuality.

Beha, Christopher, "Thomas Mann on the Artist vs. the State," *The New York Times* (September 17, 2021), sec. Books. www.nytimes.com/2021/09/17/books/review/reflections-of-a-nonpolitical-man-thomas-mann.html.

Bergson, Henri, *Creative Evolution*, trans. Arthur Mitchell (Mineola, NY: Dover, 1998)

Bergson, Henri, *The Creative Mind*, trans. Mabelle L. Andison (New York: The Citadel Press, 1992)

Bergson, Henri, *Time and Free Will: An Essay on the Immediate Data of Consciousness*, trans. F. L. Pogson (Mineola, NY: Dover, 2001)

Blank, Hanne, *Straight: The Surprisingly Short History of Heterosexuality* (Boston, MA: Beacon Press, 2012)

Clemente, Matthew, "The Multiplicity of Man: Beyond the Postmodern," in *misReading Plato: Continental and Psychoanalytic Glimpses Beyond the Mask*, ed. Matthew Clemente et al. (London: Routledge, 2022)

Dorland, William Alexander, *The American Illustrated Medical Dictionary* (Philadelphia, PA: W. B. Saunders, 1901)

Feyerabend, Paul, *Against Method* (New York: Verso Books, 2010)

Freud, Sigmund, *The Standard Edition of the Complete Psychological Works of Sigmund Freud, Volume XIII (1913–1914): Totem and Taboo and Other Works*, trans. James Strachey The Standard Edition of the Complete Psychological Works of Sigmund Freud 13, 1955. https://pep-web.org/browse/document/SE.013.0000A?page=PR0005.

Halperin, David M., "Is There a History of Sexuality?" *History and Theory*, 28, no. 3 (1989), 257–274

Johnston, Blair, "Salome's Grotesque Climax and Its Implications," *Music Theory Spectrum*, 36, no. 1 (2014), 34–57

Mann, Thomas, *Death in Venice*, trans. Michael Henry Heim (New York: Ecco, 2004)

Manoussakis, John Panteleimon, "Dying to Desire: Soma, Sema, Sarx, and Sex," in *Somatic Desire: Recovering Corporeality in Contemporary Thought* (Lanham, MD: Lexington Books, 2019)

Plato, *The Laws*, trans. Trevor J. Saunders (Harmondsworth: Penguin, 1975)

Plato, *The Republic of Plato*, trans. Allan Bloom (New York: Basic Books, 2016)

Plato, *Symposium*, trans. Alexander Nehamas and Paul Woodruff (Indianapolis, IN: Hackett, 1989)

Strauss, Richard, *Salome* (New York: Metropolitan Opera, 1965)

Wilde, Oscar, *Salome*, trans. Lord Alfred Douglas (Tonawanda, NY: Broadview Press, 2015)

11
Division and Proto-Racialism in the *Statesman*

John D. Proios

Introduction

In Plato's *Statesman*, the Eleatic Stranger applies a specialized method of inquiry—the "method of collection and division," or "method of division"—in order to discover the nature of statecraft. This chapter articulates some consequences of the fact that the method is both a tool for identifying *natural kinds*—that is, a tool for carving the world by its joints (*Phaedrus*, 265b–d)—and *social kinds*—that is, the kinds depending on human beings for their existence and explanation. (This notion of "social kind" is drawn from Haslanger,[1] which is meant to be intuitive, general, and compatible with acknowledging that there may not be boundaries between natural and social kinds as they are traditionally conceived.) The Stranger uses the method to identify the *natural* structure of *social kinds* in political society. This is significant, because it connects Plato to contemporary work seeking to articulate how blurred lines between nature and society can be the basis for pernicious social and political aims. I am guided by Haslanger's idea that a principle of feminist metaphysics is the question of how oppressive and exploitative social and political projects can claim to draw authority from the way the world is "by nature."[2] One of my goals is to illuminate the extent to which the method of division allows us to identify Plato as an early historical forerunner of *racialism*, the construction of an ideology according to which humanity divides into races differentiated by heritable physiological, cultural, and intellectual traits as a way of vindicating oppressive and exploitative social systems.[3] This is similar in spirit to contemporary work on Aristotle's idea of a "slave by nature" (*Politics*, I.2–7).[4]

My argument attempts to balance two competing strands. On one hand, Plato often thinks that aspects of society require fundamental rethinking,

DOI: 10.4324/9781003201472-14

reform, or rejection. On the other hand, his alternatives can be deeply worrying.⁵ I argue that the Stranger's collections and divisions in the *Statesman* reflect each of these strands by constituting a *revisionary naturalizing project*.⁶ I defend an interpretation of the Stranger's claim, much discussed in the literature, that the division of *humankind* into *Greek* and *barbarian* is unnatural (*Politicus*, 262c–263a). I argue that, in the Stranger's view, this division reflects subjective illusion and prejudice rather than the fundamental, and teleological, structure of human social organization, which concerns how human beings *rationally cooperate to self-produce as a species*. In this respect, I argue that the Stranger uses the method of division to reject common proto-racial ideology about human difference. Nonetheless, the Stranger's alternative, I suggest, is proto-racial in another way. Through a brief consideration of the Stranger's affirmative and complex division of kinds in the city, I argue that he reintroduces naturalistic foundations for unjust social hierarchies through his alternative theory of natural kinds and human social teleology.

Greeks and Barbarians

The method of collection and division is a tool for producing taxonomies, such as the collections and divisions of "craft" in the first part of the *Sophist* (218e–236d).⁷ The Eleatic Stranger divides "craft" into "productive" and "acquisitive" and further subdivides "acquisitive craft" eight times in order to produce one complete division, for instance (*Sophist*, 218e–221c). Plato frequently emphasizes that part of the point of practicing collection and division is to keep clear the names, definitions, and organizational relations among kinds in a discussion, since we are liable to become confused, and fall into contention, if we do not keep clear *what* we're talking about (*Sophist*, 218c–d; *Politicus*, 262d–e, 275e; *Philebus*, 15a, 15d–16a; *Phaedrus*, 263a–b). He describes the full and expert practice of the method as carving kinds by their joints, like a skilled butcher, thereby introducing an idea of what would later be called a "natural kind" (*Phaedrus*, 265d–e).⁸

The distinction between skilled and unskilled division is important early in the *Statesman*, where the Stranger identifies several flawed divisions, such as the division between Greek and barbarian. The Stranger and his interlocutor, Young Socrates, agree to try to define statecraft by dividing knowledge (ἐπιστήμη, *Politicus*, 258b) or craft (τέχνη, 258d), until they "locate" the statesman (258c). In this vein, knowledge divides into theoretical (γνωστικός) and productive (πρακτικός; *Politicus*, 258b–e), and statecraft falls within the theoretical branch, which further divides into the purely discerning (κριτικός) and the directive (ἐπιτακτικός; 259e–260b). Statecraft is a "self-directive" kind of theoretical knowledge (260c–261a), which divides into those aimed at something inanimate coming into being (e.g., a house, a cloak) and something animate coming into being (e.g., grapes, a flock; 261b–c). Finally, the Stranger divides the animate-orientated knowledge into a kind that rears individuals (such as horse grooming) and a kind that rears collectives (such as shepherding; 261d–e), and places statecraft within the latter kind.

This sets up the Stranger's criticism of a significant mistake in the division, which is the basis for his claim that the division of humankind into Greek and barbarian is misguided. The mistake arises when Young Socrates proposes to divide collective-rearing knowledge thus: "It seems to me that there is one sort of rearing of human beings [ἀνθρώπων], another of wild beasts [θηρίων]" (*Politicus*, 262a). According to the Stranger, Young Socrates makes the mistake of separating "one small part from many great ones . . . separate from forms [εἴδους]." He recommends instead that "we should make the part [μέρος] at the same time a form [εἶδος]," which constitutes division "according to forms" (262a–b). In order to expose young Socrates' mistake, the Stranger then compares the faulty division to two others, including dividing *humankind* into *Greek* and *barbarian*:

> It's like this: if someone tried to divide *humankind* [τἀνθρώπινον γένος] in two in this way, he would divide like the way that the many people here divide, separating *the Greek* [τὸ Ἑλληνικὸν] as one apart from everyone else, while the collective of all the other kinds [γένεσιν], who are unlimited, not interbreeding, and not sharing the same language with each other, they call it "*barbarian*," with a single name. On account of the same, single name, they think it is one single kind [γένος].
>
> Or: if someone took himself to divide *number* according to forms and in two, by cutting off *10,000* from all the rest, distinguishing it as one form, and giving to all the rest one name, and on account of the name also thought that this kind came to be a separate one apart from that.
>
> (*Politicus*, 262c–e)

In the first comparison, the Stranger likens Young Socrates' division to the way that "the people here" separate "the Greek" from the "barbarian." In the same way that these people (mistakenly) think they divide according to forms because "barbarian" is a single name for what is treated as a single class of people, Young Socrates mistakenly thought that "wild beast," because it named what he took to be a single class of animate beings, constituted a real kind (*Politicus*, 263c–d). In the second comparison, the Stranger makes the same point, but in the case of dividing "number" into "10,000" and "not-10,000." Both cases involve cutting off a "small part" in opposition to "all the rest" and not dividing "according to forms."

The central project of this paper is to offer an interpretation of the Stranger's critique of the division of humankind into Greek and barbarian as a way of illuminating Plato's relationship to proto-racialism. By *proto-racialism* I mean identifying racialist ideas in Plato while acknowledging the historical difference from modern racialism. On one hand, I understand "racialism" as the construction of an ideology according to which, as Appiah defines it,

> we could divide human beings into a small number of groups, called "races," in such a way that the members of these groups shared certain fundamental, heritable, physical, moral, intellectual, and cultural characteristics with one another that they did not share with members of any other race.[9]

However, whereas Appiah distinguishes between *racialism* as a set of propositions and *racism* as the further practice of using them to uphold social hierarchies,[10] I do not make such a distinction. Rather, I will understand racialism as a theory about humankind in virtue of which it is seen as appropriate for some of the racialized peoples to be subordinate in society.[11] It is in principle possible to identify racialism in this sense before the emergence of modern European colonialism. For instance, Robinson details how

> [a]t the very beginnings of European civilization. . . [was] a social order of domination from which a racial theory of order emerged; one from which the medieval nobilities would immerse themselves and their power in fictional histories, positing distinct racial origins for rulers and the dominated.[12]

In this way, we may engage in what Kamtekar calls "cross-cultural comparison" regarding us and Plato, in which we seek to determine how culturally distinct "concepts or social forms" are "closer to or more distant from each other."[13] Nonetheless, given the different human peoples involved, the different forms of oppression and exploitation, and the distinctness of modern racial concepts (such as the significance of *skin color*), I seek to identity *proto*-racialism in Plato.[14] I aim to locate ideas about *natural* difference—which likely involves heritability—to justify or explain oppressive and exploitative social hierarchies.[15]

The division of humankind into Greek and barbarian is one of the most plausible claims to proto-racialism in the ancient Mediterranean world.[16] It emerged with the development of a Greek nationalist consciousness ("Hellenism"), as part of the anti-Persian propaganda resulting from conflict with the Persian Empire.[17] Moreover, the idea of the barbarian combined social subordination with a naturalistic account of difference. On one hand, the peoples thought of as barbarians—such as Thracians, Lydians, Scythians, Phrygians, and others in west Asia and Europe—were seen as typical chattel slaves (a regular practice in fifth-century Athens).[18] On the other hand, this social and economic position was conceptualized within an ideology of natural barbarian "mental inferiority,"[19] conceptualized by an ancient "environmental theory," according to which social traits varied according to climate.[20] In *Airs, Waters, Places*, Hippocrates claims that the "temperate climate" of Asia causes its inhabitants to be "milder and gentler" (§12), and the "more uniform" seasonal changes make Asians less "warlike" than northern Europeans (§16), for whom extreme seasonal changes, and hotter and colder climates, instill "wildness, unsociability, and spirit" (§23). Although the environmental theory does not seem to imply direct heritability (as opposed to region-specific causes), it captures something like heritability by supposing that the environmental causes of difference operate via internal physiological mechanisms (i.e., humors).[21] Moreover, the purpose and function are similar to racialist attributions of heritable traits: Hippocrates seeks to explain why the non-Greek peoples are different from, and are inferior to, Greeks in a way that captures an intergenerationally stable character.

Indeed, the proto-racialist nature of ancient environmental theory comes out clearly in Aristotle, who uses the theory thus:

> The nations in cold regions, particularly Europe, are full of spirit but somewhat deficient in intelligence and craft knowledge. That is

precisely why they remain comparatively free, but are apolitical and incapable of ruling their neighbors. Those in Asia, on the other hand, have souls endowed with intelligence and craft knowledge, but they lack spirit. That is precisely why they are ruled and enslaved. The Greek race, however, occupies an intermediate position geographically, and so shares in both sets of characteristics. For it is both spirited and intelligent. That is precisely why it remains free, governed in the best way, and capable, if it chances upon a single constitution, of ruling all the others.

(*Politics*, VII.7, 1327b19–38)

As a consequence of natural human differences due to climate,[22] Aristotle claims that Northern Europeans are "deficient in intelligence" and "full of spirit," and so "free" but "apolitical"; Asians are "endowed with intelligence" but lacking "spirit" and so are "ruled and enslaved"; and Greeks are in the happy middle, endowed with both intelligence and spirit, such that they are "free, governed in the best way," and capable of "ruling all the others." Aristotle is also well known for his defense of a "slave by nature" (*Politics*, I.2–7), including his deliberations on the status of non-Greeks as fit for slavery (1252b5–8).[23] Hence, because of how it uses ideas about human groups differing by nature in ways that explain intergenerational social patterns, especially to justify forms of social, or social and political domination, it is reasonable to treat the Greek–barbarian distinction as proto-racial.

Moreover, the distinction is reflected in many Platonic texts (*Menexenus*, 239b, 245d–e; *Laws*, 692e–693a; *Republic*, 469b–471b).[24] For example, Aspasia, the speaker of the *Menexenus*, explains that Greeks are "naturally inclined to hate the barbarians, through being purely Greek with no barbarian admixture [ἀμιγεῖς]. For people who are barbarians by nature [φύσει] but Greeks by law ... do not dwell among us" (*Menexenus*, 245d, modified translation). In other words, Aspasia explains the social and political conflict between Greeks and non-Greeks as due to immutable physiological differences, including the idea of Greeks being pure of barbarian "admixture."[25] The Stranger's targeted distinction between Greek and barbarian plausibly draws on this same tradition. Indeed, he proposes Lydians and Phrygians as possible kinds into which to divide humanity (*Politicus*, 262e–263a). Moreover, his comparison of Young Socrates' division to an intelligent crane exalting itself (263d) points to the common understanding of barbarians as mentally inferior and thus fit for enslavement.

Some Other Intelligent Animal

My central goal is to articulate the Stranger's critique of the division between Greek and barbarian in terms of the methodological and political aims of the *Statesman*. I argue that the critique illustrates the Stranger's *revisionary naturalizing project*, which involves both rejecting elements of existing social arrangements (including distinctions like Greek–barbarian) while providing an alternative natural framework for justifying oppressive and exploitative human hierarchies.[26]

Scholarship on the Stranger's three examples of bad divisions (human–beast, Greek–barbarian, 10,000–not 10,000) focuses on how each division is not "according to forms" by identifying abstract, general rules of valid division. Many suggest that all three divisions are defective because at least one of the sub-kinds is "negative," that is, it lacks a "common character" or an "inner affinity,"[27] "parity or internal coherence,"[28] a "positive determinate" feature, a "natural property,"[29] or "a non-negative intension."[30] Yet this interpretation is challenged by the Stranger's acceptance of negative kinds (e.g., the "not-large") as genuine in the *Sophist*, and as we saw, the Stranger divides self-directive knowledge oppositionally, into the kinds set over the "animate" and the "inanimate."[31] Instead, the Stranger clearly states that the methodological error in Young Socrates' division is that he failed to recognize that collective-rearing was already concerned with only a subset of all animals. *Animal* had already been divided into *wild* and *domesticated* upon arriving at *collective-rearing knowledge* (*Politicus*, 263e–264a). Yet, I suggest, the same flaw is not obviously true of the two examples of unnatural divisions: the divisions of humankind into Greek and barbarian and of number into 10,000 and not-10,000 do not mistakenly divide an *already divided* kind.

I suggest that the common thread may be found in the Stranger's allegation that the division between the collective rearing of humans and of beasts is based on psychological prejudice rather than methodological principle. For, the Stranger claims, it is just as open to another animal possessing intelligence to distinguish themselves as a single kind set apart from other animals. Yet, it is clear that would be a mistaken division that serves only to flatter the animal:

> If there were some other intelligent [φρόνιμόν] animal, for instance as the crane appears to be, or some other such creature, by naming things,

perhaps, on the same bases as you, it would posit cranes as one kind in opposition to all the other animals, and [thus] exalt itself; collecting all the other animals along with human beings into the same kind, it would name them nothing other than, perhaps, "wild beast."

(*Politicus*, 263d)

Like the crane, the Stranger implies that Young Socrates relied on an idea about mental capacity as the relevant difference for dividing their target—from a methodological standpoint, this explains the "rush" that led to dividing *animal* twice. Young Socrates attributed superior intellectual capacity to humans as opposed to non-human animals, thereby "exalting" his own kind, like the crane, and inducing a methodological error. In this respect, the Stranger's critique echoes Appiah,[32] who diagnoses racial prejudice as a "cognitive incapacity" and "lack of impartiality" and who suggests that "one can be held responsible for not subjecting [such] judgements . . . to an especially extended scrutiny."[33] According to the Stranger, judgments of intellectual superiority with respect to one's own kind can give the false appearance of an oppositional division between that kind and an indiscriminate contrast seen as inferior in some way. By identifying *subjective illusion* as the cause of this division, the Stranger points to the irrationality of dividing a "small part" from "all the rest."

In the same way that the crane and Young Socrates propose divisions on the basis of a prejudice about the intelligence of their own kinds, it's plausible that the Stranger understands *Greeks* ("the people here") to "exalt" themselves as distinctive from non-Greek people ("barbarians"), implicitly or explicitly because of Greek mental superiority.[34] The Stranger thus undermines a prejudiced model of dividing humanity. Moreover, he provides an alternative theory of human division that reflects both his views about the metaphysics of natural kinds and his revisionary theory of social teleology. This can be seen in the Stranger's response to his own criticism, namely, that it is "safer" to divide "through the middle," which makes it more likely that one will divide "according to forms" (*Politicus*, 263b) "I suppose it is finer, more according to forms, and into two, if one were to divide number into odd and even, and in turn the kind of human being into male and female" (262e).

It is outside the scope of this chapter to examine adequately the methodological and metaphysical advantages of so-called dichotomous division[35]

Nonetheless, the Stranger later sanctions non-dichotomous division in the form of division "by limbs" (*Politicus*, 287b–c), which appears to divide "small parts" off, not from an indiscriminate contrast, but from other, causally coordinate kinds in a teleological system of causes (e.g., 280a–283a, 287e–289c). Accordingly, I suggest that the Stranger's lesson is not about abstract, general criteria of valid division (although he may gesture to some)[36] but about the parts of the world the divisions access and represent.[37] The Greek–barbarian and human–beast divisions represent oppositional distinctions based on illusions of superiority. Yet, structurally similar divisions may be admissible, when they access and reflect the right parts of the world. I maintain that natural divisions identify *causally coordinated kinds in a teleological process*. The Stranger's critique illustrates the need for this methodological principle, as well as a substantive human teleology, whose causal profile the division must capture.

Dividing Humankind by Nature

I maintain that "safer" division captures causal relations in a teleological process, such as humankind's internal relations of *rational cooperation as self-producers*. This analysis of human teleology is articulated, I claim, in the Stranger's myth of human origins (*Politicus*, 269c–274e), which he provides after failing in the first attempt to define the statesman. According to the myth, there are two modes of cosmic generation or becoming (γένεσις) and, correspondingly, two modes of human social organization (271d–272d). In the first mode (the "age of Chronos"), humans are cared for by an overseeing god, who tends to their needs as a shepherd does their flock (271d–e), whereas in the second mode (the "age of Zeus"), we are no longer able to come to be "on account of another's agency" but must be self-controlling or autonomous (αὐτοκράτωρ; 274a).[38] Under the latter conditions, the Stranger describes how humans emerge from a pre-social state of suffering in which they lack "resources and expertise" (ἀμήχανοι καὶ ἄτεχνοι; 274c). Gifts from the gods allow humans to transition from this condition into the one observed today: "fire from Prometheus, crafts from Hephaestus . . . seeds and plants from others: all the things that have established human life came to be from these" (274c–d). This is the distinctive form of social organization partially constituting the distinctive mode of becoming of humanity, which is an imitation of the cosmos as a whole (273e–274a).³⁹ The Stranger describes several different ways in which all animate beings are autonomous in this way, which I discuss later. Nonetheless, I suggest that, as a whole, the distinctive mode of generation of human beings in the age of Zeus is a kind of *self-production*, in which human beings individually and collectively act to continue as a species through various forms of coordination, such as the crafts, agriculture, and education.⁴⁰

The myth's emphasis on human self-production provides resources to explain the Stranger's affirmative suggestions about how to divide humankind. I argued earlier that, based on the Stranger's introduction of a non-dichotomous form of division, natural divisions access and represent the teleological causal processes structuring the world. Similarly, I have argued elsewhere that the division of *oral sound* into the letters identifies the causal kinds involved in the production of oral speech (*Philebus* 17b, 18b–d).⁴¹ This helps explain Plato's analogy between kinds and bodies, which the Stranger highlights as dividing not "in two" but "according to the limbs, like a sacrificial animal" (*Politicus*, 287b–c). Indeed, he illustrates division "by limbs" with the example of dividing the kinds of crafts relating to clothing, which articulates how the crafts cooperate in a shared production process (kinds as "co-workers" or "cooperators," σύνεργον; 280a–b), including which kinds are "contributory" or "co-causes" (συναίτιος), and which are direct causes of the "thing itself" (281d–e). In the present context, I propose that the Stranger's two examples of natural division—odd and even, male and female—divide kinds in their capacity as parts of a productive process, which the Stranger's myth then articulates in the case of human beings.

For example, I suggest that the Stranger sees male and female as natural kinds of humans because they causally coordinate in (at least) *reproduction*, which is part of the broader human activity of self-production out of which society emerges. As we saw, according to the myth, rather than being tended to and cared for by an overseer god, we engage in autonomous self-rule. The gods' gifts (crafts, fire, agriculture) are paradigm examples of how we engage in this mode of generation. But, prior to the intervention of the gods' gifts, the Stranger claims that "pregnancy, birth, and rearing," for all animals, came to conform to the mode of generation of the cosmos as a whole during this cycle (*Politicus*, 273e–274a). In this sense, reproduction and the social function of rearing are kinds of the broader activity of human self-production. Indeed, Sara Brill argues that reproduction is both an imitation of the cosmos and the conditions out of which political organization arises:

> Alongside the resources for self-preservation provided by techne, human self-rule comes to expression in the act of generating ourselves from ourselves . . . sexual reproduction . . . is treated as a form of mimesis, an imitation of the self-rule of cosmos . . . it is from this form of generation that political life follows, as it is from this act that family, *politeia*, and the differences that make the Age of Zeus recognizable as our own emerge.[42]

In other words, in the Stranger's view, reproduction is one way that human beings engage in self-production, as it is a form of reproducing humankind in socially coordinated ways.[43] This is not fundamentally different from how craft, agriculture, and politics constitute self-production. Different divisions of humankind should reveal these distinctions. But, following Brill, I maintain that reproduction is a distinctive form of self-production and part of the groundwork for political organization. As such, I suggest that the division of humankind into male and female is preferable because it identifies how human beings play distinct roles in the processes the Stranger identifies as forming the basis for human society.

An advantage of my interpretation is that it connects the Stranger's first critique, which prompts the analysis of the Greek–barbarian division, to his second critique, which prompts the myth. According to the second critique, the previous divisions failed to identify the statesman uniquely, because they failed to distinguish the statesman's unique manner of rule from the external rule of a herdsman (267e–268c, 274e–275c).[44] In my interpretation, both critiques demonstrate that division must articulate and respect how human beings differ insofar as they engage in the distinctive mode of generation in our current cosmic cycle.

It also seems to me that the division of number into odd and even is preferable because an arithmetician must know these types in their capacity as making two different kinds of contributions to arithmetic operations. Indeed, in the *Philebus*, Socrates maintains a broad continuity between the productive and theoretical branches of knowledge (*Philebus*, 55c–59e). Arithmeticians engage in the same practices of measurement that are essential to each branch of knowledge, including carpentry, as such (55e, 56c–57a). In this way, it's plausible that both number and humankind are divided "naturally" when the division proceeds according to teleological relations from the perspective of an intelligent agent. Sorting number into "odd" and "even" captures these relations.

Division in the City

I have argued that according to the Stranger's method and metaphysics of natural kinds, dividing humanity into Greek and barbarian is flawed because it does not analyze us into our different cooperative kinds in the teleology of social organization. The common supposition that non-Greeks are mentally inferior is in error about what it means to engage in intelligent activity, which the myth articulates as collective self-production. Yet, I maintain that the Stranger's revisionary project is still proto-racial, insofar as it provides *naturalistic foundations* for oppressive and exploitative social hierarchies, which is an essential element of racialism.

This can be seen in his use of the non-dichotomous mode of division to identify the kinds in the city, and with them, the natural division of society. As we saw earlier, the Stranger articulates non-dichotomous natural division as *teleological*: it captures the relations of causal cooperation in the productive process of a craft. By using this method to divide the city, the Stranger identifies seven co-causal kinds of producers, such as those who produce food, vehicles, tools, and weapons (*Politicus*, 287e–289c). Among direct causes are different kinds of servants (289c–290d), including people who are bought and sold as possessions (289d–e), free merchants (289e–290a), day laborers (290a), heralds (290b), and priests (290c). The Stranger's division proceeds in this hierarchical fashion, identifying more and more fundamental contributors to the city's organization, such as the generals, lawyers, educators, and judges (*Politicus*, 303e–305e).[45] The statesman is distinguished as the person in charge of determining the right time for setting craft in motion,[46] thereby exercising a supervisory capacity over the city as a whole (305c–e).

At the end of the dialogue, the Stranger further claims that part of the statesman's job is to interweave two natural kinds of human being, the courageous and the temperate, who are distinguished by heritable traits (*Politicus*, 307e–308a, 310c–d) and naturally hostile to each other (306a–308b). Here Plato clearly invokes the ideological tradition we saw earlier, distinguishing naturally hostile social groups demarcated by traits typically associated with non-Greek barbarians (i.e., northern Europeans and west Asians; *Politicus*, 306c–308a). Moreover, the Stranger claims that *intermarriage* (i.e., socially coordinated reproduction) is necessary in order to appropriately weave the two kinds together in order to produce a happy city, repeatedly invoking ideas about heritable difference and the need to "mix" (310b–e). In this way, the Stranger reintroduces elements of the proto-racial ideas we saw earlier (e.g., politically significant heritable difference) but in a way that reflects the revisionary social teleology of the dialogue, including a rejection of the ethno-nationalist concept of a barbarian.[47]

Nonetheless, these final divisions provide a new framework for naturalizing oppressive and exploitative social arrangements. We saw earlier that, according to the Stranger, the natural division of the city captures *hierarchical* causal relations, which is the framework for how he understands chattel slavery, among other kinds of labor in the city. In this sense, the Stranger portrays the natural structure of society such that there are always laborers and a variety of other kinds of producers supporting various kinds of elites, such as generals, politicians, and lawyers. Moreover, in a disturbing part of the dialogue, the Stranger claims that the statesman must identify those who are incapable of natural courage or temperance and execute, exile, or otherwise severely punish them, whereas he "subjects to the class of slave those rolling in stupidity [ἀμαθίᾳ] and baseness" (*Politicus*, 309a). The reference to stupidity illustrates how the Stranger has *co-opted* the ethno-nationalist charge of mental inferiority for his theoretically refined justification for slavery.[48] In this way, while rejecting common proto-racial ideas about human nature and difference, the Stranger reaffirms the idea that chattel slavery is justified by the intellectual inferiority of the enslaved and, more broadly, that there is a natural, in some cases heritable, human hierarchy that should be enforced by state violence.[49] Hence, although I have suggested that the Stranger's claims reflect Plato's concern to revise our understanding of society as part of the world's natural structure, his alternative appears to reintroduce and preserve, rather than reject and root out, the naturalization of oppressive human hierarchy.

Acknowledgments

I thank Fran Fairbairn, Rachana Kamtekar, Zeyad El Nabolsy, and Jeremy Reid for valuable feedback on this chapter, and Joshua Wilburn for sharing his manuscript so I could better understand environmental theory in the *Statesman*.

Notes

1 Haslanger, "Ontology and Social Construction."
2 Haslanger, "Feminism in Metaphysics," 157. See Mills (1997) on "naturalizing" fictions about human origins used to justify racial systems. Conversely, Spencer (2014: 1036, cf. 2019: n.10) writes of his biological racial realism: "if individuals wish to make claims about one race being superior to another in some respect, they will have to look elsewhere for that evidence." See also Outlaw (1990: 61–68) and McCoskey (2012: 3–5).
3 For more on this, See Appiah (1996: 54–55, 1990: 4–6), Haslanger (Gender and Race: (What) Are They? (What) Do We Want Them to Be?: 236–238), Kamtekar (2002: 6), McCoskey (2012: 31–32), and Robinson (1983), as well as the following discussion.
4 For example, Kamtekar (2016), El Nabolsy (2019), and Rosivach (1999: 142–148).
5 This tension is a frequent theme in Annas (1981: esp. chapter 7). See also Kamtekar (2002: 5), Kasimis (2016), Sartorius (1974) & Zack (2018: 3–5). I aim to overcome some of the challenges raised for allegations of Plato's elitism, for example, in Vlastos (1980). Cf. Mills (1990: 3–5).
6 Cf. the discussion of women's natures in *Republic*, 452d–457d.
7 Cf. Moravcsik (1973: 179), Henry (2011: 253).
8 The method involves "leading together into one form [μίαν ἰδέαν] things seen at once scattered every which way" (*Phaedrus*, 265d), and "dividing according to forms [κατ' εἴδη], the number there are by nature [κατ' ἄρθρα ᾗ πέφυκεν], and trying not to splinter any part, in the manner of a bad butcher" (265e). See Cohen (1973), Henry (2011), Moravcsik (1973), and Muniz and Rudebusch (2018).
9 Appiah, *Race, Culture, Identity*, 56.
10 Appiah, "Racisms," 6–10
11 Following Haslanger (Gender and Race: (What) Are They? (What) Do We Want Them to Be?: 236–238) on racialization, cf. McCoskey (2012: 31–32).
12 Robinson, *Black Marxism*, 83. Robinson (1983: 81–84, 45–53, 116–122) locates racial ideas about "blood" and "origin" as ideological forces in European conquests, such as the English exploitation of Ireland. See also Appiah (1996: 56–61).
13 Kamtekar, "Distinction Without a Difference?," 2.

14 Cf. El Nabolsy (2019: 257–258) for a similar strategy.
15 In this way, I hope to avoid the "anachronism" identified by Zack (2018: 3) of interpreting "earlier forms of human hierarchy or status, as racial systems, where and when there were not yet fully developed ideas of human races as hereditary physical systems."
16 McCoskey (2012: 54) argues that the "collapsing of all human variation into a single racial opposition—Greek vs. barbarian—is the closest parallel in antiquity to the modern racial binary of 'black' and 'white.'"
17 McCoskey, *Race: Antiquity & Its Legacy*, 49–58.
18 See Rosivach, "Enslaving 'Barbaroi' and the Athenian Ideology of Slavery," 129: "it is clear from our sources that when Athenians thought about slaves they habitually thought about *barbaroi*, and when they thought about *barbaroi* they habitually thought about slaves."
19 Fisher, *Slavery in Classical Greece*, 93, 86–87. Cf. Rosivach (1999: 148–152, 157), McCoskey (2012: 54)
20 McCoskey, *Race: Antiquity & Its Legacy*, 46–49.
21 McCoskey, *Race: Antiquity & Its Legacy*, 46.
22 See Leunissen, *From Natural Character to Moral Virtue in Aristotle*, 7–8 for discussion.
23 Cf. Kamtekar (2016), El Nabolsy (2019), and Rosivach (1999: 142–148).
24 Kamtekar, "Distinction Without a Difference?," 3.
25 It does not matter whether Aspasia in fact endorses this view.
26 My proposal is meant to find a middle way between reductively sociological and overly decontextualizing readings of Plato (cf. Vlastos 1980). Thanks to Zeyad El Nabolsy for emphasizing this to me.
27 Miller, *The Philosopher in the Statesman*, 20–21.
28 Franklin, "Dichotomy and Platonic Diairesis," 10.
29 Moravcsik, "Plato's Method of Division," 171.
30 Cohen, "Plato's Method of Division," 189, critically.
31 The Stranger also seems to permit negatively defined forms at *Politicus*, 258c.
32 Appiah, "Racisms," 5–6.
33 Ibid., 9. I am grateful to Fran Fairbairn for calling this to my attention. Cf. Franklin (2011: 10).
34 Moreover, following Rosivach (1999: 147), the human–beast distinction may be related to the Greek–barbarian distinction, in that the ideology according to which non-Greeks are natural slaves placed them "between" human beings and domesticated animals.
35 Plato elsewhere emphasizes the importance of opposition as a specific form of difference (*Philebus*, 12c–13d), and of difference as location on a range of opposites (*Philebus*, 24c–d), which may help explain why dichotomous division locates real kinds that may then be naturally divided non-dichotomously (*Politicus*, 279c–281a).
36 Young Socrates' misstep (dividing animal twice) seems to violate a general principle of valid division.

37 Cf. Moravcsik (1973: 179) and Henry (2011: 253).
38 See Lane, *Method and Politics in Plato's Statesman*, 101–111, for discussion of other-rule and self-rule.
39 Discussed at length in Gardner and Yao (2020).
40 This is broadly consistent with the Marxist notion of production—see Wills (2018: 230–231).
41 See Proios, "Plato on Natural Kinds." I believe that this model of division reflects the fundamentality of craft in Plato's ontology, and specifically his conception of *intelligence* as the cause of *coming-into-being* (*Philebus*, 23c–27c, 53c–54c).
42 Brill, "Autochthony, Sexual Reproduction, and Political Life in Plato's *Statesman*," 44.
43 I will not be able to examine the significance of the Stranger's naturalistic ideas about gender and sexuality, but I note that they are worth further analysis.
44 Following the interpretations in Lane (1998) and Gill (2012).
45 Cf. division as akin to sifting metals for gold, *Politicus*, 303d–e.
46 The statesman's knowledge of "timing" is discussed at length in Lane (1998).
47 I am grateful to Jeremy Reid for a helpful discussion here.
48 Hence, Rosivach (1999: 149) and Fisher (1993: 93) observe this passage as part of the Athenian ideological tradition for slavery.
49 The issue is not, as Annas (1981: 171) puts it, that Plato "is assuming normal Greek life as his background (a life in which the need for slaves was not questioned)" but that Plato has developed a theoretical and naturalistic justification for slavery and other forms of oppression and exploitation. Cf. Kamtekar (2016: 155).

Bibliography

Primary Texts (English Language Translations)

Aristotle, *Politics*, trans. C. D. C. Reeve (Indianapolis, IN: Hackett Publishing Company, 1998)

Hippocrates, *Ancient Medicine. Airs, Waters, Places. Epidemics 1 and 3. The Oath. Precepts. Nutriment*, trans. W. H. S. Jones (Cambridge, MA: Harvard University Press, 1923)

Plato, *Complete Works*, ed. John M. Cooper (Indianapolis, IN: Hackett, 1997)

Primary Texts (Greek Language)

Plato, *Phaedrus*, in *Platonis Opera, Tomus* II, ed. John Burnett (Oxford: Oxford University Press, 1901), 223–295

Plato, *Politicus*, in *Platonis Opera, Tomus* I, ed. E. A. Duke (Oxford: Oxford University Press, 1995), 474–559

Plato, *Sophist*, in *Platonis Opera, Tomus* I, ed. E. A. Duke (Oxford: Oxford University Press, 1995), 385–471

Secondary Texts

Annas, Julia, *An Introduction to Plato's Republic* (Oxford: Oxford University Press, 1981)

Appiah, Kwame Anthony, *Race, Culture, Identity: Misunderstood Connections* (The Tanner Lectures on Human Values 17, 1996), 51–136

Appiah, Kwame Anthony, "Racisms," in *Anatomy of Racism*, ed. David Theo Goldberg (Minneapolis, MN: University of Minneapolis Press, 1990), 3–17.

Brill, Sara, "Autochthony, Sexual Reproduction, and Political Life in Plato's *Statesman*," in *Plato's Statesman: Dialectic, Myth, and Politics*, ed. John Sallis (Albany, NY: SUNY Press, 2016), 33–50

Cohen, S. Marc, "Plato's Method of Division," in *Patterns in Plato's Thought*, ed. J. M. E. Moravcsik (Boston, MA: D. Reidel Publishing, 1973), 181–191

El Nabolsy, Zeyad, "Aristotle on Natural Slavery: An Analysis Using the Marxist Concept of Ideology," *Science & Society*, 83, no. 2 (April 2019), 244–267

Fisher, N. R. E., *Slavery in Classical Greece* (London: Bristol Classical Press, 1993)

Franklin, Lee, "Dichotomy and Platonic Diairesis," *History of Philosophy Quarterly*, 28, no. 1 (2011), 1–20, www.jstor.org/stable/25762153.

Gartner, Corinne, and Yau, Claudia, "The Myth of Cronus in Plato's *Statesman*: Cosmic Rotation and Earthly Correspondence," *Apeiron*, 53. no. 4 (2020), 437–462, https://doi.org/10.1515/apeiron-2017-0047

Gill, Mary L., *Philosophos: Plato's Missing Dialogue* (Oxford: Oxford University Press, 2012)

Haslanger, Sally, "Feminism in Metaphysics: Negotiating the Natural," in *Resisting Reality: Social Construction and Social Critique* (Oxford: Oxford University Press, 2012), 139–157

Haslanger, Sally, "Gender and Race: (What) Are They? (What) Do We Want Them to Be?" in *Resisting Reality: Social Construction and Social Critique* (Oxford: Oxford University Press, 2012), 221–247

Haslanger, Sally, "Ontology and Social Construction," in *Resisting Reality: Social Construction and Social Critique* (Oxford: Oxford University Press, 2012), 83–112

Henry, Devin, "A Sharp Eye for Kinds: Collection and Division in Plato's Late Dialogues," in *Oxford Studies in Ancient Philosophy* (Oxford: Oxford University Press, 2011), 229–255

Kamtekar, Rachana, "Distinction Without a Difference? Race and Genos in Plato", in *Philosophers on Race: Critical Essays*, ed. J. Ward and T. Lott (London: Blackwell Press, 2002), 1–13.

Kamtekar, Rachana, "Studying Ancient Political Thought Through Ancient Philosophers: The Case of Aristotle and Natural Slavery," *Polis: The Journal for Ancient Greek Political Thought*, 33 (2016), 150–171, doi 10.1163/20512996-12340077

Kasimis, Demetra, "Plato's Open Secret," *Contemporary Political Theory*, 15, no. 4 (2016), 339–357

Lane, Melissa S., *Method and Politics in Plato's Statesman* (Cambridge: Cambridge University Press, 1998)

Leunissen, Mariska, *From Natural Character to Moral Virtue in Aristotle* (Oxford: Oxford University Press, 2017)

McCoskey, Denise Eileen, *Race: Antiquity & Its Legacy* (Oxford: Oxford University Press, 2012)

Miller, M., *The Philosopher in the Statesman* (Las Vegas, NV: Parmenides Publishing, 1980)

Moravcsik, Julius M. E., "Plato's Method of Division," in *Patterns in Plato's Thought*, ed. J. M. E. Moravcsik (Boston, MA: D. Reidel Publishing, 1973), 158–180

Muniz, Fernando, and George Rudebusch, "Dividing Plato's Kinds," *Phronesis*, 63, no. 4, (2018), 392–407, doi:10.1163/15685284-12341355Mills, Charles, "Getting Out of the Cave: Tension Between Democracy and Elitism in Marx's Theory of Cognitive Liberation," *Social and Economic Studies*, 39, no. 1 (1990), 1–50

Mills, Charles, *The Racial Contract* (Ithaca, NY: Cornell University Press, 1997)

Outlaw, Lucius, "Toward a Critical Theory of 'Race'," in *Anatomy of Racism*, ed. David Theo Goldberg (Minneapolis, MN: University of Minneapolis Press, 1990), 58–82

Proios, John D., "Plato on Natural Kinds: The Promethean Method of the *Philebus*," in *Apeiron* (forthcoming), https://doi.org/10.1515/apeiron-2020-0060.

Robinson, Cedric J., *Black Marxism: The Making of the Black Radical Tradition* (London: Zed Press, 1983)

Rosivach, Vincent J, "Enslaving 'Barbaroi' and the Athenian Ideology of Slavery," *Historia: Zeitschrift für Alte Geschichte*, 48, no. 2 (1999), 129–157, www.jstor.org/stable/4436537

Sartorius, Rolf, "Fallacy and Political Radicalism in Plato's 'Republic'," *Canadian Journal of Philosophy*, 3, no. 3 (1974), 349–363

Spencer, Quayshawn, "How to be a Biological Racial Realist," in *What Is Race? Four Philosophical Views* (Oxford: Oxford University Press, 1994) 73–110

Spencer, Quayshawn, "A Radical Solution to the Race Problem," *Philosophy of Science*, 81 (2014), 1025–1038

Vlastos, Gregory, "Class Ideology and Ancient Political Theory: Socrates, Plato, and Aristotle in Social Context by Ellen Meiksins Wood and Neal Wood," *Phoenix*, 34, no. 4 (1980), 347–352

Wills, Vanessa, "What Could it Mean to Say, 'Capitalism Causes Sexism and Racism?'" *Philosophical Topics*, 46, no. 2 (2018), 229–246

Zack, Naomi, *Philosophy of Race* (London: Palgrave Publishing, 2018)

Hunting in Plato
On Noticing

Donald N. Boyce

> Then, Glaucon, we must station ourselves like hunters [κυνηγέτας] surrounding a wood and focus our understanding, so that justice doesn't escape us and vanish into obscurity, for obviously, it's around here somewhere. So look and try eagerly to catch sight of it, and if you happen to see [ἴδῃς] it before I do, you can tell me about it.
>
> —*Republic*, 432b

Introduction

A footnote in the chapter-opening passage of Paul Shorey's translation of the *Republic* quotes Thomas Huxley and David Hume, who say, "There cannot be two passions more nearly resembling each other than hunting and philosophy."[1] Shorey goes on to jest, "The elaboration of the image here is partly to mark the importance of justice *and partly to relieve the monotony of continuous argument*." I will risk blasphemy in saying that while justice is important to Plato's project, the hunting metaphor is actually more critical since it illuminates the structure of knowing wherever and whenever it occurs. While we welcome relief from the "monotony of continuous argument," there is something more here—not just for philosophy and hunting but also for all forms of knowing—especially psychoanalysis.

While much ink has been spilled over the erotic metaphor for knowing in Plato's thought, perhaps, in part, because of its "stimulating" or "rousing" perceptibility in the Platonic corpus, there has been little attention given to its more rugged counterpart, hunting. This is perhaps due to the plurality of English words for the Greek *διωκω* (to hunt, to pursue, to persecute, to follow, to seek after, to chase) and translators who justly value readability and the freshness of language over stilted philosophical consistency and rigor.

It often takes Plato using more explicit words like θηρευτής or κυνηγέτας for the imagery to come through.[2] The metaphor appears everywhere in Plato. From the *Euthyphro*—a text about who is hunting or "persecuting" who—to the *Republic*, an attempt to hunt the smaller (justice in man), by way of the larger (justice in a city). By turning our attention to what exactly it is that Plato is pursuing with the hunting metaphor, we can make the process more explicit, cultivate it and improve it.

Put briefly, "hunting" is Plato's image for the activity of "knowing," knowing, in both philosophy and psychoanalysis as well as wherever it happens, since "knowing" "itself by itself" must share the same essential "shape" or "look." In other words, we are looking for a unity. We say with Plato as he has Socrates say so many times to so many different interlocutors, "I asked you *for one thing* and you have given me many; I wanted something simple, and I have got a variety" (*Theaetetus*, 146d). In his book *Insight*, the Jesuit philosopher Bernard Lonergan points out that knowing, in every instance of it, has the tripartite structure of "experience, understanding, and judgement." Truth, in this sense, is intimately subjective, but the structure is the same. This is what Lonergan calls the "dynamic" foundation for knowledge that is *dis*covered by knowing about knowing. More properly, it is knowing oneself as a knower and *attending to oneself in the activity of knowing*—it is a taking possession of oneself.

Because of the role experience plays in understanding, and our "incredible" (δεινός) ability to carry experience hidden within us, we must like Socrates to Glaucon, focus our minds in brutal attention on ourselves. We are, like Glaucon and Socrates, surrounding a "wood" or a "shrub" (θάμνος)—some mass or shape that is deficient in form, a "mutilated memory" as Augustine might call it in Book X of the *Confessions*. Once we have it surrounded, we then focus our mind and attention to try to catch sight of it. The crack of a stick in the forest is the pinch of pain that seems meaningless or unconnected. Instead of ignoring it, we must be like hunters seeking prey. In the *Meno* Socrates says,

> I do not insist that my argument is right in all other respects [i.e., the myth of recollection], but I would contend at all costs both in word and deed as far as I could *that we be better men, braver and less idle, if we believe that one must search for the things one does not know,*

rather than if we believe that it is not possible to find out what we do not know and that we must not look for it.

(86b)

There is something in us—something we are "pregnant" with to use the language of the *Theaetetus*—that we must "hunt." We must attend to its "tracks" and "traces"—for the analyst, the pain the patient betrays—and "purify" it.

In this account, there is an intimate connection between Plato's famous "diatribe against the body" in the *Phaedo* and the task of psychoanalysis: both are methods for purifying "ideas" or forms of their "bodily contamination"—their accidents or associations. As Plato says after reinterpreting death philosophically in the *Phaedo*,

> then he will do this most purely who approaches each with thought alone, without associating any sight with his thought, or dragging in any sense perception with his reasoning, but who, using thought, tries to *track down* each reality pure and by itself, freeing himself as far as possible from eyes and ears, in a word, from the whole body, because the body confuses the soul and does not allow it to acquire truth and wisdom whenever it is associated with it.
>
> (*Phaedo*, 65e, trans. modified by Eric Perl)

The first part of this chapter highlights four essential structures of the hunt for Plato and in antiquity. The second part explores two concrete applications of the hunting metaphor—both different "species" of knowing—the first in the experience of knowing as described by the philosophy of science and the second knowing as it takes place in a therapeutic case study.

Four Essential Structures

In order to return "to the things themselves," this portion of the chapter illuminates four essential structures of the hunt that appear in all forms of hunting. These structures give form or shape to the unity that is hunting "itself by itself." These structures are not always present in the same degree in all particular kinds of hunting but instead are like different threads of a quilt that appear more dramatically in some particular quilts than others. In short, there are particular types of hunting that "image" the form "hunting" to which we are attempting to ascend better or more fully than others. While there are many connections to be drawn between what happens after knowing or the hunt (e.g., when Socrates describes the philosophical task as "good butchering" in the *Phaedrus*, 266, or the description of knowing as "feasting" in the *Phaedrus*, 247e), we "take aim" at the hunt itself rather than the activities that correspond with its outcome. The four structures explored are (1) the role of tracks/traces, (2) the element of danger, (3) the preparatory nature of hunting, and, finally, (4) how hunting is the work of the gods.

Tracks/Traces

The first and most obvious aspect of hunting is the idea that hunting is about following the "tracks" or "traces" (ἴχνος) of whatever is being hunted. This happens in obvious ways in bow hunting and less obviously in fishing. In both cases, however, the skilled hunter can *re*cognize the signs of the unities they are pursuing. For example, the bow hunter with the animal's imprint or mark on the forest (e.g., where a deer lies or defecates), the fisherman with water currents or seasonal patterns.

While the metaphor of track or trace shows up all over the Platonic dialogues, sometimes ethically and conventionally as in the *Phaedo*, 115b, where Socrates suggests living in the "tracks" or "trace" of the philosophical life they've put forth, and sometimes more metaphysically and ambiguously as in the *Timaeus*, 53b, where Plato says that the four elements before being proportioned and measured had a certain "trace" of what they do now, we will center our discussion of tracks and traces on Plato's discussion of them in the *Republic*.

For Jacques Derrida, one very well acquainted with the Platonic corpus,[3] presence is always the play of "traces." In brief, traces are not "inherently" meaningful in themselves for Derrida but are meaningful only within a broader context. Traces, at least for Derrida, represent the way that meaning is constantly deferred. For example, when we look for a word in a dictionary and are then quickly forced to look elsewhere in the dictionary for the other words used to describe the word we were originally looking up. Since traces do function as "effects" or "conventions" of the code of traces, they are at least able to convey meaning in some way.[4] The simplest example that shows up often in deconstruction is the way that "mother" is only a trace of other traces "father," "son," "daughter," and so on *ad infinitum*. "No more an effect of than a cause, the 'trace' cannot of itself, taken outside its context, suffice to bring about the required transgression [the presencing of a being that escapes the play of difference]."[5] And furthermore,

> we must allow the trace of whatever goes beyond the truth of Being to appear/disappear in its fully rigorous way. It is a trace of something that can never present itself; it is itself a trace that can never be presented, that is, can never appear and manifest itself as such in its phenomenon.[6]

Given Derrida's account of "trace," this is bad news for the philosophical hunters who pursue with the intent to arrive at or eventually "bag" their prey.[7]

Both Plato and Derrida hold a similar view regarding the way tracks or traces appear in language (for Derrida, language *is* the play of traces). However, Plato seems to suggest that these traces or tracks actually result in an arrival of some sort—there is a judgment that must take place where we commit ourselves to action. For example, when Socrates says in *Crito*, 54d–e, "Let it be then, Crito, and *let us act in this way*, since this is the way the god is leading us." The first example of "trace" we explore is at *Republic*, 430e–431a. Socrates suggests here that the word *self-control*, despite its logical ridiculousness, has left a "track" or "clue" to what moderation is, namely, that there is both a better and a worse part of the soul. But just as Plato, with his use of *Khora* in the *Timaeus*, picks up a trace left *in* language by something that has withdrawn *from* language in Derrida's opinion,[8] so *Plato picks up a trace in "trace" that Derrida has let withdraw from language*: namely, the unity conveyed when ιχνος is translated as "*track*." In order to read, in the spirit of Derrida, ιχνος "otherwise," making way for the otherness Derrida champions but here covers over, we must unearth ιχνος in its original Platonic fullness and unity.

While "trace" for Derrida communicates the absence of being, since its only pressencing is a pointing to other *different* traces, "track" for Plato is an oriented anticipation or fore-structure of the being to come. While "track" in Plato also communicates a kind of present absence—for example, the hunter who feels the closeness of the animal who made the track—it also represents an end to the play of traces, without necessitating an end to openness itself. In other words, the track is an oriented openness toward being rather than a constant pointing where presence is differed to what are effectively other, different tracks or traces. This is not to say that forms are not complexes of interrelated characters, that there are not structural relationships between forms, or that some forms don't have this relationship *as* their intelligible structure or whatness,[9] but that the infinite play proposed by Derrida *misses the unity and distinctness of ιχνος as a "track."*[10] In fact, ιχνος as "trace" obscures and does violence to the original metaphor. To apply "trace" in Plato to the deconstructionist's example of "mother" mentioned earlier, there is actually a finite network of relations that make up this form, and therefore, the word *does* escape the "play of traces" by aiming at or pressencing the thing itself *qua* its various, but specific and distinct, relations. The point is not that the network of relations is static or that there would be a radical closure to a new experience or new data around what it means to be "mother" but that in the heat of the hunt, a judgment delayed is a judgment poorly made.

Plato describes this idea most succinctly and rather subtly with a seemingly out-of-place reference to the hunting metaphor in the *Republic*, 462. Shortly after laying out the way in which the guardians of the hypothetical just city will have all their wives and children in common,[11] Socrates says, "And isn't the next step to examine whether the system we've just described *fits into the tracks* of the good and not into those of the bad?" (*Republic*, 462a). Not surprisingly, Socrates seems to suggest that for justice to "fit into the tracks of the good" means for the system *to be one rather than many*, to be ιχνος as Platonic "track" more than the Derridean "trace" of infinite deferral and multiplicity. Socrates dives right into determining whether the system described "fits into the tracks" of the good, "Is there any greater evil we can mention for a city than that which tears it apart and makes it many instead of one? Or any greater good than that which binds it together and makes it one?" (*Republic*, 462a).

Where our first example of "trace" in the *Republic* was used by Plato to describe the "something there" that a particular word carries, or images, that has not yet been made entirely explicit, here in a similar vein, trace seems to function as the "mark" or being of a form.[12] Taking both passages together, it is this phenomenological self-feeling *of a unity* or "look," there to be *dis*covered, that is precisely what Plato seems to mean by "trace" or "track." While Socrates may not have a hold of justice itself by itself entirely at this point yet, he knows something, *that is, some unity*, is there and is prepared to make a judgment and live his life in accord with that judgment. By metaphorically putting the unity that has been caught so far in the footprint of the good he is able to see if it "fits," or even more accurately how much it "is"—how much being it has—since the good is not reality but the condition of reality (*Republic*, 509b). Another picture-thought that might illuminate the metaphor even better is the way one can lay a piece of tracing paper with a particular pattern on it on top of a piece of paper with another pattern on it to see if both patterns match or line up. If the system put forth does not fit into the pattern of the good, it is unlikely that it "is" (i.e., is a pattern) at all, and instead of being a unity capable of being tracked by the philosophical hunter, it dissolves into an unhuntable manyness, and the great hunt of being is a farce with no end or object.

Danger

The second essential structure of hunting is that there needs to be some level of danger or risk for the hunt to be a *real* hunt. Plato is explicit when he says the hunter should not use snares or nets in *Laws*, 823 and 824.[13] The hunt—if it is to be a true hunt, rather than just an image of hunting—*should* be dangerous. Most of the depictions of the hunt in antiquity (at least human hunting according to Judith Barringer, who analyzes vase paintings from Plato's time), depict *collective* hunts.[14] When unraveling the unconscious, there are no snares or nets we can set, but we must go at it in community with a trusted support network that holds our being—a being undone in its *dis*covery—together.

Plato takes the dangerousness of the hunt seriously when he, like Xenophon before him, advocates the use of a hunting dog.[15] The very fact that the great hunt of being is *not* a farce or infinite pursuit of what is effectively an unpursuable manyness means philosophical hunters can train "hunting dogs" to help them pursue being. Plato recommends just this in the *Republic*, and without the greater context of using dogs in the hunt in ancient Greece, the passages in which Plato refers to the guardians as "puppies" or "dogs" to be trained can be quite awkward. We begin by very briefly exploring Plato's distinction between wolves and dogs in the *Sophist* and try to highlight its importance for the hunting metaphor and then conclude the section with a discussion of raising puppies or guardians in the *Republic* in order to emphasize the absolute centrality of the existence of a unity pursued for the hunting metaphor.

Throughout his dialogues, Plato uses the distinction between wolves and dogs to describe the difference between philosophers and sophists.

The Visitor in the *Sophist* admits a similarity between the philosopher and sophist:

> And [so also is there a similarity] between a wolf and a dog, the wildest thing there is and the gentlest. If you're going to be safe, you have to be especially careful about similarities, since the type we're talking about is very slippery.
>
> (*Sophist*, 231d)

Through the lens of the hunting metaphor, wolves pursue "many" or whatever they can find, whereas dogs with great discipline, leaving all periphery pursuits aside, hunt the unity they were trained to track—in the case of the philosophical hunting dog they pursue unity itself. Although wolves are also hunters of a sort, they hunt whatever image they happen to come across. Wolves indiscriminately and selfishly hunt for physical sustenance wherever and however they can find it even if it means devouring (other) human beings.[16] Just as the sophist relies on an image of dialectic and philosophy for οὐσία (both their economic sustenance and *their being*), wolves rely on an image of the hunt for sustenance (both physically and metaphorically) in ways that dogs who have learned to hunt as an end in itself do not.

In the *Republic*, Socrates makes the explicit connection between youths being trained to know beauty itself by itself in order to be philosophical guardians of the city and dogs trained in the hunt:

> Do you think that, when it comes to guarding, there is any difference between the nature of a pedigree young dog [σκύλακος] and that of a well-born youth? What do you mean [Socrates]? Well, each needs keen senses, speed to catch what it sees, and strength in case it has to fight it out with what it captures. They both need all these things. And each must be courageous if indeed he's to fight well.
>
> (375a)

The Greek "What do you mean?" (τὸ ποῖον λέγεις) draws our attention to the fact that Socrates is "making" a metaphor, image, or "poem" (from ποιέω, "to make," the verb form of the adjective ποῖον) here and is not to be taken literally. Taken philosophically the puppy or guardian who participates in the great hunt of being must be intellectually perceptive with the mind's eye, quick to find tracks or traces, quick-witted, and painfully persistent in their inquiry or "hunt" for its own sake.[17] Not only does the guardian have the ability to "endure hunger, cold, and the like and keep on till it is victorious," not ceasing until it either wins or dies, but it also is capable of being "called to heel by the reason within him, like a dog by a shepherd" (*Republic*, 440d). The *unity of the guardian's intention* requires both the courage to persevere in inquiry despite troubles and hardships and the ability to heel to reason in a way that the scavenging wolf does not or, at best, only "images."[18]

Finally, the dialogical nature of Plato's texts—the fact that philosophy is done best in groups and from different perspectives—and the fact that Socrates' own hunt is a particularly deadly one are just more evidence of the dangerousness of the philosophical hunt.

Preparatory

The third essential structure of the hunt is the idea that hunting, like philosophy, is merely preparatory: hunting for war or adulthood, philosophy for life. This is not to say that philosophy or knowing is only concerned with the practical pattern of experience but that knowing always involves a judgment—"Now that we know, what should we do about it? How then should we act?"

While there are many relevant texts from Plato that could be used to argue for the importance of philosophy for life, in particular the good life, one of the more subtle ones is Socrates' critique of Ion in the dialogue that bears Ion's name. The complex Greek name "Ion" contains in nascent form a whole host of different "tracks" or threads that Plato's critique of the poet takes in his short text *Ion*. First, the common reading of Ion's name is that it is connected to the image of "magnet." This view is explicitly stated in the text. Repositioning Ion's view of his profession into a theological context, Socrates tells him, "[T]hat's not a subject you've mastered—speaking well about Homer; it's a divine power that moves you, as a 'Magnetic' stone moves iron rings" (*Ion*, 533d). While one would think that having a "divine power" is a good thing, Plato goes on to compare Ion to the Corybantes who "are not in their right minds (ἔμφρονες) when they dance" (*Ion*, 533e).[19] "Not in their right minds" or "unthinking" can be seen here as a veiled way of saying that they are "stupid." For Plato, the way that humans resemble the gods is not by being mouthpieces of the gods but by letting reason or intellect guide their actions.[20] In other words, knowing—whether that be in philosophy or in psychoanalysis—is not the end of the story but instead is preparatory.

Next, while there are many other possible readings of the name "Ion" in the Platonic whirlpool of meaning,[21] the connection between Plato's *Ion* and Euripides's *Ion* helps support the idea as it is developed by Plato in other texts that Ion's issue is theological in nature.[22] Drawing on Euripides again in this section to place Plato's critique within a theological context helps recover how problematic Ion's life is; Ion's profession is actually only a symptom of this deeper, theological issue Plato is critiquing.[23] In Euripides's play, Ion is the secret daughter of Creusa and Apollo who was abandoned by Creusa at birth. He is then saved by Apollo and raised by Apollo's priests. Ion grows up singing Apollo's praises in his opening monologue, stating that Apollo is "like a father" to him. Ion's mother's husband, Xuthus, adopts him after consultation with Apollo's oracle, which results in a string of attempted murders: first, Creusa, assuming Ion is the son of Xuthus from an affair tries to kill Ion; then Ion, upset about the attempted murder, tries to kill Creusa.

While there is a treasure trove of connections between Euripides's *Ion* and Plato's, the most obvious is the idea that *Ion is the son of a god and does not know it*. Through a literary technique that would have been obvious to the readers of Plato during his time, Plato shows that Ion, a rhapsode of a poet, completely misses the fact that he does not need to imitate an imitator of the divine, but instead has the divine *within him*.[24] This is a rare glimpse of Plato's philosophy of contemplation, or "hunting" for action. Instead of the escapist, impractical philosopher Plato is often painted as, in *Ion* we see Plato upset with the "impracticality" of the rhapsode. The issue is that he does not know, and therefore do, anything. Pressing Ion to say what he *does* know since he talks about so many things he doesn't, Socrates says, "Now, since you know the business of a general, do you know this by being a general or by being a good Rhapsode?" Ion replies, "I don't think there's any difference." Socrates, shocked at Ion's arrogance and stupidity replies, "What? Are you saying there's no difference? On your view is there one profession for rhapsodes and generals, or two?" Ion, to Socrates' disappointment but for the sake of consistency, replies, "I don't think there's any difference" (*Ion*, 540e). Plato's issue here is not that Ion is a rhapsode or imitator of a poet but that he is a human being who does not act out of reason or intellect—*he does not realize and act of the divine within him* or see the difference between knowing knowledge as content and knowledge as the ability to make a judgment. Hannah Arendt echoes the critic that Plato is driving at here in *Ion*: that attributing one's action to the divine without any recourse to reason results in the end of responsibility. Instead, she says, one should, like Solomon, pray for an "understanding" heart.[25]

Ion's problem for Plato is not that he is a poet per se, but that his participation in the hunt serves no higher purpose—it cultivates no values or virtues and is merely about "the thrill." Ion is the type of rhapsode who only cares about rote memorization of the information in the poems he recites to please the appetitive nature of audience. As a coming-of-age ritual, the hunt, like knowing, is about coming into oneself, and *re*alizing the divine is "within us." It is *re*cognizing, like Euripides's Ion, that we are not orphans, lost in the world, but the sons and daughters of a god. This leads us to the next essential structure of the hunt: while animals image hunting, true hunting—that is, hunting for sport—is not the work of animals, but gods.

The Work of the Gods

The last essential structure of the hunt is one we've already mentioned above in our discussion of how the hunt is preparatory or serves some higher purpose. It is a structure only "imaged" by lower forms of hunting (e.g., hunting for sustenance) and is the idea that hunting for sport is a uniquely human activity and therefore divine in some way. We started to see this in the previous section on the hunt as preparatory when Socrates starts to push Ion into thinking—into making a judgment. By Plato's time, hunting was no longer an activity done out of necessity, but was, according to Judith Barringer, held up as an exemplification of aristocratic virtue and the masculine, "Nicomachean" ideal.[26] Xenophon refers to it as "the noblest activity."[27] In art, the Greek gods are often depicted as hunters—and not just Heracles, Artemis, or Pan, whom we traditionally think of as hunters, but all the gods as well.

In *Euthyphro*—the hunting text—the problem is not that Euthyphro is a hunter but that he is hunting the wrong kind of thing, his father. When Socrates asks Euthyphro if he's the defendant or the persecutor in *Euthyphro*, 3e, Euthyphro replies, "I hunt" (διώκω). When asked whether he hunts someone who will easily escape him, Euthyphro betrays the fact that he takes Socrates question literally—as an actual hunt—and says, "No, for he's quite old" (*Euthyphro*, 4a). In other words, Euthyphro's father is too old to run from the young hunter Euthyphro. In the rest of the text Socrates, performatively tries to take Euthyphro on the right kind of hunt, that is, the hunt for piety itself by itself. Socrates preliminary acceptance of piety as the gods doing "many fine things" through us, is abandoned prematurely by Euthyphro, who says, "Some other time . . . for I am in a hurry now, and it is time for me to go" (*Euthyphro*, 15e).

The hunt Socrates tries to take Euthyphro on is one Euthyphro simply does not have time for. It is the hunt that we are able to participate in or "image" because of the divine-in-us. In the *Theaetetus*, 176, Plato succinctly describes what it means to "escape earth," and it's not what Plato's more fundamentalist readers might expect. He says, "That is why a man should make all haste to escape from earth to heaven; and escape means becoming as like God as possible; and a man becomes like God when he becomes just and pious, with understanding" (*Theaetetus*, 176b). This philosophical "hunt" for "looks," "patterns," or "forms" is what helps us become just and pious with understanding. This pursuit of being that takes place throughout Plato's corpus and our attention to the activity knowing is what it means for humans to be (like) God. At every turn, Plato is prodding the reader to hunt in the true sense, that is, to "think" and judge rather than persecute.[28]

Applications

Now that we have laid out some of the essential structures of the hunt in Plato, I want to briefly ask the nagging question: why the metaphor? Plato talks about hunting, Freud talks about hunting,[29] everyone talks about hunting whenever they use language that shouldn't be interpreted literally. "Pursuing" is just this metaphor we use in everyday life and just as much in English as in ancient Greek. In short, it's because we *need* the images. And instead of avoiding them, we should cautiously attend to them, looking through them to the truth. Aristotle famously calls this "insight to phantasm" in Book III of *De Anima*. We can get to forms in and only with images that are their reflections. In a similar vein, an "indirect" method is often needed—a story or image that is more approachable for ethical cultivation. Psychoanalysis bears this out in a more obvious way in the truism that you cannot mount a direct assault on the repressors.

The first application comes from the philosophy of science where "hunting" occurs in more clear and obvious ways. The second application is more relevant for the broader context of these essays on psychoanalysis, and we will therefore go more slowly. My hope is that by looking at a therapeutic case study that, once explained as a hunt, will hopefully *en*courage the reader on their own hunt(s).

Philosophy of Science

The experience of knowing, when observed or described, looks for reason—for being—and assumes it where there doesn't appear to be any. The ancient *fides quarans intellectum*, on this account, is actually an accurate description of the scientific method. We have faith in some reason or reasonableness prior to our *dis*covering it. In knowing, like hunting, one can "catch sight" of something through noticing. The philosopher of science, Ian Hacking, describes this phenomenon when he attributes progress in science to "noticing."[30] Science, like philosophy and psychoanalysis, is about *noticing*—catching a glimpse of something amiss—a rustling of leaves not blown by the wind that might indicate some animal we are hunting. Why is that mold preventing the growth of staphylococcus, or why do we need some reference to the gods when we talk about piety? These tracks or traces are traces of unities. Science is actually most effective and makes the greatest leaps when it is "pulled up short," to borrow Gadamer's phrase from his hermeneutics in *Truth and Method*, when the data—our experience—*don't* fit the existing paradigm or horizon and instead interrupt or rupture it. In Hacking's words, "only the observant can make an experiment go, detecting the problems that are making it foul up, debugging it, noticing if something unusual is a clue to nature or an artifact of the machine."[31] If scientists, plagued by the industrialization of science, thought of themselves more as "hunters surrounding a brush" than workers in an assembly line, we may have more scientists in possession of themselves as well as more scientific discoveries. Hacking, in describing what made Caroline Herschel such a great scientist, could very well be describing a great hunter:

> I think Caroline Herschel (sister of William) discovered more comets than any other person in history. She got eight in a single year. Several things helped her to do this. She was indefatigable. Every moment of cloudless night she was at her station. She also had a clever astronomer for a brother. She used a device . . . that enabled her, each night, to scan the entire sky, slice by slice, never skimping on any corner of the heavens. When she did find something curious "with the naked

eye," she had good telescopes to look more closely. But most important of all, she could recognize a comet at once.... She was indefatigable not because she specially liked the boring task of sweeping the heavens, but because she wanted to know more about the universe.[32]

Indefatigable, the willingness to hold one's place "at a station," and the use of instruments or tools (rather than traps) to vigilantly scan one's environment are all just as relevant for hunters as they are scientists.

As noted earlier, the infinite deferral of presence obscures the original metaphor of "track." There is a *web* of "footprints" that lead to a unity. Whether we can actually capture and kill the unity, or the unity kills us—literally as in our eventual death, or metaphorically in the way Derrida and Socrates describe the gift of death—is another question.

Therapeutic Case Study

While science provides a really clear, perhaps rarified, look at how the hunting metaphor can aid us in our knowing, the second example, a therapeutic case study, affords us the opportunity to slow down and connect Plato's recurring image with psychoanalysis more thoroughly.

In this case, an otherwise healthy undergraduate student moves away from home for college. In a long-distance relationship, he becomes increasingly mistrustful and controlling of his significant other. The pain from his significant other developing other relationships while she is away is too much to bear, and the patient begins to shut himself off from developing his own relationships in the hope that his significant other will do the same. The pain eventually becomes too much to bear, and the patient contemplates taking his own life. Instead, he angrily stabs the Miracle at Canaan in his Bible multiple times with a pen. He is encouraged to seek medical help and reluctantly does. He is curious why there is so much jealous anger, particularly as it relates to alcohol. The patient decides to transfer to a college closer to home the following year, and the summer before, he finds himself in pain sitting on the back stairs of his family home. He remembers his parents fighting but is unsure about what. Instead of fleeing, he sits in it, vaguely remembering his father saying something like, "Why don't you just go be with John?" but is still not sure what it means—he remembers running up the very stairs he sat on and hearing a slamming door. Later that year in therapy, he uncovers the meaning of the memory: his mother had had an affair when he was young, and it was impacting his romantic relationships. Afterward, more memories that had been buried with this key memory come rushing forward. For example, picking his mother up from the hospital with his family and his confusion about why a small coin, later discovered to be from Alcoholics Anonymous, was something to be proud of. The hatred of alcohol, the insecurity, the jealously, and the anger all were tracks of some forgotten unity—in this case a trauma that had been forgotten only to rear its head again later as pain.

First, the case study shows how belief or hope in the fact that these tracks or traces lead to some unity can actually be a matter of life and death. The tracks or traces allow the patient to "transcend" oneself in time to *re*-collect or *re*-member the immemorial. As Porphyry says,

> [i]f you would practice to *ascend into yourself*, collecting together all the powers which the body has scattered and broken up into a multitude of parts unlike their former unity to which concentration lent strength. You should collect and combine into one the thoughts implanted within you, endeavoring to isolate those that are confused, and drag to light those that are enveloped in darkness.
>
> (*Ad Marcella*, 10)

Second, there is danger in this hunt. While "noticing" can drive various dangers to the scientists' careers when they start pushing the boundaries and limits of a particular paradigm, the danger in this therapeutic case study is even more dramatic. Plato makes it clear in the *Republic*, 514–517, that we prefer shadows to the brightness and painfulness of true being. There needs to be a kind of reckless commitment to the hunt—to finding the unity that has been scattered at any and all costs—for the hunt to be successful.

Furthermore, therapy without a strong support network—family, friends, or the therapist—can be frivolous at its best and perilous at its worst. The final connection here is that therapy, like hunting, requires the use of a "hunting dog"—in this case the analyst—who bears the imprint of reason and can "sniff out" where and how truth is hiding. The hunting dog, at least for a time, functions as "man's best friend" during the untangling process. Similar to the Guardians, the analyst must go through therapy—this kind of imprinting—themselves. Everyone is a wolf until they've undergone this purifying process of freeing something like the idea of "alcohol" from its bodily associations. We are slaves until therapy—theological or secular—frees us through the purification of ideas.[33]

Third, it is a hunt whose aim is not the content of the forgotten memory but the self. In other words, the hunt is about (re)becoming a self. Its "rite of passage" is a return. The activity of the hunt, like the activity of knowing in each instance, does something to us. Whether we realize it consciously or not, there are virtues and habits cultivated through this hunt. For example, the humility that comes with the practice of a radical openness rather than defensiveness when it comes to how a new experience should be weighed into understanding and judgment or the courage to recognize we make a judgment regardless of whether we have all "the facts" or necessary experience. The hunt, philosophy, and psychoanalysis are not ends in themselves but instead are all preparatory for the good life.

Fourth and finally, this hunt or purification is the work of the gods. It is a being at home with oneself (i.e., one's soul) that, like the divine, is technically not in space *or time*. The soul, as Plato tells us mythically in the *Meno*, can hold things we don't remember at a particular point in time—it holds things forgotten that we can *re*collect when the proper material phantasms are put in place.[34] While these are the squares for the slave boy in the *Meno*, it can also mean using the physical location of trauma to *re*member the mutilated memory. It is our having the divine in us that allows us to answer Meno's paradox psychoanalytically. How do we know what we don't know? Pain. How do we know when we've found it? Pain's relief.

Conclusion

By making explicit the process of knowing through an analysis of the hunting metaphor in Plato as well as following Plato's encouragement that there is some "unity" that the tracks and traces of pain indicate, we will get better at the activity of knowing. Getting better at this activity of knowing means getting better at knowing ourselves and knowing Others. That we, with the help of our therapist or priest, can train ourselves to catch when we are acting not out of reason but some passion, that is, something the body undergoes. At the very least, this can give us some footprint of what it looks like to "bless those who hunt us" and "hunt the love of the Other."[35]

Notes

1. See *Science and Education: Essays by Thomas H. Huxley*, Volume 6, 166. "Here no doubt lies the root of his antagonism. The quarrels of theologians and philosophers have not been about religion, but about philosophy; and philosophers not unfrequently seem to entertain the same feeling towards theologians that sportsmen cherish towards poachers. 'There cannot be two passions more nearly resembling each other than hunting and philosophy,' says Hume. And philosophic hunters are given to think, that, while they pursue truth for its own sake, out of pure love for the chase (perhaps mingled with a little human weakness to be thought good shots), and by open and legitimate methods; their theological competitors too often care merely to supply the market of establishments; and disdain neither the aid of the snares of superstition, nor the dover of the darkness of ignorance."
2. For example, *Republic*, 373b and 432b; *Symposium*, 203d; *Lysis*, 206a; and *Sophist*, 221d.
3. For example, *Plato's Pharmacy*, in which Derrida highlights the use of "pharmakon" throughout Plato's writings or *Of Grammatology*, Part 1, Section 2, "Linguistics and Grammatology."
4. See *Deconstruction in a Nutshell: A Conversation with Jacques Derrida*, "Khora: Being Serious with Plato," Ed. John Caputo.
5. Derrida, *Speech and Phenomena*, 141.
6. Ibid., 154.
7. This is related to the concept of the Messianic in Derrida. On one hand, we are always, forever waiting for the Messiah to come, and on the other hand, "the Messiah is not some future present; it is imminent and it is this imminence that I am describing under the name of messianic structure" (Derrida, *Deconstruction in a Nutshell*, 24).
8. Derrida, *Reading De Man Reading*, 567–569.
9. See the beginning of *Parmenides*, 130–133, for ways that a young Socrates and Parmenides trip up over some of these rather superficial objections to Plato's metaphysics.
10. The image of a footprint is helpful in that it represents a self-contained whole or unity that in a certain sense images the thing itself.
11. Many forget that the whole purpose of thinking through a hypothetical just city in the *Republic* is to catch the "look" of justice in something larger *in order to intellect justice in the smaller* (i.e., the justice of a man).
12. Even the idiomatic phrase "the mark of the form" is yet another example of this "track" or "trace" metaphor.
13. See "Our next step will be to address the young people with prayer—'O friends, would that you might never be seized with any desire or craving for hunting by sea, or for angling, or for ever pursuing water-animals with creels that do your lazy hunting for you, whether you sleep or wake" (*Laws*, 823). And "[t]hus there is left for our athletes only the hunting and capture of land-animals. Of this branch of hunting, the kind called night-stalking, which is the

job of lazy men who sleep in turn, is one that deserves no praise; nor does that kind deserve praise in which there are intervals of rest from toil, when men master the wild force of beasts by nets and traps instead of doing so by the victorious might of a toil-loving soul" (*Laws*, 824).

14 Barringer, "The Hunt in Ancient Greece," 51.
15 See, for example, Xenophon's *Cynegeticus*.
16 Plato refers to the tyrant who murders citizens as a "wolf" in *Republic*, 565d, making the connection between the tyrant and the sophist explicit in that they are both some kind of metaphorical cannibals.
17 Again, if a dog becomes a wolf or tyrant (as mentioned earlier in reference to the *Republic*, 565d), it will be a "savage to each other and to the rest of the citizens" (*Republic*, 375b).
18 While there may be some relevance of the Socratic clause "by the dog" that shows up throughout the Platonic corpus to this great hunt of being we are exploring, we must remain persistent and focused on our own hunt of the hunting metaphor and leave a further exploration to a later date.
19 See also "he [the poet] is not able to make poetry until he becomes inspired *and goes out of his mind and his intellect is no longer in him*. As long as a human being has his intellect in his possession, he will always lack the power to make poetry or sign prophecy" (*Ion*, 534b). Italics my emphasis of "καὶ ἔκφρων καὶ ὁ νοῦς μηκέτι ἐν αὐτῷ ἐνῇ."
20 This is all over the Platonic corpus, but a personal favorite concise formulation is found in *Theaetetus*, 173b. "That is why a man should make all haste to escape from earth to heaven; *and escape means* becoming as like God as possible; and a man becomes like God when he becomes just and pious, *with understanding*." Italics my emphasis.
21 For example, exploring the connection between Ion and the Ionians or connecting Ἴων to ἰών (I am going), a crack at Ion as someone who is concerned with becoming rather than being. Unfortunately for the sake of space, we will avoid a more in-depth analysis of "τὸν Ἴωνα χαίρειν" the first three words of the dialogue that bear a resemblance to both ὦνα ('O god') and τον-ι ("the" but also, as a prefix, "stretch"). There also may be a connection to female form of "donkey" or "ass" (ὄνος).
22 While it is difficult to date the Platonic dialogues, it is commonly accepted that Plato started writing in 399 BCE after Socrates' death (see *Plato Complete Works*, "Introduction," xii). Euripides's *Ion* was written between 414 and 412 BCE. For a more in-depth discussion of the connection between Euripides and Plato, see Sansone, "Plato and Euripides," 35–67.
23 We say Euripides "again" because the first picture Plato paints of the magnetic is also from Euripides.
24 There is a certain sense in which the demiurge from the *Timaeus*, the orderer of the universe, is active in all of us insofar as we "use" intellect.
25 "Solomon prayed for this particular gift [an understanding heart] because he was king and knew that only an 'understanding heart' and not mere reflection

or mere feeling, makes it bearable for us to live with other people, strangers forever, in the same world, and makes it possible for them to bear with us" (Arendt, *Essays in Understanding*, 322). See also Arendt, *Responsibility and Judgement*, Part I on Responsibility.
26 Barringer, "The Hunt in Ancient Greece," 7–8, and *Chapter One: Hunting, Warfare, and Aristocrats*.
27 Xenophon, *Cynegeticus*, 6.13.
28 Students who read the *Apology* for the first time either hate Socrates or love him. For the students who hate him, I ask whether Plato has successfully manipulated them into being a part of the unthinking mass steered not by reason but by passion.
29 For example, when Freud says in Lecture 2 of the *Introductory Lectures on Psychanalysis*, "So do not let us underestimate small indications; by their help we may succeed in getting *on the track* of something bigger."
30 Hacking, *Representing and Intervening*, Chapter 10: Observation, 167–185.
31 Ibid., 185.
32 Ibid., 180.
33 Cf. Spinoza's *Ethics* whose goal is just this process.
34 I am greatly indebted to Dr. Eric Perl for these mythic readings of Plato's thought.
35 *Romans*, 12:13, Translation mine.

Bibliography

Arendt, Hannah, *Essays in Understanding* (New York: Schocken Books, 1994)
Arendt, Hannah, *Responsibility and Judgement* (New York: Schocken Books, 2003)
Aristotle, *The Complete Works of Aristotle*, Vol. 1 (Princeton, NJ: Princeton University Press, 1984)
Barringer, Judith M., *The Hunt in Ancient Greece* (Baltimore, MD: John Hopkins University Press, 2003)
Derrida, Jacques, *Deconstruction in a Nutshell: A Conversation with Jacques Derrida*, trans. John Caputo (Bronx, NY: Fordham University Press, 1997)
Derrida, Jacques, *Of Grammatology*, trans. Gayatri Chakravorty Spivak (Baltimore, MD: John Hopkins University Press, 1976)
Derrida, Jacques, "Plato's Pharmacy," in *Dissemination*, trans. Barbara Johnson (Chicago, IL: University of Chicago Press, 1981)
Derrida, Jacques, *Reading De Man Reading*, ed. Waters and W. Godzich (Minneapolis, MN: University of Minnesota Press, 1989)
Derrida, Jacques, *Speech and Phenomena, and Other Essay's on Husserl's Theory of Signs*, trans. David Allison and Newton Garver (Evanston, IL: Northwestern University Press, 1973)
Freud, Sigmund, *Introductory Lectures on Psychoanalysis*, trans. James Strachey (New York: W.W. Norton, 1977)

Gadamer, Hans-Georg, *Truth and Method*, trans. Joel Weinsheimer and Donald Marshall (New York: Continuum Publishing, 1999)

Hacking, Ian, *Representing and Intervening: Introductory Topics in the Philosophy of Natural Science* (Cambridge: Cambridge University Press, 2012)

Hegel, Georg Wilhelm Friedrich, *Phenomenology of Spirit*, trans. A. V. Miller and J. N. Findlay (Oxford: Oxford University Press, 1977)

Huxley, T. H., *Collected Essays Vol. 6* (New York: D. Appleton and Company, 1894)

Plato, *Complete Works*, ed. John M. Cooper (Indianapolis, IN: Hackett, 1997)

Porphyry, *Ad Marcella*, trans. Alice Zimmern (London: London Priority Press, 1910)

Sansone, David, "Plato and Euripides," *Illinois Classical Studies*, 21 (1996), 35–67

Spinoza, Baruch, *Ethics*, trans. Edwin Curley (New York: Penguin Books, 1996)

Xenophon, *Cynegeticus: On Hunting with Dogs* (Scotts Valley, CA: CreateSpace Independent Publishing Platform, 2017)

Part IV

Aesthetics as Final Philosophy

13

The Philosophical Poet and the Poetic Philosopher

M. Saverio Clemente in Dialogue with Richard Kearney

> The main point was that Socrates was trying to prove to them that authors should be able to write both comedy and tragedy: the skillful tragic dramatist should also be a comic poet.
>
> —*Symposium*, 209c–d

I went down to the Kearney residence from Boston College—the university that the eminent philosopher Richard Kearney and his wife, Anne, have called home for over two decades—on a gray fall afternoon. The autumnal leaves were unbinding themselves from their branches and fluttering skyward before spinning down in circles and settling on the sod. When I approached the door of their cozy New England house, I was greeted by a note directing me to walk around back. There, it said, I would find the philosopher reading and writing in the leisure of his garden. As I made my way around and let myself through a small wooden gate, I saw that the yard was enshadowed by an enormous tree. Not a plane tree, I thought. Perhaps a yew. Then I saw Richard before he saw me. He was making one final pass at his forthcoming novel, *Salvage*, before sending it off to the press. Anne was back on campus teaching art to undergrads. Her sketches and paintings, I observed through an open window, adorned every wall of the house. There was a bowl of clementines on the table next to Richard, and when he looked up, he lifted the bowl and offered me one. At first I refused, but, with his typical Irish hospitality, he insisted—"Eat." And, as we peeled back the skins of the sweet, ripe fruit—he joined me in devouring one too—I found that there was something in the sharing of that simple meal that opened us both to the conversation that unfolds in the pages ahead.

M.SAVERIO CLEMENTE: Thanks for doing this, Richard.

RICHARD KEARNEY: Delighted.

MC: One of the themes that comes up a lot in the volume is how Plato can be read as an artist as much as he can be read as a philosopher—the importance of aesthetics for his philosophy. But rather than go straight to Plato, I'd love to talk to you a little bit about what artistic creation means for you as someone who writes novels, poetry, fiction, and philosophy. How do you see these things working together and informing one another? What does it mean to be a philosophical artist and an artistic philosopher and how does that relate to your work?

RK: I suppose initially it goes back biographically to when I was in a bit of a dilemma when I left boarding school, high school, and was deciding what to do at university. And I was sort of split between doing drama and acting at the Abbey Theatre School in Dublin or philosophy. I wrote to the director of the theater and told him my situation and he wrote back and said, "Look, go to university and study philosophy, because you can always come back to drama later in life but you can't return to philosophy." So I went to college and studied philosophy and literature. But I never went back to drama, except that I think that philosophy can become a sort of performance. And literature is obviously dramatic. So I guess there's always been that sort of crossover from the beginning. And my choice of subjects—philosophy and literature, English literature, English and French literature—has made me sort of ambidextrous in my approach. On the one hand, there's the systematic, speculative philosophy, academic scholarly philosophy. And then on the other hand, there's the fiction—the novels, the poetry, the work I've done in TV and film and video, you know, continuing with the Guestbook Project and even approaching teaching as a kind of performance. I've always loved the big classes—now that I'm older, I'm getting tired and quite happy to have 20 or 30 students, but I used to love the buzz when I was teaching and there were no excuses. Nine o'clock on a Monday morning, teaching existentialism to a hundred students—you have to perform.

MC: I wonder how this performative element, this dramatic approach to teaching philosophical texts, has shaped your writing.

RK: Well, I think I've tended to keep the literary and the philosophical relatively separate in my writing. There have been books that have sort of crossed over, books like *On Stories* and such, which bring in quite a bit of literature and examples from literature and film. But never experimental writing like Derrida's "Circonfession." Unreadable. It's a brilliant experiment, but, you know, it actually kind of schizophrenic because you have Geoffrey Bennington on the top of the page, trying to capture Derrida in systematic, speculative academic language, logistical, as serious as, you know, sort of computer code language. And then on the bottom, you've got Derrida's diaries and journal entries and that's confessional, experimental. But the two never really meet. And so I've always been fascinated by how Derrida experiments with speculative philosophy. But there are two parts of his brain—left brain, right brain—and I'm not sure they ever successfully come together. And this is true of a lot of philosophers. There was Heidegger the speculative philosopher and Heidegger the poet. But his poetry is awful. You know, Sartre did his philosophy and his novels, but they were separate. De Beauvoir, likewise. Separate. Merleau-Ponty always wanted to write a novel, wrote a novel, never published it, but it was there. That doesn't mean there isn't a certain literary quality in their work. You know, ditto for Irigaray and Lacan and even in Levinas there's a certain literary quality. But it is still, strictly speaking, relatively rigorous speculative philosophy throughout the continental tradition, from Husserl on. The analytics—they don't even try. The aesthetic, the religious, the ethical is dismissed. As Wittgenstein says, on those topics—*just silence*. Whereas continental philosophy does try to muddy the waters while keeping the two missionaries relatively parallel. But they are distinct, if not totally so. Hence my predilection for continental philosophy, because it does have a leaning toward the poetic and the literary, particularly when it comes to saying what you can't say. And that really is the inheritance from the nineteenth century, from Nietzsche and Kierkegaard. But really this sort of literary philosophy begins with Plato. Maybe even Heraclitus, I don't know. But certainly with Plato there's already the mixing up of the literary and philosophical. And that's his genius. You only have to compare him to Aristotle, who on one level I'm much more partial to in terms of his conclusions—the primacy of touch over sight, for instance—compare him to Plato and you'll see the difference in artistic merit. You know, Plato in his conclusions is more spectral. The human being is the one who stands up, who looks up.

MC: The stargazer.

RK: The stargazer. The one who is no longer quadruped, no longer mixing it up with animals and plants and trees and the things of nature. In that way, Plato's really emphasizing the gaze of the speculative philosopher who is moving toward the ideas, which is quite spectral. And yet, he contradicts himself by being the writer, a poet. There's a paradox there. What you have is an artist who's condemning the artists, in the *Republic*, but doing so by means of a fictional dialogue, by means of similes and allegories and fictional characters—Callicles, Thrasymachus, Meno, whoever. The Stranger. And from my point of view, that has something to do with the failure of rational, spectral philosophy to grasp what it intends to grasp. You can't actually look at the sun. So you need poetics to do so. Philosophy stops where fantasy takes over.

MC: You know, Nietzsche says in *Birth of Tragedy* that Plato invents a new art form with the Dialogues, the novel. And then, of course, he tried himself to write a philosophical novel, *Zarathustra*—he insists it's his best work, but I tend to think it's his worst . . . the jury's still out. But you make an interesting point when we're talking about contemporary philosophers, let's say from Husserl on, where they will be poetic in their philosophy, they will at times even write works of fiction, but there is a distinction, a line drawn between these two ways of knowing, ways of thinking, between the philosophical and the imaginative, that in some ways isn't there for Plato. Of course, Plato will say that there must be a line. But if you just look at the Dialogues themselves and how performative they are, how dramatic—that line doesn't seem to exist. He says very interestingly in the *Phaedrus*—Socrates, when he's going to give his second speech in favor of *eros*, says: *It's not me speaking. It's Stesichorus*. Stesichorus was the name of a poet but the name itself means "director of the chorus." And so you have this kind of image of Plato as the one directing the chorus in the Dialogues, all these different characters, a kind of a symphony of voices coming in and playing off one another. And I wonder why you think it is that we follow what Plato says—that there's a hard distinction between *logos* and *mythos*—rather than following his example of melding the two, the two working together so closely. Because it seems like we've taken him at his word more than followed him in his deeds.

RK: There are two things I would say about this. One is the distinction between Platonic Dialogues and, for example, works of unambiguous fiction—say, Aristophanes and Sophocles, the comic and tragic. The difference is that dramatists make no truth claims. They're writing "as if" it were the case. And that "as if" makes all the difference. Nobody says, "Oh, Oedipus is right, Jocasta is wrong! Iphigenia has a better argument than Agamemnon." That doesn't matter. So clearly there *mythos* trumps *logos*. Not that there isn't a particular truth specific to or proper to *mythos*. As Aristotle says in the *Poetics*, *mythos* can get to some truths better than facts can. And in a sense, the *mythos* in Plato gets to the essential truths Aristotle is talking about. Plato's Dialogues, I think, don't make a claim to historical factual veracity. I mean, we don't know whether Socrates existed or any of these characters existed for that matter.

MC: Some of their names are just too on the nose to believe they did. Antiphon, for instance. Or Polemarchus. It would be like if a thief in real life was named "Steele."

RK: Right. But even if they did, no one is going to bring a libel case against Plato for saying that they said these things because we know we're entering into a dramatic dialogue. That said, while there is *mythos* as opposed to historical chronicle, there is still within the Dialogues a gesture at the primacy of *logos*. In other words, if you compare Sophocles to Socrates, there's *logos* and *mythos* in both, but in Sophocles the "as if" trumps the argument whereas in the Dialogues, I think, the opposite is true. *Mythos* is there. *Mythos* contaminates, to use Derrida's words—paradoxes and ironies and all that come and go—but nonetheless there are persuasive arguments being put forth. The reader is being asked to weigh the arguments and see whose are stronger. They are philosophical Dialogues; they are not fictional Dialogues. In Sophocles, it's "as if" we know. Oedipus, who is the hero and the protagonist, is living in ignorance. But Socrates is not living in ignorance and we as readers are not meant to believe that we know better than Socrates. The fatal flaws of the tragic actors are apparent in drama. But it seems to me that when we're reading Socrates, we don't say, "Ha! We know Socrates is wrong here and he doesn't know what's going on, but we know what's happened." No, with Socrates we kind of feel, well, if you say these things and make these claims then you're responsible for what you say, even if you end up dying. You don't feel that it's tragic for Socrates because the Dialogues are not works of tragedy. He knows what he's doing. Even though he begins with the confession of ignorance, he doesn't end with the confession of ignorance. He goes knowingly to his death. So I think that is an important difference, that there isn't a complete conflation or confusion of *logos* and *mythos*.

MC: I want to ask you about an idea that has come up for me recently while teaching the *Republic*. It's along the same lines, I hope you don't mind. We'll keep talking about Plato the artist and the relation of art and philosophy, how they work together. In Book X, when Socrates is doubling down on the need to get rid of the poets, he says very interestingly to Glaucon something like, *Let's ask Homer: "Homer, if you're a true artist, where are the students you've made better? What laws have you influenced that have made a city better?"*—

RK: Like Solon.

MC: Exactly. *"How have you set up a* polis, *a world, structured things such that, you know, it's been for the better?"* And then there's a line from the *Laws* that our friend Will Hendel recently showed me. I want to read it to you. The Athenian is talking about the relation of the poet to the lawgiver and asks what lawgivers should tell the poets who want to enter their city. Here's what he says the lawgivers should say: "Most honored guests, we're tragedians ourselves, and our tragedy is the finest and best we can create. At any rate, our entire state has been constructed so as to be a 'representation' of the finest and noblest life—the very thing we maintain is most genuinely tragedy. So we are artists and actors in the finest drama, which true law alone has the natural powers to 'produce' to perfection" (817b–c). And so reading that against what I was just saying about the *Republic*, I've wondered recently if you could read Plato as saying that the highest form of art is not the kind of writing that Homer produces but to have your art actually shape the world, the *polis*. That politics is the highest form of art. Because what you're doing is not creating a fictional world. You're creating the real world.

RK: Well, of course this is exactly what Mussolini thought, what Hitler thought, what Napoleon thought. The aestheticizing of politics is fascism. The politicizing of art is communism. So says Walter Benjamin. From that point of view, Plato in Sicily is a fascist. The first totalitarian philosopher. Now, we're not the first to say that. Karl Popper, for instance, denounced Plato as a tyrant. So in a way that seems to me quite a dangerous route to go, to make the *polis* your work of art. You know, Hitler wanted to be a painter. He was thrown out of art school because he was terrible. So he actually created a terrible painting called the Third Reich and imposed it on an unsuspecting populace. Bad art. He got rid of all good art and replaced it with his vision and it was monstrous. So I think that's kind of dangerous at one level. At another level, where I would be sympathetic to that reading, would be that there is a *technē*, an art of making in politics—that can't be denied. I'd be interested to know the word Plato used in Greek. You see if he's saying that law too is a creation of the human mind and imagination, I'm with him. I think he's right—that's Kant. Everything is the result of the productive imagination, according to Kant, because it's a mixing of the sensible and the intelligible. And so in that sense, you could say, well, Plato is already, in that extraordinary little passage, anticipating the productive imagination. You know, there's the rational imagination and then there's the artistic imagination, the logical and aesthetic. In that way, it's a bit like deconstruction. Derrida says deconstruction doesn't begin with *Writing and Difference*. It begins with Plato and Aristotle. It's already there in the text. By the same token, the productive imagination doesn't begin with Kant and Shelley and Wordsworth and Coleridge, it's already there in Plato. So it would make sense to find traces of that in the Dialogues, traces which deconstruct the traditional, Platonic, metaphysical reading, the hierarchical reading.

MC: It's interesting to go back to where you started in your response—an idea we touched on a bit earlier as well—which is how many philosophers and politicians are failed artists. Plato, of course, burned all his dramas after meeting Socrates. And so, I'm interested to push a little further on this—

RK: Churchill painted 100 paintings.

MC: Yes. There's so many examples. Nietzsche composed music and envied Wagner, wanted to be Wagner. Boethius couldn't stop writing poetry even when Lady Philosophy denounced the muses as whores. The *Confessions* is Augustine's *Aeneid*. So we see this in philosophers and political leaders alike—in the statesman, in the tyrant—we see the artistic impulse, which is incapable maybe of living up to what the artist does and so exerts itself in a different sphere. But there's a real envy of art and the artist.

RK: Yes. There's penis envy in Freud and artist envy hidden in every philosophy. Maybe if philosophers could write poetry, they wouldn't philosophize. Look, we all desire to be poets and we all are poets in a sense. But the choice and vocation for philosophy does take us somewhat off course. Not completely. There's always a creative imagination at work, we've admitted that with Plato. But there is something still different about reading a work as true and reading it *as if* it were true. At one level, to do philosophy is to be more responsible, in the sense of leaving behind poetic license, play, where one can be self-obsessed, narcissistic, bipolar—the madness of the artist. Philosophy is moving from play to . . . politics, maybe. The real world. The practical world. Away from fantasy. So there is a certain license that the philosopher forgoes. Artists are touched by fire. But when we do philosophy—or when we do politics—we leave the childlike, the infantile, the crazy behind. We bracket the poetic—at least to an extent—we bracket faith and political ideology and instead pursue what we think to be true.

MC: Maybe as a kind of final question, we've been talking a lot about the relation between art and philosophy and how philosophers use the tools of the artist in the service of philosophy, but I want to reverse course for a moment. As we were just talking, I was thinking of one of my favorite poets, T.S. Eliot, who, of course, was getting his PhD in philosophy and quit to become a poet. David Foster Wallace was getting a PhD in philosophy and quit to become a novelist. And even the poets Eliot admires, he calls them the "metaphysical poets," that is, the philosophical poets—they're the ones with the most to say. So, just as there is the poetic philosopher—Nietzsche, for instance, or Camus—there is also the philosophical poet. But something distinguishes them. When we look at Nietzsche and at Dostoevsky, we know which side of the divide to place each of them on. Dostoyevsky is a philosophical novelist, but he's a novelist. He's not a philosopher. And Nietzsche is not a poet. So I guess I'm curious if you have any thoughts on where that dividing line between these two different ways of knowing or even different approaches to artistic creation can be found?

RK: I want to come to that. But before I do, I want to say something about how philosophy uses poetry or literature or imagination to serve philosophy. It does so to make ideas creative and living, but also to make ideas accessible. You and I teach philosophy to undergrads. You begin the semester with the Dialogues, you don't begin with Aristotle. Even teaching the *Poetics*—it's impossible. You can't read the *Poetics*. It's just dead on the page. It's dry. The dry rocks of mathematics, as Joyce says in *Ulysses*. So we need Plato and Plato's use of the rhetorical, the imaginative for philosophical purposes. It's true of Pascal. It's true of Montaigne. It's true of Nietzsche and Kierkegaard. It's true of Sartre, even though he kept his novels, strictly speaking, separate. When he writes in *Being and Nothingness* about bad faith, those descriptions are quasi literary.

MC: Sartre's always telling stories. He's describing the waiter. He's searching for Pierre in the café.

RK: Yes, exactly. So, that's the point I want to make about communication and accessibility. If you want to be read, write philosophy in a literary way. Not as literature, because if you're trying to do that then you become a novelist.

MC: Or a bad poet.

RK: Or a bad poet and a bad philosopher. Now, back to the other thing. How does one distinguish between a philosophical poet and a poetic philosopher? I want to come back to my distinction again between telling it as true and telling it *as if* it were true. In philosophy, no matter how poetic, there is a philosophical claim. In poetry . . . I mean, if you go to Dostoevsky and say, "You're wrong! Ivan's arguments are false!" he'd say, "I agree. I'm not Ivan." "No, but Alyosha's arguments are false and Dmitri's too." "I agree. I'm Alyosha. I'm not Dmitri." But a philosopher, for the most part—maybe Plato is kind of at the edge here—does not say, "I didn't write that. That's not me." A philosopher who makes an argument and signs his name to it is responsible for what he says. A philosopher has a responsibility to say what he or she means. Now, some philosophers will try to get away with it. Lacan, for instance, says things like "Well, it's not me speaking but my unconscious speaking through me." But Lacan developed a whole system—the symbolic, the real, the imaginary—which he signed his name to. Just as Barthes signed *Death of the Author*. If you said to him, "Hey, Roland, what do you mean death of the author?" and he said, "Well, that's not me who wrote that but my character"—you'd feel cheated. Because, you know, you signed your name to that and made an argument. So stand by it.

MC: Kierkegaard comes the closest to walking the line because he writes under pseudonyms. He doesn't sign his work. He lets someone else sign it.

RK: That is different.

MC: That is different.

RK: That's definitely different. And he's obviously doing that for a reason. It's a bit of Socratic irony. But just as behind the scenes, Plato is directing the whole chorus and yet we still know that Socrates is his favorite, his main ventriloquist's dummy, so too does Kierkegaard have his favorites. Silencio, for instance, rather than the Hilarious Bookbinder. Or Climacus over Anti-Climacus. And not only that, in his signed works, he says something like, "Hey, secretly and off the record, I'm a religious writer. Yes, I've written ethical and aesthetical works under pseudonyms but if you want to really know what I'm after, it's the religious." So that's what makes him a philosopher.

MC: That he has a stance. He makes a claim.

RK: He has a stance and makes a claim. And even though he doesn't want to make it systematic, like Hegel, he does want us to choose and what he wants us to choose is the religious.

MC: Whereas for the poet, it really is about play. It's a game.

RK: Yes. As Joyce says, nobody has been raped by a novel. In other words, I'm not Molly Bloom. I'm not saying, you know, let's all have rape fantasies. I'm describing the rape fantasy of a character, a fictional character who could exist and who we look at *as if* this person exists but whose thoughts and ideas I do not necessarily condone.

MC: There is no moralizing. Maybe it's a moral distinction.

RK: It's poetic license. Yeah. There's no morality in a poem. A philosopher who advances anti-Semitic ideas is different than a character in a novel doing the same thing. A character is not meant to be taken seriously or believed, which is why we don't burn the book.

MC: That's why you read Conrad, but not his contemporaries who were advocating for the ideas we see on display in *Heart of Darkness*, let's say.

RK: Yes, that's because the novel is not advancing a truth claim. It's not saying, "This is how we should behave or what we should believe." It's a work of fiction. So I think there's a moral and an epistemological distinction in terms of truth claims and value claims that we expect from philosophy, at least minimally, that we don't expect from literature. Now, Plato, to go back to your original point, by mixing up the poetic and philosophical, allows for more gray area—but it's not anything goes. Not every character is equal in their truth claims. Even if Alcibiades—you know, the poetic, the Bacchic, the drunkard, the artist—even if he bursts into the *Symposium* and interrupts the philosophical dialogue and upends the entire conversation, well, the text doesn't end with him.

MC: It ends with Socrates.

RK: It ends with Socrates. Socrates is the only one who's still awake. The poets have fallen off to a drunken sleep. The philosopher outlasts his rivals. Socrates alone is left.

As the conversation wound down, Anne entered the garden. She was done teaching for the day and asked Richard if he might fetch us a little wine. He excused himself to grab a bottle from the kitchen, and Anne and I began discussing the works of one of her favorite writers, Marcel Pagnol. As we spoke, she reached across the table and helped herself to a clementine.

In Search of the Natural Beginning

A Conversation with Stephen Mendelsohn and John Sallis

The question and the problem of beginning is a recurring theme in the writing and the teaching of John Sallis—especially as it arises in connection with the Platonic Dialogues. The question of beginning, as Sallis has noted, is perhaps nowhere more pressing and puzzling as it relates to the notion of the "natural beginning," which is given voice in the form of an injunction issued by the astronomer Timaeus in the dialogue named after him. According to Timaeus, "[w]ith regard to everything it is most important to begin at the natural beginning" (*Timaeus*, 29b). This imperative prompts Sallis, in the prologue to his *Chorology*, to ask the following series of questions:

> Where, if anywhere, is the natural beginning—in what kind of where? When was it? Across what interval of time must it be recalled in order that one begin with it? Is it a beginning *in* time or a beginning *of* time? Is this beginning—this origin (ἀρχή)—with which one is to begin sufficiently manifest at the beginning that one can begin straightaway with it? Or is it perhaps the case that what is manifest in the beginning is not the natural beginning, so that, instead of *beginning* with the natural beginning, one could only *arrive* at it by way of a discourse capable of bringing it to light?[1]

Thinking about this question of the natural beginning along with Sallis but perhaps in a different register in the context of the interview with Sallis to follow, and reflecting on my long time (nearly a decade now) as a student of Professor Sallis, I find myself cast back in memory to the "natural beginning" of my time as a student of John Sallis—especially in relation to the Platonic Dialogues. As is the case in the context of the *Timaeus*,

DOI: 10.4324/9781003201472-18

locating this "natural beginning" is indeed not such a simple or straightforward project.

In one sense at least, in a very straightforward way, the question is readily settled. My time as a pupil of Sallis began in September 2013, at Boston College, the first time I set foot in his classroom, anxiously awaiting the lecture series on Plato's *Phaedo* yet to come. In yet another sense, however, especially as it relates to Sallis's teaching of the *Phaedo* specifically, I find that the question of this beginning, the beginning of my time with Sallis, is not and perhaps cannot be so easily resolved—not at all. For in this initial recollection of Sallis's *Phaedo* class, I cannot help but think back to another time, an earlier time in my life, and a different classroom altogether. There I was an undergraduate sophomore at Providence College. I had just declared philosophy as a second major—still not really knowing or understanding what philosophy is—but certain that it was something I wanted to spend a great deal of time with in the wake of my initial encounter with it. It was in my course on ancient philosophy in October 2008 that, as we were working through Plato's *Phaedo*, I believe my time as a Sallis student truly, albeit indirectly, began. As our professor was walking us through the narrative of the dialogue, in addition to the major moments throughout, he went into a lengthy digression about a certain Plato scholar who had, in a lecture course some time ago, made the case that the entirety of the *Phaedo* is, both thematically and dramatically, framed by the myth of Theseus—with Socrates enacting the role of Theseus himself. This "certain Plato scholar" was, of course, none other than John Sallis himself—although I did not know him or the significance of his name at the time. So suddenly for me, as many seem to say of their initial encounter with Sallis's work on Plato, a whole world within the already expansive world of the Platonic Dialogues had been opened up. While it would be five more years until I was fortunate enough to hear Sallis speak about the *Phaedo* directly and in person, I knew that the way that I would approach the Dialogues had changed—now so profoundly aware of the unfathomable depths and layers that lie beneath the surface of the texts themselves.

Sallis began his 2013 course on the *Phaedo* with a kind of a promise, a promise that he was going to tell us a story. Specifically, he meant the story of the *Phaedo*, or, better yet, the story *behind* the surface-level narrative of the *Phaedo*. Over time, I have come to believe that Sallis could just as easily preface any of his readings, classes, or writings on the Platonic

Dialogues with just the same promise—a promise that he has made good on time and again for any who have read his work or have had the pleasure of hearing him speak.

And so it is with this little story in mind—the story of my own initial encounter with Sallis's reading of Plato—that I would like to frame this interview.

STEPHEN MENDELSOHN: The contributions to this volume are gathered from readers and scholars of Plato who work primarily through the lens of contemporary continental thought. In this regard it seems only fitting that the work will be framed in part by this interview with you—given the immeasurable debt that we owe to you and your own work on Plato, which, for all of us, has opened the way for this kind of approach to the Dialogues of Plato.

In that vein, I would like to open with a question that is somewhat biographical in nature regarding your groundbreaking text on Plato's Dialogues, *Being and Logos*. I would like to ask you to revisit the Introduction to that work, in which you make the case that it has become a matter of utmost *necessity* to clear away the sediment that has been heaped upon the Platonic corpus over the course of centuries—in the form of Latinized translations and mistranslations of many pivotal Greek terms and in many of the various "Platonisms," which have sprung up around this sediment as a result. At the time, readings of Plato which emphasized the importance of the dramatic and political details of the Dialogues had been gaining some traction. But what you call for in *Being and Logos* goes much further than this insofar as it is an attempt at an even more *originary* reading of the text—one which seeks to disclose as much as may be possible for a contemporary audience, the ancient Greek experience of the Dialogues. My question is, What was it in your research and in your experience at the time that led to your impending sense of necessity and even urgency that such an originary reading of the text must be (and must still) be ventured?

JOHN SALLIS: At the time when I was preparing *Being and Logos*, the scene of Platonic interpretation was much bleaker than we might today suppose it to have been. So-called Platonism (a potpourri of vague generalizations) had covered over the Dialogues to the point that careful reading of them seemed to have become superfluous.

Even more obstructive than the construction of this Platonism was the approach fostered by analytic philosophy. This approach, which aims almost exclusively at exposing what it takes to be the arguments in the Dialogues, has even today not been abandoned in all quarters. It was the adherents of this approach whom I wanted to provoke when in *Being and Logos* I wrote that there were perhaps no arguments in the Platonic Dialogues.

In fact, in the early 1970s hardly any interpreter of the Dialogues took seriously the dramatic dimension of these texts. One of the most striking exceptions was Jacob Klein, whose commentary on the *Meno* broke through the encrusted views in order to return to the Dialogues themselves and to engage in a line-by-line reading attuned to the Greek text. Yet, in *Being and Logos*, I attempted not just to bring to light the dramatic dimension but also to show by means of a micro-reading how the Dialogues release an interplay between multiple dimensions: place (Piraeus, for example), time (the *Sophist on the day after the Theaetetus*), dramatic development (Alcibiades's entrance to the symposium), deeds (erga; Socrates educating Glaucon), and mythical elements (descent into Hades). At the same time, I wanted to bring the Dialogues, as multidimensional, to bear on the fundamental philosophical determinations of Greek thought (such as being and logos), but as they could be recast outside the Latinate translations and interpretations.

SM: In *Being and Logos*, one of the primary questions you seek to address by way of the Platonic Dialogues is: "what is philosophy?" You propose that this question may be approached by way of a subsequent guiding thread of two further questions: "Who is the philosopher?" And, more specifically, "Who is Socrates?" It would be wonderful to have you respond to a further question, perhaps set in relation to this guiding series of questions which you trace so carefully throughout your treatment of them in *Being and Logos*. The question is, "Who is Plato?" We have come to know Socrates primarily through various historical accounts of his life and, of course, through his appearances as a character and Dialogues written by his contemporaries, Plato and Xenophon. In these accounts and depictions, the Socratic mode of philosophy is one which seems very much bound up with and lived out in relation to the Athenian community—although oftentimes from the perspective of someone who is an outsider at the same time; however, Plato's philosophical approach, by way of his writings, seems to be something radically different from Socrates' direct engagement in and with the Athenian *polis*. In the Dialogues, Plato is at once able to preserve the memory of Socrates for future generations and to establish—perhaps even found—a philosophical community that has spanned the globe and been given renewed life across the generations since his time. How do you see the work of Plato as related to, and yet perhaps distinct from, the life and work of Socrates, especially in relation to the questions: "Who is the philosopher," and "What is philosophy?"

JS: Nietzsche is succinct: "Socrates, he who does not write." To this description one can counterpoise another: Plato, he who only writes. The complementarity can be filled out still further. Socrates does not write, but he appears almost everywhere, both in topographical terms (he wanders all around Athens questioning whomever he meets) and in textual terms (he appears as a character in most of the Dialogues). Plato writes; he is the author of all the Dialogues, yet he never appears in any of the Dialogues; there is only the briefest mention (only three times) of his presence or absence. One might well suppose that it is in terms of this complementarity that the question, "Who is the philosopher?" can be answered—or at least rendered less undecidable. In other words, the question is perhaps best taken up in reference to the dyad, writing/appearance or logos/phenomenon and to the possible ways in which this dyad can be composed.

While Plato is one who writes, who only writes, he remains withdrawn from his writings, from the Dialogues. He is the entirely withdrawn author, withdrawn as if he were dead to these writings; and to this extent we may never be in a position to answer the question, "Who is Plato?" As a result all the narrated Dialogues are, to the extent of the narration, double-authored, authored both by the narrator and by Plato. In some cases the dialogue and the narration, the discourses by the two authors, respectively, almost coincide. As in the *Republic*, in which the entire dialogue after the first word is both narrated by Socrates and written by Plato. This coupling is, I believe, exemplary.

SM: Given Plato's radical act of self-effacement from the very Dialogues that bear his name as author, do you believe that there is anything like a "Platonism" or a "Platonic philosophy" that can be derived from the Dialogues themselves? Do you think that there is any core of thought that joins the Dialogues together into something like a unity (although certainly not a "systematic" unity)? Or do you believe that the Dialogues form more loosely something like a constellation or set of constellations which, although certainly related to one another in various ways, resist the derivation of something like a center or central set of grounding thoughts or ideas that the Dialogues are somehow meant to convey—either independently or taken together?

JS: As goes without saying, the expression "Platonic philosophy" is so vague that any significant discourse about that which one intends by the expression has to be much more closely determined. But if it is a matter—still too vague—of asking whether there is a set of fundamental principles or established theses, the answer is yes and no. It is yes, because, as even the most cursory look at the Dialogues will show, there are certain determinations that are addressed. I deliberately avoid the word *concept*, since on this point I agree with Heidegger that in Greek thought there are no concepts—that is, as I would formulate it, it is Greek thought that first makes it possible to delimit anything like a concept. The Dialogues do address such themes as being (*Sophist*), knowledge (*Theaetetus*), virtue (*Meno*). But what is absolutely decisive is that at the very core of all these discourses there is questioning in play—like the nothing coiled up within the heart of being. The questioning is not always of the simple form "What is. . . ?" This is perhaps nowhere more evident than in the *Parmenides*, which repeatedly issues in aporias, and in the *Timaeus*, in which the second discourse undermines what was to have been the character (the temporality) of the first discourse. Even more radically, Timaeus's discourse on the chora undermines that very discourse—that is, the questioning undermines itself as the kind of questioning it is and points therefore to the need for a transition to another kind, a bastard kind, of discourse. Here there are no established principles but rather questioning in motion around that which is to be thought.

SM: I would like now turn to your general hermeneutic approach to the Dialogues. In your teachings and your writings about Plato (as well as in our discussions), you consistently adhere to the notion that, as a matter of hermeneutic principle, each dialogue really ought to be treated on its own—as something of an independent unity or whole. Each of the Dialogues is able to be taken up in its own right and on its own terms. You often say that any attempt to draw connections between one dialogue and another—whether dramatically or thematically—ought to be done rather sparingly and, even then, only with the utmost care that one is speaking to what is central to each.

In the opening to your interpretation of Plato's *Theaetetus*, which appears in the chapter titled "Monstrous Wonder. The Advance of Nature" in your 2016 book, *The Figure of Nature*, you mark a distinction between what you call the chronology and the topology of each of the Platonic Dialogues. There you suggest that it is the chronology which seems to be the most prominent locus of each dialogue's connection to one another—at least in their dramatic element. Yet, even there you say that

> [t]hough the chronology has the effect of extending the compass of the dialogue beyond its direct words and deeds, it is established and thus displayed within the dialogue itself and in many instances through correspondence with indications internal to the other pertinent Dialogues. In this sense it is an *internal* chronology even though its function is to refer the dialogue outside itself, beyond itself, establishing thereby a set of relations between the dramatic time of a dialogue and those of certain other Dialogues or events.[2]

You then go on to articulate the topography of a dialogue, which you say is comprised of "three distinct moments:" (1) "the articulation or partitioning of the dialogue," (2) "the directionalities operative in the dialogue," and (3) "the texture of the dialogue . . . constituted by the way in which different textual dimensions such as words and deeds as well as the various modes of discourse . . . are layered or woven together."[3] In light of this important distinction, I would like to afford you a space here, if you would like, to offer further commentary on why it is so important to let each Dialogue speak for itself and on its own terms, especially when the temptation to draw connections between Dialogues that might end up being either spurious or superficial is often times so readily available to the reader of the Dialogues.

JS: It is necessary to let each dialogue be taken on its own terms because—quite simply—each is a dramatic whole. To move casually from one dialogue to another would be almost like moving in this way among the Shakespearean dramas—from *A Midsummer Night's Dream* to *King Lear*, supposing that the actions of a character such as Bottom could throw light directly on the plight of Lear. On the other hand, I do not regard each dialogue as absolutely apart from all others. There are certainly relations between some Dialogues, but those relations are attested most directly by various dramatic aspects. An internal chronology links a number of Dialogues, as I have shown in *Being and Logos*. Topographical links can also be indicative, for example, the trilogy that takes place near a gymnasium where, as the first dialogue begins, Theaetetus has been exercising. There are also forms of questioning and philosophical determination that link certain Dialogues (here again the trilogy is exemplary), but in these cases a great deal of care needs to be taken, because of the often monstrous shape of the questioning.

SM: Changing gears just a bit, quite a bit really—I would like to wade into the issue of politics, especially since you have, relatively recently, taught courses on both Plato's *Statesman* (fall 2015—alongside a parallel conference and book publication)[4] and Plato's *Republic* (spring 2020) at Boston College. As you know, there has been a recent resurgence of books, articles, and reflections on Plato's *Republic* in particular in response the current political climate both in the United States and across the globe. Generally, I would like to provide you with a space here to offer any thoughts or reflections you might have as to why and how this renewed focus on Plato's Dialogues which deal specifically with politics might be viewed as being both fitting and timely. More specifically, I would like to ask you, in your own estimation, whether or not any potential solution or resolution to what many have begun to view as a worldwide political crisis might be gathered from Plato (not necessarily just from the *Republic*). This crisis has been defined by prominent political figures in the United States and abroad as something of a resurgent competition between democracies and both emerging and well-established autocracies worldwide. The general terms of this debate are that in increasingly polarized and partisan democracies there is an emerging inability for them to achieve consensus or even respond to other crises, such as the global climate crisis, in effective and meaningful ways. This in turn has given rise to the argument that only autocrats and autocracies can get anything done in the realm of politics. Is there anything to be garnered from this renewed turn toward the political elements of the Platonic Dialogues and the various models and treatments of government contained therein that you believe might offer a way through this global crisis of governance? What lessons do Plato's Dialogues contain that might be of some help, some assistance to us now?

JS: This question of politics, ranging all the way from Plato to contemporary issues is much too vast to be dealt with in the present context. I would simply—and without commentary—point to three loci in the Dialogues that might be regarded as bearing on these questions and concerns. The first is, of course, the description of the tyrant in the *Republic* and, along with this, the account of how democracy can deteriorate into tyranny. Our recent experience of our national political scene has made us acutely aware of how easily such tyranny can arise and has spurred reflection on how those who further such decay of political life can be limited in their effect. The second source to which I would point is the *Statesman*, specifically to the description of the statesman as the one who is able to weave together the various strands of citizens in the *polis*. This is a description that can counter the divisiveness that is all too prevalent today in the US. The third source is the *Timaeus*, which, especially through the chorology, can provide insight into how we need to rethink the very sense of nature so as to found a basis from which to address the threat of climate change.

I have attempted to address some of these concerns in a new book titled *Ethicality and Imagination*.

SM: The power of imagination is, of course, central to much of your work on figures from Plato to Kant and beyond. The imagination is a very difficult and nuanced topic wherever and whenever it appears in philosophical discourse, so I would like to direct your attention to just a particular moment of interest in it as it appears in Plato's Dialogues. Images abound in the Platonic corpus, whether in the various myths and stories told by Socrates and other speakers throughout, or even as specific modes of instruction, exploration, or elucidation drawn up by and for many of the interlocutors who appear in the Dialogues.

Images and the power of imagination—which both attends to and in some instances generates images itself—have a potentially duplicitous nature that Socrates, at the very least, seems to be aware of even as he makes repeated use of them in philosophical dialogue. That is, especially in moments like the central books of the *Republic*, Socrates acknowledges that we are oftentimes utterly dependent upon images in our various attempts to strive for the disclosure of the truth of a certain matter or idea—especially in conversation with others. On the other hand, as is discussed in Book X of the *Republic*, images always remain at a certain degree of removal from the truth and can even potentially lead us *away* from the truth when images are not recognized as such. I wonder then if you would say that images and the power of imagination are together something of a *pharmakon* in the Platonic treatment of them: they can be both a remedy and a poison with respect to the human condition—in this case our ignorance. And if this is the case, why then are images and the imagination still so necessary, so central to the pursuit of philosophy, especially as it is depicted within the Platonic Dialogues? Also, please feel free to use this space to offer reflections on why imagination has been such an important and recurring theme for you in your own work on Plato and beyond.

JS: In my book *Force of Imagination* I have traced the history of what is meant by the word imagination from Greek thought to the most recent discussions. Obviously I cannot repeat or even summarize that account here. So, I will limit what I say to a single matter, a matter—as so often—of translation. In the presentation of the divided line Socrates designates the lowest segment of the divided line by the term *eikasia*. In the criticism of art in Book X the word used is *phantasia*. Once this difference is noticed, the apparent duplicity vanishes. One realizes that it is produced by inattentiveness to the Greek words; the translation as imagination simply conflates the two words and the powers designated by them. *Eikasia* is not a matter of just calling up images, as when I say that I imagine a unicorn. Rather, eikasia names the power (*dunamis*) of looking through an image in such a way as to recognize that it is an image and thus to catch sight of the original that it images. Thus the prisoners in the cave come to recognize—presumably with the help of a teacher—that the images they see on the inner wall of the cave are merely images of the things passing behind their backs. It is a matter, so to speak, of movement through the images to the original. This is something quite different from what one understands today by the word imagination. In Book X of the *Republic*, it is a matter of phantasia, which is the incapacity to discern the original through the image—that is, an inability to see the image as an image. It is when this incapacity is in force that one mistakes an image for the original and thus fails to recognize the painting, for example, as a mere image.

SM: I would like to close with a question in relation to some of your latest work—much of which has been concerned with the idea of nature. Some recent examples of this work can be found in your 2016 books, published simultaneously, *The Figure of Nature* and *The Return of Nature*, and your very recent book, *Songs of Nature*, published in 2020, which contains your philosophical reflections on the work of globally renowned Chinese artist, Cao Jun. In each case, you show a deep concern with various ways in which nature may be encountered, experienced, and thought through from a philosophical point of view. In these works, you very delicately attempt to bring these various modes of encountering nature—the artistic, the ancient, and the philosophical—to light for your readers. In your treatment of the idea of nature, you also reflect on the emergence of *monstrosity* or the *monstrous* from within the confines of nature. You identify monstrosity as something that seems inherently paradoxical insofar as it is something that appears to us as *excessive*, as the manifestation of nature somehow exceeding its own natural limits and limitations, somehow still emerging *within* the domain of nature. And this is a phenomenon that you show throughout the course of *The Figure of Nature* that the ancient Greeks, in their philosophy, poetry, and artwork, were acutely aware of and attuned to. It seems to me, and you have indicated this in some of your more recent teaching and writing, that we human beings are now faced with something of a dual monstrosity of our own making. On one hand, there are the excessively violent and destructive forces that human beings have released upon nature, from within nature. On the other hand, nature seems to have mounted its own sort of monstrous response to the excesses of human activity, namely in the forms of storms, floods, fires, and other environmental anomalies, which have been occurring across the globe with an alarming increase in frequency and intensity. I would like to ask what you believe is so important, what might be gained or even regained, by taking up the Platonic encounter with these various forces of nature which now threaten the entirety of the environment that we live in. Just as in *Being and Logos*, one of your primary goals is to begin to sweep away much of the sediment that has been heaped upon the Platonic corpus over the centuries, I wonder if, so too, there has been a kind of sedimentation that has occurred in the human encounter with nature. Does your work on nature in general and in Plato and the ancients specifically constitute—at least in part—yet another effort to sweep away the sediment—in this case that has been heaped upon the very way in which we relate to nature itself. In short, do these works attempt to clear the way for a more originary encounter, not just with Platonic philosophy but also with nature itself?

JS: Questions concerning nature have been at the center of much of my recent work. By the title of my recent book *The Return of Nature* I want to express precisely the incursions by which humans and nature collide with each other. On the one hand, there is the technological assault on nature, which Heidegger diagnosed already in the middle of the last century. What, it seems to me, he did not grasp sufficiently is the extent to which this assault is driven by unbridled capitalism (and no less by its symmetrical opposite). On the other hand—and this is what it is most urgent to think through—there is the return of nature, its assault in monstrous forms upon humans and the very means by which they live. What I have tried to show is that these two assaults in their opposition are inseparable—that is, that we will never be able to address the "ecological crisis" until we address the technological assault on nature and the economic-political system that drives this assault.

The dialogue that bears most directly on such questions of nature is the *Timaeus*. In my book *Chorology* I have attempted to show that the chora in its indeterminateness and its eruptive power runs throughout all the things of nature and limits the exploitation to which nature will yield. In other books I undertake to show how this ultimate inviolability of nature is most powerfully set before our eyes by elemental nature, by earth, sky, ocean, air.

Notes

1 Sallis, *Chorology*, 4. The translation from *Timaeus* 29b is from Sallis. Cf. Also Sallis, *Plato's Statesman*, 1 and Sallis, *The Verge of Philosophy*, 11–12.
2 Sallis, *The Figure of Nature*, 59, my emphasis.
3 Ibid., 59–60.
4 See *Plato's Statesman: Dialectic, Myth, and Politics*, edited by John Sallis (Albany, NY: SUNY Press, 2017).

Bibliography

Sallis, John, *Chorology* (Bloomington, IN: Indiana University Press, 1999)
Sallis, John, *The Figure of Nature* (Bloomington, IN: Indiana University Press, 2016)
Sallis, John, *Plato's Statesman* (Albany, NY: SUNY Press, 2017)
Sallis, John, *The Verge of Philosophy* (Chicago, IL: The University of Chicago Press, 2007)

15
Plato's Final Dialogue
David Roochnik

He's in bed, a blanket over him, up to his chin. There's a wool covering on his head, but he's still cold. He sleeps much of the time. When he's awake, he allows only a few of the many people hoping to visit him to enter his room. His sister, Potone. Her son, and his successor as head of the Academy, Speusippus. And Artemis, a slave who has served his family for nearly all her fifty years.[1] She is the only person with whom he actually talks—he just listens to the others—but only when they are alone.

"Speusippus visits me every day," Plato says.

"Yes, I know," Artemis replies.

"He's a dunderhead, I'm afraid. For years, he was too intimidated to say much to me, but now he's a regular chatterbox. I suppose because he's so pleased with himself. I've named him as my successor. He and my sister know this, and of course you do too, but please, don't say a word to anyone else. I've written him into my will, and I want the announcement to be made after I'm gone—which will be soon."

"Got it, Chief," she replies without a hitch.

She's been calling him "Chief" for decades.

She was seventeen, slender and tall, almost gangly, with bright eyes radiating intelligence. He was forty-eight, a broad-shouldered man, as his old wrestling coach used to say.[2]

On a hot summer afternoon, she entered his office. He typically spent this time of day talking with students in the courtyard, and so she was surprised to find him sitting at his desk. His head was buried in his hands. He looked beaten.

"Are you okay, sir?" she asked.

He was startled, and at first, he did not recognize her. "Oh, I'm sorry," he said to her. "Artemis isn't it?"

"Yup, that's me."

"Is this your day to clean?"

"Yup," she said. "Same day every week."

"Right, of course. I'm sorry, I should have remembered."

He stood up slowly from his chair.

"Oh no, sir, there's no need! I can come back tomorrow."

"It's all right," he said. "You don't have to change your schedule. I'll leave for an hour or two."

"But you look tired, sir, and it's very hot outside. Why don't you lie down on your couch, and I'll bring you some cool water. I can clean tomorrow morning when you're in class. Really, it would be no trouble."

"You're right," he sighed. "I am tired. The geometry class was grueling today. Thank god Axiotheos was there. He saved me from making a big mistake in a proof I was outlining, and after the lecture he volunteered to help the students who were struggling, and I could get away. She's a blessing."

Her alert eyes narrowed in puzzlement, but she didn't say anything.

"You're sure it's no inconvenience to clean tomorrow?" he asked her, slumping into his chair.

"Nope, not at all. It just means I'll have this afternoon off," she replied cheerfully.

Her smile, which revealed a slight gap between her two front teeth, was effortless, bright, and warm. She was gorgeous.

"And what will you do with your free time?" he asked gently.

"Oh, I don't know," she said. "Maybe take a walk down the road, through the olive grove."

"But it's awfully hot, isn't it?"

"I don't mind," she said. "I'll wear a hat and walk slow. And bring a jug of water."

"I think the heat got to me when I was teaching," he said. "The classroom has no ventilation. After the first hour it was hard to breathe."

"And I bet it didn't smell too good either," she replied with a laugh. "All those boys sweating together."

He smiled. "I didn't notice the smell, but I suppose you're right."

"I love smells," she continued. "Only the nice ones, of course, not the nasties like stinky sweat. Sometimes I ask myself, which is better: taking a warm bath or smelling hyacinth? And you know what I think?"

"What?" he asked.

"Smelling hyacinth, and you know why?"

"No, why?"

"The reason my bath feels good is because I feel bad before I take it. I mean, I'm pretty grubby after a day of cleaning classrooms, and the bath refreshes me. It feels great to get clean because it feels terrible to be dirty. But then, after the bath, I start getting dirty all over again, and if I didn't get dirty, I'd never want to take a bath. Same goes with a nice meal. I'm starving by dinnertime, and that's why it feels good to fill myself up. But then I get empty and have to do it all over again. And if I never got hungry, I wouldn't want to eat. Smell's not like this. I don't have to feel bad to enjoy smelling something nice, and I don't feel bad afterward either. It's not like drinking wine. A fragrance just hits me, and I smile, and when it's gone it leaves no pain behind. It just comes, itself by itself, for free—which is one reason why I like walking through the grove in the summer. So many wonderfuls! Sage, thyme, boxwoods, crisp and dry."

Delighted by the young woman's free flow of thought, he listened carefully.[3]

"I'm sorry, sir," she said. "I shouldn't be blabbering."

She did not, however, look the least bit embarrassed. Instead, she seemed to be amused at herself. "Not at all," he replied. "You've cheered me up. I will take your advice and lie down for a while. Why don't you go take your walk, enjoy your free time, and come back tomorrow morning when I am in class?"

"Righto, sir!" she said. "Well, bye-bye, then."

"Bye-bye," he replied, his look lingering as she walked toward the door. "Then."

A few days later he fell ill. He was a strong man, but he had been working too much and sleeping too little. For the first time in anyone's memory, he canceled his lectures and took to bed with a fever. Without being asked to, she tended to him. She wiped his forehead with a cool sponge. She freshened his bed, fed him some lukewarm broth, filled his jug with fresh water. He smiled appreciatively but did not speak.

When she entered his room on the third day, he was sitting up in bed reading a book. She blurted, "You're better, sir!"

"Yes, much better. You were an excellent nurse, Artemis, and I thank you very much."

"It was a pleasure. You know sir, if you don't mind me saying, you need to change a few things in your life. First, you work too hard. You should take a nap in the afternoon instead of talking to your students after class—especially when it's hot. They can wait, and then you'll have strength for the rest of the day. And you need to get some exercise. You should go to the gym at least three times a week. It'll help you sleep better at night. And make sure you eat well balanced meals! Lots of greens with olive oil, and not too much honey or wine."

He smiled. "Maybe you're right," he said. "Starting tomorrow I will take a nap in the afternoon."

"Promise?"

"Yes, Artemis, I promise."

"Good move, sir!" she said cheerfully. "You'll feel better, I'm sure."

The next day Plato announced to his class that he would no longer be available to them for questions after his lectures. Instead, he would be returning to his office, and he did not wish to be disturbed. He would, however, be available to talk in the evenings, when it wasn't so hot.

A few minutes after he settled on his couch for his mandatory nap, she entered the room. Without knocking. He looked surprised, but not alarmed, to see her. She smiled at him. When she undid the tie holding her brown hair, it rolled and flowed down her breast. Then, without a moment's hesitation, she took off her clothes, and walked to his couch. Her step was light and cheerful. Entirely comfortable in her own skin, sure of herself, she stood next to him. When he moved over to make room, she lay down next to him.

From that day forward she always called him "Chief," at least when they were alone—which they were almost every afternoon for thirty years.

❖

"I'm right, aren't I? Speusippus is a bore, isn't he?" Plato asks Artemis.

His voice, which has always been thin, is now even weaker. She must lean close to him in order to hear. He's glad; he can smell her hair.

"Not my place to judge," she says. "But let's put it this way. I wouldn't attend one of his lectures if you paid me."

He chuckles, which leads to a coughing fit. She helps him take a few sips of water and after a minute or two he calms down.

"My nephew likes to gossip, and the sad truth is I don't mind," he says slowly. "His stories are easier to digest than a philosophical argument."

"Depends on the argument, doesn't it, Chief?"

"I suppose," he says. "Anyway, Speusippus tells me the whole city is waiting for me to die, eager to learn who will be the next head of the Academy. He says all sorts of rumors are spreading."

"It's true."

"Apparently Philo is telling people I'm being devoured by lice. How strange. Lice may be annoying, but they can't hurt you. It's probably more dangerous for a man to bite a louse than to be bitten by one."[4]

"Do you remember the louse-catcher in the *Sophist*?" she interjects enthusiastically. "That one was delicious."

He does remember . . . vaguely.

He had been agonizing for months over the *Sophist*. His hope was that this dialogue would expose the limitations of technical thought. Or, as Artemis had put it, the limits of analysis. As much as he admired mathematics, the quintessentially analytic discipline, he was convinced it was incapable of addressing the most pressing of human questions, the ones Socrates had taught him must be asked, even if they cannot be answered. As Artemis had once said, numbers neither laugh nor cry.

He created a character, the Stranger from Elea. A serious thinker, and very much the professor, he practiced a method, which he called division. To illustrate it, he began with a mundane example: the fisherman. The Stranger's first step was to identify a general concept under which the fisherman could be subsumed. Since he was a skilled professional, he possessed a *technê*, technical knowledge or expertise. Second, the Stranger announced that there were two forms of *technê*. The first he called the productive, which, like carpentry, brings into being something that did not previously exist; the second, the acquisitive, acquires things already in existence. Fishing belonged to the latter.

Next, there were two forms of the acquisitive *technê*: in the first, there is a voluntary exchange between two parties; the second is coercive. Next, he divided the coercive branch into fighting and hunting. Fishing belonged to the latter. On and on the conceptual divisions proceeded, until they finally ended with this:

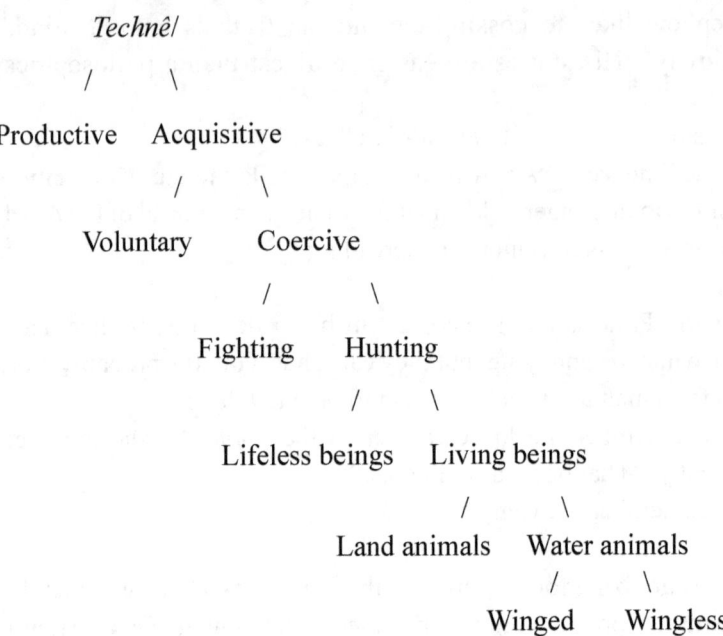

A definition had been reached: fishing is a hunting *technê* whose objects are wingless water animals.[5]

He showed her the sketch, and the draft he had been working on, and, as usual, before finishing it, she began to ask questions. It wasn't clear, she said, whether the target of this division was the fisherman or the *technê* of fishing. These are not the same, she insisted. The former is flesh and blood; the latter, an abstraction. And why did the Stranger's division leave out animals that can fly, namely, birds, but then classify them as a species of water animals? Was he wedded to the binary? If so, wouldn't such rigidity cripple his attempt to understand?

Plato smiled with delight. He explained that he was building these gaps into the division precisely to invite the reader to ask such questions.

"And read this," he said excitedly. He turned to a passage later in the text. Here the Stranger was discussing what he called the *technê* of discrimination. Its first cut distinguished the worse from the better; his second, like from like. The former is purification, and it has two forms: one separates the worse from the better in the body; the second does the same work in the soul.

```
                    Discrimination
                   /              \

        Like from Like    Better from Worse
                            (purification

                             /        \

                           Body       Soul
```

Now, while the reader's attention is naturally drawn to psychic purification, which is where they expect to find philosophy itself, Plato had the Stranger go into some detail with the body. Medicine and gymnastic, he said, were two examples, but so, too, was the lowly *technê* of the bath-keeper, who is an expert in sponging!

"The *technê* of sponging," she said with alarm. "You gotta be kidding me!"

"Just keep reading."

She did.

After a couple of minutes she looked up, her eyes blazing with excitement. "Wow! You nailed it!"

"Maybe," he said cautiously. "I was worried it might be heavy-handed."

"Nope!" she said confidently. "You let him show his cards, and then hang himself in the process!"

She read the passage aloud.

> My method of argument treats both the *technê* of medicine and of sponging as the same. For both are forms of purification, even though the former benefits us greatly, while the latter only a little. The goal of my method is to gain insight about what is alike and what is not alike in all forms of *technê*, and for this reason it honors them all equally. Because of their similarity as *technai*, it does not treat some as more ridiculous than others. For example, if someone, in trying to clarify what hunting is, uses the example of generalship, the method does not count the general as more dignified than the louse-catcher.[6]

"The louse-catcher! Now who the hell is an expert in catching lice?" she said, trying to stifle her laugh. "I mean, the only people I've ever seen doing it are nurses taking care of children. Or mothers."

Plato smiled mischievously.

"According to the Stranger, a human being is no different from a louse," she continued. "And he seems to be proud of himself, as if he's a tough guy who's not afraid to deflate our pretensions to being something special in this universe. You nailed him, Chief. He's a bloody dehumanizer!"

Retrieving the various moves he made in the *Sophist* is far too difficult for him, and he quickly stops trying.

"I don't know what I did to offend Philo," he says. "Perhaps it was years ago when I reprimanded him in a seminar. He'd been answering my questions before I had even finished asking them. He was loud and aggressive, and he interrupted other students. It's a kind of bullying I detest, and I lost my temper. 'Can you please let someone else talk!' I barked at him. He didn't say another word. I don't usually speak to students that way."

"Sorry, Chief, but it wasn't Philo you barked at. It was Philippus. When you told me the story, you were nearly trembling with rage."

"Philippus? Really?" he asks. "Doesn't matter. Whoever he was, he must have been seething all these years, and now he's getting his revenge. Imagine, me being devoured by lice."

"Guys like him are a dime a dozen," she says.

"Indeed," he answers, agreeing. "Here's another one. Hermippus claims I ate too much fish at a wedding, and now my stomach is killing me.[7] Well, it's true, I did go to a wedding feast just before I got sick, but I don't remember whose it was. Maybe my niece's daughter? She's a nice girl, isn't she? And I probably did eat some fish. But, honestly, I only took a few bites."

"As usual, Chief," she says gently, as she takes his hand. "And, yes, it was your niece's daughter, Archeanassa."

He stares at her hand with such longing that she wants to cry.

"He's resented me for a long time," he says. "Hermippus is a poet, or at least he thinks he is, and he never forgave me for writing the *Ion*. He thought I was making fun of him when I had Socrates criticize the poets for being inspired, possessed, out of their minds.[8] Like so many of my readers, he thought Socrates was no more than my mouthpiece. The fools never bother to ask themselves why I wrote dialogues in the first place. Instead of explaining to my readers what I think and why, instead of speaking in my own voice, I created characters and placed them into specific settings where they talked to particular people. Every line I wrote has to be read with this fact in mind. Still, readers like Hermippus insist on identifying Socrates with me, his author. No finesse. When they bump into something they don't like, they attribute it to me and then condemn me for having written it."

His voice sputters.

She has heard this complaint many times, especially during the past two weeks when he has been bedridden. Still, she squeezes his hand more tightly, as if to give him the energy to repeat it again.

"Nothing wrong with being out of your mind once in a while, is there, Chief?"

"Not at all," he says. "As usual, Aristotle got it right. He said my dialogues were in between poetry and prose.[9] And Olympiodorus compared my dialogues to swans, flying from tree to tree, eluding their hunters. They resist definitive interpretation."

He pauses, looks thoughtful. "But you know what?"

"What, Chief?" she says quietly.

"I've never seen a swan in a tree. Have you?"

"No." She chuckles softly. "But I do remember one afternoon when you woke up wild-eyed from a dream. You told me that you had just seen a newborn swan in your lap, and the bird suddenly sprouted feathers and with a sweet little cry flew away."[10]

"I don't remember," he said, annoyed with himself.

She chuckles again. "Well, I sure do. The symbolism wasn't exactly subtle. You had a quite an erection, my friend."

"I did?" he asks, amused at the story, wishing he could remember.

"A mighty oak!" she says, this time with a full throaty laugh.

He laughs too, but his cough quickly overwhelms him. When it finally dies down, he whispers to her, "Stop it with the jokes, would you please."

She smiles. "Not sure I can promise you that, Chief, but I'll try my best."

He nods.

"Man, you didn't do much laughing when we first got together," she says. "You were one serious guy."[11]

"Either that or maybe you weren't very funny back then."

She laughs. "Sorry, Chief, but I've been funny since I was born. It's how I charmed your father. Even when I was just three or four, he thought I was marvelous. I had so much energy. I was either talking or running.

He was tightly wound, your father, but I could always make him laugh. He gave me the name Artemis and made sure I learned how to read and write."

Plato grimaces when she speaks of his father. He changes the topic.

"Now why," he asks, "would Hermippus say I ate too much fish at a wedding? Do you think he wants to remind folks I've never been married? This bothers some people, you know. They think the job of a good citizen is to produce more citizens, which I haven't done. In their eyes this makes me politically suspect."

"Well, they're not all wrong, are they, Chief?" she asks gently.

For a brief moment he looks sad.

"Or maybe he wants to suggest I'm impotent," he continues. "They used to tell a terrible story about my father. They said he tried to force himself on my mother but was unable to complete the act. When he ceased his assault, Apollo appeared to him in a dream. The next day she was pregnant. So I was the result of some sort of coupling between an impotent rapist and a virgin mother."[12]

"People don't know what to make of you. They feel threatened. You're too much for them."

"But not for you?"

"No, but I'm special."

He smiles, a little. "Apparently," he continues, "Molon is saying I had affairs with all sorts of men. Aster, Alexis, Phaedrus, Agathon. He even claims I wrote love poems to them!"[13]

"Little do they know," she says.

"Indeed," he replies. "I've always preferred women, both in bed and everywhere else. I have two as students, you know."

Of course she knows.

"And one of them, Lastheneia, helped me a lot when I was writing the *Symposium*. I asked her to become my coauthor, but she refused. She wouldn't even let me dedicate it to her."

Plato pauses, lost in thought.

"Anyway," he continues, "I made Speusippus promise me she can continue her work in the Academy after I'm gone. He didn't look happy, but he said he would abide by my wishes."

She grimaces but does not say anything.

Although they have never discussed it, she knows he has granted her freedom in his will and provided her with a comfortable income. On one hand, she doesn't care. Her life has been good. On the other, she is relieved. She won't have to take orders from Speusippus.

"And Axiothea is a terrific geometer," Plato continues. "When she first came to study with me—and god knows when that was—she dressed like a man, called herself Axiotheos, and to this day she thinks she has me fooled. But I've known for years."[14]

He pauses again, closes his eyes, goes into himself for a minute, or more.

"Molon is a fool," he continues when he returns. "Still, what he's been saying about me and Dion is painful. For it's true, I did love him."

Now a surge of energy seems to be moving through him.

"I know," she says softly.

"He was the best of the best.[15] Smart, eager to learn, full of energy. And he cared, oh my, did he care. And not just about philosophy. But about other people. He wanted to make a difference in the city, and he believed, he actually believed, he could put my ideas into practice. He thought the two of us together could teach Dionysius how to be a good ruler, and he convinced me to go to Syracuse and advise him. And I did, two or three times, even though I hated sailing. Deep down I knew it was crazy. My ideas aren't meant to be applied, at least not the way Dion thought they could be. My city was in speech, a paradigm, laid up in heaven, not here on earth.[16] But Dion, well, he could charm a snake. It's not enough, he told me, just to talk. We had to act, change the world, make it better. He made me feel selfish—like my father used to do—which is why I sailed to Sicily that last time. God knows when, but I was already old. Sick to my stomach the whole trip, I did nothing but lie on my cot, only getting up to vomit. Just to gratify Dion. Huge mistake.

"Karudendra, the poet from Lesbos, once said my *Phaedrus* was inspired by Dion and that I changed my ideas about madness and love because of my infatuation with him.[17] Nonsense, of course, but I did love him. He was the best of the best. I don't know, maybe I did have sex with him. But I doubt it."

"Sometimes it's easy to forget that stuff, Chief. Just a few minutes of friction."

She chuckles. He does not.

"My god, Artemis, they cut Dion down like a dog—which means I was right when I had Socrates say at his trial that no one who cares about justice itself will survive for long if he enters politics. No, the best thing is to find a quiet place to talk with a few intelligent people, and talk about justice, and beauty, and the good, there. Not in the Assembly."[18]

"A place like the Academy," she says.

He does not register her remark. His old face is flushed. "My father would have been appalled if he heard me."

He's been talking about his father a good deal recently, and often the deep past is more vivid to him than what happened minutes ago. This causes Artemis to wonder about memory. Is it somehow connected to a part of the body, like an old piece of wax so hard that it can no longer absorb a new imprint? She tells herself to ask Aristotle what he thinks.[19]

"My god," he says, interrupting her thoughts, "he was furious with me when I started spending time with Socrates. He called him a parasite who gave nothing back to his city. Every night at the dinner table, he would remind me and my brothers, over and over again, that we were descendants of King Codrus,[20] and that it was our duty to continue our family's tradition of service to Athens."

He pauses and looks troubled.

"He was loud," he finally says, "but he never hit us. Except for all those lectures about politics, he never talked to us either."

He pauses again.

"My brother had it worse than me, though. I could always escape into my daydreams, but Glaucon couldn't. While I would sit at the dinner table, tuned out, not saying a word, he would challenge our father, just to get him mad, and then the two of them would end up screaming at each other. My father held Socrates personally responsible for turning Glaucon away from politics.[21] He probably would have voted guilty had he been on the jury."

He closes his eyes, but they tighten, as if he is looking for something.

"Glaucon didn't end well," he says. "We weren't close, you know."

Of course she knows.

"He died many years ago, and I don't remember what I felt. I suspect it wasn't grief."

He pauses.

"It's a good thing the old man is gone. If he could see what I've become, if he could see me with a woman like you, he'd think I was trash, irresponsible, selfish, no true Athenian. And maybe he'd be right."

He looks crestfallen and exhausted.

"Come on, buck up, buckaroo," she says softly. "Being selfish isn't necessarily bad. It depends on what you think the self is. Your version of the self was dialogical, not atomic, and that's how you've lived your life. Teaching, talking to other people, especially to the young, and even to women. No problem if a guy like you is selfish, because you've got a good one. You followed in Socrates' footsteps, my friend, and—"

"I never liked him, you know," he interrupts, his energy suddenly restored.

She smiles.

"Really?" she says, feigning surprise.

He ignores her sarcasm. "Speusippus said someone is spreading the rumor that I'm delirious, and I'm begging Socrates to forgive me for not being with him in his jail cell on the day he died. It's true, I wasn't there. I was home, sick. But the truth is—and I've never told anybody this—I wasn't that sick, and the jail wasn't far from my house, and I could have mustered the strength to visit him if I really wanted to. Cebes and Simmias made a long trip. Aeschines and Antisthenes were there. Of course, Megacles, his great buddy, was too. But not me, and you know why?"

"Why?" she says agreeably, having heard it all before.

"I didn't want to."

He falls silent for nearly a minute. She fears she is losing him. But then he resumes.

"I never understood what he saw in Megacles," he says. "I think he made his money in leather. I overheard them talking once, and you can't imagine how crude their language was. And the way they laughed together! Like drunken swineherds! Well, Socrates himself didn't come from much of a family either. His father was a stoneworker, and his mother a midwife. Still, why did he like Megacles more than me? Because I came from a privileged family? Was he jealous of me because I was rich and young?"

"And handsome, with the broad shoulders of a wrestler," she says merrily.

"My god, he was fierce!" he says, ignoring her. "He'd sink his teeth into a question and not let go, and if he needed to talk all night, that's what he do. Totally focused, nothing else mattered. But he was stone cold and a bully. You either played by his rules or you didn't play at all. Such a hard man! If you weren't a philosopher, you were a nobody. He really meant it when he said the unexamined life is not worth living for a human being. My god, how cruel! It means the vast majority of people lead worthless lives!"

He begins to cough but not for long.

She asks him, "Did he actually say that, Chief, or did you give put those words into his mouth in the *Apology*?"[22]

"Eh, what's that?" he asks, looking befuddled.

She does not repeat the question, although she is genuinely curious.

He rests for a minute. "He turned me around, though," he continues. "Before I met him I assumed my life would unfold in the Assembly and on the battlefield, like everyone else. But listening to him talk, watching him tear people to shreds, especially big shots—like *politikoi* and technocrats—made me realize they didn't know what they were talking about. Nor, I had to admit, did I. It felt like the ground under my feet was giving way. *Aporia* he called it, and he convinced me it was good. I hung on his every word. He made me want to be a philosopher. But not like him. No, from the beginning I knew I couldn't possibly be like him.

"He had huge hands, a stoneworker's hands, and a thick strong body. I was thick and strong too, but my body was gym-built. His was just his."

He closes his eyes for nearly a minute and seems to be dozing.

Suddenly springing back to life, he says, "I was a good wrestler, you know. But not as good as some people think. They say I competed in the Isthmian games.[23] Flattering but not true. Yes, I was strong and quick—hard to believe now that I'm peeing into a diaper and can't move my legs—but I lacked the killer instinct. The great ones, like Socrates, they hate to lose, but I didn't. I always tried to win, but I didn't really care as much as I should have. For me it was the joy of competition, not the laurel wreath that went to the victor. There were a few times when, just because I knew I was better than my opponent, I lost interest, and then I was the one to get pinned. And I never got angry when I lost to an opponent who was better than me. Still, I loved wrestling. I learned more about religion from it than I did from all the silly ceremonies."

She wants him to slow down and explain, but fearing she would impede his jumpy monologue, she refrains. She wonders whether the light burns bright just before it goes out.

"Before meeting him," Plato continues, "I thought I'd become a playwright, and I even wrote some tragedies when I was young. People say I burned them after I heard Socrates speak.[24] But it's not true. I still have those plays somewhere in the house. Maybe you know where they are. I may have written some comedies too. I can't remember. Maybe they were funny."

"I bet they were funny, Chief."

"I doubt it. I wrote them before I met you," he says to her with great affection.

"Right." She chuckles. "They probably weren't funny at all. But your dialogues do have their moments."

He does not smile. He may not have heard her.

"Like when you had Socrates say that Meno was surrounded by a swarm of virtues. Like bees. That was pretty funny. I mean, that guy was a big creep. Or when you had those men pushing each other to make room for the beautiful Charmides to sit next to them on the couch, and one of them actually falls! Or when Socrates was teaching Hippothales, who's madly in love with Lysis, how to deliver a seduction speech. But he demonstrates this on Lysis himself. Poor old Hippothales, he doesn't realize that after Socrates, he no longer stands a chance![25] Crazy stuff. You had some juice back in the day."

"He never wrote a word, you know," he says. "As if his thoughts were so precious he couldn't tarnish them by putting them on papyrus or scratching them into wax."

"But you nailed him in the *Phaedrus*!" she says enthusiastically. "When Socrates goes on and on about how terrible writing is. He says it ruins our memories since we can just look stuff up in a book, instead of looking inside ourselves, and that writing makes us seem smart even when we're not. And he's so afraid of misinterpretation. He says a book is like an orphan, alone in the world, and it has no one to protect it from the bad readers who will distort it. You know, quote lines out of context. Writing is inferior to in-the-flesh conversation, where I can correct you if you misunderstand me, and you can do the same for me, and I can adjust what I'm saying to your needs. If I'm talking to an old male philosopher—like yourself, for instance—I say one thing, but if I'm talking to a lowly slave girl like myself, quite another. And if I think someone is just plain incapable of understanding, I can walk away. Talking is flexible, writing is rigid, and its one size fits all. It's like a painting. Says the same thing to everybody.[26]

"Fantastic stuff, Chief! The most famous critique of writing ever written! How cool is that? They're gorgeous, your dialogues."

In her excitement, she lets go of his hand, stands, and begins to wave her arms. Fortunately, she catches herself quickly, sits back on the side of his couch, and clasps his hand once more. Her touch brings him back.

"Socrates depended on Megacles to pay his bills, you know," he says as if he didn't hear a word of what she said. "He didn't have a drachma to his name. He was never home for Xanthippe and his children. I say if you're going to have a wife and children, you're obligated to take care of them. He didn't do that. I'm not sure he even knew they were there.

"I didn't like him, and I didn't want to be like him, and that's why I didn't go to the jail cell. Yes, I was sick, but I could have made the trip. But something kept me in my bed that day. Back then I had no idea what. Now I do. He didn't need me. He had Megacles."

He pauses, presses the bony index finger of his right hand against the bridge of his nose, goes inside of himself for nearly a minute.

She waits patiently.

"My father was wrong," he says when he opens his eyes. "Socrates wasn't the parasite. I was. I took all I could get from him and gave nothing back. I didn't go to his jail cell. He didn't need me. I didn't love him. But I did respect him, and I made him young and beautiful in my dialogues.[27] If Speusippus manages to preserve my writings, he'll be remembered. Thanks to me. Not Megacles."

"And not to Xenophon either.[28] You may not have loved him, Chief, but my god, you honored him mightily. You were loyal."

He grunts softly.

"How did the writing go this morning, Chief?" Artemis asked cheerfully.

"Not too bad," Plato replied.

"Still working on the *Agathon*?"

"Yes."

"Well, I'm going to say it one more time, and I don't care if it pisses you off. You should change the title. Agathon doesn't deserve top billing, and you know it."

"But I love the play on words. *To Agathon*. The Good. Of course, he's not good at all, which makes it perfect."

"I get it, but this dialogue doesn't focus on him or any other character. Not even Socrates. I mean, you gave Aristophanes pride of place by putting him smack in the middle. You know, he's the fourth of the seven speakers."

"He's serious competition for Socrates. For philosophy."

"And he's funny as hell," she said. "And then you had Alcibiades crash the party and put the kibosh on Socrates' ascent passage."

"Diotima's ascent passage, please," he said.

"Whatever. The point is, this dialogue is not like the *Euthyphro* or *Crito* where there's only one guy he's talking to. Or like the *Laches* or the *Lysis*, where the title points to the most interesting character, even if he's not the main speaker. No, it's more like a chorus. Seven speakers, and each of contributing to the whole. Please don't call it the *Agathon*."

He looked thoughtful. "What should its title be then?"

"Why not call it the *Symposium*. The drinking party."

"Tell him, it was for his own good," he says abruptly. His voice is getting weaker.

"Tell who?" she asks.

"Aristotle. I did it for his own good. He needs to do things his way, not mine, maybe run his own school. I had to push him out of here. He and Speusippus never got along, you know. Tell him this. Please."

She can feel his hand in hers, trying to squeeze.

"Of course I will," she says softly. "Don't worry, he'll understand. I promise."

Although he was sixty, Plato was still a vigorous lover, at least on those few occasions when he was in the mood, which he had been that afternoon. Afterward, they were lying on the couch talking, their shoulders touching as they gazed at the ceiling.

"You should see this kid, from up north somewhere. He's really something," he said.

"Yeah, how so," she asked languorously, as if she did not want to awaken from a pleasant dream.

"He gets everything and fast. He's only been here a few months, and he's read all my dialogues already. And he's been asking me questions about them. Respectful, but I can tell he wants to sink his teeth into me."

"Just like me," she said as she yawned.

"Yes, just like you," he said, and he kissed her on the cheek. "No, I take it back. No one's like you. You're *sui generous*."

"What's that mean?"

"One of a kind."

"Sweet," she said.

"But this kid, Aristotle, he's only seventeen . . ."

"Same age as me when I met you!"

"Yes, I suppose he is. Anyway, I get the feeling he'll be able to do anything he puts his mind to. He's studying astronomy, geometry, comparative anatomy, Sophocles's tragedies, and the Athenian constitution."

"And your dialogues," she interjected.

"Yes, those too. You should see him when he's reading. His body is completely still, and his eyes never turn away from the book. I've never seen anybody so comfortable sitting in a chair. And I've heard from other students that he stays up most of the night reading. I'm sure his mind is more powerful than mine."

"Watch the rash judgment, Chief. He's got plenty of time to go wrong."

"I suppose, but I'm pretty sure he's the real thing. This morning, I saw him standing next to a bush. Hyacinth, I think. Full bloom, and bees buzzing like mad in the flowers. He was looking at them when I went for my walk, and he was still looking when I returned. I coughed to get his attention. He was startled, but when he saw it was me, he nearly ran to my side. Without saying hello, he asked me if I had ever noticed that bees continually cross their front legs. I certainly hadn't, but before I could say a word, he launched into his theory. He told me that because they have hard, weak eyes, they need to clear away anything that lights upon them, and they use their feet to do this."[29]

"I guess," she said, completely uninterested.

"When he's not busy in the field or with his books, he's talks up a storm. I'm going to have to put a bridle on him at some point.[30] But, my god, his energy! There's something remarkable about him, and I can't quite put my finger on it. He seems to be—I don't know—at home in the world. Yes, that's it! He likes every part of it, and that's why he's interested in everything. Studying makes him happy."

"Cool," she said, wanting him to stop talking.

"I could never do what he does. I'm not comfortable sitting, and I can't stand still for hours on end, like he does when he's watching bees or dissecting cuttlefish. I'm too restless and always a step ahead of myself. I'm never at home in the world."

"Not even with me right now?" she said as she nuzzled his neck.

He chuckled. "This is as close as I come."

He began to tickle her in the ribs.

"Hey, quit it!" she said, genuinely annoyed.

He stopped.

"Do you remember that time when you had some students at the house for a little symposium?" she asked, now fully awake. "They were having a good time, but after twenty minutes, you snuck into the kitchen to hang out with me. You sat down at the table and started planning your next party. I couldn't believe my ears."

"I used to hate myself for being like that. You know, always looking to the future. I thought I was missing out on the present."

"But you're easier on yourself these days," she said as she nibbled on his ear. "You're more comfortable in your own skin. Thanks to me, of course."

He fondled her breast affectionately. "It's true. I stopped beating myself up for not being in the moment—as that numbskull Aristippus likes to say—when I came to understand that there was no moment for me to be in. Time is a flow from future to past, and the present is no more than an indivisible gateway between the two. We're temporal beings, Artemis, at our core, and painfully aware that everything we love, including ourselves, is passing away. No wonder we're restless. I guess you could say I've become more comfortable with my discomfort."

She laughed. "At home with being homeless."

"It was writing, you know, that saved me."

"How so?" she asked.

"When I was a kid, I'd drive my tutors crazy because I couldn't sit still. All I wanted was to go to the gym and wrestle or run around outside with my friends. And even as an adult, I always read too fast, and my concentration would waver. What changed things was when I started taking notes as I was reading. I remember the first time that I worked my way through Parmenides's poem. I'd copy a line and then try to explain it in my own words, and I found that it helped me stick with it and pay attention better. Writing gave my hands something to do. It relaxed me, like walking does today, and I could do it for hours. Writing made me a reader. Truth is, writing made me a thinker. Without it I wouldn't be able to concentrate."

"You know what I think, Chief?"

"No, but I hope you'll tell me, Artemis."

"That you could boil down Diotima's speech in the *Symposium* to something super simple."

"And what would that be?"

"You know how Socrates explains to Agathon that love is the desire for something we don't have, something we lack?"

"Yes. Although don't forget to add it's not only something we lack but also something we are aware of lacking."

"Exactly! Because her whole point is that what human beings are most aware of lacking, what we, like, totally don't have, is permanence. Because we can feel deep in our bones that time never stops flowing, and we know that everything we have, everything we love, is going to pass away, and soon, what we want most of all is something that lasts forever. That's why you're restless. You're never satisfied with what's standing before you because you know it'll be gone in two shakes of a lamb's tail. You always want more, you're trying to get beyond, to, you know, the Forms, changeless and eternal."

He let her words sink in. "And you don't quite approve?"

"I love it, Chief, even though hanging with Beauty Itself isn't exactly my idea of a good time."

He laughed and kissed her.

"So, this kid Aristotle . . ."

"There's more?" she said, feigning impatience.

"He loves my 'what is it?' dialogues, but I think he takes them more seriously than me. He really thinks you can get definitions, articulate an essence, or what he calls a 'what-it-is-to-be.'[31] That seems to be his favorite word these days."

"And if you ask him, what is love? What would he say?" she asked. She put her hand between his thighs.

"He'd quote Diotima, I hope. A powerful spirit, a *daimôn*, in-between, *metaxu*, the mortal and the immortal, binding them together into a whole."

"*Metaxu*. I love that word," she said.

"Burn it," he says.

His body is inert, except for his face, which is twitching with agitation. His voice is now nearly inaudible. She has to place her ear close to his mouth in order to hear.

"Burn what, darling?" she asks softly.

"The *Laws*. It's boring."

In fact, she agrees with him. It is boring and far too long. In fact, she memorized only one passage in the whole of it. "Let us be serious with the serious, and playful with the playful, and by nature only god is worthy of complete seriousness. And we humans? No more than playthings of the gods, and so let every one of us, man and woman alike, spend our lives playing as beautifully as we can."[32]

But she doesn't say this. Instead, she says, "Oh hush. Get yourself better and we'll work on it together. We can spruce it up."

She thinks he has understood, for he looks at her sadly. Then his eyes glaze over. Afraid he is leaving, she grips his hand even more tightly, as if trying to squeeze the last bit of vitality out of his aged shell.

"*Metaxu*, me and you. Remember, Chief?"

He says nothing.

"*Metaxu*. You know, in-between. What Diotima calls Eros. 'In-between the divine and the mortal, completing both, binding together the whole itself to itself.'[33] Beautiful words, Chief. Among your best. I only wish I understood them."

She cannot tell if he is breathing.

"We have so much more to talk about. It feels like we just got started," she says.

He says nothing.

"*Metaxu* me and you? You remember, don't you? It's what we would say when we wanted to go to bed. I loved hearing those words from you, Chief. People wouldn't believe how silly you could be. At least when you were with me. But that was a long time ago."

For the first time since she has been keeping vigil, she cries.

He notices.

She can sense him trying to smile, which he cannot do. But he does manage to whisper.

"No such thing."

"No such what?"

"Long time." he says. He closes his eyes.

"Right," she says, understanding what he means. Time, he used to say, was no more than an image of eternity.[34]

"Pretty crazy stuff, this philosophy of yours," she says. "But you did a good job, Chief. You kept your cool, your humor, and you always smelled good. You weren't scared; you didn't complain. But you didn't want to die. No, you liked being here, with me. You weren't like Socrates. Philosophy as the preparation for death and dying! What garbage! For you, philosophy was celebration.

"Wasn't it, Chief?"

She falls silent for a minute or maybe two. "I don't know what I'll do without you," she says quietly.

A thought, dark and unfamiliar, flits through her mind. Maybe she should plunge a knife deep into her chest and lie down next to him. But it leaves as quickly as it had entered.

"Don't worry," she says. "I'll figure it out."

Notes

1. Artemis is mentioned only as a slave manumitted in Plato's will (Diogenes Laertius, *The Lives of Eminent Philosophers*, III.42).
2. Diogenes Laertius, *The Lives of Eminent Philosophers*, III.4.
3. Socrates offers this description of smell at *Republic*, 584b.
4. Plato's thin voice (Diogenes Laertius, *The Lives of Eminent Philosophers*, III.5). Death by lice (Ibid, 41). For more on this topic, see Sergi Grau, 'How to Kill a Philosopher: The Narrating of Ancient Greek Philosophers' Deaths in Relation to their Way of Living,' 365.
5. This is an oversimplified version of Plato's *Sophist*, 219a–221b.
6. *Sophist*, 227a–b. Translation is my own.
7. Diogenes Laertius, *The Lives of Eminent Philosophers*, III.2.
8. See *Ion*, 533d–534c.
9. Diogenes Laertius, *The Lives of Eminent Philosophers*, III.37.
10. According to Alice Riginos, *The Anecdotes Concerning the Life and Writings of Plato*, 24, Olympiodorus's story is a "late Neoplatonic biography." My inclusion of it here is thus completely anachronistic. It's possible that

Olympiodorus's story originated in Socrates' dream of the swan recounted in *The Lives of Eminent Philosophers*, III.5, and which I here attribute to Plato himself. The swan, Riginos reminds us, is "Apollo's sacred bird." I follow Mensch in her translation of *The Lives of the Eminent Philosophers* (2018), 146.

11 Diogenes Laertius, *The Lives of Eminent Philosophers*, III.26.
12 Ibid., III.2. The Greek here is quite difficult to unravel. My colleague, Steve Scully, suggests this: "Rather than meaning that he did not succeed in forcing her (unlikely meaning here because of the kai), it means that he raped his wife (and, we can presume, that he impregnated her) but that he did not 'succeed' in 'winning her.' Then, following Apollo's advice, he stayed away from her until she gave birth."
13 Ibid., III.29.
14 Ibid., III.46.
15 Plato's *Seventh Letter*, 327b.
16 See *Republic*, 592b.
17 This is a reference to Marth Nussbaum's interpretation of the *Phaedrus* in her *The Fragility of Goodness*, Chapter 8.
18 *Apology*, 32a.
19 Aristotle will have an answer for her. See his *On Memory*, 450b.
20 Diogenes Laertius, *The Lives of Eminent Philosophers*, III.1.
21 Ibid., III.29.
22 *Apology*, 38a.
23 Diogenes Laertius, *The Lives of Eminent Philosophers*, III.4.
24 Ibid., III.5.
25 Meno and the bees (*Meno*, 72a). The bench escapade (*Charmides*, 155c). That Socrates is teaching Hippothales how to seduce Lysis: *Lysis*, 206b. That Lysis is captivated by Socrates—that is, by philosophy—is suggested at 213d.
26 See *Phaedrus*, 274e–276a
27 Plato's *Second Letter*, 314c.
28 Diogenes Laertius, *The Lives of Eminent Philosophers*, III.34, 36: Plato was not on good terms with Xenophon and Aristippus.
29 Aristotle, *Parts of Animals*, 683a20.
30 Diogenes Laertius, *The Lives of Eminent Philosophers*, IV.16.
31 *To Ti Ên Einai* in Greek.
32 *Laws*, 803c.
33 *Symposium*, 202e.
34 Diogenes Laertius, *The Lives of Eminent Philosophers*, III.73. This is likely a reference to the *Timaeus*, 37d: "time is a moving image of eternity."

Bibliography

Diogenes Laertius, *The Lives of Eminent Philosophers*, trans. R. D. Hicks (Cambridge, MA: Harvard University Press, 1972)

Diogenes Laertius, *The Lives of Eminent Philosophers*, trans. Pamela Mensch (Oxford: Oxford University Press, 2018)

Grau, Sergi, 'How to Kill a Philosopher: The Narrating of Ancient Greek Philosophers' Deaths in Relation to their Way of Living,' *Ancient Philosophy*, 30, no. 2 (2010)

Nussbaum, Martha, *The Fragility of Goodness* (Cambridge: Cambridge University Press, 1986)

Riginos, Alice, *The Anecdotes Concerning the Life and Writings of Plato* (Leiden: Brill, 1976)

Who Is the Philosopher King?

Jean-Luc Beauchard

> Not many of us are literary giants or prophets, who enjoy the license of throwing off petty academic conventions.
> —Philip W. Rosemann

Appearing in another's book is a bit like sitting for a painter's portrait. The moment the thing is done, you're linked with whoever stands behind the work, your names are tied together, your fates forever intertwined. This is to be the first academic volume in which my writing appears, and so, when the editors kindly invited me to offer some closing remarks, I immediately began to wonder with whom I was agreeing to associate myself. Of course, I've known Will and Bryan for many years and have gotten to know Matt more recently, if only at a "social distance." Still, I feel that if I'm to have the final word on their work, I need to know what it's about and to articulate as clearly as possible the aims and aspirations of the editors. To do so, I must play the part of reader, not friend. Because, as Socrates tells Polemarchus, it is possible to be mistaken about who one's friends really are. Being a careful reader, however, means being harder to trick. The good reader, one of our editors insists, is schooled in the art of detection.[1] The good reader is a skeptic. Therefore, unlike many of Socrates' interlocutors who seem to always miss what he is saying, I propose to end this volume with a piece that makes explicit the ideas hinted at in the pages that precede it.

And so, like the most confident of Plato's creations, allow me to accept the editors' offer to enter into deeper dialogue with their work by declaring: "You won't get away with doing harm unnoticed and, failing to get away unnoticed, you won't be able to overpower me in the argument" (*Republic*, 341b). Yet, unlike Thrasymachus, that surprising man, I won't follow up on this assertion by simply smiling and nodding in agreement with whatever suggestion—no matter how contradictory, no matter how farcical—the editors deem worthy of spewing forth (350e). No, I won't let these would-be Socratic ironists go unquestioned. Instead, I will put them on trial, using their own words and works against them. (That is, according to one editor anyway, the philosophical thing to do).[2]

In preparation for this essential task, I have spent the past few months reading and rereading the drafts of this manuscript and have also made my way through many of the editors' other published works. And, having done so, I believe I am now prepared to tell you, good reader, what this book is about. The thing that holds these three Momuses together, as far as I can tell, and makes them a sort of unholy or at least irreverent and amoral trinity is the notion that aesthetics should function as "first philosophy," that is, philosophical investigation and artistic creation are not distinct *technê* but are actually synonymous with one another.[3] The idea seems to have originated in Bryan's reading of Nietzsche, although it appears as the final subheading in Matt's first book, *Eros Crucified*, as well. According to Bryan, Nietzsche insists that "man [sic] must turn his life into a work of art, and he must do so as an artist does: by transforming the mundane into something beautiful."[4] Will echoes this poetic *mis*reading in his afterword to the same Nietzsche volume in which Bryan's essay appears—the suggestively titled *misReading Nietzsche*—when he writes: "Nietzsche is masterly in his ability to transform the true and terrible into the true enough and delightful."[5] But where did Nietzsche learn this art of philosophical creation? At whose feet did he sit to become so subtle a poet? Matt, in his chapter in this volume, suggests in an endnote that Nietzsche is "one of those rare readers of Plato who not only picked up on the game but actually joined in." For him, Plato is responsible for the idea that aesthetics is, first, philosophy. Plato is the cheery "minor poet" (to again quote Will's afterword) who may or may not have harbored major artistic aspirations (according to Matt's essay above).

Or at least that's what these three jesters would have us believe. The careful reader, however, will approach such assertions with the suspicion typically reserved for one's enemies. The good reader will even wonder if these Jesuitical young scholars haven't been trained in the philosopher's true art, sleight of hand. Take for instance Matt's seemingly innocuous statement that "one would expect readers to be wary of an author who publishes under multiple names." He says this in relation to the writings of Kierkegaard—or at least he *seems* to. But in the pages of this very volume, he authors pieces under multiple names; his opening chapter is penned by "Matthew Clemente," his dialogue with Kearney appears under the pseudonym "M. Saverio Clemente."[6] How to untangle the web? One might, looking at a list of his other works, assume that Clemente publishes philosophy under his Christian name and fiction under his *nom de plume*, works that deal with truth deserve a true author, works of fiction, a false one. That seems to hold—and perhaps even to align with Kearney's responses earlier—until one considers that *misReading Nietzsche* appeared as coedited by "M. Saverio." In his essay from that volume, "Disciple of a Still Unknown God," Clemente espouses what might be called *autophilosophy*, a kind of philosophical autobiography similar to the current trend of autofiction sweeping through literary circles. But if there is no stable self, no unified soul, as Clemente contends in this volume, then whose life is being thought through in this self-referential (might we say solipsistic?) philosophy? Not to mention that *autofiction* is, of course, a genre of fiction, leading us to wonder what relation to truth autophilosophy might have.[7]

Now consider Will's contribution to this volume. The first chapter in Part III: "The Desire of Ethics," it suggests that Socratic ethics has more to do with *seeming* good than *being* good. Forget that no serious Plato scholar to date has held this position—one wonders if Hendel might not see this as a badge of honor rather than a critique—what his argument amounts to is Ethics = Aesthetics. So again everything collapses back into art. What does this mean practically? For Cocchiara, such "aestheticism can be understood as an existentialism."[8] The fundamental human task is to live life as beautifully as possible. I won't get hung up here on the horrors that such an approach to living, unmoored as it is from social or ethical restraints, might lead to. (Kearney astutely notes the aesthetical proclivities of the Third Reich.) Instead, I shift my focus to the curious assertion Matt's chapter makes that this perspective has the power to somehow bring us "beyond the postmodern." Neglecting the fact that every major modern and postmodern thinker has prized aesthetics above all else, the skeptical reader might be forgiven for wondering aloud how exactly artistic creation can take us beyond our gluttonous, overindulged yet never chastened postmodern malaise.

Let's see what clues Clemente provides. What we need, he says at the start of his essay, is a "new and noble ideal." The language is again reminiscent of Nietzsche, so much so that one might take his project to be a mere repetition and expansion of Nietzsche's, as say Foucault's clearly is. But something interesting happens at the end of the work, something that suggests another possibility. Commenting on the artist's desires as articulated by Socrates in the *Phaedrus*, Matt writes that "those strivings will form in [the artist] a new and noble ideal, the creation of a previously unimagined art, an art that points us, if we let it, beyond the postmodern, toward that which creates the world anew (cf. *Letter II*, 314c; *Cratylus*, 432b–c)." Here again we have the *new and noble ideal*, only this time we are directed to look at two passages from Plato. The first, which John Panteleimon Manoussakis expounds on in his outstanding Preface to this volume, speaks of the works of Plato as having been written by an "idealized and youthful Socrates." Manoussakis tells us that this might just as easily be translated a "young" (νέος) and "beautiful" (καλός) Socrates. Well, so, too, might it be translated a "new" (νέος) and "noble" (καλός) Socrates. Why that matters becomes clear if we turn to the second passage Clemente cites which appears in the *Cratylus*. There, Socrates asks:

> Would there be two things—Cratylus and an image of Cratylus—in the following circumstances? Suppose some god didn't just represent your color and shape the way painters do, but made all the inner parts like yours, with the same warmth and softness, and put motion, soul, and wisdom like yours into them—in a word, suppose he made a duplicate of everything you have and put it beside you. Would there then be two Cratyluses or Cratylus and an image of Cratylus?

To this, Cratylus responds: "It seems to me, Socrates, that there would be two Craryluses."

What we have, I believe, is the suggestion from Clemente that the kind of art that can get us beyond the postmodern (and its irony and its solipsism and its despair) is the kind that can create new and noble *characters*, that can bring those characters to life, that believes it can lift them off the page and bring them into the world with "all the inner parts" and "motion, soul, and wisdom" of real human beings. Such characters, the passing reference to *Don Quixote* makes clear, are the true authors of their stories. After all, just as Plato argues that Socrates—his fictional, artistic creation—is responsible for the Dialogues, so, too, does Cervantes tell us that "every man is the child of his own works"[9]—that is, it is the job of the good character to create his author, not the other way around. But this raises more questions than it answers. In the first place, how are we to move from the theory that aesthetics is, first, philosophy—that ethics *is* aesthetics and that all philosophy can be understood as art—to the creation of such ennobling art? And, what is more, how is such an ideal *new*? How is it any different from that which every author from the time of Homer to today has tried to realize with his art, postmodern authors included? In what way does it bring us "beyond the postmodern"? What writer of fiction has not set out to create realistic characters? Who wants to leave his works dead on the page?

In his interview with Kearney, Clemente points out that Socrates adopts the moniker "Stesichorus" in the *Phaedrus*. This he interprets as an admission by Plato that the founder of Western philosophy desires to be the director of the chorus of characters in the Dialogues, the "god" posited in the earlier quote from *Cratylus* who creates real, flesh and blood human beings capable of outliving their author and attaining the kind of immortality Diotima promises when she says that the offspring of poets are "more beautiful [καλός] and more immortal" than human children. "Everyone would rather have such children than human ones, and would look up to Homer, Hesiod, and the other good poets with envy and admiration for the offspring they have left behind—offspring, which, because they are immortal themselves, provide their parents with immortal glory and remembrance" (*Symposium*, 209c–d). There is no question that this is the desire of every author. But the truth is that it takes a Plato or a Dostoevsky or a Joyce to achieve such a noble goal. And while the editors of this volume seem to believe that throwing off ethical or metaphysical commitments in order to view aesthetics as first philosophy is a fundamental step on the path of ushering in a new age of artistic creation, this reader, for one, remains unconvinced.[10]

Notes

1 Clemente, *Eros Crucified*, xii–xiii.
2 See Clemente, "God on Trial: The Impious Philosopher as Would-be Detective."
3 Read Clemente's interview with Kearney carefully and you will begin to suspect that his questions are not really questions but rather subtle suggestions meant to elicit certain responses and lead his interlocutor to certain,

preordained conclusions—the view that "true philosophy is invented," as Zeppa, a former student of Clemente's, so finely puts it.
4 Cocchiara, "Aesthetics as First Philosophy," 6.
5 Hendel, "Afterword: A Hint for Philosophers," 169.
6 Note, too, that in that dialogue it is he, Clemente, and not Kearney who brings up Kierkegaard's use of pseudonyms as that which distinguishes him from other philosophers, claiming that "Kierkegaard comes the closest to walking the line" between philosophy and art.
7 To make matters slipperier still, let us not forget that the Kearney dialogue—conducted by "M. Saverio"—presents itself as a transcript of an actual conversation, not a fictive one, and yet opens with a descriptive staging reminiscent of Plato.
8 Cocchiara, "Aesthetics as First Philosophy," 5.
9 Cervantes, *Don Quixote*, 48.
10 And he is hardly the only one. As the review from which the epigraph that opens this chapter is taken so rightly notes of Clemente's work, "the author of a dissertation (defended at Boston College in 2019) must demonstrate an ability to control his material and write about it in a lucid, well-structured fashion." Rosemann, "Book Review," 259.

Bibliography

Cervantes, Miguel de, *Don Quixote*, trans. J. M. Cohen (New York: Penguin Classics, 1950)

Clemente, M. Saverio, "Disciple of a Still Unknown God or Becoming What I Am," in *misReading Nietzsche*, ed. Clemente and Cocchiara (Eugene, OR: Pickwick Publications, 2018), 151–165

Clemente, Matthew, *Eros Crucified: Death, Desire, and the Divine in Psychoanalysis and Philosophy of Religion* (London: Routledge, 2019)

Clemente, Matthew, "God on Trial: The Impious Philosopher as Would-Be Detective," www.3-16am.co.uk/articles/god-on-trial-the-impious-philosopher-as-would-be-detective

Cocchiara, Bryan, "Aesthetics as First Philosophy: Nietzsche, the Artist, and His Work," in *misReading Nietzsche*, ed. Clemente and Cocchiara (Eugene, OR: Pickwick Publications, 2018), 4–16

Hendel, William, "Afterword: A Hint for Philosophers," in *misReading Nietzsche*, ed. Clemente and Cocchiara (Eugene, OR: Pickwick Publications, 2018), 167–170

Plato, *Complete Works*, ed. John M. Cooper (Indianapolis, IN: Hackett, 1997)

Rosemann, Phillip, "Book Review: *Eros Crucified: Death, Desire, and the Divine in Psychoanalysis and Philosophy of Religion*," *International Journal of Philosophical Studies*, 29, no. 2 (2021), 259–263

Index

Abraham 125–126
Adeimantus 24, 101–103, 105,
　152–153, 157, 160–161, 167–168
Agathon 7, 180, 262, 268–269, 272
Alcibiades xviii, 18–19, 26, 179, 239,
　243, 269
antilogia 69, 71, 74–75
apodeixis 39–43
Apollo 18, 24, 128n6, 216, 262,
　275n10, 275n12; temple of 36, 73
aporia 118, 124–125, 246, 266
Arendt, Hannah 216
Aristophanes xvi, 29n29, 70, 72, 179,
　233, 269
Aristotle 29n29, 49n14, 70, 75, 78–79,
　169nn11–12, 188, 192–193, 218,
　231, 233, 235, 237, 261, 264,
　269–270, 272, 275n19
Aspasia 193, 202n25
Augustine 8, 208, 235
author i, ii, iii, iv, vii, viii, x, xxiii–iv,
　3–32, 186n7, 229–239, 279–281,
　281n1, 281n2, 281n3, 282n6, 10

Badiou, Alain 69
barbarism 105, 189–196, 198–200,
　202n16, 202n18
Barthes, Roland 237
Beauvoir, Simone de 231
being and becoming 20–21, 43–44, 46,
　48, 73–74, 86–87, 115–120,

　123–128, 129n10, 129n22, 164–165,
　167, 183, 185, 190, 196, 203n41,
　211–214, 218–219, 221–222,
　224n18, 224nn20–21, 243, 245,
　257–258, 279
Benjamin, Walter 234
Bennington, Geoffrey 231
Bergson, Henri 183–185
Bloom, Allan 29n25, 102, 114n3
Borges, Jorge Luis xvii, xix–xx,
　xxiinn9–12

Callicles 26, 79, 80–82, 133, 135–136,
　138, 142–143, 145–146, 152–154,
　159–162, 164, 166–167, 170, 232
Campbell, Joseph 47, 49–50n23
Camus, Albert 11–12, 28n13, 28n18,
　29n19, 96–97, 236
Cephalus 87, 90–91
Cervantes, Miguel de xix, 25, 281
Chaerephon 139, 141, 145
character ix, x, 30n35, 277–282
Charmides 26, 267; *see also* platonic
　dialogues, *Charmides*
Chesterton, G.K. xvi–xvii
Cimon 81
colonialism, European 191

δαιμμρεα, τ (daimon, divine sign) 44,
　115, 121–125, 127–128, 129n18, 273
Dawkins, Richard 34–35

Delian League, the 71
democracy 21, 70, 81, 181, 247–248
Derrida, Jacques 4, 116, 210–212, 220, 223n3, 223n7, 231
Descartes, Rene xxin2, 33
diaeresis 108
dialectic 45–48, 77, 135, 137, 142, 180, 184, 214
Diodorus of Sicily 73
Diogenes Laertius 73, 274nn1–2, 274n4, 274n7, 274n9, 274n11, 274n20, 274n23, 274n28, 274n30, 274n34
Diotima xx, 60, 161, 180–181, 183, 269, 272–273, 281
Dostoevsky, Fyodor 11, 236–237, 281
Durkheim, Emile 173

education: in *Republic* 15–17, 40, 61; in *Statesman* 110; in *Symposium* 181–182
eikasia 249
elenkos 74
Eliot, T.S. 171n19, 236
Emerson, Ralph Waldo 3–6, 28n1
Empedocles 73–74, 78
Epicureanism 78, 175
epistemology 34, 36, 119, 161, 184, 238
ergon 47, 49n20
eros xix, 7, 12, 18, 26, 28n9, 44, 46, 75–77, 110–113, 121, 176–178, 179–180, 182–185, 232, 273
erotic desire *see* eros
Eryximachus 179
Euripides 23, 216–217, 224nn22–23
Euthyphro 90, 92–93, 96, 217–218; *see also* virtues, the, *Euthyphro*

Faust 123, 130n27
Ferber, Rafael 117–118, 128n7, 129n8
Feyerabend, Paul 15, 182
flattery (κολακεttery 139, 142–146
Foucault, Michel 4

Freud, Sigmund xxiv, 8, 10, 12, 14, 28n8, 28n9, 28n11, 28n14, 174, 181, 218, 225n29, 236

Gadamer, Hans-Georg 219
Giacosa, Giuseppe 56
Glaucon 15, 28n12, 61, 94–96, 102–103, 111, 117–118, 122, 128n6, 167–169, 207–208, 234, 243, 264
gnosticism 53
Gorgias 69, 71–77, 79–80, 82–83, 133–134, 136, 138–139, 141, 145, 151–160, 162, 167
guardians of Kallipolis 15, 17, 29n21, 56, 58, 212–215, 221

Hegel, G.W.F. 78, 121–122, 128, 238
Heidegger, Martin 231, 251
Heraclitus 231
Hesiod 40
Hippocrates 192
Homer xxi, 40, 57–58, 88–89, 215, 234, 281
homoerotic desire *see* eros
Hume, David 207, 223n1
Husserl, Edmund 231–232

immortality of the soul xvi, 41–42, 72
immortal soul, the 42, 82–83, 151, 165, 170n18
Irigaray, Luce 231
irony 7, 76–77, 124, 151, 161, 179, 184, 238, 280

James, William 4

kairos 137
kalos (καλαλ) xx–xxi, 280–281
Kierkegaard, Soren 13, 24–25, 30n31, 125–126, 231, 237–238, 279, 282n6

La Boheme 51–52, 55–56, 61–67
Lacan, Jacques 29n26, 80, 180, 184, 231, 237

Levinas, Emmanuel 115–128, 128n2, 128n3, 129n10, 129n13, 129n18, 130n33
life of the gods, the (*ho bios theois*) 71, 78
logos 37–43, 45–48, 49n9, 70, 72, 86–89, 91, 97n1, 119, 133–137, 138–144, 147, 151–152, 154, 232–234, 243–244
Lonergan, Bernard 208
Lucian 73
Lyotard, Jean-Francois 4–5
Lysias 45, 77, 120, 121

MacIntyre, Alasdair 53–54, 170n14
Mann, Paul Thomas xxiin4, 30n36, 174–175
marxism 11, 203n40
McCoy, Marina 97n5, 136–137, 140, 144–145, 147
medicine 79, 108, 155, 157, 166, 259
meme 34–36
Meno 26, 127, 130n40, 232, 267; Meno's paradox 169n13, 222; *see also* platonic dialogues, *Meno*
Merleau-Ponty, Maurice 231
metaxu xix, 273
mimesis 59, 70, 76, 198
Montaigne, Michel de 33, 237
Murdoch, Iris 54
music 9, 29n9, 37, 52, 54–57, 59–60, 155–157, 160, 162, 235
myth 58, 82, 109, 134, 141–142, 144, 146, 183, 196–199, 208, 222, 241, 248
myth of Er 79, 86, 90, 96–97
mythology *see* myth
mythos 37–48, 232–234

Nabokov, Vladimir xvii, xix
Nehamas, Alexander 77
neoliberalism 11, 21
Neoplatonism 36, 59, 78, 274n10

Nietzsche, Fredrich xv, 28n1, 35–36, 48–49, 49n3, 50nn23–24, 74, 80, 232, 235–236, 244
noble lie, the 16, 183
nous 43–44

ontology 117, 127–128, 161–163, 165, 170n17, 203n41

palinode xvi, 38, 41, 43, 47, 124
Parmenides 73, 223n9, 272; *see also* platonic dialogues, *Parmenides*
parrhesia 140–141
pederasty 77, 120, 176, 181–184
Pericles 70, 81
Phaedrus 75–78, 119–121, 126–127, 128n3, 129n17, 142–143, 179, 262–263, 267; *see also* platonic dialogues, *Phaedrus*
phantasia 249–250
pharmakon (φ(αρακον, τκ) 36, 49, 86, 223n3, 249
phenomenology xxiv, 212
philosopher king 19, 21, 23, 27, 102, 105, 111, 114n2, 179, 182, 185
philosophy: analytic 4, 231, 243; continental 4, 231, 242
phronesis 108, 111, 114n8
Plato: parodic reading of *xiv-xvii, xxi-xxii*; *see also* platonic dialogues; platonic letters
platonic dialogues: *Apology* xx, 22, 27, 29n28, 36, 71, 101, 104, 122, 124, 130n30, 136–138, 141, 147, 225n28, 266, 275n18, 275n22; *Charmides* xxiin4, 6–7, 11, 18, 275; *Euthydemus* 74, 122; *Gorgias* 26, 72, 74–77, 79–82, 133–139, 141–146, 151–158, 159–161, 164–165, 169n4; *Hippias Major* and *Minor* 74; *Ion* 215–216, 224n19; *Menexenus* 193; *Meno* 18, 26, 74, 79, 127, 151, 170, 208, 222, 243, 245; *Parmenides* xx,

223n9, 245; *Phaedo* v, xvi, xx,
  19, 26, 37, 72, 170n18, 209–210,
  241; *Phaedrus* xxiin4, 1, 26–27,
  38–47, 49n6, 49n21, 60, 75–78,
  81, 115–116, 119–122, 126–127,
  128n1, 130n23, 130n29, 142–143,
  189, 201n8, 210, 232, 275n17,
  275n26, 280–281; *Philebus* 18, 189,
  197–198, 202n35, 203n41; *Politicus*
  (*see Statesman*); *Protagoras* 18,
  71, 74, 154; *Republic* xvi–xviii, 4,
  7–9, 12–19, 21–30, 37, 40, 49n22,
  52, 55–61, 72, 75–76, 79, 85–97,
  101–114, 115–119, 122, 126–127,
  151, 153, 165–171, 176, 179–183,
  193, 201n6, 207–208, 210–215,
  221–224, 232, 234, 244, 247–250,
  274n3, 275n16, 277; *Sophist* 70,
  74–75, 77, 102, 107, 114n2, 189,
  194, 213–214, 223n2, 243, 245,
  257, 260; *Statesman* 101, 107–113,
  114n2, 189–191, 193–197,
  199–201, 202n31, 203n45,
  247–248; *Symposium* xv–xvii, xix,
  xxiin10, 7, 9, 18–19, 23, 26–27,
  60, 120, 179–183, 223n2, 229, 239,
  243, 262, 269–272; *Theaetetus* 71,
  78, 122, 208–209, 218, 224n20,
  243, 245–246; *Timaeus* 210–211,
  224n24, 240, 245, 248, 251
platonic letters: *Letter II* xix–xx,
  xxiin8, 27, 280; *Seventh Letter*
  275n15
poetry xiv, 23–27, 37, 51–52, 54–58,
  76, 170n18, 215–217, 224n19,
  231–232, 234, 236–239
Polemarchus 87, 109, 165, 257
polis 8–9, 13, 16, 18–20, 22, 26, 29,
  40, 82, 85–86, 90, 95, 104, 108,
  110–111, 234–235, 244, 248
Polus 79–80, 133, 138–142, 151–154,
  157–160, 162–166
Popper, Karl 235

Porphyry 221
Protagoras 71–72, 78–79; *see also*
  platonic dialogues, *Protagoras*
psychagogia 76–77
psychoanalysis 80, 207–209, 218–220,
  222
Puccini, Giacomo 51–52, 56, 61

Rabelais xvii–xviii, xxiin5
racialism 188, 191–192, 199
recollection 5, 76, 142, 208
relativism 69, 71
rhetoric 48, 69, 72, 74–77, 79–81,
  109–110, 119–121, 133–134,
  136–147, 147n9, 179, 237
Russell, Bertrand 4

Sallis, John 104, 107, 170n16, 171n25,
  240–242
Sartre, Jean-Paul 20, 97n2, 231, 237
science, philosophy of 218–220
Silenus xviii, 179
slavery 26, 80, 152, 170n18, 188,
  192–193, 200, 202n18, 203n48,
  203n49, 253, 268, 274n1
Socrates xv, xvii–xviii, xx–xxiii, 7,
  9–14, 16–19, 21–23, 25–26, 37–39,
  41–45, 47–48, 52, 57–61, 69–72,
  74–83, 85–96, 97n1, 101–109,
  111–113, 101–128, 129nn17–18,
  129n21, 130nn24–26, 130n31,
  130n40, 133–147, 147n10, 151–168,
  170nn16–18, 171n22, 179–180,
  182, 186, 189–191, 193–195, 198,
  202n36, 208, 210–212, 214–218,
  220, 223n9, 224n22, 225n28, 229,
  232–235, 238–239, 241, 243–244,
  249, 257, 260–261, 264–269, 272,
  274, 275n10, 277, 280–281
socratic irony 24, 179, 184, 238
sophistry 45, 48, 69–78, 81–83, 102,
  104–105, 107, 109, 151–153,
  160–161, 163–165, 166–168,

169n13, 179, 213–214, 224n16; *see also* platonic dialogues, *Sophist*
Sophocles 29n19, 233, 270
Speusippus 253, 256–257, 262–264, 268–269
Spinoza, Baruch 16, 78, 80, 225n33
Stesichorus 232, 281
Stranger from Elea, the 74–75, 107–111, 188–191, 193–200, 202n31, 203n43, 232, 257–260
Strauss, Leo 6, 26–27, 28n3, 28n5, 29n22, 30n40, 168n4, 170n14, 171n19
syllogism 162, 164

techne 76, 110, 143–144, 147n9, 198, 235, 257–259, 278
telos 28n14, 136, 165, 175
Themistocles 81
Thrasymachus 26, 75, 80, 93–96, 152, 165–167, 232, 277
Thucydides 70, 73
Tolstoy, Leo 54
tragedy xiv–xv, xviii, 23, 26, 69, 73, 76, 82, 229, 233–234, 267, 270
tyranny 23, 86, 90, 93–95, 97, 176, 248

universalism 72

virtue *see* virtues, the
virtues, the 81, 126, 140, 222; in Aristotle's *Nicomachean Ethics* 169n12; in Aristotle's *On Sophistical Refutations* 75; courage in *Republic* 57, 214–215; in *Cratylus* 280; in *Euthyphro* 92–93, 96, 217; in *Gorgias* 72, 73, 79–80, 81, 133, 137–138, 141, 144–145, 155–160, 162; justice in *Euthyphro* 96, 208; in *Laws* 182; in *Meno* 79, 127, 245, 267; moderation in *Crito* 211; in *Phaedo* 72, 209; in *Phaedrus* 44–46, 48, 143; piety 123, 219; in *Protagoras* 70–72, 75; in *Republic* xvi, 14, 19, 23–24, 26, 27, 59, 72, 87, 90–91, 94–96, 103, 106, 109, 111, 165–168, 169n7, 207–208, 212, 223n11; in *Statesman* 109, 199–200; in *Symposium* 18, 23, 60, 179, 181, 183; temperance in *Phaedrus* 44; in *Theaetetus* 70–72, 218, 224n20; virtue in *Apology* 136–137, 147; wisdom in *Apology* 141; in Xenophon's *Memorabilia* 70, 75

Wallace, David Foster 236
Whitehead, Alfred North 4
Wilde, Oscar xxiin4, 173, 175
Wittgenstein, Ludwig 231

Xenophon 70, 127, 217, 224n15, 243, 268, 275n28

Yunis, Harvey 123, 129n17, 130n23

Zeus 134, 139, 141–142, 144, 146; the age of 196–198